THE
UNDESERVING
POOR

Praise for *The Undeserving Poor, Revised Edition*

"Michael Katz has done a magnificent job of revising his classic text. It draws on a remarkable range of new material while retaining the clarity, historical perspective, and ethical sensibilities of the original. Everybody, from beginning student to seasoned expert, has something to learn from this important book."—Alice O'Connor, University of California, Santa Barbara

"This is social history at its best. Katz excavates the political and ideological battles over what we should do to lift people out of poverty and into the middle class. Like a good drama, it is filled with fascinating people: politicians, writers, policy wonks, activists, academics, philanthropists, and journalists. Their personalities, interests, ideas, and conflicts have shaped how we view the poor and what we do about poverty. Katz makes it all come alive in this absorbing and well-written book." —Peter Dreier, Chair, Urban & Environmental Policy Department, Occidental College

"The original edition of *The Undeserving Poor* profoundly influenced two generations of poverty scholars and policy-makers. Full of fresh research and thoroughly re-written to incorporate the insights of feminist scholars, critical race theorists, economists, geographers, political philosophers and poverty historians, this new edition is as indispensable as the first. At a time when poverty rates are skyrocketing, Katz's insight and vast knowledge are more critical than ever."—Annelise Orleck, author of *Storming Caesars Palace: How Black Mothers Fought Their Own War on Poverty*

THE
UNDESERVING
POOR

AMERICA'S ENDURING
CONFRONTATION WITH POVERTY

BY
MICHAEL B. KATZ

SECOND EDITION

FULLY UPDATED AND REVISED

OXFORD
UNIVERSITY PRESS

OXFORD
UNIVERSITY PRESS

Oxford University Press is a department of the University of Oxford.
It furthers the University's objective of excellence in research, scholarship,
and education by publishing worldwide.

Oxford   New York
Auckland   Cape Town   Dar es Salaam   Hong Kong   Karachi
Kuala Lumpur   Madrid   Melbourne   Mexico City   Nairobi
New Delhi   Shanghai   Taipei   Toronto

With offices in
Argentina   Austria   Brazil   Chile   Czech Republic   France   Greece
Guatemala   Hungary   Italy   Japan   Poland   Portugal   Singapore
South Korea   Switzerland   Thailand   Turkey   Ukraine   Vietnam

Oxford is a registered trademark of Oxford University Pressin the UK and certain other
countries.

Published in the United States of America by
Oxford University Press
198 Madison Avenue, New York, NY 10016

© Michael B. Katz 2013

Library of Congress Cataloging-in-Publication Data
Katz, Michael B., 1939–
The undeserving poor : America's enduring confrontation with
poverty / by Michael B. Katz.—Second edition.
pages cm
ISBN 978–0–19–993395–2 (hardback : alk. paper)   1. Poor—United States.
2. Poverty—United States.   3. Discrimination—United States.
4. Economic assistance, Domestic—United States.   I. Title.
HC110.P6K28 2013
362.5'80973—dc23
2013007311

1 3 5 7 9 8 6 4 2
Printed in the United States of America
on acid-free paper

For Michael Harrington
1928–1989

CONTENTS

PREFACE

———❦———

"THERE IS A FAMILIAR America. It is celebrated in speeches and advertised on television and in the magazines. It has the highest mass standard of living the world has ever known," wrote Michael Harrington in 1962 in *The Other America*. While Americans in the 1950s agonized over the consequences of their affluence, "there existed another America. In it dwelt somewhere between 40,000,000 and 50,000,000 citizens of this land. They were poor. They still are." They did not suffer poverty "in the same sense as those poor nations where millions cling to hunger as a defense against starvation," but "tens of millions" of them at the "very moment" he wrote were "maimed in body and spirit, existing at levels beneath those necessary for human decency." They were "hungry.... without adequate housing and education and medical care." Still, Harrington observed, "the millions who are poor in the United States tend to become invisible. Here is a great mass of people, yet it takes an effort of the intellect and will even to see them." Harrington's purpose was to expose this "huge, enormous, and intolerable fact of poverty in America."[1]

Harrington wrote to arouse the conscience of a nation. His book was a sensation. It has sold over a million copies. It is alleged to have played a role in rousing President John F. Kennedy to plan an attack on poverty. In important ways, the war on poverty that followed Kennedy's assassination transformed the landscape of poverty in America. By 1973 the poverty rate had dropped from 22 percent at the time Harrington wrote, to 11.1 percent—poverty's nadir in America. By 2011 poverty had drifted upward: 46.2 million Americans lived below the official income poverty line. They were 15 percent of the population—an extraordinary, unacceptable share—but much lower than when Harrington called the nation to account.

Poverty remained a "huge, enormous, and intolerable fact." Unlike the era when Harrington wrote, Americans seemed to remain not only oblivious to its extent but hostile to any frontal assault by government. Poverty had become so much a third rail in American politics that it received almost no mention by presidential candidates and most other politicians. In part, the increased economic segregation in where Americans lived rendered much poverty hard to see, and municipal governments tried to force homeless persons and beggars away from shiny, revitalized city centers. But the barriers to visibility were psychic as well. The statistics were well publicized and easily accessible. Americans, for the most part, chose not to pay them much attention or act on their implications. All this was very strange at a time when massive increases in inequality and insecurity rendered the well-being of ordinary Americans more and more precarious.

How to account for the relative invisibility and political toxicity of poverty as a public issue in twenty-first century America is a topic about which historians, sociologists, economists, political scientists, and pundits surely will argue. This book does not attempt a comprehensive answer. Rather, it focuses on one necessary component of any explanation: how Americans have thought and talked about poverty and how they have put poverty talk into action. For more than two hundred years, one theme has run through this American response to poverty. It is the idea that some poor people are undeserving of help because they brought their poverty on themselves. This belief can be traced in what has been said about poor people; it can be located, as well, by identifying who was, and who was not, given assistance in times of need. The identity of the undeserving poor has shifted with time and context, but the category has endured.

The key words in the subtitle of this book have been chosen with care. They are "enduring" and "confrontation." Enduring points to the stubborn persistence of poverty in American history. Poverty is deeply rooted. Before the twentieth century, the nation lacked both the economic surplus and policy tools to eradicate it; all that could be hoped for was to ameliorate the condition of the poor by keeping them from perishing from starvation, wretched housing, and disease. That situation began to change in the twentieth century with what one historian has called the "discovery of abundance" and with increasingly sophisticated methods for transferring income, delivering services, and providing the essentials of a decent life. For about a decade, this combination of abundance and method backed by popular support and political will worked spectacularly well.[2] Since then, poverty has been allowed to grow once again, not, it must be emphasized, as the inevitable consequence of government impotence or economic scarcity, but of political will.

Confrontation, the second key term in this book's subtitle, has multiple referents. It refers to the continuing confrontation with poverty throughout the nation's history. It includes both ideas—whose importance and consequences must not be underestimated—and the actions of both public and private sectors. It embraces, as well, ideas and actions emanating from the political Right as well as the Left, both of which have been constant players in the nation's confrontation with poverty.

As a practical matter, the use of labels for political Right and Left is inescapable in moving between sides of the political spectrum, as this book does, without repeatedly interrupting the story, even though labels obscure shades of meaning. In telling this story, I often use the terms "liberal" and "liberalism." These, of course, have had multiple meanings over the centuries, from the classic liberalism emphasizing individual freedom and unfettered markets to "New Deal liberalism" with its emphasis on activist government. It is in the latter sense that I use the term. In this book it is a shorthand for a political position that stresses the role of an active government in directly promoting the economic and social well-being of citizens through public policy. It contrasts with conservatism understood as a position more skeptical of the legitimacy and capability of government and more reliant on markets to solve public problems. The terms also have taken on meanings with respect to social issues that on the surface appear to contradict their positions on the role of government in economic affairs.

Liberalism in general stands for reduced governmental interference with individual freedoms, especially in matters of conscience and sexuality. Conservatism has come to imply a far more authoritarian government intrusion into civil liberties and private lives. These, of course, are rough and ready definitions that skirt over subtleties, changes over time, and overlaps between positions. But they do highlight real tendencies in modern politics identifiable in the stories told in this book and, for this reason, constitute a defensible shorthand.

To emphasize, as this book does, that large numbers of poor people throughout the nation's history have been labeled as undeserving is to say that poverty has been viewed as a problem of persons. Its roots lie in personal deficiencies—moral, cultural, or biological. This tendency to view poverty as a problem of persons, I contend, offers the oldest and most enduring answer to the question, what kind of a problem is poverty? But it is not the only answer. Poverty has been written about, as well, as a problem of place, resources, political economy, power, and market failure. These answers are important because each has carried—and continues to carry—different implications about the direction and priorities for actions against poverty. In this book, I pay attention to each of them. But I look behind them as well. Each of them tells a causal story about the origins of poverty. They do not address the enduring meta-questions of why we should care about poverty, whom we should help, and the consequences of our actions.

Three perennial issues frame discussions of poverty's origins. They have coursed through every debate on poverty during more than two centuries. The first of these is who to help. This problem has been partly about the allocation of finite resources and partly about the exercise of moral judgment: who deserves to be provided with cash, food, housing, medical care, or other goods and services? The second issue is the impact of relief, welfare, or charity on individual behavior. It is what the economists call moral hazard. Does the availability of help undermine incentives to work, marry, and maintain a stable family life? The third issue is ethical. What do we owe each other? Beyond our families and immediate communities, what are the limits of our social obligations? The great debate about the answers to these questions has structured poverty talk and action since before the nation was born through to the present, and we will encounter it again and again throughout this book.

This is a book with a purpose. It wants to enlighten readers about the persistence of poverty as both a fact and an issue. It tries to show poverty's complexity and to provide readers with a framework for understanding the politics of poverty. It hopes to convince readers that ideas really do have consequences and that alternatives always have existed—history is the story of choice, albeit constrained, not inevitability. Poverty remains a national disgrace in part because of the way we define and think about it—which, in turn, shapes the energy we put into its eradication. Or, as Charles Darwin admonished in 1839 in *The Voyage of the Beagle*, "if the misery of our poor be caused not by the laws of nature, but by our institutions, great is our sin…"

I

The Undeserving Poor: Morals, Culture, and Biology

THE UNDESERVING POOR HAVE a very old history. They represent the enduring attempt to classify poor people by merit. This impulse to classify has persisted for centuries, partly for reasons of policy. Resources are finite. Neither the state nor private charity can distribute them in unlimited quantities to all who might claim need. On what principles, then, should assistance be based? Who should—and, the more difficult question, who should not—receive help? Answering the questions means drawing lines separating individuals into categories and defending arbitrary distinctions that discriminate among people, none of whom can survive by themselves with comfort and dignity. In practice, honest and perceptive officials have recognized the impurity of all distinctions: No classification can be applied easily or satisfactorily to real people. For reasons of convenience, policy has collapsed into artificial categories the continuum on which poor people have been arrayed.

How to draw the boundaries between who does and who does not merit help is one of the three great questions that run through debates about poverty since the late eighteenth century. The second is, how can we provide help without increasing dependence or creating what economists call moral hazard? The third is, what are the limits of social responsibility? What do we owe to the poor and to each other? This chapter focuses on the first question; later chapters take up the second and third.

The identity of the undeserving poor, as this book shows, has varied throughout American history. At times, men—allegedly drunk and lazy—have dominated; at other points, women—unmarried mothers, especially women of color—have been the focus; frequently, immigrants—for instance, Mexicans in the 1930s and the undocumented in the early twenty-first century—have been part of the group; and African Americans often have found themselves included as well. In studying the undeserving poor, one methodological point is very important. Who fits within the category at any point in time is evident not only by discovering what has been said and written about them, but, at least as important, by identifying how groups of poor people have been treated—in practice, who has been excluded from private and public charity.

The terms used to describe the undeserving poor—whether based on morality, culture, or biology—serve to isolate and stigmatize them. The undeserving poor, the culture of poverty, and the underclass are moral statuses identified by the source of dependence, the behavior with which it is associated, its transmission to children, and its crystallization into cultural patterns. Empirical evidence almost always challenges the assumptions underlying the classifications of poor people. Even in the late nineteenth century, countervailing data, not to mention decades of administrative frustration, showed their inadequacy. Since the 1960s, poverty research has provided an arsenal of ammunition for critics of conventional classifications. Still, as even a casual reading of the popular press, occasional attention to political rhetoric, or informal conversations about poverty reveal, empirical evidence has remarkably little effect on what people think. Part of the reason is that conventional classifications of poor people serve such useful purposes. They offer a familiar and easy target for displacing rage, frustration, and fear. They demonstrate the link between virtue and success that legitimates capitalist political economy. And by dividing poor people, they prevent their coalescing into a unified political force. Stigmatized conditions and punitive treatment, moreover, provide powerful incentives to work, whatever the wages and conditions.

The belief that poverty results from personal inadequacy assumes that poverty is a problem of persons. There are, in fact, as the rest of this book will illustrate, a number of other answers to the question, what kind of a problem is poverty? Before the twentieth century, the idea that poverty is a problem of persons—whether deserving or undeserving—remained intertwined with the biblical idea that poverty is always with us. With production limited and population pressing on resources, poverty appeared ingrained within the human condition.[1] When this fatalistic idea of poverty as a result of universal scarcity began to crumble in the early twentieth century under Progressive-era economists' "discovery of abundance," a wholly new dilemma emerged. If poverty was unnecessary, then what accounted for its stubborn persistence? Why were so many people poor? The most straightforward answer unbundled the two strands: scarcity and individual deficiency. With scarcity off the table, individual failings marked persons as all the more undeserving in a world of possibility where poverty no longer was inescapable. This idea—we might call it the *irony of optimism*—carved a hard edge of inferiority into ideas about poor people. That is one reason why the idea that poverty as a problem of persons persists with such tenacity, despite whatever evidence social scientists produce.

The idea of poverty as a problem of persons comes in both hard and soft versions. The soft version portrays poverty as the result of laziness, immoral behavior, inadequate skills, and dysfunctional families. The hard version views poverty as the result of inherited deficiencies that limit intellectual potential, trigger harmful and immoral behavior, and circumscribe economic achievement. The soft view, which is the older of the two, holds out the possibility of individual escape from poverty. The hard side, also rooted in the nineteenth century, is deeply pessimistic. Neither the soft nor hard side have resulted in much sympathy for poor persons throughout American history other than children, widows, and a few others whose lack of responsibility for their condition could not be denied. These were the deserving poor. Today they are most often referred to as the working poor, and in recent years they have elicited sympathy and support from public programs. The others have been thought to have brought their poverty on themselves; they are the undeserving poor.

The Origins of the Undeserving Poor

Before the twentieth century, it would have seemed preposterous to imagine the abolition of poverty. Resources were finite; life was harsh. Most people, as the bible predicted, would be born, live, and die in poverty. The questions, then, were who among the needy should be helped? What should they be given? How should relief or charity be administered? The answers by and large were not moral, because poverty entailed no disgrace. Rather, from the time of the Elizabethan poor law, policies in England and America reflected two other ways of classifying poor people. The first of these represented an attempt to answer the enduring question, what are the limits of our social obligations? Of primary importance was the division between neighbors and strangers. Responsibility extended to family and community; there it ended. This was the point of the settlement provisions in both English and American poor laws, which required communities (defined variously as parishes, towns, or counties) to assist their permanent members. Others who might fall into need within their borders should be shipped to their places of origin. Settlement laws reflected a state of limited mobility in which most people belonged to some identifiable community. They reflected, too, the permeable and blurred boundaries between family and community in agricultural villages where markets and wage labor had not hardened distinctions and redefined relations.[2]

No aspect of the poor laws caused as great confusion and litigation as the settlement provisions. The restriction of public and private charity to neighbors resonated with deep cultural preferences, but in practice it proved almost impossible to do. As migration and mobility increased, as people wandered from town to town in search of work, who could say with authority to what community someone belonged? The complex attempts at definition all failed, and the result was cruelty and expense. In winter, local authorities shunted sick or old people from one town or county to another, and the expense of transporting them, or of defending against their claims in court, consumed a large share of the tax money raised for relief. Indeed, the modification of the settlement laws became a primary goal of poor law reform in the early decades of the nineteenth century. Still, despite the modification, settlement continued as both a legal and emotional issue, as in the resistance to national welfare standards, the resentment of dependent outsiders allegedly drawn to states with relatively generous welfare benefits, and the reluctance to provide benefits to immigrants.[3]

Another distinction originally attempted to separate the genuinely needy from rogues, vagabonds, and sturdy beggars. It translated over time into the restriction of aid to the impotent and the exclusion of the able-bodied. This principle, so transparently reasonable on the surface, also proved administratively impossible to implement. In both England and America, rising costs for poor relief in the late eighteenth and early nineteenth centuries convinced critics that in fact the able-bodied had penetrated relief rolls, and a great object of poor law in both countries became to remove them. This task remained far more difficult than imagined.

In his report on the poor laws of the Commonwealth of Massachusetts in 1821, Josiah Quincy, future mayor of Boston and president of Harvard University, pointed out that the principle on which the laws rested divided the poor into "two classes": first, "the impotent poor; in which denomination are included all, who are wholly incapable of work, through old age, infancy, sickness or corporeal debility." Second were the "able poor...all, who are capable of work, of some nature, or other; but differing in the degree of their capacity, and in the kind of work, of which they are capable." No one disagreed about helping the impotent, but the able poor were another matter: "From the difficulty of discriminating between this class and the former, and of apportioning the degree of public provision to the degree of actual impotency, arise all the objections to the principle of the existing pauper system." The problem could not be solved by legislation, because

> There must be, in the nature of things, numerous and minute shades of difference between the pauper, who through impotency, can do absolutely nothing, and the pauper who is able to do something, but that, very little. Nor does the difficulty of discrimination, proportionally, diminish as the ability, in any particular pauper, to do something, increases. There always must exist, so many circumstances of age, sex, previous habits, muscular, or mental, strength, to be taken into the account, that society is absolutely incapable to fix any standards, or to prescribe any rule, by which the claim of right to the benefit of the public provision shall absolutely be determined.[4]

Quincy's language points to another enduring classification: the distinction between the poor and paupers. Paupers originated as an administrative category. They were recipients of public relief. Although by itself poverty carried no stigma, pauperism did. During the early nineteenth century, the distinction between poverty and pauperism hardened, and commentators increasingly attributed the latter to moral sources. A few years after Quincy had written his report, a Philadelphia committee of the Guardians of the Poor, reporting on poor relief in other cities, asserted: "The poor in consequence of vice, constitute here and everywhere, by far the greatest part of the poor.... From three-fourths to nine-tenth of the paupers in all parts of our country, may attribute their degradation to the vice of intemperance."[5] In 1834 the Reverend Charles Burroughs, preaching at the opening of a new chapel in the poorhouse in Portsmouth, New Hampshire, admonished his audience:

> In speaking of poverty, let us never forget that there is a distinction between this and pauperism. The former is an unavoidable evil, to which many are brought through necessity, and in the wise and gracious providence of God. It is the result, not of our faults, but of our misfortunes.... Pauperism is the consequence of willful error, of shameful indolence, of vicious habits. It is a misery of human creation, the pernicious work of man, the lamentable consequence of bad principles and morals.[6]

The transmutation of pauperism into a moral category tarnished all the poor. Despite the effort to maintain fine distinctions, increasingly poverty itself became not the natural result of misfortune, but the willful result of indolence and vice. As Walter Channing pointed out in 1843, to the "popular mind" poverty "is looked to solely as the product of him or of her who has entered its dreadful, because dishonored, uncared for, or unwisely cared for, service. Let me repeat it, the causes of poverty are looked for, and found in him or her who suffers it."[7]

The redefinition of poverty as a moral condition accompanied the transition to capitalism and democracy in early nineteenth-century America. It served to justify the mean-spirited treatment of the poor, which in turn checked expenses for poor relief and provided a powerful incentive to work. In this way the moral definition of poverty helped ensure the supply of cheap labor in a market economy increasingly based on unbound wage labor. The moral redefinition of poverty followed also from the identification of market success with divine favor and personal worth. Especially in America, where opportunity awaited anyone with energy and talent, poverty signaled personal failure. The ubiquity of decently paid work and opportunity, of course, were myths, even in the early Republic. The transformation in economic relations, the growth of cities, immigration, the seasonality of labor, fluctuations in consumer demand, periodic depressions, low wages, restricted opportunities for women, industrial accidents, high mortality, and the absence of any social insurance: together these chiseled chronic poverty and dependence into American social life.[8]

Persistent and increasing misery did not soften the moral definition of poverty. Neither did the evidence available through early surveys or the records of institutions and administrative agencies, which showed poverty and dependence as complex products of social and economic circumstances usually beyond individual control.[9] Instead, the definition hardened until nearly the end of the nineteenth century. As a consequence, public policy and private charity remained mean, punitive, and inadequate. Predispositions toward moral definitions of poverty found support in the latest intellectual fashions: in the antebellum period, in Protestant theology; after the Civil War in the work of Charles Darwin and early hereditarian theory; and in the twentieth century in eugenics. So deeply embedded in Western culture had the distinction between the deserving and undeserving poor become that even writers on the Left invoked it automatically or translated it into their own vocabulary. Marxists wrote about the "lumpenproletariat" and even the Progressive reformers who, starting in the 1890s, rejected individual explanations of poverty, unreflectively used the old distinctions. Robert Hunter, a socialist whose widely read book *Poverty* (published in 1904) traced dependence to its structural sources, used the hoary distinction between poor people and paupers ("Paupers are not, as a rule, unhappy. They are not ashamed.... They have passed over the line which separates poverty from pauperism"). He asserted that "the poverty which punishes the vicious and the sinful is good and necessary.... There is unquestionably a poverty which men deserve."[10] (Not all Progressive-era writers on poverty agreed with Hunter. In 1908, in one of the first articles on poverty in a scholarly journal, poverty expert Lilian Brandt wrote that most poverty resulted from "some form of exploitation or...some defect in governmental efficiency." To be sure, some "natural depravity" and "moral defects" resulted in dependence, but they "may not be large enough to constitute a serious problem."[11])

The moral classification of the poor survived even the Great Depression. Poverty lost much of its moral censure as unemployment reached catastrophic levels, but the idea of relief remained pejorative and degrading. The unemployed turned to the state for help usually only as a last resort, after they had exhausted all other possibilities. President Franklin Delano Roosevelt could hardly wait to move the federal government out of the business of relief, which it had reluctantly and temporarily entered in 1933. The foundation of the social welfare edifice erected by his administration became a distinction between public assistance and social insurance (relief based solely on need versus universal programs such as Social Security) that assured public policy would continue to discriminate invidiously among categories of poor people.[12] At the same time, social workers and public officials in the Southwest deliberately constructed needy Mexican immigrants as the undeserving poor, thereby justifying encouragement of their "voluntary" repatriation and, when that failed, deportation.[13]

During World War II and the 1950s, poverty received little explicit attention from social scientists. However, controversies about Aid to Dependent Children—federal matching grants to states popularly known as "welfare"—and other aspects of public assistance showed that the moral classification of poor people had persisted.[14] In the nineteenth century, asking for relief became a sign of individual failure; no label carried a greater stigma than pauper. By the second half of the twentieth century, some groups in need of help had been moved out of the pauper class. Most elderly people, workers disabled in accidents, and the unemployed (not to mention veterans, always a special category) could claim help as a right through social insurance. Others, notably single mothers, remained dependent on public assistance—morally tarred, as always, by their association with relief as well as by their allegedly promiscuous sexuality and, increasingly, their race.[15]

Assaults on the character of unmarried, welfare-dependent mothers escalated throughout the last half of the twentieth century, culminating, as Chapter 4 explains, in the 1996 "welfare reform" legislation. Seen as lazy, immoral "welfare queens" happily soaking up public money while transmitting a culture of dependence to their children, they stood out in public rhetoric as the quintessential undeserving poor. (For a time, with the decline in the "welfare" rolls after the passage of the

1996 legislation, criticism of poor single mothers softened as many were forced into low-wage jobs, but by the end of the first decade of the twenty-first century, fueled by the research of social scientists, criticism had come roaring back.) If, however, the lens is shifted from rhetoric to action, two other groups come into focus in the picture of the undeserving poor. The first is a subset of immigrants. The construction of Mexicans as the undeserving poor during the 1930s persisted, augmented by the huge influx of immigrants from Latin America and Asia triggered by the repeal of nationality-based quotas in 1965 and subsequent legislation. Disproportionately poor, immigrants'—and not just from Mexico—place among the undeserving poor also became clear with legislation in 1996 denying them public benefits for which they had previously been eligible. The other undeserving poor were young black men. In fact, men in need always had elicited less sympathy than women. It is true, as historians have shown, that since its inception, social insurance has favored men. But nineteenth and early twentieth century responses to men in need for the most part represented them as lazy alcoholics who had brought their misery on themselves. Variously labeled tramps, hoboes, and vagabonds, they elicited harsh local ordinances criminalizing their behavior. Early in the twentieth century, to take one example, Buffalo, New York, contained several homes for needy women and not one for men. Children, in fact, more readily took in their needy mothers than fathers, which is why men were found more often in poorhouses than women. There was no federal or state assistance for men comparable to the mothers' pensions of the early twentieth century. In the late twentieth century, chronically jobless black men had few places to turn for assistance and, instead of support, training, or work, found themselves incarcerated in astounding numbers, pushing America to the top of the list of nations in rates of imprisonment. Incarceration had become the welfare state for black males, signifying more than any rhetoric their place among the undeserving poor.[16]

The Culture of Poverty

In the early 1960s intellectuals and politicians rediscovered poverty. Sustained economic growth and myths of affluence had hidden the stubborn persistence of deprivation and dependence; Americans appeared shocked to discover that between 40 and 50 million among them were, by any objective measure, poor.[17] To interpret the meaning of these no longer avoidable and disheartening facts, social scientists drew on a new concept: the culture of poverty. The culture of poverty did not have the classification of poor people as its primary purpose. Still, it served the same end. For most writers observed that the culture of poverty did not capture all poor people. Rather, it placed in a class by themselves those whose behaviors and values converted their poverty into an enclosed and self-perpetuating world of dependence. Although some of its exponents located the sources of poverty in objective factors such as unemployment, the new concept resonated with traditional moral definitions. The culture of poverty could not quite sanitize the poor; their ancient odor seeped through the antiseptic layer of social science. They remained different and inferior because, whatever their origins, the actions and attitudes of poor people themselves assured their continued poverty and that of their children.

Not surprisingly, by the 1970s the culture of poverty had become a conservative concept, thought of as a justification for mean and punitive policies, harshly and sometimes unfairly attacked from the Left. But its political history is much more complex, for the culture of poverty originated among liberals who advocated more active, generous, and interventionist policies on behalf of the poor. As such, the concept reflected a larger strand in the liberalism of the time: the assumption that dependent people were mainly helpless and passive, unable without the leadership of liberal intellectuals to break the cycles of deprivation and degradation that characterized their lives.

In *Poverty Knowledge*, her magisterial history of poverty and social science in the twentieth century, Alice O'Connor interprets the culture of poverty as the result of two strains within postwar social science: the behaviorist revolution and the Cold War-induced concepts of development and modernization. The behaviorist revolution grew out of "the quest for an interdisciplinary, methodologically rigorous science of human behavior, with the ability to predict as well as describe." With funding by the federal government and major foundations, behaviorism "assumed the dimensions of an organized movement...leading to a vast expansion of the resources and institutional infrastructure for behavioral research." Behaviorism was revolutionary because it broke with the "Progressive Era tradition of industrial and social survey research" and "reflected a broader change in the political economy of affluence" that "set the stage for individualizing poverty as a social problem, locating its origins in individual behavior rather than in economic and social arrangements, and tracing its 'pathology' to individual personality." Behaviorists, including sociologist Seymour Martin Lipset and anthropologist Margaret Mead, identified a core American national character oriented toward achievement, "acquisitive, individualistic, and fixed on the future" as the source of "prosperity and democratic practice." In this context, the "lower class" emerged as un-American. "Lower-class deviance, deprivations, and even political ideology... were looking more and more like personality deficiencies inculcated by lower-class mothers in the young."[18] With the most advanced scientific tools, behaviorists rediscovered the undeserving poor and placed most of the blame for its reproduction on poor mothers.

"If World War II had opened the door to a behaviorist 'revolution' in social science," claims O'Connor, "it was the Cold War that truly paved the way for direct investigation of the culture and psychology of 'the poor' as a distinguishable social group. For it was the Cold War that generated the need and the justification for opening up a whole new world—the 'third world'—for technical assistance and applied behavioral research in the name of international aid to the poor." "Modernization," the crucial concept guiding programs of international development, broke with anthropologists' stress on the exotic, primitive folkways of peasant cultures. Instead, modernization theory identified their poverty as the principal barrier to "a more modern, democratic way of life." What held third world cultures back, the Harvard psychologist David McClelland argued, was the absence of "a single personality trait" he labeled the achievement motive or "n Achievement," which formed "the engine behind *all* the great civilizations in Western history." In McClelland's theory, behaviorism combined with the imperatives of Cold War foreign policy goals to promote a "vision in which the individual personality, manufactured by the family, was the central driving force, and in which the family, reduced to its psychological function, was sharply divided into maternal and paternal breadwinning roles." This was, remarkably, a vision for development that disregarded "the facts of political economy and ... the economic agency of women and the family in the developing world." Other social scientists extended the blend of behaviorism and Cold War modernization theory from the third world to the "rural coal towns and mill towns of the United States" where they located "a superstitious, often fundamentalist 'pre-modern' worldview that left villagers passive, submissive, hostile to outsiders, and unable to share in the national wealth." Liberals found in this "dead hand of tradition" not only the source of deep and persistent poverty but of reactionary politics as well. In the early 1960s, according to O'Connor, "the elements of rural traditionalism and lower-class urban culture became conflated into a single, undifferentiated concept of a culture of poverty that deviated from the American middle-class norms."[19]

The anthropologist Oscar Lewis introduced the idea of the culture of poverty in his ethnographic portraits of Mexicans and Puerto Ricans.[20] "In the idea of the culture of poverty," claims O'Connor, Lewis "extended" the "logic" of behaviorally based modernization theory "across national, racial, and ethnic lines."[21] The culture of poverty, he stressed, differed from "economic deprivation ... or the absence of something." Rather, it was a "way of life ... passed down from generation to generation along family lines." It could be found in both urban and rural settings and in different regions and nations because it represented a series of "common adaptations to common problems."[22]

Those problems flourish in cash economies where wages are low, unemployment high, social and political organization of the poor undeveloped, kinship bilateral, and dominant class values stress "the accumulation of wealth and property, the possibility of upward mobility and thrift, and ... personal inadequacy or inferiority" as the source of low economic status. In these settings, the lower strata of rapidly changing societies became likely candidates for the culture of poverty because of their alienation and marginality.[23] Lewis stressed the adaptive role of the culture of poverty: It serves to "cope with feelings of hopelessness and despair which develop from the realization of the impossibility of achieving success in terms of the values and goals of the larger society." Nonetheless, its perpetuation "from generation to generation" crippled children because it leaves them psychologically unprepared "to take full advantage of changing conditions or increased opportunities which may occur in their lifetime."[24]

For Lewis, the culture of poverty had several key features. Among the most important was "the lack of effective participation and integration of the poor in the major institutions of the larger society" and their consequent apathy, hostility, and suspicion. Nor do the members of the culture of poverty form very many organizations of their own. Indeed, he wrote, "the low level of organization...gives the culture of poverty its marginal and anachronistic quality in our highly complex, specialized, organized society. Most primitive people have achieved a higher level of socio-cultural organization than our modern urban slum dwellers."[25]

A distinctive family life also characterized the culture of poverty: "the absence of childhood as a specially prolonged and protected stage in the life cycle, early initiation into sex, free unions or consensual marriage, a relatively high incidence of the abandonment of wives and children," and maternal dominance. Dominating individual psychology were a "strong feeling of marginality or helplessness, of dependence, and of inferiority" coupled with a battery of other traits:

> a high incidence of maternal deprivation, of orality, of weak ego structure, confusion of sexual identification, a lack of impulse control, a strong present-time orientation with relatively little ability to defer gratification and to plan for the future, a sense of resignation and fatalism, a widespread belief in male superiority, and a high tolerance for psychological pathology of all sorts.[26]

Lewis stressed the distinction between poverty and the culture of poverty. In this, he echoed the old distinction between poverty and pauperism, which as we have seen was a staple of social thought from the late eighteenth century onward. In the United States, he argued, only 20 percent of the poor remained trapped within the culture of poverty. Both anthropological and historical evidence gave many examples of impoverished people untouched by the latter. For the most part, they escaped for one of a variety of reasons: the lack of stratification within their societies (as with hunting and gathering tribes); their integration into the larger society through formal organizations (as with castes in India); an emphasis on literacy and voluntary associations (as with the Jews of Eastern Europe); or, Lewis speculated, political leaders who inspired confidence and hope. "On the basis of my limited experience in one socialist country—Cuba— and on the basis of my reading, I am inclined to believe that the culture of poverty does not exist in socialist countries." When poor people became class-conscious or joined trade unions, when their outlook became "internationalist," they left behind the culture of poverty because any "movement...which organizes and gives hope to the poor and effectively promotes solidarity and a sense of identification with larger groups, destroys the psychological and social core of the culture of poverty."[27]

Lewis understood the culture of poverty's "positive adaptive function," but did not romanticize it. He found it "a relatively thin culture. There is a great deal of pathos, suffering and emptiness among those who live in the culture of poverty."[28] Lewis understood how his portrait of the culture of poverty among Puerto Ricans could offend those who have dedicated themselves to eliminating poverty and who are trying to build a positive public image of an often maligned minority group. He knew the "danger that my findings might be misinterpreted or used to justify prejudices and negative stereotypes...which, unfortunately, are still held by some Americans." Clearly, his intent was otherwise. To improve the conditions of people trapped within the culture of poverty, "the first step is to know about them," he asserted, quoting a popular Puerto Rican saying: " 'You can't cover up the sky with your hand.' Indeed, you can't cover up slums, poverty, and ugliness."[29]

Despite his intentions, Lewis's definition of the culture of poverty lent itself easily to appropriation by conservatives in search of a modern academic label for the undeserving poor. At the same time, it also pointed in a radical direction. For the quickest and surest way to eliminate the culture of poverty was through the organization of its members. Lewis's stress on the pivotal role of organized militancy links the culture of poverty to the stress on the "maximum feasible participation" of the poor that characterized the War on Poverty in the early 1960s. For him pride, organization, and class (or racial) consciousness led swiftly away from the culture of poverty. In other words, Lewis understood that poverty resulted in part from a lack of power. In the United States, the great example for Lewis was the civil rights movement. In the third world, it was revolution.[30]

Michael Harrington was the first major author to apply the culture of poverty concept to the United States, although, wrote Lewis, "he used it in a somewhat broader and less technical sense than I had intended."[31] In *The Other America*, published in 1962, a pivotal book in the rediscovery of poverty in the 1960s, Harrington defined the contemporary poor in the United States as "those who, for reasons beyond their control, cannot help themselves." "Poverty in the United States," he wrote, "is a culture, an institution, a way of life.... The family structure of the poor... is different from that of the rest of the society.... There is... a language of the poor, a psychology of the poor, a world view of the poor."[32] Harrington's call to action against poverty lacked Lewis's appreciation of the potential of organized militance and assumed the passivity of the poor. Only the intervention of sympathetic elites could begin to lift poor people out of their degraded and helpless condition. The first step was to arouse the conscience of the nation, and this was the purpose of his book. Indeed, the great service of Harrington's *Other America* was to render poverty visible. Harrington, points out Harold Meyerson, saw "what almost everyone else had missed: that 40 million Americans in a nation of 176 million were poor."

> The new middle-class majority that had moved to suburbia bypassed the decaying inner cities on the recently built interstates, kept their distance from the African American ghettos, never encountered the migrant farmworkers, and failed to see (at least in aggregate) the millions of impoverished elderly. None of these groups had political power or a visible collective presence: they had not found a way to announce their existence. So Harrington did.[33]

As the culture of poverty entered the lexicon of American social science, it framed interpretations of public policy issues. Most notable was educational discourse in which the culture of poverty concept, redefined as cultural deprivation, explained the learning disabilities of economically disadvantaged youngsters.[34] To educators, cultural deprivation necessitated major changes in schooling, which ranged from "readers and materials more attuned to the experiences and problems of lower socioeconomic groups" to methods of instilling "school know-how" in which culturally deprived children were especially deficient, pedagogy that drew on their "physical approach," techniques for combatting their anti-intellectualism, and balancing the "female school" with masculine influences.[35] Cultural deprivation underpinned the War on Poverty's Operation Head Start, which sought to counteract the familial and environmental disadvantages of poor children through intensive pre-school education.

Other liberal social scientists shared key assumptions of the culture of poverty. Most important was the image of poor people both past and present as dependent—passive, lacking the will and organizational capacity to attack the sources of their exploitation and degradation. Historian Oscar Handlin wrote of the Irish immigrants to mid-nineteenth century Boston: "No other contemporaneous migration partook so fully of this poverty-stricken helplessness." Indeed, "degradation by poverty was almost inevitable under the circumstances of Irish life in Boston." Want "insinuated itself into personal habits, perverting human relations and warping conceptions of right and wrong." Boston's Irish, moreover, reflected the impact of Ireland's harsh agrarian economy and Catholic religion: "Their utter helplessness before the most elemental forces fostered an immense sadness, a deep rooted pessimism about the world and man's role in it."[36]

Stanley Elkins compared slaves to the inmates of concentration camps. The force of oppression disintegrated their personalities and transformed them into "Sambos," passive grinning subhumans who tried to please their masters. The "Elkins interpretation of slavery," writes John Cell, "was part of the American liberalism of the postwar era.... Under segregation, though obviously not so rigidly as during slavery, a closed-behavior system has supposedly continued. And, especially in the South, black people on the whole had continued to submit to it."[37] Psychologist David McClelland's theory of development, as we have seen, pointed in the same direction—characterizing poor people's lack of n Achievement motivation as the source of the passivity that retarded their economic progress.

The culture of poverty solved two intellectual problems. First, it provided a justification for America's Cold War intervention into third world societies. Without the aggressive intervention of the West, third world societies locked into backwardness by the culture of poverty could not put themselves on the road to economic development and political democracy. In this way, the culture of poverty played a role similar to the idea of Manifest Destiny in the mid-nineteenth century and the racial arguments used to justify America's imperial activities a half century later.[38] Second, the culture of poverty helped explain why poor people failed to rise up in protest on the streets or through the electoral system. The false consciousness offered by Marxism appeared increasingly facile and patronizing. The culture of poverty, by contrast, offered a complex and subtle interpretation of the process that connected the objective sources of exploitation with the psychology and behavior of everyday life. Its emphasis on the development and transmission of adaptive coping strategies preserved some dignity and rationality for the poor even as it deplored the culture that resulted and stressed the importance of intervention by sympathetic elites.[39]

From the Culture of Poverty to the Black Family

In the early 1960s the resurgent interest in poverty did not focus initially on cities or on race. Michael Harrington's *Other America*, for instance, paid most attention to rural poverty, and the Kennedy Administration's early concern with poverty concentrated on Appalachia. However, as Chapter 3 shows, after 1964 the civil rights movement and urban civil violence refocused the lens on poverty. Poverty increasingly appeared an urban problem most seriously afflicting blacks, even though most poor people were white.

President Lyndon B. Johnson's commencement speech at Howard University on June 4, 1965, signaled the shifting focus of anti-poverty efforts. The "great majority of Negro Americans—the poor, the unemployed, and the dispossessed," said Johnson, "are another nation. Despite the court orders and the laws, despite the legislative victories and the speeches, for them the walls are rising and the gulf is widening.... The isolation of Negro from white communities is increasing rather than decreasing, as Negroes crowd into the central cities and become a city within a city.... Negro poverty is not white poverty. Many of its causes and many of its cures are the same. But there are differences—deep, corrosive, obstinate differences—radiating painful roots into the community, the family, and the nature of the individual."[40]

Johnson based his remarks on a hitherto confidential report, *The Negro Family: The Case for National Action*, which had been submitted to him in March 1965. Its principal author was Daniel Patrick Moynihan, then assistant secretary of labor in the Office of Policy Planning and Research of the Department of Labor.[41] Moynihan's report, finally published in the fall, became one of the most controversial documents in the history of American social science.[42] Moynihan drew on the work of early black sociologists, especially E. Franklin Frazier, and the recently completed *Dark Ghetto* by black social psychologist Kenneth Clark.[43] His explanation for worsening poverty among urban blacks did not name the culture of poverty; nor did he mention Oscar Lewis or Michael Harrington. Nonetheless, informed readers could not miss the striking parallels between Lewis's culture of poverty and Moynihan's cycle of poverty—the "subculture...of the Negro American" and "tangle of pathology" (a phrase borrowed from Clark).[44] Moynihan's report outraged black leaders and a great many of their white supporters. Because most critics distorted the report, the debate generated more passion than insight. One result was to accelerate the burial of the culture of poverty as an acceptable idea in liberal reform and research for close to a half century.[45]

Moynihan, points out James T. Patterson, "was a reformer who believed that poor people had to receive substantial government help." But this did not lead him to dismiss "the power of cultural forces.... He worried that racist and economic pressures had driven many poor Americans, especially blacks, so far into the depths that they were in great danger of passing on a host of dysfunctional behaviors to future generations." At the same time, "he also believed that unemployment was the major source of instability within poor families, and that government could and should act to improve their chances in life."[46]

Moynihan argued that the Civil Rights Act of 1964 had fulfilled "the demand of Negro Americans for full recognition of their civil rights." Now, Negro Americans would press "beyond civil rights." They would want their equal opportunities to produce "equal results, as compared with other groups." This would not happen without special effort because two forces undermined blacks' legitimate aspirations for equal results. One was "the racist virus in the American bloodstream that still afflicts us"; the other was the toll of "three centuries of sometimes unimaginable mistreatment." The most difficult fact for white Americans to understand, emphasizes the report, is that conditions within "the Negro American community in recent years" had not been improving. On the contrary, they were worsening. The fundamental problem with black communities was "family structure." The evidence, still a bit tentative admitted the report, was "that the Negro family in the urban ghettos is crumbling." A middle class had managed to save itself, but "for vast numbers of the unskilled, poorly educated city working class the fabric of conventional social relationships has all but disintegrated...So long as this situation persists, the cycle of poverty and disadvantage will continue to repeat itself." Only a massive federal effort could reverse the pathology afflicting the lives of black Americans. Its goal should be "the establishment of a stable Negro family structure."[47]

Moynihan used several indexes to demonstrate the disintegration of the black family: "Nearly a quarter of urban negro marriages are dissolved"; "Nearly one-quarter of negro births are now illegitimate"; "Almost one-fourth of negro families are headed by females"; "The breakdown of the Negro family has led to a startling increase in welfare dependence."[48] As Lee Rainwater and William Yancey point out, Moynihan's dismay at trends in black family structure reflect the influence of Catholic social welfare philosophy emphasis on "family interests" as the "central objective of social welfare and of social policy in general."[49] The influence of the family in "shaping character and ability," wrote Moynihan, "is so pervasive as to be easily overlooked. The family is the basic social unit of American life; it is the socializing unit. By and large, adult conduct in society is learned as a child."[50] By definition, children raised in female-headed families could not learn conduct appropriate to American life. "Ours is a society which presumes male leadership in public and private affairs," asserted Moynihan. "The arrangements of society facilitate such leadership and reward it. A subculture, as that of the Negro American in which this is not the pattern, is placed at a distinct disadvantage."[51]

The current condition of black Americans resulted from a variety of forces. The unique brutality of American slavery, Moynihan argued, had destroyed family life among blacks and crippled black males, and trends after the Civil War had reinforced the assault on black masculinity. "The very essence of the male animal, from the bantam rooster to the four-star general, is to strut. Indeed, in 19th century America, a particular type of exaggerated male boastfulness became almost a national style. Not for the Negro male. The 'sassy nigger' was lynched."[52] The rapid transformation of American blacks from a rural to an urban population had accentuated the deterioration of black family life. When urbanization occurs "suddenly, drastically, in one or two generations," as it did among blacks, observed Moynihan, "the effect is immensely disruptive of traditional social patterns."[53]

Black male unemployment heightened the disorganizing impact of slavery's legacy and rapid urbanization. "The fundamental overwhelming fact is that negro unemployment, with the exception of a few years during World War II and the Korean War, has continued at disaster levels for 35 years." Employment affected family patterns profoundly. During the periods when jobs for black men had been relatively plentiful, "the Negro family became stronger and more stable. As jobs became more and more difficult to find, the stability of the family became more and more difficult to maintain."[54] The American wage system added to the other factors eroding black family stability. Although it offers relatively high incomes for individuals, it rarely ensures "that family, as well as individual needs are met." Alone among industrial democracies, America failed to supplement workers' incomes with family allowances. Because black families have the largest number of children and the lowest incomes, "many Negro fathers literally cannot support their families. Because the father is either not present, is unemployed, or makes such a low wage, the Negro woman goes to work." This "dependence of the mother's income" further undermined the position of the father and deprived the children "of the kind of attention, particularly in school matters, which is now a standard feature of middle-class upbringing."[55] For Moynihan, therefore, male unemployment and underemployment remained key issues.

The result of these trends, as Moynihan saw it, was a self-perpetuating cycle of poverty, which he described provocatively as a "tangle of pathology."[56]

> In essence, the Negro community has been forced into a matriarchal
> structure which, because it is so out of line with the rest of American

society, seriously retards the progress of the group as a whole, and imposes a crushing burden on the Negro male and, in consequence, on a great many Negro women as well.

Moynihan naturalized patriarchal gender roles as the standard from which black families had departed. "A fundamental fact of Negro American family life is the often reversed roles of husband and wife." He cited with alarm a research study that purposed to show that in "44 percent of the Negro families studied, the wife was dominant, as against 29 percent of white wives." This matriarchal family pattern that inverted natural sex roles proved insidious because "it reinforces itself over time." Moynihan found problematic the education gap between black female and male students. "There is much evidence that Negro females are better students than their male counterparts." These educational "disparities...carried over to the area of employment and income." In one quarter of black families "where the husband is present, is an earner, and someone else in the family works, the husband is not the principal earner." In comparable white families, the proportion was 18 percent. "More important, it is clear that the Negro females have established a strong position for themselves in white collar and professional employment, precisely the areas of the economy which are growing most rapidly and to which the highest prestige is attached." Moynihan turned black women's strengths and accomplishments into evidence that they had subverted the natural order of gender relations. Rather than cause for admiration, black women's achievements emerged as reasons for deep concern because by reproducing matriarchy, they weakened black men and perpetuated the tangle of pathology in the nation's urban ghettos.[57]

Housing segregation worsened the situation because it prevented stable middle-class black families from escaping the "cultural influences of the unstable ones."[58] Besides matriarchy, the "tangle of pathology" revealed itself in "the failure of youth" (defined by poor school performance and low scores on standardized tests); delinquency and crime; the failure rate on the Armed Forces Qualification Test; and the alienation of black youths, reflected in staggering unemployment rates, "narcotic addition," and isolation from white society. "The present generation of Negro youth," observed Moynihan, "growing up in the urban ghettos has probably less personal contact with the white world than any generation in the history of the Negro American."[59]

Only a program of national action could begin to undo the "tangle of pathology." Its object should be "to strengthen the Negro family so as to enable it to raise and support its members as do other families."[60] Moynihan purposefully omitted specific policy recommendations. His audience was the administration; he wanted to persuade the president and his advisors to mount a coordinated attack on the forces retarding the economic progress of black Americans. Clearly, this goal influenced his choice of language, his provocative metaphors, and the lack of balanced argument. As Rainwater and Yancey observe, an alternative approach to poor urban black families would concentrate on how "particular family patterns" help individuals adapt to deprivation and survive "in the one world in which they must live." (This has been, precisely, the approach of urban ethnographers.) From this point of view, some of the very behaviors that appear "pathological" assist families "to make as gratifying a life as possible in the ghetto milieu." Had he emphasized the positive aspects of black family patterns, Moynihan might have avoided some of the criticism his report provoked.[61] But this was not possible. The problem with Moynihan's presentation extended deeper than rhetoric. It lay, as we shall see, in his incorrect beliefs about the legacy of slavery, patriarchal view of the family, and emasculating impact of strong women. It is not surprising that the report initiated a major debate on the black family in which Moynihan became the villain.

Major newspaper accounts omitted Moynihan's emphasis on unemployment as the major source of family disorganization. Scholarly commentators relied on newspaper accounts rather than on the original report, distorted Moynihan's arguments, and offered as their own alternatives views Moynihan either explicitly or implicitly shared.[62] Moynihan's report aroused passionate hostility because it intersected with the second phase of the civil rights movement, which emphasized black pride and power. In this context, his thesis "deeply embarrassed" advocates of increased black political power because his stress on social pathology contradicted claims of black achievement.[63] Criticism of Moynihan did not result solely from misreading his report. It reacted as well to his misreading of history and patriarchal assumptions, which, as Chapter 2 explains, violated the racial and gender premises of the politics of liberation nearing their zenith at the time Moynihan wrote and, indeed, remain deeply offensive to African American women to this day.

The attacks on Moynihan highlight the swelling reaction against cultural explanations of poverty and other ideas that assumed passivity and disorganization among the poor.[64] Although Moynihan rarely used the word "culture," clear parallels exist between his report and early descriptions of the culture of poverty. Critics associated his argument with theories of cultural deprivation. Both Moynihan and culture of poverty theorists located the perpetuation of poverty in attitudes and behaviors transmitted from one generation to the next. Both stressed the origins of those behaviors in the legitimate frustration and alienation bred by blocked opportunities; and both used similar indicators to identify the "culture of poverty" or "tangle of pathology": a high proportion of female-headed families, unrestrained sexuality, an inability to defer gratification, and an apathetic withdrawal from social involvement.

Moynihan did not share Oscar Lewis's emphasis on the adaptive, strategic role of poverty culture. Nonetheless, a casual reading could easily lump both views together as attempts to use cultural explanations to reinforce sophisticated versions of the old idea that poverty resulted from individual behavior. To their critics, Lewis's families caught in the culture of poverty, educators' culturally deprived children, and Moynihan's black families all seemed mid-twentieth-century euphemisms for the undeserving poor. The ironic outcome of Moynihan's report, therefore, was to sweep the black family off the agenda of policy research and to hasten the culture of poverty's amputation from its liberal origins. The idea of such a culture, however, did not disappear. Instead, it became a conservative rationalization for cutting welfare until, in the first decade of the twenty-first century, "culture" staged a stunning reentry into mainstream poverty research.

Culture as a Conservative Idea

Even in the late 1950s and 1960s, liberal social scientists did not have a monopoly on cultural approaches to poverty. Among the more conservative writers who also developed cultural interpretations of poverty, the political scientist Edward Banfield became the most prominent. At the same time that Oscar Lewis first described Mexican villagers as trapped in a culture of poverty, Banfield used culture to explain the failure of economic development and modernization. Banfield did not share Lewis's belief that political mobilization could destroy the culture of poverty, and when he extended the fatalistic implications of his interpretation of a "backward society" to American cities, Banfield stressed the futility of liberal reform. Published shortly after the Moynihan report, Banfield's book helped cement the association of culture with conservatism. It foreshadowed the major themes in conservative writing about poverty and welfare during the next two decades.

In 1958 Banfield published an account of the Southern Italian village Montegrano under the title, *The Moral Basis of a Backward Society*.[65] In Montegrano he found a cultural pattern, which he labeled "amoral familism," that inhibited corporate action and perpetuated the miserable lives of its peasants. Banfield identified "amoral familism" as behavior consistent with a simple rule: "Maximize the material, short-run advantage of the nuclear family; assume that all others will do likewise."[66] Montegranesi never joined together to sponsor projects such as the improvement of roads; the village had no voluntary charities; most residents said that no one was "particularly public-spirited"; there was no "stable and effective [political] party organization; villagers remained reluctant to help one another; and friends were "luxuries" they felt they could not afford. The example of Montegrano showed that "technical conditions and natural resources" did not inevitably result in the formation of economic and political associations that sponsored development. Instead, the intervening force of culture caused people to live and think in "ways...radically inconsistent with the requirements of formal organization."[67]

Because their family-centered ethos prevented them from acting "concertedly or in the common good," better incomes, argued Banfield, would do little to "make the atmosphere of the village less heavy with melancholy." Indeed, it would probably worsen the situation, because without "accompanying changes in social structure and culture, increasing incomes would probably bring with them increasing frustration."[68] By 1970 Banfield had extended his pessimistic forecast for social and cultural change to American cities.[69] Like the Montegranesi, the American urban lower class remained trapped by a culture that inhibited advancement and perpetuated pathology. Without transgressing against democratic and constitutional rights, government could do little to alter the situation. In fact, most of its well-meaning interventions had been ineffective or harmful.

Banfield belittled the then-fashionable despair about American cities and argued that no urban crisis in fact existed. On most measures, conditions within cities had improved. Even the number and "relative disadvantage" of "the poor, the Negro, and others who stand outside the charmed circle" had decreased. As a result, "a great many so-called urban problems" were really conditions that we either "cannot eliminate or do not want to incur the disadvantage of eliminating."[70] One reason those conditions remained intractable was, as in Montegrano, their anchor in lower-class culture.

To Banfield, class exerted a major influence on "the city's form and the nature of its problems." To whatever source they traced class, he argued, all definitions stressed its expression in a "characteristic patterning that extends to all aspects of life: manners, consumption, child-rearing, sex, politics, or whatever." No agreement existed on the core principle that unified each cluster of traits. For his purposes, and from a policy standpoint, "the most promising principle seems to be that of psychological orientation toward the future."[71] Banfield located four classes in America: upper, middle, working, and lower. The distinction between the working and lower class played a pivotal role in his analysis, because he wanted to separate the poor into groups defined by their psychology and behavior. "The reader is asked to keep in mind," he advised, "that members of a 'class' as the word is used here are people who share a 'distinct patterning of attitudes, values, and modes of behavior,' *not* people of like income, occupation, schooling, or status. A lower class individual is likely to be unskilled and poor; but it does not follow from this that persons who are unskilled and poor are likely to be lower class."[72]

Banfield defined the lower class person by his "time-horizon." (Note the use of the male pronoun. Banfield describes class behavior almost exclusively in male terms.)

The lower-class person lives from moment to moment, he is either unable or unwilling to take account of the future or to control his impulses. Improvidence and irresponsibility are direct consequences of this failure to take the future into account...and these consequences have further consequences: being improvident and irresponsible, he is likely also to be unskilled, to move frequently from one dead-end job to another, to be a poor husband and father.[73]

The lower-class person was also impulsive. "Bodily needs (especially for sex) and his taste for 'action' take precedence over anything else—and certainly over any work routine." With a "feeble attenuated sense of self," suffering from "feelings of self-contempt and inadequacy," he remained "suspicious and hostile, aggressive yet dependent," lacking the ability to maintain a stable relationship with a mate, without attachment to community, neighbors, or friends, and with no interest in voluntary organizations or politics. Because the women in the characteristically female-headed lower-class households were usually impulsive and incompetent, boys drifted into gangs where they learned the "extraordinarily violent" style of lower-class life. Lower-class life, in fact, was not normal, and lower-class people emerged from Banfield's account as less than fully human. "In the chapters that follow, the term *normal* will be used to refer to class culture that is not lower class."

In his interpretation of the origins of the lower class, Banfield repeated a common but incorrect version of urban and ethnic history usually labeled "the last of the immigrants thesis." "The *main* [emphasis in original] disadvantage" of the contemporary Negro, wrote Banfield, was "the same as the Puerto Rican's and Mexican's: namely, that he is the most recent unskilled, and hence relatively low-income, migrant to reach the city from a backward rural area." As with other immigrants, blacks had been attracted to cities by a "job, housing, school, and other opportunities." As poor as facilities in cities were, they were "better by far than any he had known before." Cities were "not the end of his journey but the start of it." Indeed, "Like other immigrants, the Negro has reason to expect that his children will have increases of opportunity even greater than his."[74]

Banfield did not deny the force of race prejudice. Instead, he argued that its intensity and institutional embodiment had lessened. As a consequence, the problems facing contemporary blacks had more to do with class than race. (Chapter 5 takes up the issue of the history of black social structure and the question of black "progress.") Indeed, he expected that "under favorable conditions Negroes can be expected to close the gap between their levels of welfare and those of whites much faster than most people would probably imagine." He predicted that "the movement of the Negro up the class scale appears as inexorable as that of all of other groups."[75]

Casting blacks as the last of the immigrants results in important consequences for policy. It links their advancement to patience, not government intervention or special policies that favor them over others. Cities, Banfield argued, develop according to their own internal logic—determined by the three "imperatives" of rate of population growth, transportation technology, and distribution of income—which place "stringent limits on policy." Government interference might speed up or slow down the process of growth, but it cannot change it.[76] In fact, it often has made problems worse.

One of those problems, Banfield wanted to clarify, was poverty. He argued that urban poverty seldom originated in cities. Cities attracted poor people, and migrants imported poverty. As a term, however, poverty covered a condition with "four degrees": destitution, want, hardship, and relative deprivation. No one within cities was destitute any longer. That is, no one lacked "income sufficient to assure physical survival and to prevent suffering from hunger, exposure, or remediable or preventable illness." Even want had nearly disappeared, and in only a few decades there would "almost certainly" be none.[77] The modern problem of poverty, therefore, had more to do with relative deprivation, with "income *level* [rather] than...income *distribution*" [emphasis in original].[78] Even though the contemporary poor remained no more relatively deprived than their counterparts a decade before, they thought "the gap to be wider." This accentuation of discontent resulted largely from the well-meaning, though misguided, liberalism of the War on Poverty, which, by focusing on income differences, "probably engendered and strengthened feelings of relative deprivation."[79]

Banfield realized that absolute poverty still existed among the people once called "undeserving." Now, as he observed, new terms like "troubled," "culturally deprived," "hard to reach," "chronically," or "multiproblem," carried the same connotation. This poverty reflected both lack of money and the "extreme-presentist orientation" of the lower class. Beyond the boundary of the lower class, "poverty in the sense of hardship, want, or destitution" now generally resulted from "external circumstance—involuntary unemployment, prolonged illness, the death of the breadwinner, or some other misfortune." Among the lower class, however, its proximate cause was "ways of thinking and behaving that are, in the adult, if not elements built into personality, at least more or less deeply ingrained habits."[80]

All the problems of the lower class melded in fact into one problem: "the existence of an outlook and style of life which is radically present-oriented and which therefore attaches no value to work, sacrifice, self-improvement, or the service to family, friends, or community."[81] The Italian peasants of Montegrano at least owed a fierce loyalty to their immediate family. The American urban lower class lacked even this small, redeeming virtue.

Not surprisingly, therefore, none of the programs directed toward lower-class reformation in recent years succeeded; only policies unacceptable in a constitutional democracy (such as semi-institutional care, separation of children from parents, or preventive detention based on statistical probability of criminal behavior) could even begin to eradicate it. In their absence, the lower class would replenish itself and continue to generate serious urban problems at a rate far exceeding its size.[82] Government, Banfield feared, would only exacerbate the problem, because its "growing multitude of programs" created an unstoppable "bureaucratic juggernaut" that had no effect on the core of the problem. If the government needed a symbol for its policies, what was preferable "in every way" to a Freedom Budget or Marshall Plan was a "useless dome."[83]

Banfield's work revealed the conservative potential within cultural theories of poverty. Without Lewis's faith in the transformative power of political mobilization, the culture of poverty led neither to socialism nor to a liberal war on poverty. Instead, its logical outcome was the "benign neglect" advocated as a response to urban problems by Daniel Patrick Moynihan when he served in the Nixon administration and the translation of "lower class" into a new synonym for undeserving poor.[84] In fact, Banfield's argument contained all the essential themes of the conservative attack launched on poverty and welfare in the 1980s (and described in Chapter 4): the "last of the immigrants" thesis as a description of American history; the gradual disappearance of physical want; the damage done to the poor by liberal government policy; and the preeminent role of culture and behavior in the perpetuation of misery. In the 1960s and early 1970s, these ideas conflicted with proud and militant independence movements (discussed in Chapter 2) that fought for civil rights and national liberation. They resonated, however, with the idea that poverty was in part a problem of biology and that the undeserving poor were the product of faulty genes as much as, or more so than, toxic environments.

The Biological Inferiority of the Undeserving Poor

In 1866 the Massachusetts Board of State Charities, which had oversight of the state's public institutions, wrote, "The causes of the evil ['the existence of such a large proportion of dependent and destructive members of our community'] are manifold, but among the immediate ones, the chief cause is inherited organic imperfection,—vitiated constitution or *poor stock*."[85] This was the hard version of poverty as a problem of persons. It arose as a response to institutional failure. Beginning in the early nineteenth century, reformers sponsored an array of new institutions designed to reform delinquents, rehabilitate criminals, cure the mentally ill, and educate children. Crime, poverty, and ignorance, in their view, were not distinct problems. The "criminal," "pauper," and "depraved" represented potentialities inherent in all people and triggered by faulty environments. Poverty and crime, for instance, appeared to cause each other and to occur primarily in cities, most often among immigrants. This stress on the environmental causes of deviance and dependence, prominent in the 1840s, underpinned the first reform schools, penitentiaries, mental hospitals, and, even, public schools. Residential institutions, where possible, were to be located outside of cities and governed by "moral therapy," a mild regime that avoided corporal punishment and other harsh sanctions. Public schools, advocated Horace Mann and his allies, should substitute a pedagogy based on appeal to the interests of children, identification with the teacher, and soft sanctions for the prevailing regime of corporal punishment, drill, and extrinsic motivations.[86]

By the mid-1860s it had become clear that none of the new institutions built with such optimism had reached their goals. They manifestly failed to rehabilitate criminals, cure the mentally ill, reeducate delinquents, or reduce poverty and other forms of dependence. The question was, why? Answers did not look hard at the failures in institutional design and implementation or at the contexts of inmates', prisoners', and patients' lives. Rather, they settled on individual-based explanations: inherited deficiencies. The emphasis on heredity in the 1866 Massachusetts State Board of Charities reflected the views of one of its most influential members, Samuel Gridley Howe, founder of the Perkins Institute for the Blind, whose discouragement with the results of the Institute had led him to believe that the blind were mentally inferior and to stress the influence of heredity on mental and physical capacity.[87] Howe's pessimism and emphasis on heredity reflected a parallel move away from environmental causation in theories of insanity, evident, even, in popular novels that touched on the genesis of crime. The Board of State Charities explained that "vitiation or imperfection of stock" originated from two sources: "First, lack of vital force; second, inherited tendencies to vice. The first comes from poor nutrition, use of stimulants, or abuse of functions on the part of progenitors [in other words, the inheritance of acquired characteristics later known as Lamarckianism]. The second comes from their vicious habits of thought and action. The first, or lack of vital force, affects mainly the dependent class, and lessens their ability for self-guidance." The Board supported its belief that the inheritance of acquired characteristics reproduced the undeserving poor as well as criminals, the mentally ill, and other depraved and dependent individuals with scientific evidence from physiologists that emphasized the toxic impact of large amounts of alcohol, which stimulated "those organs or those functions" evident in the "animal passions, and represses those which manifest themselves in the higher or human sentiments which result in *will*." This submission to "animal passions" resulted in the terrible outcomes for posterity evident in the state's dependent, delinquent, and defective population.[88]

The State Board's gloomy emphasis on heredity did not lead it to pessimistic conclusions, however. It believed, rather, in the body's recuperative power over time. Vice had a standard deviation that, if not exceeded, could be eradicated by the body's natural capacity for healing. "The intemperate and vicious classes," argued the Board, "do tend to point in the wrong direction, but the tendency is not yet so established that they point simultaneously. They are still susceptible to the influences of education, and or moral and religious training, and these should be brought to bear on them." In place of despair, the Board promised "we may, by taking thought, during two or three generations, correct the constitutional tendencies to disease and early decay." In fact, the Board, surprisingly, still believed that the persistence of crime and poverty was "phenomenal—not essential in society... their numbers depend upon social conditions within human control." The "important truth" to be "presented in every aspect on and on every proper occasion" was this: "the numerical proportion of the dependent and criminal classes to the whole population is subject to conditions within human control, and may be rapidly increased or lessened by the action of society." The Board had revealed the source of social pathologies through the scientific study of heredity; through the scientific study of society it would excavate the laws governing its prevention. The scientific vehicle, which its secretary Frank Sanborn helped found in 1865, was the American Association for the Promotion of Social Science. The practical vehicle was advocacy of public programs that would remove the inheritable sources of deviance and dependence. The Board advocated: "improvement of dwellings; encouragement to ownership of homesteads; increased facility for buying clothing and wholesome food; decreased facility for buying rum and unwholesome food; restriction of exhausting labor; cleanliness in every street, lane, and yard which the public arm can reach... and many like measures." The Board had started out with an ideology prefiguring eugenics and ended with one anticipating Progressivism. Its early bridge between heredity and environmentalism, or biology and reform, remained one crossed by reformers for only a relatively short time until it was broken by social Darwinism. It was rebuilt in the early twentieth century until demolished once more by eugenicists and their successors and then reconstructed yet again in the early twenty-first century by the proponents of epigenetics.

By the 1920s, two initially separate streams converged in the hard-core eugenic theory that justified racism and social conservatism. "Eugenics," initially coined in 1883 by the English scientist Francis Galton, denoted "the 'science' of improving human stock by giving 'the more suitable races or strains of blood a better chance of prevailing speedily over the less suitable.'" The word itself derived from a "Greek root meaning 'good in birth' or 'noble heredity.'" Galton pioneered the mathematical study of heredity, basing his theories on studies of probability, first developed with sweet pea data in 1876.[89] Social Darwinism composed the other stream. Social Darwinists attempted to apply the theory of Darwinian evolution to human behavior and society. Many "insisted that biology was destiny, at least for the unfit, and that a broad spectrum of socially deleterious traits, ranging from 'pauperism' to mental illness, resulted from heredity."[90]

In the United States, eugenic "science" owed more to the genetic discoveries of Gregor Mendel, first published in 1866 but unrecognized until the end of the century, than to mathematical genetics as practiced by Galton and his leading successor Karl Pearson. In 1904 Charles Davenport, the leading US eugenics promoter, used funds from the newly established Carnegie Corporation to set up a laboratory at Cold Spring Harbor on Long Island. Cold Springs, according to historian Daniel Bender, "revitalized the marriage between biology and the social sciences," which "had gone sour with the advent of Weismanism and the rediscovery of Mendel's laws of inheritance." Anticipating Mendel, August Weismann, the German biologist, had advanced the theory that "essential traits were inherited through...'germ plasm,' an internal substance unaffected by the environment." Davenport looked forward to the "new era" of cooperation between the sociologist, legislator, and biologist who together would "purify our body politics of the feeble-minded, and the criminalistic and the wayward by using the knowledge of heredity."[91]

In the United States, the application of evolutionary and genetic ideas to social issues gained traction in the late nineteenth century as a tool for explaining and dealing with the vast changes accompanying industrialization, urbanization, and immigration. "Herbert Spencer's triumphant 1882 tour of the United States," observes Bender—Spencer was the leading spokesman for social Darwinism—"marked the growing importance of evolutionary thought within and beyond the academy. Hailed as a hero, Spencer was feted with banquets, including a feast on the last night of his tour at Delmonico's in New York, the city's toniest restaurant."[92] "In 1908," reports Daniel Kevles, "the American geneticist Raymond Pearl noted that eugenics was 'catching on to an extraordinary degree with radical and conservative alike, as something for which the time is quite right.'"[93] In 1913 a writer in the *Yale Review* tried to explain the "new 'cult' of eugenics" by pointing to both the "rediscovery of Mendel's laws" and "the growing demands on the taxpayers" caused by "a rapid and steady increase in the ratio of pauperism, insanity, and crime to the whole population."[94]

Darwinists viewed the "unfit" not only as unworthy losers but as savage throwbacks to a primitive life. "A host of poverty experts, settlement workers, reformers, socialists, and eugenicists," observes Bender, "cast paupers, tramps, and prostitutes as 'savage survivals.' Immigrant children in street gangs as well as working women found themselves compared to men of the lower races. Ominously, like the lowest animals, racially inferior humans seemed to be breeding faster than their moral and economic betters."[95] Hereditarian beliefs thus fed widespread fears of "race suicide," giving an urgency to the problem of population control. The "ignorant, the improvident, the feeble-minded, are contributing far more than their quota to the next generation," warned Frank Fetter of Cornell University.[96]

Eugenics drew support from both conservatives and progressives. Conservatives found in eugenics justification for opposing public and private charities that would contribute to the reproduction of the unfit. Davenport, for instance, pointed to a strong role for heredity in a number of diseases and in conditions such as alcoholism and "feeblemindiness"—"a catchall term of the day, used indiscriminately for what was actually a wide range of mental deficiencies." He "similarly reduced pauperism to 'relative inefficiency [which] in turn usually means mental inferiority.'" "Reformers and eugenicists shared, above all, a faith in the explanatory power of evolution and individuals, most notably birth control activist Margaret Sanger, crossed fluidly from one campaign to the other."[97] Settlement workers, argues Bender, saw "the immigrant working class" standing "on a precipice with degeneracy looming in the abyss on the other side." Like their predecessors on the Massachusetts State Board of Charities decades earlier, they reconciled their belief in the biological foundation of physical and moral degeneration with their commitment to the power of environment in shaping character and behavior through "a kind of neo-Lamarckianism that posited that acquired characteristics were passed on to future generations." Their role combined weeding out the irredeemable with providing a social environment in which adults would build character and acquire habits that they would transmit to their children. Social worker James Reynolds emphasized, "we are helping to prevent the continuance of evils whose triumph would mean the pauperizing or degradation of another generation."[98]

Immigration restriction was one campaign that drew support from progressive reformers as well as from conservatives. Davenport, for instance, reserved his heaviest fire for the new immigrants pouring into America, all of whom he believed came from biologically different races. They would, he expected, "rapidly make the American population 'darker in pigmentation, smaller in stature, more mercurial...more given to crimes of larceny, kidnapping, assault, murder, rape, and sex-immorality.'" One possible solution was state-enforced sterilization; another was immigration restriction. Davenport's colleague, Harry Laughlin, who directed the Eugenics Records Office at Cold Spring, established with money from Mrs. E. Harriman in 1911, became the principal advisor to the congressional committee that recommended the nationality-based immigration quotas in the 1920s.[99]

Nonetheless, by the 1920s, cracks appeared in the bridge that linked hereditarians and environmentalists. Hereditarians took an increasingly hard line, manifest especially in the use and interpretation of intelligence tests and the advocacy of sterilization. The French psychologist Alfred Binet, "an acoloyte of Galton's quantifying aims," developed the first intelligence tests in France in the early twentieth century at the request of the French government, which sought a means for identifying mentally deficient children. In 1880 American psychologist Henry H. Goddard brought intelligence tests to the United States, where he first applied them at the Vineland, New Jersey, Training School for Feeble-Minded Boys and Girls—he was the director of its new laboratory for the study of mental deficiency. Goddard extended his studies, intro-ducing the classifications "idiot," "imbeciles," and "morons," and even-tually published *The Kallikak Family: A Study in Feeble-Mindedness* in 1912, which he followed in two years with *Feeble-Mindedness: Its Causes and Consequences*. The feeble-minded lacked "an understanding of right and wrong and the power of control." Some of them became paupers "because they found the burden of making a living too heavy." Feeble-mindness, he was certain, constituted "a condition of mind or brain which is transmitted as regularly and surely as color of hair or eyes."[100] "After Goddard instituted IQ tests for immigrants upon their arrival at Ellis Island," reported Stephen Jay Gould, the great critic of hereditarian-based theories of intelligence, "he proclaimed more than 80 percent of them feeble-minded and urged their return to Europe."[101]

Other psychologists picked up Goddard's work on intelligence test-ing, extended it to other populations, and experimented with different methods. Lewis Terman at Stanford, one of the most prominent and a proponent of the hereditarian view of intelligence, introduced the term "IQ," which stood for "intelligence quotient," a concept devel-oped in 1912 by William Stern, a German psychologist. Intelligence testing, which at first aroused skepticism and hostility, received a tre-mendous boost during World War I, when a trial of the tests on more than 1.7 million people during the war dramatically brought them to public attention. "The army tests," according to historian Paula Fass, "demonstrated the feasibility of mass testing, and as one text-book on testing noted, 'The possibility of measuring an individual's intelligence by a short and simple test has captured the imagination of school people and of the general public'...the army tests were a significant administrative breakthrough, but the headline-grabber and contemporary interest involved the results."[102] The tests purported to show that nearly one-fourth of the draft army could not read a news-paper or write a letter home and that "the average white draftee—and, by implication, the average white American—had the mental age of a thirteen-year-old." Blacks, the tests claimed to show, had the average mental age of a ten-year-old.

Davenport, Goddard, and others blamed the results for whites on the immigration of inferior races and used them as ammunition in their advocacy of immigration restriction. One significance of these tests lay in their alleged demonstration that intelligence as well as "mental deficiency" was "genetically determined." The implications for policy were stark. "Terman and other psychologists were quick to point out that opening up avenues of opportunity to the children of the lower socioeconomic groups probably made no sense; they did not have the I.Q. points to compete."[103] These ideas worked their way into public education in the 1920s, underpinning the educational psychology taught in teacher preparation courses and the massive upsurge in testing used to classify students, predict their futures, and justify unequal educational outcomes. After the war, "the same group of psychologists who constructed the army Alphas [the name of the Army intelligence tests] developed the National Intelligence Test." Sales were astonishing: more than 575,000 copies in the first year and more than 800,000 the next year, 1922–23. "By 1922," reports Fass, "it was competing with other tests of a similar kind. In 1922–23, over 2,500,000 intelligence tests were sold by just one firm which specialized in their development and distribution."[104] In the minds of its prominent advocates, intelligence testing was linked with beliefs that science had demonstrated the primacy of heredity over environment and that the immigration of inferior races was driving America toward a dysgenic future. In 1923 Terman told the National Education Association in Oakland that one of the "most significant batteries of tests" measured "certain traits of moral character likely to be associated with delinquency and incorrigibility.... in the traits measured by these tests our gifted children ranked high.... The conclusion is that here as elsewhere gifted children are superior to the common run.... Children of so many superiorities could hardly have acquired them all through environmental influences. Nor have they, for their heredity, too, is demonstrably superior." But "two facts of serious portent should be mentioned. (1) The racial stocks most prolific of gifted children are those from northern and western Europe and the Jewish. The least prolific are the Mediterranean races, the Mexicans and the Negroes. (2) The fecundity of the family stocks from which our gifted children come appears to be definitely on the wane."[105]

Eugenics entered public policy through its influence on immigration restriction, public education, and, as well, state sterilization laws. Indiana passed the first of these in 1907. By the end of the 1920s, twenty-four states had passed laws permitting the sterilization of the mentally unfit. First in the Virginia Supreme Court in 1925 and then in the US Supreme Court in 1920, the case eventually known as *Buck v. Bell* tested the constitutionality of state sterilization. The case originated with a sterilization order issued against Carrie Buck, born out of wedlock to a mother certified as feebleminded and herself committed to the Virginia Colony for Epileptics and the Feebleminded. Buck's court-appointed legal guardian challenged the sterilization order. In preparing its defense, Virginia officials "consulted Harry Laughlin at the Eugenics Records Office" who, without ever having seen Buck or her mother in person, "provided an expert deposition that Carrie's alleged feeblemindedness was hereditary." Another staff member at the Eugenics Records Office, Arthur Estabrook, also provided evidence for the state. The Supreme Court, by a vote of 8-1, upheld the Virginia Statute, declaring "sterilization on eugenic grounds was within the police power of the state, that it provided due process of law, and that it did not constitute cruel or unusual punishment." Writing for the Court, Justice Oliver Wendell Holmes issued his famous (or infamous) dictum: "Three generations of imbeciles are enough."[106]

Even before the 1920s, strains between eugenicists and reformers had opened fissures in the consensus around the heritability of mental and character defect. Eugenicists' commitment to "germ plasm" pulled them away from the environmental neo-Lamarckianism on which reformers depended. Criticisms surfaced at conferences held at the Race Betterment Foundation, started by cereal millionaire J. H. Kellogg in Battle Creek Michigan in 1914, 1915, and 1928. "Advocates for reform found themselves face-to-face with eugenicists and both presented competing visions of race betterment. It became clear that the emerging science of the 'germ' favored eugenics." Attempts to chart a middle ground between the two failed, signaling the victory—albeit temporary—of the eugenicists and the need for the reformers to find other grounds to support their emphasis on the environmental sources of social pathologies.[107]

Biochemistry and the rise of the Nazis combined to drive eugenics into eclipse and disrepute after the 1920s. The more research revealed about the complexity of human genetics, "the less did eugenics—even much of the reform variety—appear defensible in principle, or even within scientific reach." The American Eugenics Society told several newspaper editors that Hitler's 1933 sterilization law "showed great courage and statesmanship." German eugenicists flattered their American counterparts by pointing to the debt that they owed them. In 1936 the University of Heidelberg awarded an honorary doctorate to Harry Laughlin. The American writer, eugenicist, and virulent anti-communist, Lothrop Stoddard, traveled to Germany in 1939, "where he was—to the distaste of many American readers—heartily received by the Nazi leadership, including Adolf Hitler himself."[108]

The fall of eugenics left the field open to environmentalist explanations. Nurture rather than nature became the preferred explanation for crime, poverty, delinquency, and low educational achievement. The emphasis on environment fit with the emergent civil rights movement, which rejected racial, or biological, explanations for differences between blacks and whites—explanations that had been used to justify slavery, lynching, segregation, and every other form of violent and discriminatory activity. Hereditarian explanations fit badly, too, with the optimism underlying the War on Poverty and Great Society that, as Chapter 3 shows, assumed the capacity of intelligent government action to ameliorate poverty, ill health, unemployment, and crime.

Nonetheless, by the late 1960s a new eugenics began to challenge the environmental consensus. Its appearance coincided with the white backlash against government-sponsored programs favoring African Americans and the disenchantment following on what appeared to be the failure of programs of compensatory education designed to make up for the culturally deficient home life of poor, especially poor black, children. "No single publication did more to precipitate the revival," claims Kevles, "than Arthur R. Jensen's 1969 article in the *Harvard Educational Review*, 'How Much Can We Boost IQ and Scholastic Achievement.'"[109] Once again, institutional and programmatic failure became the grounds for invoking science-based theories of the limits imposed by genetic inheritance. Jensen began with the unequivocal assertion, "Compensatory education has been tried and it apparently has failed." He continued:

> Compensatory education has been practiced on a massive sale for several years in many cities across the nation. It began with auspicious

enthusiasm and high hopes of educators. It had unprecedented support from Federal funds. It had theoretical sanction from social scientists espousing the major underpinning of its rationale: the 'deprivation hypothesis,' according to which academic lag is mainly the result of social, economic, and educational deprivation and discrimination—an hypothesis that has met with wide, uncritical acceptance in the atmosphere of society's growing concern about the plight of minority groups and the economically disadvantaged.[110]

Despite this massive investment of resources, "the chief goal of compensatory education—to remedy the educational lag of disadvantaged children and thereby narrow the achievement gap between 'minority' and 'majority' pupils—has been utterly unrealized in any of the large compensatory education programs that have been evaluated so far." His question, thus, was, "Why has there been such uniform failure of compensatory education programs wherever they have been tried?" The short answer—and Jensen's article consisted of 123 pages bristling with statistics and summaries of scientific literature—was that they ran up against a genetic wall. Poor, minority children lacked the intelligence to profit from them. The diagnosis of the problem, he argued, needed to begin *"with the concept of the IQ: how it came to be what it 'really is'; what makes it vary from one individual to another; what can change it, and by what amount"* [emphasis in original]. For Jensen, intelligence had a "specific meaning...namely, the general factor common to standard tests of intelligence....probably best thought of as a capacity for abstract reasoning and problem solving." As such, it was largely inherited. Jensen quoted with approval the 1905 pronouncement of Edward L. Thorndike, perhaps the most prominent educational psychologist of the early twentieth century: "In the actual race of life, which is not to get ahead, but to get ahead of somebody, the chief determining factor is heredity." The "preponderance of evidence" gathered since Thorndike's time had "proved him right, certainly as concerns those aspects of life in which intelligence plays an important part." After a review of the available data, Jensen concluded that "the composite value" for the heritability of intelligence "is .77, which becomes .81 after correction for unreliability....This represents probably the best single overall estimate of the heritability of measured intelligence that we can make." (Unfortunately for his case, Jensen had relied for his most important evidence on twin-studies by Cyril Burt, a prominent British educational psychologist, which, in the early 1970s, were revealed as fraudulent by Princeton psychologist Leon Kamin.) From this data about the heritability of intelligence, Jensen drew the unavoidable conclusion that class and race variation in intelligence reflected primarily genetic rather than environmental differences. This is why the IQ changes produced by compensatory education programs, he argued, were so small.[111]

"The reaction to Jensen's article," reported Harvard psychologist Richard Herrnstein and conservative writer Charles Murray, "was immediate and violent. From 1969 through the mid-1970s, dozens of books and hundreds of articles appeared denouncing the use of IQ tests and arguing that mental abilities are determined by environment, with the genes playing a minor role and race none at all. Jensen's name became synonymous with a constellation of hateful ways of thinking."[112] Nonetheless, the controversy over Jensen breathed new life into research and writing on the influence of heredity on intelligence and seeped into the rationales for failure offered by educators. (I recall sitting in a meeting in the early 1970s with a high-level Toronto school administrator who, in a discussion of the low achievement of poor students, said, in effect, "well, Jensen has told us why.") In 1971 Nobel laureate physicist William Shockley told the National Academy of Sciences, "Diagnosis will, I believe, confirm that our nobly intended welfare programs are promoting dysgenics—retrogressive evolution through the disproportionate reproduction of the genetically disadvantaged." Herrnstein wrote in *The Atlantic* that "the tendency to be unemployed may run in the genes of a family about as certainly as bad teeth do now."[113] Harvard zoologist E. O. Wilson, a leading authority on insect societies, helped found the new field of sociobiology, which, he wrote, focused on "the study of the biological basis of social behavior in every kind of organism, including man."[114] This new emphasis on heritability, however, met strong scientific as well as political criticism and failed to clear away the taint that still clung to eugenics and genetically-based theories of race, intelligence, and behavior. The idea that the undeserving poor were genetically inferior had not been wiped from the map by any means, but it remained muted, unacceptable in most academic circles.

In 1994, in their widely publicized and discussed *The Bell Curve*, Herrnstein and Murray—whose notorious *Losing Ground* (discussed in Chapter 4) had served as the bible for anti-welfare state politicians—challenged the reigning environmentalist view of intelligence. Their 800-page plus book reported and elaborated on "six conclusions regarding tests of cognitive ability...that are now beyond significant technical dispute."

1. There is such a thing as a general factor of cognitive ability on which human beings differ.
2. All standardized tests of academic aptitude or achievement measure this general factor to some degree, but IQ tests expressly designed for that purpose measure it most accurately.
3. IQ scores match, to a first degree, whatever it is that people mean when they use the word *intelligent* or *smart* in ordinary language.
4. IQ scores are stable, although not perfectly so, over much of a person's life.
5. Properly administered IQ tests are not demonstrably biased against social, economic, ethnic, or racial groups.
6. Cognitive ability is substantially heritable, apparently no less than 40 percent and no more than 80 percent.[115]

Success in American society, they argued, was increasingly a matter of the genes people inherit. Intelligence, in fact, had a lot to do with the nation's "most pressing social problems" such as poverty, crime, out-of-wedlock births, and low educational achievement. It was true, they admitted, that whites growing up in the worst socioeconomic circumstances are far more likely to fall into poverty than those growing up in the most advantaged family. *"But low intelligence is a stronger precursor of poverty than low socioeconomic background."* Poverty, they argued, "is concentrated among those with low cognitive ability," which, itself, was largely inherited. It also was racially tinged because blacks, they found, revealed lower cognitive ability at every socioeconomic level. Evidence "pointing toward a genetic factor in cognitive ethnic differences is that blacks and whites differ most on the tests that are the best measures of g, or general intelligence."[116]

With the cognitive elite producing fewer children and the nation overrun by immigrants with low IQs, Herrnstein and Murray saw only a dysgenic future for America divided into a wealthy cognitive elite and a growing, menacing cognitive underclass. The newly consolidated coalition of the cognitive elite and the wealthy "is already afraid of the underclass. In the next few decades, it is going to have a lot more to be afraid of." Public policy directed toward promoting an unattainable and undesirable equality through measures like affirmative action, welfare, and disproportionate education spending on the poor at the expense of the gifted only pushed the nation faster along the road to disaster. Herrnstein and Murray deployed advanced statistical techniques and drew on contemporary research to give their case scientific grounding. But stripped of its scientific veneer it revealed the persistence of some of the oldest themes in American writing on social issues: the combination of crime, poverty, ignorance, and other social pathologies into single condition with different manifestations but a common origin in inherited inferiority; the use of "science" to make its case about the heritability of human weakness; the ineffectual and perverse outcomes of well-meaning public policy; and the threatened collapse of American society under the weight of its dysgenic future.[117]

Herrnstein and Murray based *The Bell Curve* on both philosophy and science. As philosophy, they situated their argument in a long tradition of writing sympathetic to inequality as inevitable, justifiable, and, even, important to the promotion of the general welfare and happiness—"the social tradition of an Edmund Burke...the economic tradition of an Adam Smith." As science, they based almost all their conclusions on the NLYS—the National Longitudinal Survey of Labor Market Experience of Youth that started in 1979 with a national sample of participants aged fourteen to twenty-two—and the AFQT—the Armed Forces Qualification Test administered to the sample to measure cognitive ability. In *Inequality by Design*, a detailed and powerful demolition of *The Bell Curve*, Claude Fischer and his colleagues show how Murray and Herrnstein misused both the AFQT and NLYS, leaving their empirical conclusions utterly unreliable and their larger argument in shambles. *The Bell Curve*, they point out, "was attacked even as it was publicized." Despite assaults in the public media and by scholars, "the book withstood the attacks and sold hundreds of thousands of hardcover copies (perhaps a record for a book with dozens of pages of statistical tables)." For this reason, they felt compelled to reanalyze the data on which the book rested and expose its misunderstanding of inequality. Fischer and his colleagues show that Murray and Herrnstein "made major errors that exaggerated the role of the AFQT relative to social factors. For example, the AFQT is largely a measure of *instruction*, not native intelligence.... Moreover, a correct analysis of the NLSY survey reveals that the AFQT score is only one factor among several that predict how well people do; of these factors, the social ones are more important than the test scores" [emphasis in original]. "Even more importantly, *The Bell Curve* also provides an inadequate understanding of systems of inequality."[118]

Fischer and his colleagues provide many examples that undermine *The Bell Curve*'s credibility. For instance, they show that the real distribution of test scores from the AFQT did not simulate a bell curve, or normal distribution. In order to produce the bell curve they wanted, Herrnstein and Murray resorted to "a good deal of statistical mashing and stretching. Because they presumed... that intelligence must be distributed in a bell curve, they justified transforming the number of questions each test taker correctly answered until they produced the bell curve" they needed. In their analysis of the NLSY, Herrnstein and Murray had to deal with the problem that "key information was missing for many of the respondents." In the case of income, their solution was to assign to respondents "the *average* parental income reported by the other respondents. But these respondents with missing information were not average respondents." In their reanalysis of the data, Fischer and his colleagues corrected for this error, using "a more appropriate procedure." Their reanalysis showed that *"social environment during childhood matters more* as a risk factor for poverty than Herrnstein and Murray report and that it matters *statistically at least as much as do the test scores* that purportedly measure intelligence" [emphasis in original]. The "most surprising omission of all in *The Bell Curve*'s discussion of poverty is any recognition that women are far likelier to be poor than are men" with similar advantages and test scores. Inequality, they show, does not reflect the intersection of cognitive ability with the natural working of markets, as Herrnstein and Murray contend. Rather, "America's level of inequality is by design. It is not given by nature, nor by the distribution of people's talents, nor by the demands of a 'natural' market. Other Western nations face the same global competition that we do and are about as affluent as we are and yet have managed to develop patterns of inequality less divisive than ours."[119]

The Bell Curve is understood best not as a popularization of science but as an episode in the sociology of knowledge. It is hard to gauge the impact of a book on policy, but *The Bell Curve* probably had much less influence than Murray's earlier *Losing Ground. Losing Ground* fit within the boundaries of acceptable debate. It updated historic conservative positions on poverty and welfare (see Chapter 4) and reinforced the widespread hostility toward welfare expressed in the media and politics, as reflected in the 1980 election of Ronald Reagan as president. *The Bell Curve*, in contrast, hovered outside the boundaries of respectability. The weight of scholarly and political argument still tipped the scales toward environment, and hereditarian theories of causation could not escape a reflexive association with racism. Yet, the book, as Fischer and his colleagues pointed out, did sell an extraordinary number of copies for a thick, quantitatively based academic tome. (Despite the book's reliance on quantification, it is so clearly written that its argument may be followed easily by readers without statistical training.) Clearly, even if it often did not dare speak its name, the suspicion remained alive that heredity underlay the growth and persistence of the "underclass" and the black-white gap in educational achievement, which seemed to many impervious to increased public spending or reform. This suspicion was nurtured by a small set of academic researchers and some foundations, like the Pioneer Fund, which claims that it "has changed the face of the social and behavioral sciences by restoring the Darwinian-Galtonian perspective to the mainstream in traditional fields such as anthropology, psychology, and sociology, as well as fostering the newer disciplines of behavioral genetics, neuroscience, evolutionary psychology, and sociobiology."[120]

From the 1990s onward, a profusion of new scientific technologies has provided the tools with which to explore mechanisms underlying the linkages between biology and society. With astonishing acceleration, neuroscience, evolutionary psychology, genomics, and epigenetics emerged as important scientific fields—in practice, often combined in the same programs. Of the 134 graduate programs in neuroscience in place in 2009, only 40 percent existed in 1986 and 60 percent in 1991, compared to 90 percent 1998. Between 1998 and 2009 the mean number of faculty per program increased from thirty-four to fifty. Neuroscience and other biological advances promised new ways of explaining medical issues, such as the black-white gap in cardiovascular diseases, the increase in diabetes, the rise of obesity, and the origins and treatment of cancer-related disease.[121] They promised, as well, the possibility of understanding how the brain ages and how Alzheimer's disease and dementia might be mitigated or delayed.[122] Research focused, too, on how the environmental stresses associated with poverty in childhood could damage aspects of mental functioning and learning capacity with lasting impact throughout individuals' lives and, some scientists believed, beyond through the inheritance of acquired deficiencies.[123]

In its January 18, 2010, cover story, *Time* announced, "The new field of epigenetics is showing how your environment and your choices can influence your genetic code—and that of your kids." Epigenetics, the article explained, "is the study of changes in gene activity that do not involve alterations to the genetic code but still get passed down to at least one generation. These patterns of gene expression are governed by the cellular material—the epigenome—that sits on top of the genome, just outside it.... It is these 'epigenetic' marks that tell your genes to switch on or off, to speak loudly or whisper. It is through eugenic marks that environmental factors like diet, stress and prenatal nutrition," which "can make an imprint on genes," are transmitted "from one generation to the next." More soberly, the eminent child psychiatrist Sir Michael Rutter offered this definition: "The term 'epigenetics' is applied to mechanisms that change genetic effects (through influences on gene expression) without altering gene sequence."[124] The flood of scholarly research and popular writing on epigenetics justified science writer Nessa Carey's giving her book the title, *The Epigenetics Revolution*. The revolution, according to Carey, "that has happened very recently in biology is that for the first time we are actually starting to understand how amazing epigenetic phenomena are caused."[125]

Epigenetics found such a receptive audience, in part, because once again scientific advance coincided with a major social issue—this time, the "achievement gap." The stubborn persistence of a gap between the educational achievement of African American and white students bedeviled educators and appeared to elude the efforts of educational reformers. The allegedly tightening link between school success—notably higher education—and good jobs combined with the pressure on schools to improve their performance on standardized test results placed increasing urgency on the question of what it would take to reduce the gap. The meteoric increase in articles on the achievement gap during the first decade of the twenty-first century testifies to the problem's prominence in the pantheon of educational dilemmas. A search of scholarly articles turned up six references to achievement gap in 2000, twenty-nine in 2005, and sixty-eight in 2011.[126] A large literature suggested a variety of answers, most of which focused in one way or another on the handicaps associated with growing up in poverty while the proponents of hereditary explanations lurked in the background. What the environmentalists lacked was a mechanism that explained exactly how the environment of poverty was translated into low school achievement. This is what epigenetics offered.[127]

Time's breathless account ran ahead of the evidence about the heritability of acquired characteristics and limits of existing epigenetic knowledge. Even Carey, an epigenetics enthusiast, warned, writing specifically about neuro-epigenetics, "this whole area, sometimes called neuro-epigenetics, is probably the most scientifically contentious field in the whole of epigenetic research."[128] In fact, the links between childhood, poverty, and biology are exceedingly complicated and only partly understood, as serious scientists working in the area readily admit. Much of the existing evidence on the "biology of social adversity" was summed up in the October 2012 publication of the papers of a December 2011 symposium cosponsored by the National Academy of the Sciences and the Canadian Institute for Advanced Research. The papers addressed a number of key questions: "What...are the developmental and biological consequences of early exposures to penury, strife, and hardship? How do experiences of childhood adversity get 'under the skin' and affect physiological and cellular pathways leading to disease susceptibility? How are the adverse circumstances of children 'biologically embedded' into the molecular, genomic systems that determine expressions of vulnerability and resilience? Why do some children flourish, whereas most others founder in the face of severe childhood conditions?"[129] Collectively, the papers provided evidence bearing on each question, and, at the end, a number of key themes emerged reinforcing the impact of early "social adversity" on health and well-being. But many issues remained unresolved or subject to further research. As Rutter wrote:

> First, there needs to be much better conceptualization, categorization, and measurement of the several rather different forms of environmental adversity. Second, much greater use must be made of research strategies that can test environmentally mediated causal hypotheses. Third, there is a need to determine just what epigenetic changes do and do not account for.... Fourth, what do the findings on brain plasticity tell us about the neural responses to brain injury and environmental remediation? Fifth, what are the implications of [gene-environment interaction] for an understanding of the effects of environmental influences and their biological embedding? Sixth, how can preventive interventions be better informed by the biological evidence?[130]

The significance of epigenetic research on how environment alters gene expression—which has made *The Bell Curve* obsolete—according to Nobel laureate economist James Heckman, is that the "modern literature on epigenetic expression and gene-environment interactions teaches us that the sharp distinction between acquired skills and ability featured in the early human capital literature is not tenable.... Genes and environment cannot be meaningfully parsed by traditional linear models that assign unique variances to each component. Abilities are produced, and gene expression is governed by environmental conditions. Behaviors and abilities have both a genetic and an acquired character. Measured abilities are the outcome of environmental influence, including *in utero* experiences, and also have genetic components."[131] The upshot, nonetheless, is the power of early childhood experience. For Heckman, most of the gaps at age eighteen that explain adult outcomes are present by age five. "Converging evidence from neuroscience, molecular biology, genomics, and epigenetics," points out Jack P. Shonkoff of Harvard's Center on the Developing Child, "indicates that the influence of the early years can extend over a lifetime, as it affects the foundations of learning, behavior, and both physical and mental health."[132] By the time disadvantaged children reach school, the clear implication is that it is too late to remedy their cognitive deficiencies or to put them on a road to escape poverty.

Other neuroscientists, it should be pointed out, are not so sure. They view brain development as more plastic, with changes possible through adolescence and, possibly, even in old age, although they find direct evidence of early childhood disadvantage on the size of key areas of the brain, especially those that control memory and executive functions. Rutter points out, "it is now clear that the brain is intrinsically plastic right into adult life, although plasticity reduces with increasing age. The sensitive periods are not as fixed and immutable as was once thought, and they can be extended pharmacologically. . . . In addition, plasticity can be increased by vigorous extended exercise."[133] "The pathways by which socioeconomic deprivation and stress in childhood and adult development negatively influence cognitive health at later ages," report Michelle C. Carlson, Christoher L. Seplaki, and Teresa E. Seeman, "remain plastic and responsive to environment in late-life development."[134] Here, at least, are some grounds for optimism.

Epigenetics has facilitated the reconciliation of hereditarianism and reform that flourished before social Darwinism in the late 1860s and then again in the Progressive Era, before splitting apart in the 1920s. This time, however, the question of the biological ranking of "races" has remained off the table—a reflection of the impact of profound political and social change on science. Epigenetics promises to move beyond the long-standing war between explanations for the achievement gap, persistent poverty, crime, and other social problems based on inheritance and those that stress environment. It gives scientific sanction for early childhood education and other interventions in the lives of poor children. As with earlier invocations of science, popular understanding fed by media accounts threatens to run ahead of the qualifications offered by scientists and the limits of evidence. Herein lies the danger. In the past, the link between hereditarianism and reform proved unstable, and when it broke apart the consequences were ugly. Even when in place the link supported racially-tinged immigration reform and compulsory sterilization—all in the name of the best "science." Indeed, every regime of racial, gender, and nationality-based discrimination and violence has been based on the best "science" of its day. "It is when scientists and doctors insist that their use of race is purely biological," cautions legal scholar and sociologist Dorothy Roberts, "that we should be most wary."[135] In *Beyond Human Nature: How Culture and Experience Shape the Human Mind*, philosopher Jesse J. Prinz warns that "naturism"— theories that stress the biological causes of behavior—"is not just misleading; it is potentially dangerous." Naturism

> has been used to keep various groups down, and it vastly underestimates human potential. When we assume that human nature is biologically fixed, we tend to regard people with different attitudes and capacities as inalterably different. We also tend to treat differences as pathologies. We regard people who think differently than we do as defective. We marginalize groups within our borders and we regard the behavior of foreigners as unnatural or even subhuman.[136]

It is not a stretch to imagine epigenetics and other biologically based theories of human behavior used by conservative popularizers to underwrite a harsh new view of the undeserving poor and the futility of policies intended to help them. This is not the aim, or underlying agenda, of scientists in the field, or a reason to try to limit research. It is, rather, a cautionary note from history about the uses of science and a warning to be vigilant and prepared.

2

Poverty and the Politics of Liberation

IN THE 1950S AND 1960s events challenged the reigning image of poor people in American social science. In the same years that social scientists described them as passive, apathetic, and detached from politics, all over the world colonized people were asserting their right to liberation. Wars of independence attacked the vestiges of colonialism in Africa, Asia, and the Near East; guerrilla movements organized against dictatorships in Central and Latin America; in the United States, blacks who mobilized to claim their civil rights linked their cause to the politics of anti-colonialism and expanded their movement into a militant assertion of racial pride and demand for social and economic justice. And a powerful black feminism incorporated the mounting attention to women's poverty into its own politics of liberation. By the late twentieth century, the emphasis on gender equity, poverty reduction, and liberation fused in the burgeoning human rights movement represented by the United Nations-sponsored Millennium Goals and began to arc back from the Global South to the United States.

The Strange Career of "Culture"

Theories of cultural poverty and deprivation reflected hoary images of lower-class pathology that offended advocates of liberation. For all its surface liberalism, American social science seemed to sanction an image of poor people that denigrated their culture and personality, belittled their capacity for self-mobilization, and reinforced direct or indirect colonial rule. It offered them social work and therapy when they needed economic justice and political mobilization.[1] By the late

1960s and early 1970s, social scientists who supported independence movements in the Global South and civil rights, black power, and affirmative action in the United States had challenged the politics, empirical grounding, and theoretical foundation of the culture of poverty.

The implicit politics of cultural theories disturbed many critics. Social scientists sympathetic to national liberation movements argued that the idea of a culture of poverty reinforced colonial domination and obscured the structural sources of exploitation. Randolf S. David, writing from the Philippines, claimed that culture of poverty researchers, "having decided that poverty has reduced people into a sub-species of the human race, proclaim the emergence of a unique and fascinating way of life associated with such extreme deprivation." With a prurient interest in the more lurid aspects of the lives of the urban poor, social scientists had become "well-equipped peeping toms." Despite good intentions, their "romantic interest" cast the condition of the poor "as an *unalterable* given which we can only cope with, adjust to, or build our whole life around."[2] To Alessio Colombis, Banfield's portrait of a southern Italian village reflected the influence of the Cold War on American social science: "His thesis offers a pseudo-scientific cover justifying relations of exploitation and subjection resulting from the situations of domination and inequality that still exist today."[3] Alejandro Portes identified the culture of poverty as one of three major theories that portrayed Latin American slum radicalism as irrational, a "simplistic emotional response to irrational psychological needs." These theories attributed the radicalism of the poor to their cultural backwardness: "Extremism permeates these groups to the extent that they are also permeated by ignorance, social isolation, and irrational aggressiveness."[4]

David, Colombis, and Portes each proposed an alternative framework for interpreting the behavior of poor people. Portes's research on a Chilean slum showed the poorest residents most active in neighborhood councils, and he argued for the fundamental rationality of social conduct.[5] Colombis contended that Banfield neglected the constraints on villagers' behavior, misunderstood class structure, and ignored the exercise of power. His interpretation stressed their "economic, political, administrative, cultural and social subjection" and emphasized the importance of placing the local situation in the context of Italian society.[6] David also urged the replacement of cultural explanation with structural analyses that linked the roots of poverty to the dynamics of exploitation: Urban poverty "implies a relationship of dependence—a relationship which produced further underdevelopment for the poor and continued development for the affluent."[7]

Culture of poverty critics who focused on the United States offered similar objections. Walter Miller underlined the political significance that conceptions of poverty had assumed in the charged atmosphere of the 1960s. Discussions of poverty touched most of the major domestic issues of the time: the urban crisis, welfare, education, the black revolution, white backlash, and violence and crime in the streets. Unsuccessful attempts to respond effectively to these great domestic issues revealed a consistent conceptual failure in thinking about poverty and undercut attempts to formulate a coherent national policy.[8] As a result, according to Chandler Davidson, researchers and advocates had "built a one-sided case against an entire social class—the poor." Whether they were aware of the fact or not, social scientists' descriptions served the interests of the affluent and justified the inequitable distribution of wealth and income.[9] Most writing about American working-class people by sociologists, psychologists, and anthropologists, claimed Eleanor Leacock, contributed to a "picture of a people who, lacking family organization and reared without consistent and close relations with adults... are passive, have difficulty with abstract thinking and communication, seek escape from problems through relatively uninhibited expressions of sex or aggression, lack ego strength and are unable to plan for the future." Programs based on this image attempted to reduce poverty by transforming poor people into "solid middle-class citizens."[10]

Political criticism of the culture of poverty often remained fuzzy around the edges, abstracting a series of conservative implications (often from writers who considered themselves liberal) and attaching them to a broad array of writers. Some critics lumped Oscar Lewis, Michael Harrington, Frank Riessman, Daniel Patrick Moynihan, and Edward Banfield into one category.[11] Clearly, by the late 1960s, the very act of writing about cultural aspects of poverty had assumed political significance.

Many of the culture of poverty's professional critics chose to fight limited engagements. Instead of sweeping political attacks, they attempted to disprove components of the theory with empirical research. The result was a raft of case studies. For example, Leonard Davidson's and David Krackhardt's study of a large manufacturing firm's special training program for poor blacks found that employees' behavior reflected "situational realities" rather than the personalities of minority workers.[12] Frederick Jaffe and Steven Polgar lamented the cooptation of the culture-of-poverty concept as an explanation for slow progress in family planning programs. Using data from American cities, they argued the opposite case: Accessibility, rather than culture and motivation, determined program success.[13] Harlan Padfield, who examined an industrial training program for hard-core unemployed men in San Diego, also asserted that his research results undermined the culture of poverty thesis.[14]

Some of the most important empirical studies that tried to chip away at the culture of poverty idea drew on Hyman Rodman's influential notion of "value stretch," which asserted that lower-class people, without abandoning the general values of mainstream society, developed an alternative set of values that helped them adjust to their circumstances.[15] Elliot Liebow's *Tally's Corner*, an ethnography of street-corner men in Washington, DC, portrayed a "shadow system" of values that qualified Rodman's and others' "alternative system of lower-class values" in two ways. First, alternative or stretched values differed from the general system of values because they are "derivative, subsidiary in nature, thinner, and less weighty, less completely internalized." Second, its users could not automatically invoke the alternative value system; instead, it was "a shadow cast by a common value system in the distorting lower-class culture." Liebow explained the behavior of poor black men "as a direct response to the conditions of lower-class Negro life rather than as mute compliance with historical or cultural imperatives." The street-corner man did not carry an independent cultural tradition; rather his behavior reflected his attempt to achieve many of the goals and values of the larger society and his attempts to conceal his failure from others and himself.[16]

Although other scholars added empirical evidence that contradicted the culture of poverty thesis by discovering indigenous organizations and a capacity for political mobilization among poor people, the generalizability of their work remained uncertain. Ingenious defenders could reinterpret their data, dismiss them as exceptions, or incorporate them as subtle modifications within the larger culture of poverty. By itself, the empirical evidence was too limited, fragmentary, and sparse to support either side in the controversy—which made theoretical and methodological criticism all the more important. Could the assumptions, logic, and research methods of the culture of poverty thesis withstand intense scrutiny? Critics said no.

Theoretical and methodological criticisms of the culture of poverty made several arguments:[17]

1. What does the culture of poverty mean by culture? Critics point to the absence of a uniform or consistent definition and argue that culture usually becomes a synonym for subculture, itself a slippery concept. Of what is the subculture of poverty a subset? What are its boundaries? Does it evolve from a larger culture or arise as a reaction to it? Is there more than one subculture of poverty? These questions lack satisfactory answers.

2. No uniform set of characteristics identify the culture of poverty as it is used by different writers. The long lists of traits usually offered have an ad hoc quality and do not separate indicators of material deprivation from descriptions of behavior and personality. By and large, they do not identify the core characteristics which give shape and coherence to the whole.

3. Presentations of the mechanisms perpetuating the culture of poverty are usually incomplete because they reflexively assume the primacy of socialization. In other words, families pass on the culture of poverty to their children. An alternative, situational explanation is equally plausible: each generation re-adopts the behaviors associated with the culture of poverty as it adapts to similar constraints. The policy implications of this question are important because they lead either to social work and therapy or to politics and redistribution as the method for breaking up the culture of poverty.

4. Culture of poverty theories are tautologies. The pathological behavior of poor people causes their poverty, which is the source of their pathological behavior. This lack of clearly specified independent and dependent variables leaves the reasoning circular.

Most presentations of the culture of poverty, therefore, leave cause and effect hopelessly tangled.

5. The purpose of culture of poverty theories often remains ambiguous. What exactly are they supposed to explain? Family patterns? The persistence of poverty? Political apathy? The answer usually is unclear, and theories become catchalls for a loosely associated set of behaviors and material conditions.

6. Links between subcultures, social institutions, and social structures remain unspecified. The culture of poverty, if it exists, does not float in a vacuum. How is it shaped by the distribution of power and resources? How is it affected by the political and institutional structure in which it is embedded? The culture of poverty literature remains relatively silent on these questions.

7. The boundaries separating culture, class, and ethnicity remain vague in most presentations of the culture of poverty. Is the culture of poverty synonymous with the lower class? Does it penetrate other classes? What distinguishes the definition of class from the definition of culture? Are some of the behaviors identified with the culture of poverty in fact attributes of ethnic groups? Are there distinct subcultures of poverty among different ethnic groups, or does ethnic variation in the behavior of poor people contradict the idea of a culture of poverty?

8. The culture of poverty is an ethnocentric idea. It takes one set of standards—usually white, middle-class, and American—and applies them universally. In the process, it defines differences as pathologies, thereby failing to appreciate their positive, adaptive significance and the validity and coherence of other cultures or subcultures.

9. Most culture of poverty research is static: It examines its subjects at one point in time or throughout a period in which the circumstances that constrain their behavior do not alter. Its predictions about how poor people will react to a change in their constraints and opportunities rest on deductions, not evidence.

Critics of the culture of poverty raised fundamental questions, but most of them did not want to discredit attempts to link culture and poverty. Rather, they exposed weaknesses in existing formulations and pointed to questions left unanswered. Politics also shaped these debates about theory and method, as the participants well knew. Those committed to the idea that the unequal distribution of power and resources shaped and constrained the behavior of poor people wanted to redirect research and policy. In the culture of poverty literature, poverty remained a problem of persons: a set of individual and family-based traits that perpetuated poverty and inhibited achievement. To most critics of the culture of poverty, poverty was either a problem of resources—a lack of money, good education, health care—and/or a problem of political economy—a by-product of capitalist economies. For them, culture remained at best a tangent, interesting and in some vague way important, but a distraction; at worst, it justified the perpetuation of colonialism abroad and inequity at home. In the 1960s and early 1970s, the political climate favored the critics and pushed cultural questions to the margins of poverty research for roughly two decades. Writing in *The New York Times* in 2006, the Harvard University sociologist Orlando Patterson pointed to "a deep-seated dogma that has prevailed in social science and policy circles since the mid-1960s: the rejection of any explanation that invokes a group's cultural attributes—its distinctive attitudes, values and tendencies, and the resulting behavior of its members—and the relentless preference for relying on structural factors like low incomes, joblessness, poor schools and bad housing."[18] However, sociologists and anthropologists who studied poverty failed to replace culture as an organizing concept, thus marginalizing their disciplines among policy makers and facilitating the passage of leadership in poverty research to the economists (discussed in Chapter 3).

Sociologists and anthropologists never gave up on culture. In the early twenty-first century, in fact, culture staged a remarkable comeback in poverty research. The timing reflected frustration with the seeming inability of purely structural theories to account for the growth and persistence of urban poverty and family patterns among the urban poor—the increase in out-of-wedlock births, decline in marriage, absent fathers, and violence, which are discussed in Chapter 5. The eminent sociologist William Julius Wilson, whose 1987 *The Truly Disadvantaged* sparked the revival of research on urban poverty, tried to point poverty research toward a balance of structure and culture, albeit a culture stripped of the major weaknesses of the culture of poverty idea. In his 2009 *More Than Just Race*, Wilson called "for reexamining the way social scientists discuss two important factors associated with racial inequality: *social structure* and *culture*." He predicted the book would "generate controversy because I dare to take culture seriously as one of the explanatory variables in the study of race and urban poverty—a topic that is typically considered off-limits in academic discourse because of a fear that such analysis can be construed as 'blaming the victim.'"[19] Wilson takes a grounded view of culture intended to absolve it of blaming the victim or to allow it to float unmoored from institutional and economic contexts, as in too many variants of the culture of poverty thesis. For Wilson, culture "refers to the sharing of outlooks and modes of behavior among individuals who face similar place-based circumstances (such as poor segregated neighborhoods) or have the same social networks (as when members of particular racial or ethnic groups share a particular way of understanding social life and cultural scripts that guide their behavior)." Social structure and culture each exert independent influence on the production and reproduction of poverty, but, importantly, "they interact to shape different group outcomes that embody racial inequality."[20]

But the matter is not quite so straightforward. In their introduction to a special issue of *The Annals of the American Academy of Political and Social Science* (2010) supporting the use of "culture" in poverty research, Mario Luis Small, David J. Harding, and Michèle Lamont also highlight the new legitimacy of culture in poverty research. "Culture is back on the poverty research agenda," they write. "Over the past decade, sociologists, demographers, and even economists have begun asking questions about the role of culture in many aspects of poverty and even explicitly explaining the behavior of the low-income population in reference to cultural factors." They point out that a new generation of researchers who employ culture in the study of poverty differentiates itself from the older culture of poverty scholarship. "Contemporary researchers," they report, "rarely claim that culture will perpetuate itself for multiple generations regardless of structural changes, and they practically never use the term pathology." This "new generation of scholars . . . *conceives* of culture in substantially different ways. It typically rejects the idea that whether people are poor can be explained by their values. It is often reluctant to divide explanations into 'structural' and 'cultural,' because of the increasingly questionable utility of this old distinction." Even as they advocated for the reintroduction of culture into the study of poverty, Small, Harding, and Lamont curtailed its reach and problematized its distinctiveness.[21]

Small, Harding, and Lamont offer three persuasive motives for why scholarship on poverty should concern itself with culture. The first motive is "to understand better why people respond to poverty the way they do—both how they cope with it and how they escape it." The second motive "is to debunk existing myths about the cultural orientations of the poor," which rest on an astonishingly weak empirical foundation. The third motive "is to develop and clarify exactly what they mean by it—regardless of whether they believe it helps explain an outcome." Ignoring culture, they stress, can lead to bad policy—and they offer a number of examples to support this observation, and argue that, like it or not, culture is very much a part of the "policy discourse on work, marriage, crime, welfare, housing, fatherhood, and a host of other conditions related to poverty."[22]

But these reasons for using culture in the study of poverty do not answer the question, exactly what is culture? If its boundary with structure has collapsed, what remains to be pulled out of the wreckage and deployed in research? The literature on the definition of culture, of course, as they report, is huge and not all that helpful as a guide to working scholars. In fact, their advocacy of culture in poverty research ends up rejecting the usefulness of the term. "While the umbrella term 'culture' might serve as a useful shorthand to point to a constellation of issues to which poverty scholars should pay greater attention, ultimately it masks more than it reveals. At least when the purpose is to understand a specific problem." In place of culture, they recommend using "seven different but sometimes overlapping perspectives, based on seven different concepts—values, frames, repertoires, narratives, symbolic boundaries, cultural capital, and institutions" that are "narrow and distinct analytical devices...far more useful than...the concept of 'culture,' which is generally used in too vague a fashion." In the end, they stage a complete retreat, describing their editorial intent as assembling not a series of essays on "culture" but, rather, a collection designed "to convey a composite and multileveled picture of how meaning-making factors into the production and reproduction of poverty." Culture emerges as a vague umbrella term for analytic devices that show how people make meanings. This is a sophisticated, subtle, and heuristic framework for poverty research, but it is not a rehabilitation of "culture."[23]

The bad odor that wafted from "culture" in the intellectual politics of liberation stemmed from its appropriation as a tool for "blaming the victim"—the means with which to trace the poverty of individuals and families to their own shortcomings, a new method for identifying and stigmatizing the undeserving poor. Even the new culture researchers by and large failed to transcend the individualistic bias in poverty scholarship. In six of the seven analytic frames they describe, observe Small, Harding, and Lamont, "the unit of analysis.... is typically located in individuals or in groups or in interpersonal relations; by contrast, institutions are typically located either in organizations or in society at large."[24] The implicit question remained, how are poor people different and what can be done about it? Culture carried a taint, as well, because of its entanglement with Daniel Patrick Moynihan's report on the black family, with its unfortunate metaphor of the "tangle of pathology." The rehabilitation of Moynihan, in fact, was a precondition for the reentry of culture into poverty research.

Moynihan: From Demon to Seer

Conventional ideological labels fail to capture the complex political response to Daniel Patrick Moynihan's report, *The Negro Family: The Case for National Action*.[25] Moynihan, after all, identified himself with liberal politics and wanted to encourage the Johnson administration to devote more attention and resources to the problems of northern blacks. Many of the critics to Moynihan's political Left—who joined in demonizing him—were themselves, as Rainwater and Yancey point out, trying to modify the way government responded to the needs of African Americans and poor people. As much as Moynihan, they wanted to influence the president. Had the report suited their interests, these critics "would have swallowed their ideological distaste and used the report as an argument for their programs. As with civil rights leaders, the opposition of the Permanent Government (a loose synonym for the civil service, here officials concerned with welfare and labor) to the report stemmed "from organizational threats to their existence and tactical requirements" instead of ideology.[26]

Civil rights leaders applauded President Johnson's Howard University speech with its reference to the "breakdown of the Negro family structure," and they welcomed the idea of a national conference devoted to the needs of black Americans.[27] They became increasingly uneasy, however, as rumors about Moynihan's report and the conference circulated in Washington. Was it, in fact, to be a conference about the black family? Press commentary on the report, which had not been released, only fueled speculation. Then, in the summer of 1965, the Watts riot riveted attention on black ghettos and signaled the end to the first phase of the civil rights movement. Its focus on the legal foundations of discrimination required broadening outward to social and economic issues. A new generation challenged the movement's leaders and questioned both their goal of integration and nonviolent tactics. Newspaper and magazine writers fueled anger among blacks by invoking Moynihan's report (still under wraps) as an explanation of the riot, which they attributed to the deterioration of the black family.

Civil rights leaders could not subscribe to an interpretation that substituted family pathology for unemployment, inadequate housing, poor schools, and police brutality. Nonetheless, leaders' reactions to Moynihan's thesis were not uniform. Younger, militant leaders emerged as most critical. Floyd McKissick, CORE's new director, observed that Moynihan's report "assumed that middle-class American values are the correct ones for everyone in America." McKissick accused Moynihan of thinking that "everyone should have a family structure like his own," and of blaming individuals "when it's the damn system that needs changing."[28] Older leaders stressed the report's strengths as well as its dangers. Martin Luther King, Jr., for one, emphasized the opportunity afforded by public awareness of problems with black family structure "to deal fully rather than haphazardly with the problem as a whole—to see it as a social catastrophe and meet it as other disasters are met with an adequacy of resources."[29]

Civil rights leaders increasingly distrusted Johnson's administration, which did not include them in the conference planning. In fact, the president threatened to leapfrog over civil rights leaders and take leadership of the movement himself.[30] Shaken and surprised by the Watts

riot, increasingly concerned about the implications of the administration's activities, civil rights leaders began to attack the Moynihan
Report and to redirect the forthcoming conference. The black family,
they argued, should not even be on the agenda.

Clearly, this reaction to the family issue worried the Johnson administration. At the November planning conference, only one of eight
agenda papers focused on the black family. One government official
quipped that "he had been reliably informed that no such man as
Daniel Patrick Moynihan existed." Speakers attacked Moynihan, who
responded vigorously. At the conference itself in February, the black
family did not appear on the agenda, and Moynihan's report did not
appear in a bibliography that included fifteen references to Department
of Labor documents.[31]

The Permanent Government's interests differed from those of the
civil rights leaders. Moynihan's report threatened the reputation and
influence of the welfare establishment, which emphasized improving
existing programs. For Moynihan's not-so-hidden message was "that
existing federal programs in labor and in welfare were inadequate to
deal with the problems of the Urban Negro." The report also challenged
the welfare establishment's approach to civil rights, which acquiesced
in "subtle and blatant discrimination and inadequate labor and welfare
services to Negroes." Welfare officials tried to obscure their complicity
in discriminatory treatment by stressing their "color-blind" approach;
they called Moynihan's emphasis on color "reactionary rather than
radical."[32] Because government officials, unlike civil rights leaders,
could not publicly denounce the report, they used other tactics. They
circulated criticisms within government circles and developed alternative statistics. They also turned to their contacts in universities, sending summaries of the report to faculty members and soliciting replies,
which they then used to reject the report's validity. They also leaked
accounts of the report to the press.[33]

It would be misleading to dismiss the controversy surrounding the
Moynihan Report as solely a mix of organizational politics and ideological differences, for the report raised substantive issues of national
importance. Was Moynihan correct about the explosive growth in
the proportion of black female-headed households, out-of-wedlock
births, and teenage pregnancy? Elizabeth Herzog, chief of the Child

Life Studies Branch of the Children's Bureau Division of Research countered that exaggerations had distorted much less alarming patterns revealed by the data. Black families, it is true, were about 2.5 times as likely as white to be "fatherless," but the statistics did not reveal a rapid increase in recent years. After a gradual increase from 1949 (19 percent) to 1959 (24 percent), the rate remained relatively stationary at 23 percent in 1964. Therefore, contrary to Moynihan's claims, the statistics showed that "during the past twenty-five years there has been a gradual rise, preceded and followed by a plateau, but not an acute increase in the over-all proportion of broken homes among Negroes."[34]

The question, of course, was how to interpret a rise of 5 percentage points. To Herzog, it represented a minor increase, but, as Moynihan later replied, it would also be construed as a 25-percent leap. Had the issue been unemployment, this increase would have been considered catastrophic. Other critics, such as William Ryan, argued that undercounting, racial biases in statistical reporting, the differential availability of birth control, and the limited options available to poor, black, pregnant young women so qualified official rates that the trends Moynihan reported could be fictitious. In any case, events soon would undermine arguments that Moynihan had misread the trends. If he had overstated what had happened in the recent past, he was right about the future (as Chapter 5 explains).

Moynihan's exclusive focus on black domestic pathology, as his critics repeatedly pointed out, obscured the rise in female-headed families, divorce rates, and out-of-wedlock birth among whites and variations by income within ethnic groups. References to "the Negro family" casually glossed over the varieties of black families and did not compare the incidence of female heads (or other characteristics) among whites and blacks of comparable economic standing. Had he done so, critics argued, he would have discovered more similarities than differences. As it was, critics contended, Moynihan's report fueled an ideology that condemned black families in general and displaced blame for their problems from segregation, discrimination, and poverty onto alleged cultural pathology. Critics on the political Left themselves were not always consistent on the relation between class and race because they argued in opposite ways when they attacked Moynihan and Oscar Lewis. Moynihan, they claimed, confounded class and race by failing to observe the similar family patterns of blacks and whites within the same social classes. Lewis, they asserted, had erred because he assumed universal cultural patterns within social classes, when in fact they varied by ethnicity.[35]

Curiously, critics neglected a crucial empirical weakness in Moynihan's case. Moynihan showed that trends in unemployment rates and AFDC cases had diverged after 1962. Although nonwhite male unemployment had declined, the number of new AFDC cases had increased. Moynihan assumed this showed the emergence of a self-perpetuating tangle of pathology. "The steady expansion of this welfare program, as of public assistance programs in general, can be taken as a measure of the steady deterioration of the Negro family structure over the past generation in the United States." Here, Moynihan clearly was wrong. Until the mid-1960s, the number of AFDC cases had not reflected the size of the population eligible for cash assistance. In the late 1950s and early 1960s, in fact, only a relatively small proportion of eligible families received AFDC. During the years about which Moynihan wrote, advocates of welfare rights led a campaign to broaden eligibility requirements. As a consequence, the proportion of poor families receiving AFDC began to increase dramatically. Moynihan did not consider the extent to which the rising number of welfare cases opened resulted from an expansion of AFDC to previously eligible families. In fact, though, changing rates of use and eligibility standards undercut any attempt to use AFDC rates as an index of increased family disintegration.[36]

Moynihan's report also skated over normative issues. It assumed but by no means proved that matriarchal family structure and the absence of a father were "pathological." As Herbert Gans pointed out, sociologists had demonstrated an extended and surprisingly stable kinship system of mothers, grandmothers, aunts, and other female relatives among blacks. Many women who headed families, moreover, raised boys who adapted successfully and entered into stable marriages. Indeed, a family headed by a "capable if unmarried" mother could provide a healthier environment than "a two-parent family in which the father is a marginal appendage." Nor should out-of-wedlock births among blacks be evaluated in the same way as among whites, because they carried different meanings for each group.[37]

Both Moynihan and most of his critics assumed that the increase in female-headed black families resulted from choice. Moynihan wanted to find ways to break up a matriarchal culture; critics asserted its validity and strength. Few, however, asked, as did Christopher Jencks, whether in fact "the families in question are matriarchal by necessity or by choice." Jencks could find little evidence that poor blacks preferred matriarchal families; on the contrary, "there is considerable reason to suppose that they eagerly adopted the more patriarchal middle-class norm whenever they can."[38] Writing about four decades later—with the same issue still in play—Kathryn Edin and Maria Kefalas showed a strong commitment to marriage among young single mothers whose domestic aspirations remained frustrated by the unemployment, incarceration, and unavailability of marriageable men.[39]

In *All Our Kin*, anthropologist Carol Stack offered the most influential alternative view of poor black families. Like most other social scientists, Moynihan, she wrote, remained trapped within conventional definitions of family that failed to capture the domestic experience of poor black Americans. Stack's ethnographic study of families supported by welfare found "extensive networks of kin and friends supporting, reinforcing one another—devising schemes for self-help, strategies for survival in a community of severe economic deprivation." As she studied these kin networks, Stack argued for the inadequacy of the conventional definition of a family as the husband, wife, and their children. Instead, she defined family "as the smallest, organized durable network of kin and non-kin who interact daily, providing domestic needs of children and assuring their survival." Using this definition, families extended across "several kin-based households." Stack claimed that her definition made possible the identification of supportive kin networks and offered insight into how the people she studied actually "describe and order the world in which they live." Indeed, her study of kin networks convinced Stack not of the weakness or pathology of black families supported by AFDC, but rather of the "stability and collective power of family life."[40]

Controversy also swirled around the sources of the trends identified by Moynihan. Critics argued that he had substituted matriarchy for unemployment, discrimination, and racism. Benjamin Payton, director of the Office of Church and Race of the Protestant Council of the City of New York, wrote that Moynihan's greatest error lay in his "analysis of the Negro family as 'the fundamental source of the weakness of the Negro community at the present time.'" Payton located the root instead in urbanization, "its conflicts, inadequate resources and injustices."[41]

In part, critics blamed Moynihan for neglecting unemployment and related sources of black disadvantage because of early press reports about what he had written. Based on leaks from government officials and summaries, press reports highlighted the report's emphasis on family pathology and largely ignored its analysis of the economic sources of trends in black domestic life. In fact, Moynihan agreed with his critics' stress on unemployment, but his rhetorical emphasis on family structure along with the unavailability of the report's actual text fueled misconceptions and obscured potential consensus. As a result, much of the public debate on the report reflected not what it said, but what people thought it said.

In the years following the report, its historical underpinning crumbled under the weight of historical research. Moynihan's reliance on the legacy of slavery as a partial explanation of the alleged matriarchal structure of black families came under withering attack. Historian Jacqueline Jones showed how inappropriately matriarchy describes the many-sided roles of black women. Other historians discovered remarkably resilient family structures among slaves. Slavery did not destroy blacks' sense of family. To the contrary, slaves made heroic efforts to preserve family ties; during Reconstruction, freedmen traveled to find mates from whom they had been separated by slave owners, and thousands greeted the opportunity for legal marriage, denied under slavery, by solemnizing longstanding relationships. Herbert Gutman discovered a high proportion of two-parent families among blacks in the post–Civil War South and in early-twentieth-century cities. Theodore Hershberg and his associates demonstrated parallel structures among black and white families of similar wealth in late nineteenth-century Philadelphia and traced increasing rates of female-headed black families to the early death of black men forced into unhealthy and dangerous work and to the inability of poor black women to marry. Stuart Tolnay's careful analysis of census material found higher rates of two-parent families among southern- than among northern-born blacks.[42] It was conditions within the cities to which they had migrated, not slavery, that strained blacks' ability to maintain two-parent families.

Other historians demolished the "last of the immigrants" thesis by showing that black migrants to northern cities faced obstacles not encountered by any immigrant groups. Blacks entered cities in large numbers as unskilled and semiskilled manufacturing jobs were leaving, not increasing. The discrimination they encountered barred them manufacturing jobs to which earlier immigrants had been recruited and which, now, were filled much more often by white migrants from the Appalachian South. Public schools had defined their mission in part as the assimilation and "Americanization" of immigrant children; by contrast, they excluded and segregated blacks. As for welfare, white European immigrants received far more generous benefits than African Americans. Racism and federal mortgage underwriting standards enforced housing segregation. As a result, residential concentration among blacks increased at the same time as it lessened among immigrants and their children. Political machines that embraced earlier immigrants and incorporated them into the system of "city trenches" through which cities were governed excluded blacks from political power until cities had been so abandoned by industry and deserted by whites that resistance to black political participation no longer mattered. All the processes that had opened opportunities for immigrants and their children broke down for blacks. The last of the immigrants joined the legacy of slavery as another myth that had diverted attention from the origins of black poverty and excused the inaction of government.[43]

The assault on what Moynihan was alleged to have written was no surprise. His report appeared at precisely the wrong moment, if its potential receptivity is the measure. Surfacing in the heyday of the politics of liberation, its inflammatory language and whiff of cultural chauvinism guaranteed that the report would become an instant target—an example of white colonialism—for the politics of liberation and a cautionary example to poverty researchers who have troad lightly and carefully around the black family for decades. One might have expected the Moynihan Report to take its place as an episode in the intellectual politics of poverty and, over time, fade into the embrace of history. But this is not what happened. In the early twenty-first century, not long after Moynihan's 2003 death, the Moynihan Report staged a stunning comeback, refurbishing Moynihan's reputation as prescient and a seer.

A 2007 conference on the legacy of Moynihan's report at Harvard sponsored by the American Academy of Political and Social Sciences and Harvard's Sociology Department and DuBois Institute testified to the rehabilitation of Moynihan as a dishonored prophet before his time. The conference papers were subsequently published as a special issue of the *Annals of the American Academy of Political and Social Sciences* edited by Douglas Massey and Robert Sampson, two giants of American sociology.[44] From all quarters came praise for Moynihan and regret that his findings had not been heeded. "When the late Daniel Patrick Moynihan first warned of the social dangers in the decline of black families back in the 1960s, and called for government policies to help deal with these dangers," conservative sociologist Thomas Sowell recounted, "he was attacked viciously for saying something that everyone now recognizes as true because the problem has grown even worse than it was when he issued his warning. The denunciation and demonization of Pat Moynihan marked a major turning point in public discussions of racial issues. From then on, the test of what you said was no longer whether it was true but whether it was politically correct. This silenced the faint hearted—which is to say, most of academia and virtually all of the media."[45] For most researchers, black family structure and behavior—unless celebrated for its resilience and agency—became a third rail, touchable only at great risk.

In both the late 1960s and early twenty-first century, anxiety centered on the number of out-of-wedlock births and their consequences. But at the time Moynihan wrote and for the next twenty years or so, this concern was linked to a panic over a spurious "epidemic" of teenage pregnancy.[46] When even the family Cassandras no longer could deny the decline in teen pregnancy as a source of increasing out-of-wedlock births, attention shifted to the institution of marriage itself and its growing disconnection from parenthood. In both time periods, trends among blacks, whites, and Hispanics moved in the same direction, but blacks remained in the vanguard of family change and the object of most criticism and worry. It was this trend—the disconnection of marriage from parenthood, discussed in Chapter 5, which provided the groundwork for the Moynihan revival. But the revival became possible not only because of demographic trends but, as well, because of a shift in intellectual politics. The politics of liberation had faded into the past, a subject for the burgeoning historical literature on the 1960s and early 1970s, not any longer a powerful force in the academy or among public intellectuals. In the conservative ascendance, which is the subject of Chapter 4, poverty largely dropped off the political agenda, replaced by a concern with welfare dependence, which itself led straight back to the black family. Researchers concerned with poverty—especially poverty among inner city African Americans—could not avoid the consequences of family organization that the intellectual and political climate made it much safer for them to explore. Moynihan became the prophet without honor, deified almost as uncritically as he had been attacked.

In its attempt to discredit the culture of poverty and Moynihan Report—and in the process to remove culture and the black family from the agenda of poverty research—the politics of liberation fought a mostly defensive battle. But there was much more to its story. For in its development of the idea of the ghetto as colony, its links with feminism, and its eventual alliance with human rights, the politics of liberation waged struggles—some of which failed, others of which were partly successful—to alter the frames through which poverty was understood and the means with which it was attacked. The intellectual politics of liberation did more than drive cultural explanations of poverty and black families off the research agenda of social science for decades. It also offered alternate explanations for ghetto poverty in the United States and mass poverty in the Third World.

The Ghetto as Colony

"Whether one is talking about the fantastic changes taking place in Africa, Asia or the black communities of America," wrote Stokely Carmichael and Charles Hamilton in 1967, "it is necessary to realize that the current, turbulent period in history is characterized by the demands of previously oppressed people to be free of their oppression."[47] The modern black American struggle against oppression began in the 1950s and swiftly escalated into a national movement for civil rights. Its first targets were the legal bases of discrimination: segregation in public facilities, schools, and housing, and barriers to voting. With the passage of the Civil Rights Act in 1964 and the Voting Rights Act a year later, the civil rights movement reached its first goals. For the first time in American history, the federal government committed itself to extending the full rights of citizens to all black Americans.[48]

The historic achievements of the civil rights movement did not end discrimination or racism. Southern states mounted massive resistance to school integration; northern cities balked at busing students to reduce racial imbalance; whites fled to suburbs, whose exclusionary zoning ensured that all but a handful of affluent blacks would remain outside their boundaries; and, in myriad ways, the institutional racism of the world of work checked black occupational progress. Nonetheless, in every area formal barriers crumbled. Still, the civil rights movement could not rest content with its magnificent achievements. For its participants knew that racism continued to infect America's institutions and, especially in cities, that a growing number of blacks lived in terrible poverty whose roots lay in racism and exploitation.[49]

In the conventional story, black economic and political radicalism flowed from disappointment with the achievements of the civil rights legislation in a neat two-stage sequence. The history, in fact, was more complicated. Recent scholarship places "militant organizers side-by-side with nonviolent moderates" and finds the origins of "Black Power radicalism in the political activities of students and activists in the postwar era."[50] Nonetheless, after 1964, events accelerated the expansion of the civil rights movement into a struggle against the poverty and exploitation of northern ghettos. The Los Angeles Watts riot of 1965, followed by ghetto revolts in cities around the country, impelled civil rights leaders as well as politicians to reassess their strategies. Militant young blacks rejected the emphasis on integration and nonviolence at the core of the civil rights campaigns. As they argued that older civil rights leaders had ignored the forces that sustained the systematic oppression of blacks, they drew support from the young, poor blacks in northern ghettos and, as a consequence, shifted the social base of the black liberation movement away from its earlier anchor in an alliance between middle-class blacks and liberal whites. The "most significant indication of the middle class nature of the civil rights movement," wrote one militant black scholar in 1969, "was the fact that it did absolutely nothing to alleviate the grim plight of the poorest segments of the black population." The black rioters of the 1960s, he argued, "were vigorously repudiating the civil rights Negro leaders" and calling for new leadership willing to confront the problems arising from "oppression and powerlessness" and capable of speaking to the needs of the black masses.[51]

Stung by the urban uprisings, aware of the limits of integration as a strategy, challenged by new contenders for power, older civil rights leaders began to refocus their attention on urban poverty. Although they retained their commitment to integration and nonviolence, they too helped transform the black struggle into a quest for economic justice and political power. Martin Luther King, Jr., in fact, as Thomas Jackson has shown, had emphasized the economic roots of black oppression throughout his career.[52] This phase of the black liberation struggle had three overlapping components. Established civil rights leaders advocated economic redistribution, job creation, and housing reform. A new, militant Black Power movement asserted American blacks' kinship with anticolonial struggles around the world, rejected integration as a goal, and hoped to restructure American social and economic institutions, and black economists debated the source of ghetto underdevelopment and poverty, the accuracy of colonial analogies, and strategies for economic development.

In 1967 Martin Luther King, Jr., summed up a decade's achievements and outlined the tasks that remained. "In assault after assault," he said, "we caused the sagging walls of segregation to come tumbling down. During this era the entire edifice of segregation was profoundly shaken.... today, Civil Rights is a dominating issue in every state, crowding the pages of the press and the daily conversation of white Americans." Nonetheless, he stressed, "the deep rumbling of discontent in our cities is indicative of the fact that the plant of freedom had grown only a bud and not yet a flower."[53] Blacks, King pointed out, still lived "in the basement of the Great Society." Half of them lived in substandard housing; they had half the income of whites; twice as many were unemployed; their infant mortality rate was double that of whites; and twice as many blacks were "dying in Vietnam as whites in proportion to their size in the population." Blacks, as a consequence, faced a set of difficult and interrelated tasks. First was to "massively assert our dignity and worth." Another was "to discover how to organize our strength in terms of economic and political power." A third was the development of a program to "drive the nation to a guaranteed annual income." Black poverty had nothing to do with "want of industrious habits and moral fiber"; rather, "dislocations in the market operations of our economy and the prevalence of discrimination thrust people into idleness and bind them in constant or frequent unemployment against their will." The task was clear: "We must create full employment or we must create incomes." Joining his call for economic justice to his increasing criticism of the Vietnam War, King argued that if the nation can spend "35 billion dollars a year to fight an unjust, evil war in Vietnam, and 20 billion dollars to put a man on the moon, it can spend billions of dollars to put God's children on their own two feet right here on earth."[54]

King linked the struggles of black Americans to movements against colonialism throughout the world. "The deep rumbling of discontent that we hear today," he wrote, 'is the thunder of disinherited masses, rising from dungeons of oppression to the bright hills of freedom.... All over the world like a fever, freedom is spreading in the widest liberation movement in history." As in America, freedom required not only political rights but economic justice. "Like a monstrous octopus," poverty stretched "its choking, prehensile tentacles into lands and villages all over the world.... The time has come for an all-out world war against poverty."[55] King's call for a worldwide war against poverty echoed a key theme in the black American politics of liberation that predated the mid-1960s riots—but one met, according to historian Robin D. G. Kelley, "with a general conspiracy of silence against the most radical elements of the black freedom movement," which spoke of revolution, socialism, and self-determination and looked to the Third World for models of black liberation in the United States. Frequently "small and sometimes isolated," and "independent of both the white Left and the mainstream civil rights movement," these movements advanced a "vision of global class revolution" that did not grow out of the "civil rights movement's failure but existed alongside, sometimes in tension with, the movement's main ideas."[56]

Unlike the black radicals, King retained his commitment to nonviolence and criticized urban riots. "At best, the riots have produced a little additional anti-poverty money allotted by frightened government officials, and a few water-sprinklers to cool the children of the ghettos. It is something like improving the food in prison while the people remain securely behind bars." In no instance had riots gained any concrete improvement. No violent revolution would find sympathy and support from either the white or the majority of the black population, and "romantic illusions and empty philosophical debates about freedom" distracted energy from a tactical strategy for change. Here, as in his commitment to integration, King challenged the new, militant philosophy of liberation embodied in Black Power.[57]

In the summer of 1966 three leading civil rights organizations— SCLC, CORE, and SNCC—jointly sponsored a civil rights march in Mississippi. On June 17 state troopers in Greenwood ordered marchers not to pitch their tents on the grounds of a black high school. When one of SNCC's leaders, Stokely Carmichael, defied their order, the police arrested him. Released from jail only minutes before a major rally, Carmichael told an angry, militant crowd: "The only way we gonna stop them white men from whuppin' us is to take over. We been saying freedom for six years and we ain't got nothin'. What we gonna start saying now is Black Power!" His cry, writes Jack Bloom in his study of the civil rights movement, reflected "the experience and disillusionment of the civil rights workers in the South, but it was fueled by the ghetto uprisings [which started in Harlem in 1964]."[58] In fact, Black Power had deeper routes that extended back to postwar radicalism, including, for example, West Coast student activism embodied in the Afro-American Association founded at Berkeley in 1961. "While the Watts rebellions signaled a turning point, inaugurating a new militant and anti-integrationist strain of black politics," points out historian Donna Murch, "many of the social networks and ideas that formed the core of California's Black Power movement had their roots on the campuses of public colleges and universities."[59] Black Power, asserts historian Robert O. Self, "was a creative outgrowth of earlier efforts [to advance a political strategy beyond desegregation], not a radical and failed break from them."[60]

By calling for black power, militants rejected both the analysis and strategies of the civil rights coalition. One result was a new explanation for the poverty of black America: The colonialism of white America had trapped blacks in an ever-worsening poverty from which militant solidarity offered the only escape. In his influential 1962 essay, "Revolutionary Nationalism and the Afro-American," Harold Cruse explained that in the United States blacks experienced "domestic colonialism." The relationship of American blacks "to the dominant culture of the United States" paralleled "that of colonies and semi-dependents to their particular foreign overseers: the Negro is the American problem of underdevelopment. The failure of American Marxists to understand the bond between the Negro and the colonial peoples of the world has led to their failure to develop theories that would be of value to Negroes in the United States."[61]

Cruse and other writers used the colonial analogy before it was taken up by advocates of black power, who transformed it into the basis of a national movement.[62] Black Americans, wrote Carmichael and Hamilton, formed "a colony, and it is not in the interest of the colonial power to liberate them." Although blacks were legal citizens, they stood as "colonial subjects in relation to the white society." Colonialism, they argued, operated in three areas: political, economic, and social. Like other colonial masters, whites made the key political decisions that affected blacks' lives and governed them through indirect rule by coopting selected blacks to administer their decisions. As in other colonial situations, the colony existed "for the sole purpose of enriching, in one form or another, the 'colonizer.'" Outside "exploiters" entered the ghetto; bled "it dry," and left it "economically dependent on the larger society." As a result, the economic depression of black communities worsened. Here, then, was the source of black poverty, which was not only a problem of persons—individuals without enough resources to lead a decent life—but, equally, a problem of place—districts from which the resources essential to sustain viable communities had been drained.[63] This spatialization of black urban poverty endured as the signal intellectual contribution of internal colonialism—one echoed, albeit with a different politics, two decades later in the idea of concentrated poverty (discussed in Chapter 5).

In the rhetoric of black power, the colonial analogy became a brilliant and powerful strategy for galvanizing blacks into a militant national movement. As an explanation of poverty, it broke radically with liberal discourse, whether expressed as the culture of poverty, the residue of discrimination, or the lack of human capital. But was it correct? Was black America truly a colony? Could its persistent and deepening poverty be explained by the dependency theory with which radical scholars of the Third World had begun to challenge mainstream theories of economic development? These questions animated a vibrant debate among black social scientists and the few white colleagues who shared their concerns.

The colonial analogy rejected the core premise of conventional development economics: the benefits of economic growth. Radical scholars argued that wealth created by economic growth did not automatically trickle down from rich to poor. In Third World countries, poverty had spread even as economies modernized and grew. Without changes in political control, the benefits of growth always failed to reach those most in need. In fact, growth had widened the gap between rich and poor. Nor did conventional economic theories explain the economic failure of black ghettos. American economic growth had not decreased poverty among blacks. Indeed, black unemployment remained high during a period of economic expansion. Similarly, explanations of black poverty that stressed only the role of discrimination or the low educational achievement of blacks overlooked some uncomfortable facts. The passage of civil rights legislation had not ended ghetto poverty, and blacks achieved far less than whites with comparable educations.[64]

As they applied the colonial model to America, black scholars drew especially on dependency theory as developed by Andre Gunder Frank and other Third World economists. In a series of Latin American case studies, Frank illustrated his theory that conventional analyses of development and underdevelopment ignored the "economic and other relations between the metropolis and its economic colonies throughout the history of the world-wide expansion and development of the mercantilist and capitalist system." The expansion of the capitalist system had "effectively and entirely penetrated even the apparently most isolated sectors of the underdeveloped world." One result was relations of dependence that prevented development and fostered growth inequality and poverty. Ron Bailey argued that Tanzanian economist Justinian Rweyemamu's definition of dependence could be applied to the status of Africans in the United States. Dependence meant that economic development and expansion in metropolitan economies retarded growth among peripheral economies. Dominant nations used their power to monopolize markets and transfer surplus wealth from dependent nations to themselves, just as powerful white economic interests extracted and appropriated surplus wealth from black ghettos.[65]

Particularly through the work of Baran and Sweezy on monopoly capital, Marxism also influenced colonial models of ghetto economic development, although black scholars criticized conventional Marxist analyses for their lack of attention to race. The history of capitalist development, contended Baran and Sweezy, confirmed again and again that "capitalism everywhere generates wealth at one pole and poverty at the other." This was a "law of capitalist development . . . equally applicable to the most advanced metropolis and the most backward colony." Within capitalist economies, they stressed, poverty always remained rooted in unemployment and underemployment, or the industrial army, which in America concentrated in "the decaying centers of the big cities."[66]

Applied to America, the colonial model was straightforward: Ghettos export their unskilled labor and import consumer goods. Most capital within them remains in the hands of outsiders who control local businesses and export their profits. Unable to import capital, ghettos neither produce the material needed for their subsistence nor accumulate the capital essential to development. Blacks who work outside the ghetto bring back wages too low to offset the drain of their energy and resources. The result is exploitation and dependency, or what some called "domestic colonialism." Wilfred David summarized the model clearly:

> Unskilled labor is the basic productive resource of the ghetto, which is "exported" to the outside economy. Consumer goods and services are largely "imported" from outside, and with a few exceptions, the ghetto is unable to produce its needed materials. Further, it is difficult to import capital into the ghetto for use by its residents, and where such capital is employed it is largely "foreign-owned." Thus, wealth is extracted by "outsiders" as profits from the sale of consumer goods and returns to invested capital. The outward flow of cash is partially offset by the wages of "exported" labor, but the result is that no net financial accumulation takes place within the ghetto.

> This creates a situation of dependency. Much as a colony is dependent on its "mother country," so too is the ghetto dependent on the larger society for most of its material needs.[67]

Poverty among American blacks, writers pointed out, had special features. The economic forces generating black poverty, claimed Frank Davis, differ from those that create white poverty. Demand for black labor, he argued, did not increase when discrimination lessened; in both boom and depression, unemployment rates remained high among unskilled ghetto laborers. Indeed, technological change had rendered black unskilled workers "redundant." Demand for their labor in high-paying industry would decrease, thereby perpetuating low wages and poverty in the black ghetto. Urbanization as well as automation had worsened their situation. In subsistence economies, agricultural economist Frank Parsons pointed out, agriculture provided one "refuge for the poor—for all the people who can't find anything else to do." But in the United States—especially for blacks driven from the land by the mechanization of southern agriculture—refuge in a subsistence economy ceased to be "a feasible (or acceptable) alternative." The intersection of race with a dual labor market also sustained black poverty. Black workers, according to David, face a dual labor market, with primary sector jobs reserved for whites, and blacks relegated to secondary or "low-paying low status jobs." This arrangement protects workers in the primary sector from layoffs due to business cycles. And because secondary-sector jobs offer almost no opportunity for advancement, the dual labor market reinforces the subordinate position of the ghetto worker.[68]

Colonial powers always confront the problem of control; they must discover how to prevent protest and rebellion. Writers advocating the colonial analogy contended that America deployed two strategies: One was to distribute back to the ghetto a small part of the surplus extracted from its residents. The major examples were welfare and Great Society programs. (This analysis omitted much larger returns of the surplus in the form of public education, infrastructure, police and fire protection, and social insurance.) One critic labeled Model Cities programs "liberal pacifiers." The other strategy was tokenism, or the selective promotion of a few blacks to positions of influence within ghetto communities. As with colonies elsewhere, internal imperialists chose when possible to govern through indirect rule. With ghettos, according to William Tabb, "acculturated natives" acted as "middlemen between other natives and the colonist businessmen who...reside 'abroad.'" Not only did they serve the colonial power, they also exemplified the rewards of "working hard within the system." Indeed, tokenism's true purpose, according to Baran and Sweezy, was securing the loyalty of the black bourgeoisie: "If this loyalty can be made secure, the potential revolutionizing of the Negro protest movement can be forestalled and the world be given palpable evidence—through the placement of loyal Negroes in prominent positions—that the United States does not pursue a South African policy of *apartheid* but on the contrary fights for its Negro citizens."[69]

Although critics of the colonial analogy often argued that true colonies formed geographically distinct states, most black scholars rejected strict spatial separation as irrelevant. "The concentration made of a given population on a single land area," claimed Ralph H. Metcalf, Jr., only made colonization "more convenient as a result of centralization." But an oppressive country could colonize its oppressed population by exploiting them "economically, politically, and militarily, with almost the same machinery it would use with a centralized population." Although not a national political unit, wrote David, the black ghetto exists "as a geographical, economic, and social unit within its own unique psycho-pathology...The black ghetto is an economic entity covered by a glacier of poverty."[70]

Not a colony in a conventional sense, black America formed a new type of settlement, which writers labeled an internal colony. "Internal colonialist perspectives," explained Michael Omi and Howard Winant, "saw racism as an ongoing historical process which contained *both* class- and nationally based elements."[71] African Americans, writers on internal colonialism explained, had lived as colonized people before the development of urban ghettos. Indeed, from its inception, their colonization ran as a bitter stream through American history. To J. H. O'Dell, the American Revolution remained incomplete because it left slavery intact. Capitalist institutions and racist psychology had developed within a colonial framework that continued to constrain American blacks. For David, blacks' contemporary status also derived from their history in America. Study of the black ghetto, therefore, became "in essence a study of *de facto* slavery, i.e., the black ghetto economy is a *de facto* slave economy."[72] (The argument that internal colonialism represented one legacy of slavery at first glance appears to have reflected the legacy of slavery argument that black scholars and liberal whites angrily rejected when Moynihan and others applied it to black culture and family life. The difference was that Moynihan and other writers making the same point applied the argument to persons; the black advocates of internal colonialism applied it to place, which is quite different, although still an analogy in need of unpacking.)

Like other colonial populations, Ron Bailey argued, blacks usually had concentrated in places most in need of their labor: the antebellum rural South; late nineteenth-century industrializing southern cities; and twentieth-century northern manufacturing cities badly in need of semi- and unskilled labor. Now, however, automation and deindustrialization had left American blacks concentrated in urban ghettos with no vital economic function. As had occurred in numerous African states, American blacks now formed a colony no longer needed by its colonizers. They had become what some writers called a "neocolony." ("Neocolonialism" is a term coined by Kwame Nkrumah, who used it to refer to the way in which imperialist powers switch tactics—that is, substitute foreign aid and other indirect measures for repression as a means to "perpetuate colonialism while at the same time talking about 'freedom.'"[73])

Exploitation emerged as the central and most controversial concept in theories of black colonialism. Based on the Marxist definition of surplus value, exploitation referred to the use of blacks to produce wealth of which they received only a small, inadequate share. "The rate of exploitation," explained Bailey, "is the ratio of surplus value to wages." All capitalists tried to increase their share of workers' daily production. "When the share going to the worker is decreased, the rate of exploitation increases." Although capitalism resulted in the exploitation of all workers, some suffered more than others. The question was the basis of differential exploitation, or, as Donald Harris phrased it, "whether there is a systemic pattern of under-payment of black labor relative to whites *for the same task, same level of skill, and same level of productivity.*" Black proponents of internal colonization answered with a resounding yes. Indeed, Bailey claimed that only the concept of "super-exploitation" could describe the labor market situation of American blacks throughout their history. Blacks had been barred from many jobs, relegated to the "least skilled, lowest occupational categories," and paid less than whites with similar education and training for comparable work. Almost everywhere, they remained the last hired and first fired. The result of the "mechanisms, once by law and now more by custom, was black super-exploitation and impoverishment."[74]

Not all black economists agreed. Thomas Sowell, for one, traced black disadvantage to discrimination rather than exploitation. Because of discrimination, argued Sowell, a black man "born with native ability to be a chemist and earn $20,000 a year" easily could find himself a "ditch-digger making $3,000 a year." He would be "worse off than if he were in fact exploited," and policies directed toward raising his wages as a ditch-digger only would worsen his situation. For the net result likely would be that machines would replace ditch-diggers, thereby reducing his already meager income. Nor were black people robbed of very much by white America: "The real problem is that deliberate discrimination, unconscious racism and general neglect have left black people too poor to be robbed of anything that would make a difference on a national scale." For Sowell the source of oppression was not the conjunction of capitalism and racism. "Whenever one group oppresses another, it almost invariably does so by denying them opportunities for self-realization, *not* by allowing them to develop their potential and then taking away what they have produced." The answer to black poverty, therefore, lay in the hard task of blacks developing their own human capital.[75]

Nor did all radical black scholars accept the colonial analogy. Joseph Seward, who taught for seven years in Ghana, argued that the analogy usefully aroused American blacks to "our kinship to our African and Caribbean brothers-in-oppression." (Note the use of "brothers," which expresses the unreflexive sexism in the early black radical movement, discussed in the next section.) Nonetheless, the analogy was wrong on several counts because it failed to point out that African and Caribbean neocolonies could break with monopoly capitalism if they chose, while American blacks could not. Seward worried that the internal colonial analogy would end up another source of black oppression because of its increasing acceptance in "liberal ruling class thinking." One trick of the ruling class, he argued, was the use of the colonial analogy to promote black capitalism, that is, the capitalist development of ghettos by blacks themselves. Black capitalism, he predicted, would only transfer resentment from Jewish landlords to the black middle class. "Black capitalism, if it ever gets off the ground, can be expected to make black workers and slumdwellers even more anti-black bourgeoisie." American monopoly capitalism had made black people poor, and "black capitalism isn't going to change that."[76]

Like Seward, though with different politics, Sowell rejected black capitalism as an answer to ghetto poverty. "Capital," he pointed out, "is the most fluid of resources." It flows wherever profits are highest, and it had avoided the ghetto because businesses there had "on the whole done poorly," as had "the community banks which...financed them." Black capitalism, with its emphasis on artificially supported markets, added up to a new form of mercantilism, which as a strategy of economic development had been discredited historically. In Europe and America, generations had elapsed before "repeated disasters" finally led to the abandonment of mercantile policies, and black people could not afford to repeat the same process.[77]

Unlike Sowell, advocates of the colonial analogy did not rely on markets freed from discrimination for black economic advancement. Instead, they rejected liberal individualism. By focusing on individuals and individual initiatives, Frank Davis argued, the ideology of free enterprise neglected the group oppression of black people, which called for collective action. "The problem in America," wrote Guy C. Z. Mhone, "is simply that opportunities for blacks are only open to them on an individual level." Any efforts to enhance "the group upward mobility of black people only results in a redefinition of status such that blacks will remain at the bottom."[78]

Any serious attempt at liberation required "a plan to create political cadres" dedicated to organizing black people in the great metropolitan areas and developing strong, independent political organizations directed toward capturing control of all institutions that touched their lives and livelihoods. Even liberal white remedies for black poverty, claimed Charles Sackrey, failed to advocate changing the distribution of power. They failed, that is, to grasp that poverty is a problem of power as well as resources. Whites would still own and control "the productive equipment of the economy, even in areas...predominantly black; whites would also continue to make most of the laws, would still run the schools, the cities, and the counties."[79] Sackrey wrote before depopulation and white flight had turned over institutional control to African Americans in many American cities. It is a great irony of late twentieth-century history that they inherited the ostensible reins of power when depleted resources left city governments struggling just to keep their cities alive, unable even to contemplate the institutional reforms that would turn around the economic situation of black Americans.[80]

Disagreements among advocates of internal colonialism highlighted the theory's ambiguities and the different politics to which it led. These included, Omi and Winant point out, a spectrum that ran

> all the way from moderate reform initiatives to revolution and 'national liberation.' Demands for increases in the number of 'natives' occupying key posts in businesses or state institutions (police, schools, social agencies), plans to achieve 'community control' of the ghetto and barrio economies, and schemes for a two stage revolutionary process analogous to the Angolan or Vietnamese experiences, were all put forward based on the internal colonialism analysis.[81]

Internal colonialism enjoyed only a short life as the theory underlying radical black militance. As early as 1970, Murch points out, Huey Newton, a leading Black Panther theorist, "coined the term 'intercommunalism'" to replace the "Party's earlier stance on internal colonization, which defined Afro-America as a subjugated colony within the mother country." Intercommunalism "shifted the focus to 'communities' rather than nation-states." Newton had come to believe that "capitalist expansion and an increasingly integrated world system rendered the nation-state obsolete as a means of confronting power." Instead, he argued, activists should follow a "communitarian ideal in which resources would be mobilized to serve 'communities' rather than nations." With this shift, Newton was able to link the "Party's radical anticolonial and internationalist stance with its newfound commitment to reform" expressed through its "local survival programs"—breakfasts for poor children, involvement in local electoral politics, and other practical activities.[82]

By the late 1970s, debates about the ghetto as colony, like the Black Power movement with which they were so intimately connected, had faded. In the case of Black Power, one reason was the relentless assault of the FBI and other public authorities who broke up the movement through infiltration, propaganda, and jailing and killing its leaders. Even as they turned to practical reformist activity, the Black Panthers could not escape the powerful campaign of law enforcement to destroy them and discredit their activities.[83] Internal colonialism, on the other hand, fell out of favor not so much from repression as from a combination of its radical sponsorship, location outside the mainstream of American social science, and internal weaknesses. Neither the literature of internal colonialism nor Black Power left a strong institutional legacy or influence on economic and political thought. For Kelley, "describing black people as colonial subjects was a way of characterizing the materialist culture of racism; it was more a metaphor than an analytical concept."[84]

But it was much more than that. Internal colonialism's brief prominence was a significant moment in American discourse about poverty because it was the first major theory of the spatialization of urban poverty—more firmly anchored than its successor, concentrated poverty, discussed in Chapter 5, in political economy—and, also, because it offered one of the only alternatives to the liberalism of the time. (The spatialization of poverty was, of course, a long standing theme in development economics and, in the U.S., in discussions of rural, Southern, and Appalachian poverty.) To the economists and political scientists who developed the idea, internal colonialism was a deeply serious attempt to develop a theory that transcended liberalism, which, even when it avoided the culture of poverty, concentrated, as Chapter 3 shows, on microeconomic issues: how to get people off welfare, how to train the unemployed, how to prevent children from failing in school. Mainstream social scientists avoided the macroeconomic questions posed in the literature of internal colonialism: Why does America generate so much poverty? How does poverty relate to the dynamics of capitalism? Is American poverty linked to the world economy? Do the same mechanisms perpetuate poverty among American blacks and among people of color in the Third World? For advocates of internal colonialism, unlike mainstream social scientists, poverty was a problem of political economy as well as a problem of power and of space. In its combination of political economy, power, and space, internal colonialism remains unique in the intellectual history of American poverty.

Whether or not theorists of internal colonialism offered correct answers, the questions they raised remain of profound importance.[85] Their neglect has impoverished American discourse on poverty and stunted the development of a strong, Left political economy. What accounts for the lack of attention they have received? Why did internal colonialism never enter the mainstream of American debates about poverty? The easy answer is the quality of the literature. By and large, it lacked the polish found in major academic journals and did not use the advanced econometric techniques that began to dominate poverty research in the 1960s. In method as well as theory, its advocates remained outside the prevailing approach to research. Still, they formulated crucial questions; their work bristled with insights unavailable elsewhere; and their combination of political economy, power, and space is immensely heuristic. They might have laid the foundation for a generation of rigorous empirical, theoretical, and historical research. Their work pointed to an intellectual open road, not a dead end. But they suffered fatally from their association with Black Power and Marxism. Because Black Power seemed to sanction violence, outside of academic circles it faded quickly as a respectable, debatable political alternative. Nor, despite the emergence of an extraordinarily gifted group of radical economists such as those involved with the founding in 1968 of the Union of Radical Political Economists (URPE), did most economists modulate their hostility to Marxist theory or expand the questions that underlay their research.[86] (Since 1969 URPE has published the lively *Review of Radical Political Economics*, which according to *Citation Reports* ranked only 256 of 321 economic journals, a signal of the continued marginalization of radical economics within the discipline.[87])

The colonial analogy raised issues of geography, class, and power usually avoided by American social science, including the new branch of research on poverty, and its advocates lacked the cultural authority to force these issues onto its agenda.[88] At the same time, public policy also contributed to its weakening. When civil rights laws and affirmative action opened jobs and neighborhoods, individual social mobility, as so often before in American history, undercut the institutional, occupational, and residential base on which the theory of internal colonialism rested. Without support for its reformulation in the wake of changed contexts, internal colonialism became a missed opportunity to break through the barriers that have channeled American discussions of poverty and wealth in their narrow course.[89] (Today, the relative lack of attention to the concept of human capabilities as developed by Amartya Sen and Martha Nussbaum in American poverty discourse—discussed in the Epilogue—represents another missed opportunity to widen the channels.) Another opportunity to push discussions of poverty along unmapped roads, however, experienced more mixed success and a more enduring legacy. This was black feminism, which fashioned its own distinctive politics of liberation based on the triple oppression of race, class, and gender. White feminism, slow off the mark to embrace poverty as one of its issues, also in time inserted poverty into its agenda for the liberation of women.

Race, Gender, and Human Rights

Women's poverty as history

Both white women and women of color always have borne a disproportionate share of poverty. In early and mid-nineteenth century America, most white women lived on farms, where their labor was essential to the family's economy. Some supplemented farm income with the household manufacture of clothing and other articles, but the value of household manufacture declined steeply in the first decades of the nineteenth century.[90] Almost none worked for wages after they had married. Before marriage, most employed women were domestic servants; others worked in mills; a smaller number taught school; many labored as seamstresses; others were prostitutes. All these occupations paid little. After marriage, women supplemented family income in various ways: by helping their artisan or shopkeeper husbands, taking in boarders, or sewing and washing at home.[91] They depended on their husbands for their primary income. When working-class husbands died, they usually left almost no savings and no life insurance. Their widows, often with children still at home, could earn only the most meager income at customary women's work. Even farmers' widows often found themselves destitute or dependent on their children. No public programs existed on which women could draw as a right. Instead, they depended on family, charity, and sometimes meager outdoor relief or, even, the poorhouse. As a consequence, women, including single women trying to support themselves, often suffered terrible, absolute poverty.[92] Many contemporaries understood the source of women's poverty, even if they could do little to alleviate it. Most poor women, even harsh critics of relief admitted, had not fallen into poverty through indolence or intemperance. Upright widows with children and old women remained the quintessential worthy poor. But where could they turn for help? They looked first to their families. Children much more readily housed and cared for their mothers than their fathers. Men never evoked as much sympathy as women. They should have saved enough for their old age; they were cantankerous and difficult to live with; and they could not help with the housework and childcare. Women with young children or without families to care for them turned to private and public authorities. Most large towns and cities in the early nineteenth century had female benevolent societies that made small gifts to widows, who more often than widowers received outdoor relief from public sources. But in both cases the amounts were small and their continuation uncertain. Neither benevolent societies nor overseers of the poor offered help as a right; it always remained charity. (Unemployed and older men, who could not tap the same well of sympathy as women, more often depended on indoor relief, that is, the poorhouse.)[93]

Women's prospects did not improve much until the twentieth century. Life insurance became more widespread, and late in the nineteenth century, widows of northern Civil War veterans received pensions. Industrialization opened more semi- and unskilled jobs to women. Still, only a small fraction of married women worked for wages outside the home. In the early twentieth century, state governments began to introduce mothers' pensions. Although these small grants for worthy widows with children extended the responsibility of state governments, they never reached more than a tiny fraction of eligible women. Nor did the constitutional right to vote, won in 1920, directly alleviate the hardships experienced by women.[94] The situation of black women was especially dire. In 1950 9 percent of black women worked in agriculture and 42 percent in domestic service; 67 percent lived in poverty—as did 81 percent of black children and 62 percent of black men—and local welfare officials and social workers conspired to deny them benefits.[95]

Energetic women reformers from the federal government's Children's Bureau managed quietly to nationalize the mothers' pension concept in the Aid to Dependent Children provision of the 1935 legislation creating the Social Security system. Its sponsors thought that ADC would be a small program supporting widows with children, but in the 1950s its demography started to change. By the 1960s AFDC (Aid to Families with Dependent Children, as it was renamed in 1962) supported growing numbers of women whose husbands had deserted or divorced them, or who had never married. Increasing numbers of them were women of color. Hostility to the program—fueled also by an escalating Cold War-inspired antagonism toward the idea of a welfare state—mounted: southern states tacked on punitive regulations, and a welfare backlash swept northern cities. In the early 1960s, the program still supported only a modest number of women, largely because most of those eligible did not apply or because officials arbitrarily denied them relief. A combination of forces, as we have seen—the civil rights movement, the War on Poverty, and the welfare rights movement—increased the number of women on the AFDC rolls, whose size exploded. Even though the cost remained a small and shrinking fraction of the total budget for social welfare, it bore the onus of public hostility, which inflated popular conceptions of its relative cost and generosity (AFDC never lifted women over the official poverty line) and fueled myths about the poor women who turned to it for survival. AFDC clients fused gender, sexuality, and welfare dependence into a powerful image that touched deep, often irrational fears embedded in American culture. As they refused to be grateful and demanded public assistance as a right, they provoked a transformation in the historic relation between women and welfare. Poor unmarried women with children now became the undeserving poor.[96]

Unlike AFDC, other programs, serving mainly the "deserving" poor, helped alleviate women's poverty. These include Social Security extended to survivors (that is, widows) in 1939 and both increased and indexed to inflation in later years; Supplemental Social Security in 1974; Medicare and Medicaid in 1965; federal housing programs; nutritional grants to women and children with infants; the expanded food stamp program, and, in the 1990s, the Earned Income Tax Credit and child care tax credits.[97] By the 1980s, women could draw on an unprecedented array of income supports. Even though they still earned lower wages for comparable work, experienced employment discrimination, and found themselves the object of sexual harassment, legislation and the courts had begun to extend them protections. As their labor force participation soared, women entered an unprecedented variety of occupations with the result that their position improved along most of the major routes charted by the early feminists.[98]

As a result of work and government support, by the 1980s poverty among women had decreased, but no more quickly than poverty among men. The ratio of women's to men's poverty, in fact, remained stubbornly resistant to change. Poverty among women fell from 38.9 percent in 1930 to 20.8 percent in 1959 and hit its low point, 11.9 percent, in 1979 before turning upward to 12.6 percent in 1989. But poverty among men fell more quickly, with the result that the ratio of women's to men's poverty was 125 in 1959, 149 in 1979, and 137 in 1999. Even though poverty among women decreased, the proportion of women among the poor grew, leading to what writers in the 1980s labeled the feminization of poverty.[99] This increase was driven by the rise in the number of women heading households. Between 1960 and 1984, the number of poor female family heads had increased 83 percent, from 1.9 million to 3.5 million. The changes were reflected among both white and black women, but black women fared worst. In 1960 women headed 20 percent of poor white families and in 1984, 38 percent. By comparison, women headed 42 percent of poor black families in 1960 and 73 percent in 1984. These numbers were cause for serious concern because of the rise, after 1970, in the number of households headed by women. Among all families, female-headed households rose from 11 to 16 percent in 1984. For whites, the increase was from 10 percent to 12 percent and for blacks from 28 percent to 43 percent. By 1986, for the first time women headed more than half of all poor families. (Chapter 5 discusses the increase in female-headed families in later years.) In 1970 cash programs removed 19 percent of female headed families from poverty; by 1984, they lifted only 10 percent above the official poverty line—one result of the war on welfare embodied in the decline in the real value of AFDC payments after 1973. (Frances Fox Piven and Richard Cloward argued that the real increase in female-headed households was much, though an indeterminate amount, lower because changes in census categories artificially inflated the increase.)[100]

Women's poverty raised alarms in part because of its association with the growing poverty of children. Between 1979 and 1982, the proportion of children under six living in poverty increased from 18 percent to 24 percent and of six- to seventeen-year-olds from 16 to 21 percent. In New York City about 38 percent of all children lived below the nationally established poverty line uncorrected for the city's cost of living. National children's advocate Marian Wright Edelman pointed out: "Children were slightly worse off in 1979 than in 1969. But from 1979 to 1983 the bottom fell out." In 1980, 1981, and 1982 more than 1 million children per year joined the poverty rolls, and the rate of child poverty soared to its highest level since the early 1960s.[101]

The sharp increase in the proportion of women among the poor and of childhood poverty helped draw attention to women's poverty as an issue, despite the overall decline in the proportion of women who were poor. The feminization of poverty became a prominent social issue because of the interaction of women's real poverty with the energy of modern feminism and public policy. Three conditions proved especially important: the identification of the early feminist movement with affluent women; the male bias in discussions of poverty; and the Reagan administration's attack on social programs. To become a mass movement, feminism needed to incorporate working-class women and women of color—which, of course, directed its attention to poverty. As it turned to poverty, feminism confronted a discourse strikingly male-centered. Despite the historic poverty of women, most writing about poor people used male pronouns. By implication, the poverty of men appeared more real, urgent, and distressing. After 1980 the Reagan administration's policies worsened the situation of poor women. Cuts in income maintenance programs, food stamps, health care, and even the administration's early tax policy all fell heavily on women. (Male poverty also increased during the same years.) The conjunction of demographic trends, ideology, and politics transformed women's poverty into a major public issue.[102]

Historians contributed to the focus on women's poverty not only by documenting its existence and tracing its sources and trajectory but also by showing how from its inception the architecture of the welfare state disadvantaged women. The division between social insurance and public assistance at the core of the American welfare state, they have shown, reserved the best benefits disproportionately for men. The American welfare state emerged in the 1930s divided between public assistance and social insurance. Social insurance benefits were entitlements; they reflected the assumption that workers and employers paid into funds on which they drew in times of unemployment or when they retired or became disabled. (The insurance model, in fact, has been more myth than fact.) Public assistance is means tested. That is, it serves only people who meet strict income and asset requirements. Although early advocates of social insurance included benefits for the elderly, the unemployed, and the poor within their proposals, the split deliberately engineered into policy created two different types of programs. Public assistance programs became synonymous with welfare; they carried the old stigma of relief. Their recipients were the modern paupers. Social insurance benefits, moreover, always were more generous, and the gap between them and public assistance continued to widen. Social Security, for instance, came to lift most of the elderly out of poverty; AFDC boosted no one above the official poverty line. From the beginning, gender biases underscored the distinctions between these categories. Federal public assistance, ADC, was a women's program. By consigning most needy women with children to ADC, public policy ensured that they would remain poor. Social Security for decades excluded agricultural and domestic workers, two types of occupations that employed a large proportion of women (and blacks). In the beginning, Social Security did not extend benefits to survivors, that is, to widows; it reflected prior earning, which favored men; and its benefit structure disadvantaged women. At the same time, unemployment insurance contained a structural bias against women because it rested on a male model: its founders assumed it would serve male household heads and designed it in ways that overlooked the needs of women.[103]

Black feminists and the politics of liberation

Black feminists along with women welfare recipients became the first to convert women's poverty into a public issue. In 1971 a group of black and Puerto Rican female political activists in New York City founded the Third World Women's Alliance (TWWA). Like other radical women of color, they believed it necessary to build their own organization to advance the politics of liberation. Largely ignored by white feminists who missed the distinctive oppression of black (and poor) women, and exploited by radical black men in SNCC and the Black Panthers, women of color required their own platform for advancing their interests—not only in the United States but around the world. The TWWA (whose lineage extended back to the 1968 Black Women's Liberation Caucus in SNCC and its 1969 successor, the Black Women's Liberation Organization) represented one short-lived effort to link women of color around the globe in a politics of liberation.[104]

In its newsletter *Triple Jeopardy* (the title refers to the triple jeopardy of race, class, and sex that confronted women of color), published bimonthly from September 1971 through the summer of 1975, the TWWA explained that *"Our purpose is to make a meaningful contribution to the Third World community by working for the elimination of the oppression and exploitation from which we suffer. We further intend to take an active part in creating a socialist society where we can live as decent human beings, free from the pressures of racism, economic exploitation, and sexual oppression."* Its ambitious goals, which, as in most feminist politics, linked the conventionally public and private, included radical changes in family, employment, education, services, sex roles, self-defense, and "women in our own right"—the right of third-world women to determine their own lives and the demand that all organizations (including "so called radical, militant, and/or so-called revolutionary groups") deal with women as individuals valued for themselves, not through their association with particular men; and that they be "full participants on all levels of the struggle for national liberation." Their concrete demands called for "Guaranteed full, equal, and non-exploitive employment"; "Guaranteed adequate income for all"; and a reform of social services—"inadequate, unavailable, or too expensive, administered in a racist, sexist manner"—that exacerbated the indignities and frustrations faced daily by poor women. "All services necessary to human survival—health care, housing, food, clothing, transportation, and education," they contended, "should be free and controlled and administered by the people who use them." With family, in response to the widespread condemnation of "illegitimacy" and the controversy over the Moynihan report, they stressed that there "is no such thing as an illegitimate child" and called for "the continued growth of communal households and the idea of the extended family" along with "alternative forms to the patriarchal family" as well as expanded day care facilities. They also asserted their right "to decide if and when to have children" and demanded free and safe family planning, "including abortions if necessary." Control of their own reproduction meant more than access to family planning and abortions. It extended as well to the assault on black bodies. "There should be no forced sterilization or mandatory birth control programs, which are presently used as genocide against third world women and against other poor people."[105]

In September 1973 *Triple Jeopardy* focused on the role of involuntary sterilization, a legacy of the eugenics movement, which remained prevalent in the United States right through the 1970s. In "Sterilization of BLACK Women Is Common in the U.S.," the magazine cited shocking case histories from Alabama, Mississippi, Illinois, New York City, and Georgia. "On the state level," wrote the magazine, "it is the old story. Laws advocating sterilization of the poor or the 'mentally defective' have been on the books in a number of states (22 according to the ACLU) since the 1800s." But at "the local level, it is terrifying." The magazine cited the case of a "doctor who informed a number of women that they had cancer, performed hysterectomies, and used the money earned to finance a sparkling new clinic."[106]

In her powerful *Killing the Black Body*, Dorothy Roberts documents *Triple Jeopardy*'s claims, setting sterilization in the context of the attempt throughout American history to assert control over black women's reproductive behavior. During the 1930s through 1950s, involuntary sterilization of black women took place in institutions under the auspices of eugenic-inspired state laws. "The North Carolina Eugenics Commission," reports Roberts, sterilized nearly 8,000 "mentally deficient persons in the 1930s and 1940s, some 5,000 of whom were black." But most sterilization came to be practiced under different sponsorship:

> The violence was committed by doctors paid by the government to provide health care for these women. During the 1970s, sterilization became the most rapidly growing form of birth control in the United States, rising from 200,000 cases in 1970 to over 700,000 in 1980. It was a common belief among Blacks in the South that Black women were routinely sterilized without their informed consent and for no valid reasons. Teaching hospitals performed unnecessary hysterectomies on poor Black women as practice for their medical residents. This sort of abuse was so widespread in the South that these operations came to be known as 'Mississippi appendectomies.' In 1975, a hysterectomy cost $800 compared to $250 for a tubal litigation, giving surgeons, who were reimbursed by Medicaid, a financial incentive to perform the more extensive operation—despite its twenty times greater risk of killing the patient.[107]

As a practice, sterilization exposed how public policy linked together black women's alleged sexual promiscuity, unfit mothering, and welfare dependence in a toxic, frightening threat to the fiscal, social, and moral health of the nation. By their actions, even more than their words, medical practitioners of sterilization and their many supporters in public life and among ordinary citizens revealed the place of black women in the pantheon of the undeserving poor. In her history of black feminist thought, Patricia Hill Collins writes, "African-American women were deemed unworthy recipients of aid that maintained their status as permanent beggars."[108]

Black women fashioned a politics of liberation that grew out of the pattern of oppression that constrained their lives in ways that marked them as distinct from both white women and black men. One supporter quipped, "there can't be liberation for half the race."[109] Black women feminists seized on the concept of "womanism" first introduced by novelist Alice Walker. Womanism, as historian Linda Gordon explains, emphasized that black women "shared an autonomous gender system, one distinct not only from white mainstream norms but also from those of white feminists." Womanism signified "an assertion of women's rights" that "did not attempt to isolate gender from race or class issues."[110] "With the collapse of the black nationalist movement," reports historian Ruth Rosen, "African-American women felt freer to take a look at the sexism within their own community. In 1973 activists founded the National Black Feminist Organization (NBFO), which, within a year, had spawned local chapters and had held a national conference."[111] In her introduction to her anthology of African American feminist thought, Beverly Guy-Sheftall succinctly summarized the movement's common premises.

> 1) Black women experience a special kind of oppression and suffering in this country which is racist, sexist, and classist because of their dual racial and gender identity and their limited access to economic resources; 2) This 'triple jeopardy' has meant that the problems, concerns, and needs of black women are different in many ways from those of both white women and black men; 3) Black women must struggle for black liberation *and* gender equality simultaneously; 4) There is no inherent contradiction in the struggle to eradicate sexism and racism as well as the other 'isms' which plague the human community, such as classism and heterosexism; 5) Black women's commitment to the liberation of blacks and women is profoundly rooted in their lived experience.[112]

As with the broader African American liberation struggle, the actions of black women drew on a long history of activism and assertiveness, which for the most part had been ignored or suppressed in accounts of African American history and the history of social and political movements.[113] The history unearthed by the new black feminism revealed that the "matriarchy" theory of black history inverted the history of black women, turning their strength into a weakness;[114] it also showed how poverty had been integral to the experience of black women since the days of slavery, the product of overlapping pressures: the inability of black men to earn living wages, and their early death, which left black women widowed and without support;[115] educational opportunities restricted through the deliberate underfunding of black schools;[116] the confinement of black women to jobs in agriculture and domestic service—the most poorly paid employment;[117] the reluctance of public authorities and private charities to extend aid to black women;[118] the denigration of black women as unfit mothers;[119] and exclusion from the exercise of political influence through the ballot box. Because black women's distinctive pattern of oppression translated into widespread poverty, struggles against poverty composed a key component of their politics of liberation. Activist Pauli Murray, reviewing the statistics of black women's economic disadvantage, emphasized that "while all families headed by women are more vulnerable to poverty than husband-wife families, the black woman family head is doubly victimized."[120]

Black women built their theories and politics of liberation from the ground up. Their ideas about the connections among gender, race, and inequality grew out of lived experience, which also shaped their anti-poverty agenda. This generative role of lived experience in shaping consciousness, theory, and practice remained a key feature of black women's feminism. What Patricia Hill Collins labels "motherwork," for instance, "reflects how political consciousness can emerge within everyday lived experience. In this case, Black women's participation in a constellation of mothering activities, collectively called motherwork, often fostered a distinctive political sensibility."[121] "As women who had almost always worked," explained historian Ruth Rosen, black women "viscerally understood the bitter experience of economic exploitation, the nightmare of finding child care, the humiliation of caring for white women's children when their own children cried out for them."[122] "Although day care was an issue that predominantly white feminist organizations covered," reported Kimberly Springer in her history of black feminist organizations, *Triple Jeopardy* linked the need for day care not only to women's work lives, but also to the "intersection of city, state, and federal policies surrounding welfare as they impacted the well-being of communities of color."[123] Black feminist ideology, emphasizes historian Jacqueline Jones, "sprang not from abstract theoretical formulations, but from self-scrutiny and self-understanding." Toni Morrison mused that the African American woman "had nothing to fall back on: not maleness, not whiteness, not ladyhood, not anything. And out of the profound desolation of her reality she may very well have reinvented herself."[124]

As they constructed indigenous theories and strategies, poor women and men asserted the idea that welfare was a right linked directly to the exercise of first-class citizenship. In *The Battle for Welfare Rights*, historian Felicia Kornbluh reports that welfare rights activists created political theories from the materials available to them. They drew on, and transformed, Anglo-American legal and political traditions and the rights discourse of postwar United States. At the center of their approach to politics was a vision of citizenship. Welfare recipients and their allies believed that the rights for mothers that had been written into public policy in the New Deal period should apply to all low-income parents and not just to the respectable white women who had been their primary beneficiaries in the years between the New Deal and the 1960s. They saw the United States as an affluent society in which citizenship entailed access to the consumer goods that allowed children to hold their heads up in school and made women look and feel presentable. Citizenship meant full participation in the economic, legal and governmental institutions that shaped people's lives.[125]

In the late 1960s and early 1970s black women asserted their claims to welfare rights and first-class citizenship through the welfare rights movement. The National Welfare Rights Organization, NWRO, founded in 1966, was the most visible welfare-rights player on the national scene. But local welfare-rights organizations preceded it and sprang up around the country. In Philadelphia, the Kensington Welfare Right Union, founded in 1991 and led by the "firebrand" Cheri Honkala, became the most prominent poor women's anti-poverty organization.

[Honkala and the KSWU] pries open abandoned HUD buildings to provide housing for homeless families. When she and five other mothers found there was no safe place for their children to play, they took over a closed welfare office and turned it into a community center. After being held in jail for six days, Honkala and the others were found not guilty by a jury that was so impressed by the defendants that jury members asked if they could join the welfare rights group.[126]

In Las Vegas, Nevada, the extraordinary Operation Life, according to its historian, Annelise Orleck, showed that when "the lived experience of poverty is seen as a valid credential, entitling poor mothers and fathers to build their own antipoverty programs, the results can be astounding, both materially and psychologically."[127] Orleck tells the story of black single mothers who left farms in Louisiana and Mississippi for Las Vegas, Nevada, during and shortly after World War II. They ended up influencing state politics, garnering national support, and, for two decades, running a major community-based social service organization. They worked in low-income service jobs and lived in terrible poverty, experiencing the consequences of the city's racial segregation and the state's reluctance to accept federal welfare, job training, or health care funds. Galvanized by the cutback in welfare payments, they formed a branch of the National Welfare Rights Organization. National celebrities, clergy, and other supporters joined them on March 6, 1971, as they occupied the opulent Caesars Palace in protest. On March 19, federal judge Roger Foley ruled Nevada's welfare cuts illegal. Energized by success, the women studied law, entered politics, and built Operation Life, a grassroots organization that mobilized federal, state, local, and foundation funds to deliver social services, health care, job training, housing, and economic development to the city's impoverished Westside. "It had taken the women years to feel entitled to a fair shake from the government," writes Orleck. "Now they were arguing something more daring: that poor mothers deserved a voice in policymaking. They knew more about managing a tight budget than any cost-cutting legislator. They knew firsthand what poor children lack and what mothers needed to pull their families out of poverty."[128] For about twenty years, Operation Life ran its services with exemplary skill and efficiency and at low cost made possible by volunteers and minimally paid workers. Despite the success and national praise it earned, the organization struggled against unremitting opposition, which, finally, in the anti-welfare climate of the 1990s, succeeded in shutting it down for reasons of ideology and politics—not effectiveness, efficiency, or diminished need. "What is remarkable," emphasized Orleck, "is not that the women of Operation Life failed to achieve their vision, but that they went as far as they did. Their successes are astonishing not only because they started with so little, but because those who opposed them were so fierce and so relentless."[129]

Welfare rights organizing outlived the militant phase of the black women's politics of liberation, which, like the men's movement, wound down in the 1970s, unable to sustain its passion in the face of state-sponsored repression, internal conflict, and the rightward movement of American politics. "Counterintelligence Program (COINTELPRO) records indicate," Singer discovered, "that the TWWA was under investigation from December 1970 to March 1974. This investigation included at least six sources supplying the FBI with the TWWA's publication...infiltration of the organization's meetings, reports on the activities of key TWWA members, and photographs of TWWA members for inclusion in the agency's Extremist Photograph Album."[130] Black feminists faced external challenges from their struggles to show other black women that feminism was not only for white women; their confrontations with white feminists over demands to share power and "affirm diversity"; and their fights with the "misogynist tendencies of black nationalism." Added to these "were significant, inter-and intra-organizational conflicts"; "insufficient resources;" and "activist burnout."[131] At the same time, some organizations "decided to stop meeting because they felt it was time to devise new strategies of organizing. These organization sensed a rise in conservatism, and...determined that 1960s strategies would not be effective in the predicted backlash against women of color, the working poor, and people of color communities."[132]

Despite their short formal life span, black feminist organizations left a concrete legacy in empowering black women to carry on the struggle in other forums. "It may be more useful to assess Black women's activism less by the ideological content of individual Black women's belief systems," advises Collins, than "by Black women's collective actions within everyday life that challenge domination in" the "multifaceted domains" that routinely impinge on their experience. An African American mother "unable to articulate her political ideology," claims Collins, "but who on a daily basis contests school policies harmful to her children may be more an 'activist' than the most highly educated Black feminist who...produces no tangible political changes in anyone's life but her own."[133] As Springer points out, black feminists "often found their activism institutionalized in social services, governmental bodies, higher education institutions, and other organizations they could attempt to influence with antiracist and antisexist ideology."[134] Nonetheless, the early black feminists also left their legacy in a flourishing field of black feminist scholarship—a national meeting at

M.I.T. in 1994 brought together 2,010 black feminist scholars—and in many organizations dedicated to improving the lives of black women and children.[135]

In fact, black feminist writing in the 1970s and 1980s composed the starting point for the literature of "intersectionality," a term first used by Kimberly Crenshaw in her 1991 *Stanford Law Review* article, "Identity, Politics, and Violence Against Women of Color."[136] Intersectionality developed early black feminism's insights about "triple jeopardy"—the simultaneous oppressions of race, class, and gender in the lives of women of color—into a theoretical program that combined analysis of "the relationships and interaction between multiple axes of identity and multiple dimensions of social organization at the same time"—with a practical program of social and political criticism and action. For Patricia Hill Collins, intersectionality represented a mode of analysis "claiming that systems of race, economic class, gender, sexuality, ethnicity, nation, and age form mutually constructing features of social organization, which shape African American experiences and, in turn, are shaped by African Americans."[137] In the introduction to their anthology of writing on intersectionality, Bonnie Thornton Dill and Ruth Enid Zambrana explain the ambitious agenda on which the idea rests—four "theoretical interventions" that echo the themes we have seen in early black feminist writing.

> (1) Placing the lived experience and struggles of people of color and other marginalized groups as a starting point for the development of theory; (2) Exploring the complexities not only of individual identities but also group identity, recognizing that variations within groups are often ignored and essentialized; (3) Unveiling the ways interconnected domains of power organize and structure inequality and oppression; and (4) Promoting social justice and social change by linking research and practice to create a holistic approach to the eradication of disparities and to changing social and higher education institutions.[138]

For Collins, the "heady days" of intersectional scholarship were the 1970s and 1980s when it focused on questions of economic power and "trying to do something about social inequalities." After its promising beginning, however, intersectional analysis had lost its tough, cutting edge, too often turning "inward, to the level of personal identity narratives, in part because intersectionality can be grasped far more easily when constructing one's own autobiography." This inward turn also reflected "the shift within American society away from social structural analysis of social problems" and institutions, which had been abetted by the ascendancy of "poststructuralist theory" in the "American academy" with its "erasure of social structure." With their book, Dill and Zambrana refocused intersectionality on inequality and showcased its essential role in the development of theory and the analysis of policy. The goal—and it was crucial, "more needed than ever"—asserted Collins was to restore "the robust, initial vision of social justice that catalyzed intersectionality's origins."[139]

The exploitation resulting from the links between race, class, gender, and inequality limned by theorists of intersectionality found concrete expression in the care-giving occupations that had largely replaced domestic service among women of color. Care-givers for the sick, elderly, and disabled, overwhelmingly female and persons of color, experienced a combination of low pay, absence of benefits, dangerous and difficult working conditions, and job insecurity that kept them below or, at best, not far above the poverty line—a modern version of the historically oppressive features of women's work. The substitution of home-based health care for domestic work, Eileen Boris and Jennifer Klein show in *Caring For America: Home Health Workers in the Shadow of the Welfare State*, originated in the 1930s with the WPA, which funded "visiting housekeeper" positions filled mainly by African American women who helped families in poverty. The trend accelerated during the War on Poverty with the attempt to provide jobs for poor women—and move them off welfare—by turning them into care workers and, with the New Careers program, into paraprofessionals. The process of exchanging domestic labor for home aide positions was by and large completed in the 1960s, when federal funding of social services opened up huge numbers of new positions. At first, most home health aides were African American. However, the liberalization of immigration law after 1965 coincided with new employment opportunities made available to African American women by the civil rights movement, resulting in the hiring of newcomers from Latin America and other regions as home health aides and staff in nursing homes, assisted living facilities, and other entry-level care-giving positions. By and large excluded from the protections of the Fair Labor Standards Act, home health workers suffered from low pay and terrible working conditions even as their numbers skyrocketed when changes in federal reimbursement to hospitals during the 1980s resulted in shorter hospital stays and the transfer of recovery and rehabilitation to patients' homes. The story of home caregivers, nonetheless, Boris and Klein show, went in an opposite direction from the rest of the labor movement as home caregivers formed unions that enjoyed real success. "Home care workers entered the twenty-first century with a dynamic union movement—one of the few success stories of recent decades. Like public sector workers in the 1960s and 1970s, care workers for the welfare state repoliticized American labor relations."[140] Here in the militancy of home caregivers was a significant legacy of low-wage women's politics of liberation for the late twentieth and early twenty-first-centuries.

By the close of the twentieth century, the facts on the ground to which the black women's and the early white women's liberation movement responded had undergone profound shifts. The progress of black women was astonishing. As discussed elsewhere in this book, they had moved into a distinctive occupational niche in the public and quasi-public sector. Since the 1960s, their poverty rate had plummeted, and with education held constant they earned as much as white women.[141] The defining feature of their history, like the history of black men whom they outpaced in education, income, and occupation, was differentiation. While substantial numbers enjoyed true economic advance, others remained poor, trapped in the ghettos of America's cities. In 2009 roughly one of every four black and Hispanic women lived in poverty.[142]

In fact, the condition of all women remained precarious. Between 2000 and 2010, the number of women living in poverty increased by 4.9 million, and fewer of them found help in the public safety net. In 1996 TANF provided cash benefits to 68 of every 100 families with children in poverty; in 2010, the number had plummeted to 27 of 100.[143] In theory, welfare reform was replaced by work and an array of new supports such as the Earned Income Tax Credit, and these supports did raise a significant proportion of women not far below the poverty line over it. But huge numbers of women, when they worked at all, found themselves in jobs paying poverty wages and lacking benefits. In 2010 women made up a majority of low-wage workers. In food preparation and serving-related jobs, 73.7 percent of workers earned a wage at or below the poverty level; for personal care and service jobs the proportion was 56.9 percent.[144] Both of these occupations were populated disproportionately by women.[145] The politics of liberation, long faded, had been replaced by the struggle for survival, which, in truth, is the constant theme in the history of poor women—both white women and women of color.

In reality, the politics of liberation was not so much dead as transformed, melded into the international human rights movement. From its inception, black feminism linked its quest for liberation to the struggles of women in the Third World. Accounts of women's liberation struggles in Third World countries, for instance, filled many of *Triple Jeopardy*'s pages. Working for human rights on an international scale formed a key plank in the black feminist agenda. Collins writes that "women of African descent have a distinctive, shared legacy that in turn is part of a global women's movement."[146] At the grassroots, writes historian Rhonda Y. Williams, "black women activists . . . viewed their daily struggles for material well-being, representation, autonomy, and respect as part of a quest for not only citizenship rights and self-determination but also as a matter of human rights."[147] "Defining poverty as an international human rights issue," reports Orleck, members of the KSWRU "and other economic human rights organizations have traveled to the Mexican border to meet poor women who live and work in polluted and dangerous American-owned factory towns." Women helped revive poverty as part of the human rights movement, as Chapter 5 explains, and bend it back from the Global South to the United States. In its trajectory, the human rights movement has renewed the ties between the politics of liberation and the politics of poverty, though to what result remains to be seen.

3

Intellectual Foundations of the War on Poverty and Great Society

RESIDENT RONALD REAGAN FAMOUSLY quipped that the nation fought a war on poverty and poverty won. This summary judgment assented to without reservation even by many liberals is far too harsh. Through the War on Poverty and Great Society, the federal government helped millions of Americans find medical care, food, housing, legal aid, early childhood education, and income security at a level unprecedented in America's past. Poor Americans also helped themselves. The day-to-day War on Poverty took place at the grassroots in the complicated inter-actions among activists on the ground, local officials, and the federal government. Many of the gains wrested with great difficulty in these years remain in place today. The War on Poverty and Great Society did not eradicate poverty in America, but during the years when the pro-grams flourished, poverty dropped to its lowest recorded point in the nation's history. At the same time, through these programs many poor and minority women and men gained at least limited power over insti-tutions and programs that affected their lives and were set on the road to new careers. In these programs lay the origins of the black middle class and political leadership that expanded in the decades to come.[1]

The idea of a comprehensive assault on poverty had been formulated by President John F. Kennedy. On November 23, 1963, the day after Kennedy's assassination, President Lyndon Johnson met with Walter Heller, chairman of the Council of Economic Advisors, and instructed him to continue planning the anti-poverty program. Johnson used the phrase "unconditional war on poverty" for the first time on January 8, 1964, in his State of the Union message. On February 1, he appointed

Sargent Shriver, director of the Peace Corps, to direct the new anti-poverty program. For two years, he directed both agencies—highlighting the ideas and strategies shared by international and domestic development activities in the 1960s.[2]

Shriver, along with a planning committee that drew members from various branches of the federal government, developed a strategy for the program and drafted the Economic Opportunity Act (creating the OEO), passed by the Senate on July 23, 1964, and by the House on August 8. President Johnson signed it into law on August 20. At the same time, President Johnson attacked other problems, including poverty among the elderly, the lack of health insurance for old people and the very poor, and substandard housing through a dazzling array of new programs loosely grouped under the banner of the Great Society.

For its model, the poverty program located in the Office of Economic Opportunity drew heavily on Mobilization for Youth, a comprehensive program in New York City organized to combat delinquency by boosting poor minority youngsters over the structural barriers to social mobility. Mobilization for Youth influenced the formulation of the War on Poverty through the President's Committee on Juvenile Delinquency (PCJD), which adopted many of its ideas, especially its emphasis on the role of blocked opportunity and the importance of community participation, and hired some of its key staff. Economists, the new monarchs of public policy analysis, also played pivotal roles through their novel tools and macroeconomic theories about growth and underdevelopment, which they applied to both foreign and domestic policy.

The poverty war focused on programs to promote opportunity in four areas: juvenile delinquency, civil rights, job training, and education. Without doubt, the most popular, and many would argue the most successful, was Operation Head Start, which funded preschool education for poor children. The most controversial aspect of the program was community action—the requirement in Title II of the Economic Opportunity Act that the new community agencies created to receive and administer federal anti-poverty funds be "developed, conducted, and administered with the maximum feasible participation of the residents." Historians are still unpacking community action's complicated origins and rescuing its legacy.

Ideas, Bureaucracy, and Politics

Histories of the War on Poverty disagree about the relative influence of ideas, bureaucratic politics, and political strategy. Was the War on Poverty guided by a coherent response to the nature of inequity and deprivation in American society? Or did it emerge from a struggle for power among federal agencies and between old-line bureaucrats and the new administration? Was its driving force compassion for the poor, or the need to win black votes and quell the riots in America's cities?

It is possible to write a history of the early War on Poverty that stresses the primacy of ideas and goodwill. By the early 1960s, the story would begin, politicians influenced by the small but growing literature on poverty in contemporary America had determined to attack the remnants of destitution in the land of plenty. It is also possible to write about the poverty war as the outcome of bureaucratic maneuvering. Within the federal administration, at least four agencies—the President's Commission on Juvenile Delinquency, the Council of Economic Advisors, the Labor Department, and the Bureau of the Budget—jockeyed to shape and control the new initiative. In the same years, the Social Security Administration quietly pressed for one incremental benefit expansion after another, with the result that benefits increased dramatically. It is similarly possible to portray the poverty program and the expansion of social benefits as a response to great social and political forces: the migration of southern blacks to northern cities and the civil rights movement, or as a way to meet the political needs of the Democratic Party and assuage the unrest within America's cities.

All these stories are correct. The history of the poverty program is incomplete without any one of them. The difficulty is assessing their relative weight and combining them into a coherent explanation.

Some common stories about the poverty war's origins apparently are apocryphal. John F. Kennedy did not read Michael Harrington's *The Other America* and suddenly declare war on poverty. A long essay on poverty in *The New Yorker* by Dwight Macdonald, which reviewed *The Other America*, exerted a greater impact than Harrington's book on Kennedy and his advisors. Also influential was John Kenneth Galbraith's *The Affluent Society*, which stressed increased investment in the public sector and in other unmet social needs such as relief of poverty. Cloward and Ohlin's opportunity theory of delinquency (described later in this chapter) influenced the initial design of the program, and echoes of the culture of poverty thesis also ran through early discussions, even though Oscar Lewis and his writings apparently played no direct part. Nor should we forget that anti-poverty measures did not form an explicit part of Kennedy's early urban policy. Indeed, the war on poverty, influenced especially by Homer Bigart's articles in the *Herald Tribune* on rural Kentucky, at first tilted strongly toward Appalachia.[3]

The poverty program also drew on ideas formulated by reformers during the late nineteenth and early twentieth centuries. At a 1973 conference of former poverty war officials at Brandeis, David Austin, who had served as planning director of the Cleveland Demonstration Project funded by the President's Committee on Juvenile Delinquency, recalled: "There's been a long tradition... based... on an assumption that essentially the poor, in many cases seen as immigrants, essentially were to be helped up and into a stable position in society by the down-reaching hands of the well-to-do and the intellectuals." The reforms of the 1960s, he thought, represented "a rediscovery of many of the innovations of the progressive era, had many of the same characteristics and in the end were influenced very much by the same scientific philanthropy, which strongly emphasized professionalism, social theory and the idea of incorporating the poor into society without disruption and on an individual case basis."[4] In the tradition of American liberalism, early poverty warriors defined reform as education, not redistribution, and focused their slim resources on the individual rehabilitation of poor people.

In part, the formulation of the poverty program was also an exercise in bureaucratic politics, with William Cannon of the Bureau of the Budget mediating among contending units within the Executive Branch. In fact, one of the poverty war's most contentious phrases, "maximum feasible participation," emerged from bureaucratic compromise among the program's planners. Richard Boone had wanted to use the word "involvement," which others found too strong. "To my knowledge," Boone remembered, "at that point and thereafter for some time—at least in our circle-the-word 'control' was not mentioned. It wasn't part of that vocabulary. It was 'involve' and 'participate.' Those were the two terms that were used and the compromise was 'feasible.'"

Another and more serious conflict erupted over the location of the National Youth Corps and Job Corps, both of which Willard Wirtz believed to have been delegated to the Department of Labor by a "treaty in advance."[5] Bureaucratic politics also shaped anti-poverty programs at the great foundations. At the Ford Foundation, for instance, Paul Ylvisaker wasn't "altogether happy" with "that bag of opportunity theory which Pat [Daniel P.] Moynihan and others take off so much at—there's a kind of an ideology to it." Nonetheless, a common goal motivated foundation staff: "what always bound us together...we could forgive each other our theology if we knew that we were in the same rag-tag group who were taking on the establishment."[6]

Political concerns also fueled and directed the early poverty program. According to William Capron, former official of the Council of Economic Advisors and Bureau of the Budget involved in the planning and administration of the War on Poverty and Great Society programs, Kennedy "was persuaded politically that, having made his major '63 domestic program a tax cut which helps the middle and upper income people, that the next piece had to be something to help people that [sic] didn't have enough income to pay taxes." None of the former federal officials who gathered at the 1973 Brandeis conference to discuss the poverty program dissented from Capron's reminiscence, or, for that matter, from each other's enumeration of influences and tales of bureaucratic compromise. They did, however, disagree sharply about the role of the civil rights movement and race.[7] In part, the disagreements reflected the diverging perspectives of those inside and outside the administration, whose different views have shaped interpretations of the War on Poverty since early in its history.

Disagreement centered on the political impact of racial issues, for no one disputed the impact of demography on reshaping America's cities. More than any other single development, in the late 1950s and early 1960s the massive migration of southern blacks to northern cities framed the formulation of both urban and anti-poverty policy. Distinctions between the situation of earlier European immigrants and contemporary black migrants underpinned Cloward and Ohlin's interpretation of delinquent subcultures. The culture supposedly brought by black migrants shaped Moynihan's interpretation of black family structure and the mechanisms by which it helped perpetuate poverty.

The impact of migration likewise determined Paul Ylvisaker's strategy for urban policy at the Ford Foundation: "I came to that sudden perception of the city as the magnet and passage-point of great migrations," he remembered. "It was...for me an intellectual breakthrough...But at the same time it was also strategic because if you could conceive of an overarching process within which one could deal with the *Verbotens* of race relations and so forth, and where you weren't talking black immediately, which raised all the hackles, then you had much more chance of getting a program accepted."[8]

Consensus on the intellectual and strategic role of black migration did not reflect agreement on the more direct links between race, politics, and social programs. Did Kennedy and then Johnson plan their attack on poverty in response to mounting black protests? Were the War on Poverty and Great Society devices for cementing black loyalty to the Democratic Party? Opinions among those connected to policy at the time differed sharply. Adam Yarmolinsky, Shriver's deputy in planning the poverty program, denied the role of political concerns not only in the early War on Poverty, but in the Kennedy administration's stance on civil rights, which was "99 and 33/100 percent noblesse oblige" with "no concern whatsoever about holding the black vote, about an upsurge of revolt of the masses."[9]

Richard Cloward and Frances Fox Piven, the two participants at the conference least connected to actual federal policymaking, argued the opposite case. Warning against a view of history in which "the main actors were some intellectuals and some bureaucrats," Cloward reminded other participants of the events surrounding the initial discussions of anti-poverty policy in 1963: the Birmingham civil rights campaign; the March on Washington in August; the bombings in September. Throughout, Kennedy commissioned "various groups within the administration to study black unemployment and to come up with plans and so forth in order to begin to respond to what were very large political forces particularly within the Democratic party that were being activated and radicalized to some extent by the civil rights movement and by the insurgency that was beginning to take form in the cities." William Capron, referring to the Council of Economic Advisors, conceded: "We saw, literally, the March on Washington and that sure didn't do anything to cool us off on pushing this embryonic program."[10]

Yarmolinsky disagreed. "During the late winter, spring and early summer of 1964," he asserted, "we were concerned with explaining to the Congress and the public that the poverty program was in no sense a help-the-blacks program, and not only were we saying this, but we didn't think it was." In fact, planners expected the poverty program to offer "very little for blacks" because "Most poor people are not black, most black people are not poor," to cite one slogan that Yarmolinsky repeatedly inserted into speeches. In 1964 OEO "hadn't the faintest gray tinge to it. If anything, color it Appalachian if you were going to color it anything at all."[11]

Capron, disagreeing with Yarmolinsky, distinguished between political rhetoric and intellectual understanding. The reelection campaign of 1964, he recalled, was much on their minds: "We knew that it would be death...to bill any kind of program as a help-the-blacks program. But that doesn't mean that we didn't realize that this program was very important in terms of the black vote...Now, we did not articulate it that way...But we did understand that this was an important part of what was going on."[12] On occasion, the poverty program's supporters dropped their reticence about race. In April 1964, at a symposium on integration, Shriver linked the struggle against poverty to the civil rights movement as "all part of the same battle," and explained that in the congressional floor debates, the Economic Opportunity Act "sometimes was regarded as but the logical counterpart of the Civil Rights Act which had just been passed in June."[13]

At the roundtable on the War on Poverty, Piven emphasized that she and Cloward were not claiming that blacks were the *only* concern of the Kennedy administration. But, she contended, the poverty program represented in part a strategy of political mobilization designed to ensure Democratic electoral success. Documentary evidence clearly showed the prominence of black votes among the administration's priorities. Because black allegiance to the Democratic Party had weakened, even in 1960 Kennedy showed concern for the black vote. She pointed to his "famous call to Mrs. Martin Luther King, followed by massive pamphleteering about that fact in the ghettos."

Piven failed to convince David Hackett, former executive director of the President's Committee on Juvenile Delinquency, who countered, referring to his program: "We would have run it completely different

[sic] if we had followed your thesis. If it had been a political program and if the administration wanted to cater to the black vote, we would have done it completely different [sic]...We did it completely the opposite way."[14]

Nonetheless, Piven continued to press the impact of race and politics on the poverty program. All the morning's speakers, she pointed out toward the end of the discussion, had talked about "very large developments in American society having to do with race, with class and with politics." However they evaluated them, "we've raised again the question that no one wanted to discuss, which is the relationship of the specific federal programs to very broad social, economic and political developments in American society in the 1960s. That relationship, it seems everybody was saying today, did exist." In the end even Yarmolinsky agreed: "I guess I'm also agreeing with Frances," he conceded in his closing remarks, that the poverty program "was in part a response to profound...social movements in the United States. All I was saying earlier was that it was not...a concession by the executive committee of the ruling class to the rising demands of the masses."[15]

In part, the argument had revealed inevitable differences in perspective: outsiders (Cloward and Piven) stressed context; most insiders (former federal officials) remained preoccupied with the day-to-day process of policymaking and the politics of bureaucracy. Outsiders focused on broad social and political goals; insiders defended their motives. No one, it should be stressed, denied the influence of racial politics on the poverty program after 1964. They disagreed, rather, about its origins.

In *The War on Poverty: A New Grassroots History, 1964–1980*, Annelise Orleck and Lisa Gayle Hazirjian side with Piven and Cloward. "The War on Poverty has usually been seen as distinct from the southern civil rights movement," they write, "but the two historic movements were inextricably tied together."[16] They remind readers that when President Johnson described his vision for a Great Society at the University of Michigan in May 1964, "he did not shy away from acknowledging that the effort formed part of a struggle for racial justice. He evoked a future of 'abundance and liberty for all' Americans, 'an end to poverty and racial injustice....' Johnson was speaking, they underscore, "after a decade in which hundreds of thousands of men, women, and children had put their bodies on the line to end a century of legal segregation;

less than a year after a quarter million marchers had listened to Martin Luther King Jr.'s 'I Have a Dream' speech...." In one way or another, all the essays in Orleck and Hazirjian's book show the intersection of the poverty war with civil rights activity in communities throughout the country.[17] In rural Mississippi, for example, the Child Development Group of Mississippi, recounts Amy Jordan, "a network of child care and educational centers and one of the most controversial programs to emerge from the Community Action Program of the War on Poverty, began as a hopeful outgrowth of the movement schools established during the 1964 Freedom Summer campaign."[18] In Memphis, writes Laurie B. Green, the organizers of the Memphis Area Project, a War on Poverty program, viewed "the antipoverty struggle as a continuation of the black freedom movement...."[19] Robert Bauman excavates the story of three women in Los Angeles who made "signal contributions" to the city's War on Poverty. All three had "long and consistent connections to civil rights and social service organizations, giving them experiences that informed their leadership of community organizations during the War on Poverty."[20]

The insiders had based their case on narrow grounds that ignored the intertwining of civil rights and powerful grassroots mobilizations unleashed by the War on Poverty. Although no spokesperson for the civil rights movement joined the discussions that shaped the poverty program,[21] the image most insiders tried at first to convey—an intelligent, well-meaning circle of white male federal officials uninfluenced by the racial struggles (and oblivious to the gender issues in poverty) headlined in newspapers across the country—remains implausible, as in the end even the most intransigent insider agreed. Nonetheless, despite its often narrow focus, the insiders' account remains crucial because it describes the complex process by which the anti-poverty initiative moved from impulse to federal program, and without which it cannot be understood. Their perspective also illuminates key strategic decisions: Why did the administration locate the poverty program in a separate agency? Why did it label it a war?

Lyndon Johnson placed his poverty program in a new federal agency and called it a war. Neither decision represented his only alternative. He could have spread anti-poverty funds throughout existing federal departments and used his office to stimulate and coordinate new programs. He also could have promised less than total victory or framed the program in terms of inequality, income, or—for that matter—race. His choices carried profound consequences. As a separate agency, OEO remained both visible and vulnerable—a target for both Congress and a sometimes hostile public—and the federal agencies bypassed in its creation. It lasted only a decade. As an unconditional war, the poverty program raised expectations that even an adequately funded and redistributive initiative could not be expected to meet within a few years. Its own overblown promises became a principal factor in the disillusion it aroused among contemporaries and the unfavorable verdict rendered by many of its historians. That said, it is important not to blame the victim. Proclaiming war on poverty was a brave, unprecedented act on the part of an American president, an expression of optimism, faith, and idealism rarely encountered among politicians. It must be remembered that the poverty war fell short of its goals not just on account of its internal weaknesses but, as well, because the Vietnam War robbed it of necessary resources and because of the political backlash its successes provoked.[22]

In part, the War on Poverty seemed to its planners to require a separate federal agency because its projected budget was so low. As President Kennedy thought about the 1964 campaign, he planned the War on Poverty and the tax cuts as his major domestic program, William Capron remembered. And although it was not clear what the dimensions of the program would be, the sum of available money was so small that his advisors realized, according to Capron, "if you threw this into the existing bureaucracy...it was political suicide...it would be clear to everyone that it was nothing, that it was just window dressing."[23]

The poverty program also required a new agency because it assumed the inertia and incompetence of the agencies that existed. Anti-poverty strategists within the Kennedy and early Johnson administrations lacked confidence that existing federal departments could create bold and effective programs. Two alternatives emerged. The first, favored by Hackett and his associates in the President's Council on Juvenile Delinquency, was to expand the PCJD model. That meant an independent staff with money for experiments backed by the power of the president. Shriver chose a different course. He so distrusted the Department of Labor that he insisted the Job Corps be run from within the Office of Economic Opportunity. By repeating the pattern with every major OEO initiative, Shriver surrendered the possibility of reforming departments and programs within the federal government. Hackett recalled with regret that each OEO program had been built outside the system. Manpower programs, for instance, operated outside the Department of Labor; Head Start never confronted "the educational system head-on." Therefore, OEO never accomplished any basic reform in the agencies of the federal government.[24]

For William Cannon at the Bureau of the Budget, the "key decision" in the early anti-poverty initiative was the adoption of the designation, War on Poverty. The Bureau of the Budget opposed the label because it raised unrealistic expectations about the amount of money available for the new program. Nonetheless, during the Christmas holiday in 1963, Johnson decided to call the anti-poverty program a war. He chose the language deliberately: "The military image carried with it connotations of victories and defeats that could prove misleading. But I wanted to rally the nation, to sound a call to arms which would stir people in the government, in private industry, and on the campuses to lend their talent to a massive effort to eliminate this evil." As David Zarefsky notes in his excellent analysis of the poverty war's rhetoric, the military metaphor solved important political problems confronting Johnson and facilitated the passage of the Economic Opportunity Act. For one thing, it responded to the national mood after the assassination of John F. Kennedy. "Aroused by President Kennedy's untimely death," asserts Zarefsky, "many Americans longed for redemption through sacrifice."[25]

As an issue, poverty also helped the new president with delicate problems of image. Johnson needed to establish a national identity and create a positive impression by shedding his image as a Texas conservative. He also faced the task of managing the "transition between his caretaker role after the Kennedy assassination and his own presidency."[26] For this reason, he needed a program that appealed to Kennedy's supporters but had not yet been publicly labeled a Kennedy effort.

Because poverty had not yet become an important national concern, Johnson began a rhetorical campaign to alter public opinion in which the military metaphor, announced in his 1964 State of the Union message, played an important role. The metaphor of unconditional war aroused national interest and participation and placed the administration in a moral position that opponents attacked only at great risk. "When a nation is at war," points out Zarefsky, it has "acknowledged the existence of a foe sufficiently threatening to warrant attack." Characterizing opponents as "almost treasonous," the war metaphor "served as a unifying device, rallying the nation behind a moral challenge."[27]

The military metaphor proved to be brilliant political strategy. Other metaphors for the poverty program would have failed to mobilize public opinion, or aroused even more hostility among conservatives. Robert Lampman, for instance, advised Walter Heller in 1963: "Probably a politically acceptable program must avoid completely the use of the term 'inequality' or of the term 'redistribution' of income or wealth." As the military metaphor fueled the passage of the Economic Opportunity Act, it aroused the sympathy of the nation. It also aroused its expectations, which proved a huge risk for an underfunded program addressing a massive and historical social problem with little theory and no proven methods.[28]

From Structure to Service and the Hidden Jobs Program of the War on Poverty

The War on Poverty began with a structural analysis and ended up with a service-based strategy. How did this happen? As David Austin reflected in 1973, "The issue is really why a service strategy when you had a structural diagnosis." Although the most influential analyses of poverty stressed its roots in unemployment, federal anti-poverty planners deliberately avoided programs whose main purpose was to create jobs.[29] Nonetheless, as we shall see, the poverty program and Great Society sometimes deliberately, sometimes as a by-product of their other activities, created many jobs.

In his economic report for 1964, Lyndon Johnson summarized the problem of poverty in America in structural terms. His presentation drew on the detailed second chapter of a report by the Council of Economic Advisors (CEA), written primarily by Robert Lampman, an economist from the University of Wisconsin and an expert in poverty statistics.[30] Using the most detailed data yet published, the CEA's report argued that economic growth by itself would not eliminate poverty in

America. It anchored poverty in income distribution, employment discrimination, and inadequate transfer payments by government, and it proposed a comprehensive program for its reduction. "By the poor," asserted the report, "we mean those who are not now maintaining a decent standard of living—those whose basic needs exceed their means to satisfy them." It also firmly rejected explanations based on character or heredity: "The idea that the bulk of the poor are condemned to that condition because of innate deficiencies of character or intelligence has not withstood intensive analysis."[31] Those in poverty lacked "the earned income, property income and savings, and transfer payments to meet their minimum needs." Many employed people earned inadequate wages, while other poor people could not work on account of "age, disability, premature death of the principal earner, need to care for children or disabled family members, lack of any saleable skill, lack of motivation, or simply heavy unemployment in the area." For others, low pay reflected racial discrimination or "low productivity" that resulted from inadequate education and skills.

Property and savings income were most important for the elderly, but many had earned too little to save, and about half of them had no hospital insurance. Without such transfer payments as existed, many more families would have been poor. Nonetheless, only half the poor received any transfer payments at all, and the most generous payments (private pensions and Social Security) offered the least help to those employed irregularly or in the worst-paying jobs. Aside from earnings, poverty's roots, according to the report, lay in a "vicious circle." Poverty bred poverty because of "high risks of illness; limitations on mobility; limited access to education, information, and training." As a consequence, parents passed on their poverty to their children. With discrimination often an insurmountable barrier, escaping poverty proved nearly impossible for "American children raised in families accustomed to living on relief."[32]

Despite its structural diagnosis, the Council of Economic Advisors laid the foundation for a War on Poverty based on economic growth, civil rights, and new social and educational services designed to equalize opportunity. The CEA report revealed the hallmarks of American liberalism in the 1960s: an uneasy mix of environmental and cultural explanations of poverty; a continuation of the historic American reliance on education as a solution for social problems; trust in the capacity of government; and faith in the power of experts to design effective public policies. The council stressed removing handicaps that denied the poor "fair access to the expanding incomes of a growing economy" and introducing new federal programs "with special emphasis on prevention and rehabilitation." As for jobs, the council urged their indirect creation through a tax cut that would stimulate the economy.[33] In fact, as historian Alice O'Connor tells the story in *Poverty Knowledge*—her indispensable history of social science, social policy, and poverty in the twentieth century—the CEA, drawing on recent economic theory, confronted "an alternative analysis of unemployment that threatened to stop the high-growth agenda before it got off the ground. This analysis, increasingly popular among economic conservatives as well as left-liberals in the labor movement, held that unemployment was a 'structural' rather than an aggregate growth problem and hence would not respond to the simple solvent of more growth." Labor stressed "[s]tructural change, technology, and, especially, automation" as "responsible for persistently high unemployment rates" that "threatened to render industrial, low-skilled, and, especially, minority workers unwanted and obsolete." This version of a structural diagnosis of poverty received strong support in 1958 from the noted economist John Kenneth Galbraith in his book *The Affluent Society* and in 1962 from the famous Swedish social scientist Gunnar Myrdal in *Challenge to Affluence*, which proposed a "Marshall plan to eradicate poverty." It found support as well in Michael Harrington's *The Other America*.[34] At the same time, points out O'Connor, "focusing on automation, labor market exclusion, and racial exploitation as primary causes of poverty, influential leaders within the civil rights movement were also articulating a more structural concept of poverty in the early 1960s, building toward their own version of a 'domestic Marshall Plan' that would come to include job creation and income guarantees as well as more specifically race-targeted measures to combat segregation, discrimination, and the absence of capital in black urban communities."[35]

In 1961 the CEA saw its "immediate challenge" as disproving this version of a "structural unemployment analysis altogether, quashing the idea that it was impossible or undesirable to reduce unemployment without a direct government role in creating jobs."[36] In this task,

O'Connor reports, they found support in a new economics that combined an updated Keynsianism, which stressed the use of "government policy to stimulate faster economic growth and full employment" with the emphasis on market forces among neoclassic economic theorists and human capital theory, which implied that the "gains made by American workers...should be understood not as the product of institutional factors such as unions, government policy, or firm practices, but as market returns to individual investments. Similarly, individual skills and behavior, not institutional practices or sociological factors, could explain both differences in earnings and why people were poor." Adding to economic theory was the "increasing emphasis on mathematical theory and quantification, spurred along by expanding computer capacity and by sophisticated econometric" methods that supposedly lent economics scientific precision. This new economics, O'Connor stresses, gave liberals "a powerful analytic and institutional platform from which to wage a national campaign against poverty" by making "the struggle against poverty compatible with lightly managed, if not free-market, capitalist growth."[37]

In its emphasis on growth, the CEA reflected the ubiquity of the idea of growth in post–World War II America. Growth was the magic elixir that would permit the improvement of living standards for all Americans, indeed for the whole world, without economic redistribution. "Rapid economic growth, it was felt," claims political scientist Alan Wolfe, "could expand the pie sufficiently so that it would not have to be cut in a different way.... Growth was ... transpolitical."[38] It is hard to overestimate how pervasive this idea became in the decades following the war, giving liberals the means to serve progressive goals without adopting the social democratic models gaining traction in Europe. The consequences for policy were immense, and, when the idea proved a delusion, tragic for the boats that did not find themselves buoyed by a rising tide. "Growth," claimed Andrew L. Yarrow in *Measuring America: How Economic Growth Came to Define American Greatness in the Late Twentieth Century*, "was a magical word, carried from the economics profession to the broader public. It was a proxy for progress, and the creator of abundance and better living." Yarrow's JSTOR analysis of major economic journals found that the number of articles including the term "economic growth" skyrocketed from 226 in the 1940s to 2,980 in the 1950s and 6,788 in the 1960s.[39]

The decision by the Johnson administration to back away from direct job creation reflected practical politics as well as the new economics, with its emphasis on reducing unemployment and poverty through growth. An early poverty warrior, Adam Yarmolinsky, remembered, "You ask yourself, do you concentrate on finding jobs for people or preparing people for jobs. There our tactical decision was let's concentrate first on preparing people for jobs." The strategists thought the 1964 tax cut would create jobs; they believed poor people needed a long process of job preparation; and they knew that "it was less expensive to prepare people for jobs than to create jobs for people."[40]

Like other domestic and international policies of the era, this strategy assumed the continuation of growth and abundance: an anti-poverty plan that stressed increased educational opportunity and work preparation depended on the continued expansion and easy availability of jobs. Because growth would stimulate demand and enlarge the available rewards, the eradication of poverty required no painful reallocation of money and power. In the buoyant economy of the early 1960s this analysis still remained plausible, and an analysis of poverty as primarily a problem of employability reasonably could result in a relatively cheap public policy directed toward equalizing education and job preparation.[41]

Not all members of the administration agreed, however. The Department of Labor, led by Secretary Willard Wirtz, proposed a poverty program that stressed employment. Wirtz's objections drew on the Labor Department's commitment to macroeconomic policies based on reducing unemployment, where necessary, through public employment. In 1961 Arthur Goldberg, then secretary of labor, advocated a Full Employment Act of 1961, and Wirtz continued to press this Labor Department position. He "violently attacked" the CEA report, which was "published over his strenuous objection." In a memo to Theodore Sorenson, who had circulated a proposal for a poverty program, Wirtz emphasized, "*The Poverty Program must start out with immediate, priority emphasis on employment* [italics in original]." Because poverty "is a description of income," he argued, the major "single immediate change which the poverty program could bring about in the lives of most of the poor would be to provide the family head with a regular, decently paid job." Job creation did not depend solely on direct action by the federal government. The attack, Wirtz believed, should be launched principally at the local level, because "*the private forces are stronger than the public* [italics in original]." The tax bill was "an anti-poverty bill, probably the principal weapon we have." Nonetheless, the problem of unemployment demanded "special programs designed to create useful jobs." Wirtz, in common with other advocates of a poverty program, also stressed health and education, but his emphasis on job creation set the Department of Labor apart from the Council of Economic Advisors.[42]

Wirtz apparently persuaded the staff designing the poverty program, because at the last minute it added a job component. Armed with a proposal for a supplementary tax on cigarettes to finance it, Sargent Shriver presented the plan at a cabinet meeting, where Wirtz also argued vigorously on its behalf. President Johnson, however, wanted neither expanded economic transfers nor direct job creation, and he finessed the question of income transfers by appointing a commission. As for the job creation plan, "I have never seen a colder reception from the president," recalled Yarmolinsky. "He just—absolute blank stare—implied without even opening his mouth that Shriver should move on to the next proposal."[43]

Direct attacks on unemployment never had a serious chance of passage in either the Kennedy or Johnson administrations. Kennedy did not appoint the most influential advocate of Keynesian policies, John Kenneth Galbraith, to the Council of Economic Advisors. His three appointees, led by Walter Heller, did not share Galbraith's interventionist approach. Instead, they stressed aggregate economic objectives, particularly economic growth. Because they believed tax cuts would achieve their goals most efficiently, the focus of the War on Poverty and the Great Society, as Margaret Weir concludes, "shifted from the structure of the economy to the characteristics of the individual, characteristics that training was supposed to modify."[44] By default, the War on Poverty adopted the culture of poverty.

And yet, the War on Poverty and Great Society in fact did create a very large, if indeterminate, number of jobs, a large proportion of which went to minorities. One of its other accomplishments was launching a new African American political and institutional leadership. How did this happen? In part, the answer is found in the jobs provided by new programs directly associated with the poverty war; in part, by the poverty war's community action arm; and, as well, in the expansion of social services during the Great Society years. Operation Head Start was the most dramatic instance of deliberate and direct job creation by OEO. The next section will take up the community action story and the following section, the expansion of social services.

Gretchen Aguiar's pioneering research has excavated the role of Head Start in job creation. The story begins with the New Careers Movement led by Frank Riessman, a professor at Bard College, which argued for launching poor people on careers through decently paid subprofessional jobs. NCM stressed employment first, with training on the job. NCM advocates saw in the War on Poverty and its community action arm the perfect opportunity to put its ideas into practice, and it found a favorable reception in the Office of Economic Opportunity. From the outset, the provision of jobs for low income parents, almost entirely women, as teacher aides formed an integral part of Head Start program requirements. In Head Start's first summer alone, the program employed 100,000 local parents. "In his final report to Congress on Head Start," Aguiar points out, President Lyndon Johnson "praised this new emphasis on jobs for the poor. Head Start had created 'many thousands of employment opportunities for poor persons as health, community, and teacher aides. Their successful performance has led to the establishment of similar opportunities in hundreds of public and private agencies.' Head Start jobs counted as one of the program's signal achievements."[45] As well as in Head Start, the War on Poverty created jobs through its most controversial and innovative wing—the Community Action Program.

From Equal Opportunity to Community Action

As finally approved by the president, the poverty program linked two major strategies: equal opportunity and community action. As an anti-poverty strategy, equal opportunity stressed improved and expanded services, especially those related to education and job preparation—for example, Operation Head Start for preschool children and the Job Corps for adolescents. (It also led to the unprecedented infusion of federal funds into the schools attended by poor children—a result not of the poverty program itself but of the Elementary and Secondary Education Act of 1965.) Community action refers to the active participation of community residents in the formulation and administration of programs. It required the establishment of local agencies to receive and spend federal funds. As a strategy, it deliberately bypassed local political structures, empowered new groups, and challenged existing institutions.

At the outset, the theory that most influenced the poverty program joined opportunity and action in a coherent and novel explanation of juvenile delinquency. Recall the formative influence of the President's Committee on Juvenile Delinquency on the poverty program. The theoretical base of Mobilization For Youth drew on the work of the famous Chicago Areas Project as adapted by its research directors, Richard Cloward and Lloyd Ohlin of the New York School of Social Work of Columbia University.[46] Cloward and Ohlin presented their theory in an influential book, *Delinquency and Opportunity*, published in 1960. By 1964, the year of the poverty program's official origin in the Economic Opportunity Act, the book was in its fifth printing.

During the panic over adolescent behavior in the 1950s, individualist and psychological theories had begun to dominate the literature of delinquency. By contrast, *Delinquency and Opportunity* developed a self-consciously social and cultural approach closer to the criminology of the 1930s and 1940s. Cloward and Ohlin wanted to reinsert delinquency into the social and cultural matrix from which psychological theory had abstracted it.[47] Much like Oscar Lewis's portrayal of poverty, Cloward and Ohlin presented delinquency as a subculture. They differentiated between three delinquent subcultures: criminal, conflict (gang violence), and retreatist (drug-based). They then asked why the prevalence and appeal of these three variants shifted across time.[48]

Usually associated with males, delinquent subcultures, they argued, concentrated among the lower class, emerged during adolescence, and occurred most often in cities. (Note the irony of drawing on a male model of delinquency to construct a national poverty program when women constituted a huge proportion of the poverty population and, as we have seen, black women were increasingly criticized for their baleful influence on the psycho-social development of black men.) In modern urban America, they believed, unlimited and unrealizable aspirations fueled the practice of placing blame for failure on the larger social order, which in turn reduced its legitimacy and hence its restraining power. The result was an explosive discrepancy between aspiration and opportunity. Delinquent subcultures did not represent alternative value systems; rather, the adolescents within them had internalized conventional goals. Only they faced limits on legitimate means of attaining them. "Unable to revise their aspirations downward," frustrated adolescents explored "nonconformist alternatives."[49]

To account for the relative strength of the variations in delinquent subcultures, Cloward and Ohlin turned to the historical interaction between immigrants and cities throughout modern American history. They argued that in recent decades the bureaucratization of crime, decline of political machines, and slum clearance had intensified political disorganization. At the same time, the most recent arrivals in northern cities, black migrants from the South, confronted unprecedented conditions that blocked group mobility and frustrated historic processes of assimilation. With traditional social structures crumbling and mobility blocked, urban adolescents turned increasingly to crime, conflict, and drugs.[50]

Although *Delinquency and Opportunity* offered no policy proposals, the importance of both opportunity and community action was one implicit message. Expanded opportunities would close the gap between aspiration and achievement; empowerment would help combat the subcultures of conflict and retreatism that grew out of hopelessness and despair. Cloward and Ohlin, much like Oscar Lewis, offered a cultural explanation that pointed to the need for a redistribution of power downward and outward to communities of the poor.[51]

Cloward's and Ohlin's stress on community had deep roots in twentieth-century American history. It drew on the traditions of the settlement house movement, which had always encouraged active citizen participation. Early in the twentieth century, Jane Addams, with customary simplicity and eloquence, had stated one premise from which community action eventually grew: "unless all men and all classes contribute to a good, we cannot even be sure that it is worth having."[52] Indeed, as Alyosha Goldstein argues, from the start of the twentieth century through the three decades following World War II, "ideas and initiatives that centered around the idiom of community became especially significant for debates about social and economic equality."[53]

Mobilization for Youth illustrated the shift toward a focus on poverty and its consequences as it drew out the implications of *Delinquency and Opportunity* for opportunity and community action. Its 1962 summary proposal argued, "Obstacles to economic and social betterment among low-income groups are responsible for delinquency." No effort to prevent juvenile delinquency could succeed unless it offered young people genuine opportunities to behave differently. At the same time, community participation remained critical. For programs to be truly effective, residents must create and participate in them "rather than have them imposed from without by persons who are alien to the traditions and aspirations of the community." Combatting delinquency therefore required more than the expansion of opportunity: Young people would respond more positively to an adult community that exhibits "the capacity to organize itself, to impose informal sanctions, and to mobilize indigenous resources."[54]

Community action infiltrated the nascent War on Poverty through David Hackett, executive director of the President's Committee on Juvenile Delinquency, who, reports Alice O'Connor, "mobilized the juvenile delinquency and urban reform networks to put the idea into the policy pipeline, eventually leaving both community action and the poverty initiative significantly changed." As a result of his frustration "with the limitations the PCJD was encountering in its efforts to create better opportunities for low-income youth, and particularly with his difficulties in persuading old-line federal agencies to coordinate and concentrate their resources in experimental communities," Hackett put together an interagency group, which called itself "Hackett's guerrillas" because of "its aim to shake up the bureaucracy...." Hackett's guerrillas drew its members "heavily from the networks that had been forming around juvenile delinquency and urban reform since the late 1950s."[55] Four of the guerrillas, Jack Conway, Richard Boone, Sanford Kravitz, and Fred O'R Hayes, "conceptualized and developed the legislative provisions for the new community action program, including the language requiring 'maximum feasible participation of the poor.'" The first director of CAP was Conway, a trade union organizer "on loan" from the AFL-CIO.

Boone, formerly a Chicago-area police captain, Ford Foundation official, and member of the PCJD, became associate director; Boone's deputy for research and development was Kravitz, "a social work and planning professional who had staffed the PCJD...Hayes, a budget officer with the Housing and Home Finance Administration at the height of urban renewal, was in charge of CAP operations."[56] Despite their lack of experience with administering large government programs, this initial CAP leadership shared "a history of engagement in community-based reform and a growing conviction that no meaningful change would occur without basic political as well as administrative changes in the local status quo." In the agency's controversial 1965 Community Action Workbook, Boone wrote that "the poor need access to power as well as resources." Nonetheless, the guerrillas also stressed the need for "consensus-building." The "ideal community action agency," Conway "spelled out...would operate like a 'three-legged stool,' joining public officials, private agencies, and the poor in a planning process." Built into the simultaneous stress on empowering the poor and working through consensus lurked an explosive contradiction that CAP's founders chose not to confront until it nearly destroyed the program.[57]

It is misleading to grant community action too much ideological consistency. For community action emerged in practice as an ambiguous concept whose appeal rested as much in practical politics as in theory. By late 1963, Hackett, Boone, and other community advocates had persuaded administration officials of the value of a poverty program based on community action. Shriver, however, remained unconvinced. He worried about its appeal to Congress and about potential problems in coordinating "agencies, organizations, and disparate interests." Nonetheless, his resistance wore down, although for exactly what reasons remain unclear.

As Yarmolinsky recalled in an exchange with Arnold Gurin, dean of the Heller School at Brandeis:

YARMOLINSKY: I think I'd have to say that the principal factor was that when someone shows you the stripe down the middle of the road and you're not going to redefine the road, the chances are you'll include the center stripe.

GURIN: So it was really that residual?

YARMOLINSKY: It was being pushed very, very hard…There was no one in the room who said, "That is really a bad idea and we oughtn't to do any of it."…after the first day, and the first week when no one had said, "Throw it out," because it was there, we thought about it. We thought about its pros and cons. We didn't think about it on a yes or no basis. We thought about what it can be…Look, Shriver thought about it, again, primarily as a salesman. I suppose I thought about it primarily as how you would administer it; it was a fascinating administrative problem.[58]

Within the Kennedy and early Johnson administrations, a group of former federal officials recalled, community action assumed several different meanings. William Capron, for example, stressed the utility of community action as a planning mechanism. He recalled how impressed he and his colleagues were with variations in the "situation in each group of the poor" among and within cities. Because this variation required different mixes of resources, each local group should have "a major say in deciding what their highest priorities were in the way of services."[59] Community action also was a method for encouraging social experiments. Shriver's principal deputy, Adam Yarmolinsky, for one, saw it "as a way of attempting to test out a variety of solutions to the poverty problem."[60]

Community action appealed to federal planners as a technique for coordinating policy. Lloyd Ohlin stressed the need at both local and federal levels for "creating a coordinating structure that could funnel money into the new programs and use that as the carrot to bring programs together." A community action agency, continued former OEO official Fred Hayes, was a "treaty organization," an effort to bring the "school system, the city and other interests together in a new structure simply because you had no old ones that were both competent and nonsuspect."[61]

For others, community action was a form of social therapy. Community participation overcame anomie and social disorganization by energizing previously apathetic and disaffected poor people to act on their own behalf. At the same time, it promoted the success of new services by capturing the loyalty of the constituents who had participated in their planning and implementation. This was the meaning of community action in the settlement movement; it was implicit in *Delinquency and Opportunity* (whose authors taught in a school of social work); and it wafted through federal planning for the poverty program. William Cannon, formerly of the Bureau of the Budget, recalled that one "version [of maximum feasible participation] was the fact, almost in psychology, that you don't get programs well done unless you have the participation of those people who you were delivering them to."[62]

Community action had a practical appeal as well. It was a cheap strategy for attacking poverty. William Capron recalled that officials within the Bureau of the Budget knew the administration would appropriate little new money for the anti-poverty initiative, and they groped for some way to focus limited funds on a highly visible program. Clearly, a negative income tax, which Budget Bureau officials would have preferred, remained "ahead of its time." Instead, they looked for a "cheap program" that "would show us ways to get...lots of federal dollars." For this reason, "community action struck us as very attractive."[63]

Finally, community action offered a way to attack the rigid, self-protective, unresponsive, interlocking federal and local service delivery network. The heart of the War on Poverty was an institutional critique rather than a program. Community action was the method for "shaking the system" and forcing change on reluctant school administrators, welfare and employment service officials, and even settlement houses and Community Chest leaders, what Yarmolinsky called the "board ladies" and the "bureaucrats." Federal poverty warriors expected to build an alliance between mayors and poor people. They believed (naively, as Yarmolinsky admits) that mayors and their constituents wanted new services and would join forces to formulate a program "which we from Washington would insist that the bureaucrats carry out." When Frances Fox Piven asked why federal planners expected mayors to join a fight against their own bureaucrats, Henry Cohen and Fred Hayes answered, "Ah, that's the key point." They emphasized the fact that the mayors were dealing with school boards that "were almost totally insulated from them," with welfare agencies that were "run by county governments rather than by the city," with a whole range of "categorical programs," all "administered by special districts, state governments, or county governments." Community action, they believed, would enlist the support of mayors because it offered them the prospect of control over services of immediate concern to their constituents.[64] This turned out to be a costly misreading of American politics.

On the ground, in fact, community action immediately threatened mayors. From the start, the tension between empowerment and consensus-building proved an illusion. Frances Fox Piven captured the program's early novelty, radicalism, and threat.

> Some deference to "citizen participation" has always been important in legitimizing governmental action in America. But the Great Society programs went beyond token representation. They gave money to ghetto organizations that then used the money to harass city agencies. Community workers were hired to badger housing inspectors and to pry loose federal welfare payments. Later the new community agencies began to organize the poor to picket the welfare department or to boycott the school system. Local officials were flabbergasted; one level of government and party was financing the harassment of another level of government and party![65]

The urban riots that convulsed American cities—Harlem 1964, Newark 1967, Detroit 1967, and hundreds of others—fueled hostility toward the War on Poverty and, especially, toward its Community Action Program; they appeared "proof of the agency's subversive and incendiary character."[66] Employees of CAP faced accusations "of inciting riots" while "employees of flagship projects such as MFY were being labeled communist provocateurs."[67] Combined with alleged scandals in some CAP-funded programs, the riots gave mayors and right-wing critics, some of whom amplified their attacks with charges of subversion, the opening they needed to provoke congressional hearings on OEO appropriations and to amend the Economic Opportunity Act in ways that drew strict boundaries defining the limits of acceptable participation. "Almost all of these allegations," points out Goldstein, "were either dropped or proved to be false."[68] Nonetheless, anticipating Congressional action, OEO itself introduced strict limits. At the insistence of the US Conference of Mayors, it prohibited CAP employees from participating in voter registration or local political organizing. An Administration-sponsored amendment prohibited the use of federal funds for "illegal picketing or demonstrations...participation by antipoverty employees in any form of direct action in violation of the law, or in partisan political activity." Finally, in 1967, an amendment introduced by Congresswoman Edith Greene undermined the transformative potential of community action by mandating direct municipal control over CAP funds. Funds for community action now would pass through mayoral hands before they reached local groups. In its self-presentation, OEO redefined community action, dropping the radical emphasis on fighting poverty through political empowerment and stressing, instead, building community through cooperation and consensus. In its 1968 report, the National Council on Economic Opportunity wrote:

> Neither an extension of welfare nor a training ground for revolt, community action is rather a box of tools made available to communities to use where they will do the most good—along with a set of instructions on some of the infinite number of ways the tools may be used.... [Community action] provides the organizational basis for developing, planning, funding, and initiating a variety of programs designed to enable communities to develop methods of their own to break the poverty cycle. *It includes services and programs of self-help. But it acts fundamentally to move the poor so that, by their participation in a multitude of activities, they will change their pattern of life and join the mainstream of American achievement.*[69]

The definition speaks volumes. Not only were OEO and CAP emphatically not programs for the redistribution of economic or political power. They re-translated poverty from a problem rooted in unemployment, politics, and institutions to one centered in the life patterns of individual poor people that kept them outside the "mainstream of American achievement." In the end, it was poor people themselves, with the assistance of a government-provided tool box, who would have to work their own way out of poverty.

The toolbox, it should be remembered, was filled with useful instruments for constructing programs that brought improvements to the lives of many thousands of poor people. In its 1968 annual report, CAP gives examples of its achievements under the five purposes laid out for it in the 1967 amendments.

1. To strengthen community capabilities for planning and coordinating federal, state, and other assistance;
2. To improve the organization of a range of services;
3. To stimulate use of new types of services and innovative approaches in attacking poverty;
4. To develop and implement programs and projects designed to serve the poor with the maximum feasible participation of the members of the groups served; and
5. To broaden the base of poverty-related activities to assure greater participation of the members of the groups served by business, labor, and professional groups in the communities.

As its example of purpose number four—enhancing maximum feasible participation—the report pointed to neighborhood councils in Little Rock, Arkansas, whose members worked with staff and "other professionals in the community" to improve or implement an array of services. The councils also "won concessions from public officials," such as improved mail services and in one neighborhood, "an underpass to eliminate the need for children to crawl beneath and over railroad box cars going to and from school everyday." As for the fifth purpose—including representatives from local businesses, labor, and the professions—the report highlighted the work of Total Action Against Poverty, the Community Action Agency in Roanoke Valley, Virginia. The agency had partnered with the Municipal Court and HELP, a local organization, to open "a halfway house and rehabilitation program for alcoholics" and also "formed a business advisory council of the area's leading businessmen to provide one-to-one counseling assistance to job seekers who have unstable job histories" and help them find and hold jobs.[70] A long way from the initial vision of community action as shaking the system and empowering the poor, these achievements cumulatively were far from trivial in the day-to-day lives of the people served.

Nonetheless, "it would be a mistake to underestimate the significance of the OEO's mandate of maximum feasible participation" that, for all its problems, unleashed democratic energies that refused to remain constrained by official boundaries.[71] The principal players were women, a fact troubling to OEO staff who believed "that the primary purpose of poverty programs was to transform poor men into wage-earning heads of household."[72] Instead, what Orleck and Hazirjian label "mother-ist politics" underlay the implementation of community action at the grass roots. Many poor mothers were "drawn to activism by the belief that good mothers have a right and an obligation to demand that government agencies provide improved services for their children." The focus of many War on Poverty programs reinforced this idea. For poor women who headed their own households, job training programs directed at male wage earners "were of no use," and "they wanted government programs geared toward women." Nationally, motherist politics coalesced in the National Welfare Rights Organization (NWRO). The militant tactics of its local branches wrested many important victories from municipal governments, assuring that poor women received the public benefits to which they were entitled.[73]

Community Action Programs (CAPs) not only offered poor mothers services and resources for their children; they were a source of jobs. Women, point out Orleck and Hazirjian, "found alternative routes to paid work through the War on Poverty." Legal Services staff taught them that many new programs included money with which to hire poor people. "Growing increasingly sophisticated in their activism and their understanding of government programs, they pushed for federally funded jobs as Head Start teachers, school lunch aides, health outreach workers, community organizers, and screeners at local clinics." As a result, CAP facilitated women's upward mobility. "Career development...for non-professional staff members," asserted OEO's 1968 Annual Report, *As the Seed is Sown*, "is an important ingredient of community action training. CAP places a high priority on the hiring and training of residents of the target area.... [and] encourages the up-grading of non-professionals to positions of greater responsibility...Opportunities for continuing education on the part of staff members is [sic] also encouraged. The aim is to assist non-professionals in career development so that they can aspire to and achieve permanent positions involving greater economic and vocational rewards."[74]

Poor women's successful experience as workers in CAP-funded programs led them to the belief that mothers should control programs that affected their children. The motherist politics that resulted created "fresh and unlikely coalitions" between, for example, working-class black and white mothers in Durham, North Carolina; Puerto Rican and African American mothers in the Bronx; and black and Chicana women Los Angeles.[75] Poor women without high school degrees navigated byzantine city, state, and federal agencies and skillfully "played officials from different branches and levels of government against one another." They lobbied in city halls, state capitals, and the federal government. When state governments proved recalcitrant, either refusing to accept or implement new War on Poverty programs "such as food stamps, free breakfast and lunch programs, WIC, and Early Periodic Screening and Diagnostic Testing," poor mothers took their protests from the streets to the federal courts—where they won.[76]

> Across the country, untold numbers of poor mothers became politicized during the 1960s and 1970s in pursuit of better food, schools, and health care for their children. Unwilling to remain passive clients of social welfare and health professionals, they came to see themselves as the true experts on poverty and to believe that they could run poverty and community health and education programs more effectively than the supposed experts. This was the promise of maximum feasible participation fulfilled.[77]

However, this was not the revolution. Male organizers often "derided" motherist politics as "counterrevolutionary—piecemeal, temporary, and apolitical," arguing that "women's focus on service delivery undermined community action." To them, "the only permanent way out of poverty was for the poor to demand power, to overhaul the entire American system, to create revolution." Many of the poor women energized by the War on Poverty, by contrast, "were less interested in overturning the system than in becoming voices for change within it."[78] Strong arguments can be made in defense of both positions. In the end, it was motherist, not revolutionary, politics whose accomplishments in winning services, opening up careers, and politicizing poor women have proved most enduring.

Community action also raised profound questions about the role of popular participation in politics. What, in fact, did "action" mean? Was it membership in organizations that planned programs and received and distributed funds? Or was it mobilization—militant action organized around demands? How could poor people best redress the imbalance of power that helped perpetuate their poverty? In their controversial and influential *Poor People's Movements: Why They Succeed, How They Fail*, Frances Fox Piven and Richard A. Cloward offered an answer that stressed mobilization. Protests, they argued, remain unusual events. They do not erupt "during ordinary periods," but when "large-scale changes undermine political stability....It is this context that makes political leaders somewhat vulnerable to protests by the poor." During these moments of vulnerability, as in the 1930s when the Roosevelt administration needed the votes of the urban working class or the 1960s when the Democratic Party depended on the vote of African Americans in cities, insurgencies by the poor exacted concessions. Power, emphasized Piven and Cloward, derives from insurgency, not leadership or organization.

> Elites respond to the institutional disruption that protest causes as well as to other powerful institutional imperatives. Elite responses are not significantly shaped by the demands of leaders and organizers. Nor are elite responses significantly shaped by formally structured organizations of the poor. Whatever influence lower-class groups occasionally exert in American politics does not result from organization but from mass protest and the disruptive consequences of protest.[79]

When protest ebbs, politicians withdraw some concessions. "Since the poor no longer pose the threat of disruption, they no longer exert leverage on political leaders; there is no need for conciliation." But some important concessions and institutional changes remain, such as the right to join unions or the extension of the franchise to southern blacks. Because the retreat from protests' initial passion is inevitable, all "organizers and leaders" can do is to seize the moment. "They can only try to win whatever can be won while it can be won." After protest dies out, organizers find themselves incorporated into "stable institutional roles"; they become part of the established order, not sources through which poor people can continue to leverage power on their own behalf.[80]

Community organizers also believed that poor people could muster power on their own behalf through mobilization and protest, but, unlike

Piven and Cloward, they emphasized the importance of building organizations and developing leaders. The great founding figure of community organizing was Saul Alinsky, who began his work in Chicago's Back of the Yards neighborhood in the 1930s. Alinsky "recruited local leaders from the churches, block clubs, sports leagues, and unions that formed the Back of the Yards Neighborhood Council, the first of what Alinsky would call the People's Organization. Alinsky guided them to identify common interests that brought together into a large organization previously hostile ethnic groups of Serbs and Croatians, Czechs and Slovaks, Poles and Lithuanians. The council pressured, demanded, and negotiated with government officials and businesses on bread-and-butter issues such as better garbage collection, improved schools, fresh milk for children, and more jobs."[81] Like Piven and Cloward, the organizing tradition Alinsky inspired stresses concrete, local grievances, not abstract causes. Only the role of the organizer is central. Organizers bring together local people, help them define their grievances, and plan militant strategies, often called "actions" to pressure authorities. The Industrial Areas Foundation, founded by Alinsky in 1940 to train organizers, turned organizing into a profession whose members have mobilized poor people to win local, and even not so local, victories. When organizers threaten entrenched interests, however, they provoke reaction that can be vicious and devastating. This is what the history of one of the most effective community organizing networks, ACORN, illustrates. Subject for years to vicious attacks by right-wing media, ACORN, which won important national and state, as well as local, victories, finally was brought to its knees by a carefully orchestrated scam designed to discredit its integrity.[82]

Its opponents killed ACORN as a national organization, but they did not destroy community organizing. Indeed, of the several varieties of community action, the community organizing movement has emerged as the one with the most transformative potential. The remarkable PICO provides the best example. It claims many achievements in health-care access and reform, immigration policy, housing, school improvement, rural development, and other areas. Like ACORN, PICO organizes at neighborhood, state, and national levels. It even has established a policy office in Washington, DC. Founded in 1972 by Father John Baumann, a Jesuit priest, PICO originated as a regional training institute to assist neighborhood community organizing in California. Unlike ACORN, PICO works through a congregational-community model that it pioneered. Its networks embrace congregations of all denominations and faiths and now count 44 affiliated federations as well as 8 statewide networks working in 150 towns and cities and 17 states. More than one million families belong to the one thousand congregations in its networks. In 2004 the organization changed its name from Pacific Institute for Community Organizing to PICO National Network so as to underscore its national scope. It describes its strategy this way:

> PICO begins with the concrete problems facing working families, helps them to conduct a careful research process on these issues, and creates policy innovations from the ground up. These solutions come out of specific places and problems, but offer models for communities and states across the U.S. They are solutions that unify rather than divide.[83]

The Living Wage Movement underscores the transformative potential of community organizing. The idea of a living wage—"a wage," according to legal scholar William P. Quigley, "that enables a worker to earn enough to lift the worker and his or her family out of poverty"— has found advocates for well over a century. In his Address to Congress in 1937, President Franklin Delano Roosevelt asserted, "No business which depends for its existence on paying less than living wages to its workers has any right to continue in this country. By living wages I mean more than a bare subsistence level—I mean the wages of decent living." At first intertwined with the call for a minimum wage, promotion of a living wage emerged on its own as a vibrant locally based movement in the 1990s, winning its first major victory in Baltimore in 1994. An alliance known as BUILD led by a coalition of churches organized by the Industrial Areas Foundations and the American Federation of State, County, and Municipal Employees (AFSCME) convinced the city government to enact a local law requiring city contractors to pay wages high enough to lift a family of four over the poverty level. The Baltimore victory inspired similar campaigns around the country in which ACORN, as well as labor unions and religious congregations, played a lead role. ACORN developed a Living Wage Resource

Center to monitor the movement's progress and make resources available online. Other victories came quickly—within a decade 122 cities had passed living wage ordinances and campaigns were in progress in another 75.[84]

Community organizing, along with other community-based tactics, poses profound questions about strategies for social change in general, and for anti-poverty efforts in particular. How much can be accomplished at the local level? Can community-based tactics do anything at all to reduce or prevent poverty, which, after all, is a problem with deep roots in political economy and is national (indeed, global) in scope? What resources can be mobilized at the local level to create jobs and increase incomes? In political scientist Ira Katznelson's acidic account of community action on the ground in a section of New York City during the War on Poverty, community action emerges as a toothless strategy for change, at once coopted into the "city trenches" that had channeled local politics since the nineteenth century and manipulated by the city administration to cool out potential insurgencies.[85] Local mobilization, in fact, often has worked against the interests of poor people and African Americans, as in successful opposition to halfway houses and similar institutions and, especially, in resistance to racial integration. Arnold Hirsch, for one, described the violence unleashed by local neighborhood groups against African Americans trying to move into white working-class neighborhoods of Chicago, and Thomas Sugrue has charted the tactics of neighborhood associations dedicated to preventing integration in Detroit.[86] Some accounts of locality based strategies to deal with poverty-related issues, especially the role of community development corporations in building affordable housing (discussed in Chapter 5), reveal a more mixed record. As the case studies in the book edited by Orleck and Hazirjian show, the actual on-the-ground history of community-based movements contains many stories of success, while the major community-organizing networks—IAF, ACORN, PECO—can count victories that made substantial differences in the lives of poor people. The living wage campaign conducted mainly at the local level has won gains that translate directly into better incomes.[87] The same can be said for local trade union victories. Successful movements for social change in America, moreover, have started outside legislatures and built from the ground up. Abolition, temperance, women's rights, civil rights, anti-war, gay rights: all these movements grew from the grassroots, building pressure, until they found their way into state and national legislation. Finding the sweet spot where local and national work together: this is the great conceptual and strategic challenge for activists against poverty. Another way to think about the question is this: poverty is, in part, a problem of power. It persists at such high levels in the United States because poor people lack the power to take effective action against it. Community organizing provides a necessary, although not sufficient, means for mobilizing the power to press for change, first, usually, at the local level, but, aggregated, at the national level as well. Without mobilization at the grass roots, the prospects for effective action against poverty—and other huge and pressing public issues—remain dim.

Expanding Social Welfare

Neither community action nor the War on Poverty's new service programs increased the amount of money spent on redistributive social welfare programs. Nonetheless, between the late 1960s and early 1970s, the federal government expanded public social spending in five major ways. First, the Public Welfare Amendments of 1962 initiated the massive increase in government-funded social services, which not only made new and existing services much more widely available but also created a vast number of new professional and semiprofessional jobs and altered the character of the voluntary sector by making it dependent on government for funding. In real dollars, between 1960 and 1995, public spending on social services increased 500 percent. By 2009, together federal, state, and local governments spent about "$150 billion annually on means-tested food, housing, education, and social service assistance for tens of millions of working poor Americans." Programs of cash assistance, by contrast, received only about $11 billion to help 4.5 million people in need.[88]

Second, the number of persons receiving Aid to Families with Dependent Children (AFDC) exploded, partly as a result of the work of welfare activists to move eligible women onto the program rolls. Third, food stamps became more widely available and free to the poor, signaling a de facto acceptance of the right to food as an entitlement of citizenship. Fourth, through Supplemental Security Income (SSI), the aged, blind, and disabled received a guaranteed minimum income, a residual outcome of the failed campaign for a national minimum income, discussed below. Fifth, Medicaid and Medicare created a system of national health insurance for welfare recipients and the elderly, a truly major injection of a new principle into the nation's welfare state but one that remained—with the exception of medical care for children—stuck, unable to reach true universality until the Affordable Health Care Act brought it closer in 2012. Still, Congress defeated the most dramatic proposal for expanding the basis of social citizenship: Richard Nixon's guaranteed minimum income for families. In many ways, Nixon's abortive Family Assistance Plan remains the most intriguing part of the story because it was the first major attempt to overhaul the social welfare structure erected in the 1930s. As such, it rested on ideas about anti-poverty strategy that differed sharply from the service-based strategy of the War on Poverty. The Family Assistance Plan, like other varieties of guaranteed assistance plans proposed in the 1960s and 1970s, according to their major historian, Brian Steensland, "called into question deeply held assumptions about the causes of poverty, the adequacy of the labor market, and the goals of welfare reform that are rarely debated in American society but that nonetheless guide policymaking." Although the Family Assistance Plan was dressed as conservatively as possible, it was, Steensland contends, "still revolutionary. It provided benefits to two-parent families. It guaranteed all families a minimum income. And, most important, it provided benefits to the unemployed and employed poor within the same program, thereby erasing the existing distinctions between different categories of poor people."[89]

On August 8, 1969, President Richard Nixon proposed a Family Assistance Plan that would guarantee all families with dependent children a minimum yearly income ($1,600 for a family of four). He also proposed that states pay a prescribed federal minimum to disabled, blind, and elderly people eligible for public assistance. The House Ways and Means Committee held the first hearings on the bill between October 15 and November 13. At the same time, it examined a bill that would increase social benefits and link them automatically to inflation. In March the Ways and Means Committee approved the bill, and the

House passed it on April 16 by a vote of 243 to 155. The Senate proved more resistant. Throughout the next two years, the Senate sent administration proposals back for redrafting and considered alternatives. It did, however, agree to raise Social Security benefits and to broaden the food stamp program. At last, on October 17, 1972, the Senate passed a welfare reform bill stripped of the Family Assistance Plan. Instead, it created Supplemental Security Income (SSI), which folded aid for the blind, disabled, and elderly not eligible for Social Security into one program with a federally mandated income floor, and workfare (an unsuccessful attempt to link welfare to work discussed in Chapter 4).

Nixon's plan reflected proposals for a negative income tax or national minimum income advocated by many economists of that period. Its earliest major proponent was conservative economist Milton Friedman. It also had appealed to economists in the Kennedy and Johnson administrations, who considered increasing the income of poor people the most straightforward way to reduce poverty.[90] Johnson himself remained more cautious, and he fended off the advocates of an income-based approach to anti-poverty strategy by creating a national commission on income maintenance, otherwise known as the Heineman Commission.[91] Its report, *Poverty Amid Plenty: The American Paradox*, published in November 1969, offered an informed and eloquent plea for a national minimum income. Because commission members included the chairman of the board of IBM, the president of Northwest Industries, the president of Equitable Life Assurance Society, the chairman of the Westinghouse Electric Corporate, and the chairman of the Republic National Bank of Dallas, as well as professional economists, politicians, and union officials, its advocacy of a strategy anathema to many conservatives (not to mention the president who appointed it) is startling. However, for businessmen able to overcome their resistance to any expansion of government social benefits, the national minimum income meshed with important conservative goals.

The commission's main recommendation was "*the development of a universal income supplement program to be administered by the Federal Government, making payments to all members of the population with income needs* [italics in original]." Most people were poor because they "lack money, and most of them cannot increase their incomes"; only the government had the resources to provide "*some minimum to all in need* [italics in original]." The commission stressed that poverty did not result from personal failings and offered a blistering criticism of existing welfare programs, which failed to provide adequate support or incentives and demeaned recipients. Underlying their inadequacy were an ineffective strategy and outmoded assumptions. The strategy depended on services that could not "substitute for adequate incomes," "pay rent," or "buy food for a poor family." The obsolete assumption, which considered employment and receipt of welfare "mutually exclusive," had become "untenable in a world where many employable persons have potential earnings below assistance payment standards."[92]

By proposing to supplement wages, the commission staked out a new position in official American discourse on poverty and welfare. Nonetheless, despite its radical surface, it rested on premises compatible with business interests. First, it simply accepted the spread of low-wage labor as inevitable and did not recommend improving working conditions or wages. Second, it provided an "alternative to the minimum wage," as University of Minnesota economist George Stigler had pointed out nearly twenty-five years before Nixon's proposal. Thus, a negative income tax would help business by socializing the cost of labor and give economists worried about the effect of the minimum wage on the market a way to support the needy without risking inflation—this is precisely the function of the Earned Income Tax Credit (EITC), a watered-down version of a national income plan established in 1975 and expanded greatly with bipartisan support during the administration of President Bill Clinton in the 1990s.[93] (In fairness, the EITC has proved effective at moving huge numbers of families over the poverty line—although only families close to the poverty line to begin with and those having some income from work. In 2010 the EITC lifted 6.3 million people, of whom 3.3 million were children, out of poverty. Without it, child poverty would have been 25 percent higher.)

Third, in contrast to in-kind programs (ones that provided goods such as food and housing), which the commission wanted abolished, income supplements worked on market principles. The market system, argued the report, "is more effective at distributing goods and services than direct governmental distribution." Income supplements permitted "greater consumer choice" and "greater flexibility of family resources." In its emphasis on the market, the commission prefigured the attempt

to redesign the welfare state, and American social policy more generally, with a market template—a move whose hegemony, starting in
the 1980s, stretched across political party lines. Fourth, income supplements avoided the problems inherent in expanding social insurance,
which performed "an antipoverty function far less efficiently than
programs which pay benefits on the basis of need." Social insurance,
argued the commission, paid disproportionate benefits to the nonpoor
and lacked incentives. By contrast, an intelligently designed income
maintenance program would provide "financial incentives to work, and
limit incentives for family breakup." It also would reduce the administrative costs associated with direct subsidy by 15 to 30 percent.[94]

Nixon supported a family assistance plan for complex reasons.
Influenced especially by HEW Secretary Robert Finch and Daniel
Patrick Moynihan, who had joined his administration, Nixon reached
his decision by stages. He disliked both social workers and the current
welfare system, and a bold welfare reform plan offered concrete political advantages. "Why not utterly repudiate the old Democratic-devised
welfare system as socially destructive and unfair? Why not insist that a
reformed system reward those who work more than those who could
work but don't?" Nixon, assert Vincent and Lee Burke in their history of the Family Assistance Plan, "liked to think of himself as a
modern-day Disraeli, a Tory bringing social progress," and his welfare reform "offered a dazzling opportunity to win a place in history."
Nixon would gain regardless of how Congress acted: "If Congress
approved his plan, Nixon would be credited with reforming a despised
institution; if Congress balked, Nixon would get a political issue."[95]

The commission's proposals managed to anger not only many conservatives, but potential allies on the Left as well. Conservatives objected
to Nixon's plan because it would expand the number of families eligible
for benefits and because it violated their beliefs about the limited role
of government and the harmful effects of welfare. On the Left, opinion divided between those who, like Frances Fox Piven and Richard
Cloward, supported the bill as an important precedent and those, like
the National Welfare Rights Organization, who believed its benefits to
be woefully inadequate and its workfare provisions punitive.[96]

No such coalition formed to defeat the other expansions of public social provision in the same years. Because everyone grows old,

Social Security cuts across class lines and draws on the massive political power of the elderly. As for food stamps, hunger historically has moved Americans more than any form of deprivation. In 1968, after a powerful television documentary on hunger, Senator George McGovern, chair of a new Senate Committee on Nutrition and Human Needs, began public hearings on the issue. By proposing the expansion of the food stamp program, Nixon preempted what otherwise surely would have become a major political issue for the Democrats.

Through an adroit series of compromises, which assured physicians could profit handsomely, in 1965 the Johnson administration overcame enough of the historic opposition of the organized American medical profession to national health insurance to pass Medicare, national health in insurance for the elderly, and Medicaid, a program of health care for the indigent.[97] Medicare and Medicaid cemented the division of health care into the social insurance and public assistance tracks of the welfare state. America was left with an uncoordinated system of health care: private insurance for the fortunate employed, social insurance for the elderly, public charity for the indigent, and nothing at all for tens of millions others.

Unlike the other expansions of public social provision, the explosion of the welfare rolls required only modest legislative changes. In 1960 745,000 families received AFDC at a cost of less than $1 billion; by 1972 the number of families had become 3 million and the cost had multiplied to $6 billion. The reasons were several. The migration of southern blacks to northern cities increased the number of poor people dependent on cash incomes and reduced the number of subsistence farmers. Starting in 1961, Congress permitted states to extend aid to families headed by unemployed male parents. (As of 1988, only twenty-eight states had taken advantage of this opportunity, which was a minor factor in the increase.) Some states loosened the standards for eligibility. More important, mobilized by the welfare rights movement, the proportion of poor families applying for welfare increased dramatically, as did the proportion of applicants accepted, which skyrocketed from about 33 percent in the early 1960s to 90 percent in 1971. The latter event reflected the efforts of the nascent welfare rights movement to recast welfare as an entitlement, reduce its stigma, and mobilize poor people to claim assistance as a right. Indeed, welfare rights became a social movement acted out in demonstrations that pressured reluctant welfare officials and in courtrooms where lawyers successfully challenged state laws restricting eligibility.[98]

Welfare rights was a new idea in American social policy. "Prior to the 1960s," writes Rand Rosenblatt in his review of its legislative history, "recipients of benefits under programs such as AFDC were not seen as having 'rights' to benefits or even to a fair process for deciding individual cases." The achievement of welfare rights required both the mobilization of poor people and new legal doctrines. Funded by the poverty program, the Legal Services Corporation for the first time in American history provided poor people with lawyers to act on their behalf. With the example of civil rights victories in the courts, a new generation of welfare and poverty lawyers successfully challenged state laws in the Supreme Court.[99]

Welfare rights advocates won legal victories in three key areas: length-of-residence requirements, invasion of privacy practices, and unregulated state discretion over eligibility conditions and the amount of grants. Three key Supreme Court decisions dented these historic features of welfare law. *King v. Smith* (1968) struck down an Alabama rule that effectively denied public assistance to any children and their mother if the mother had sexual relationships. (The rule had defined any man with whom a recipient mother had sexual relations as the "substitute father" of her children, regardless of his relation to them.) *Shapiro v. Thompson* (1969) declared that a state residency requirement—a one-year waiting period before new state residents could receive public assistances—"penalized the fundamental constitutional right to interstate travel and thereby denied equal protection of the law." *Goldberg v. Kelly* (1970) required welfare agencies to offer clients a hearing that met "minimal due process standards" before stopping benefits.

These cases extended benefits to hundreds of thousands of women and children. According to Rosenblatt, in *King v. Smith*, the Supreme Court had estimated that the substitute father rule in Alabama alone had excluded about 20,000 people, including 16,000 children. The Court's reasoning in the *King* decision prompted many lower court rulings that struck down other exclusionary state rules. Nonetheless, by the early 1970s, a backlash against welfare rights surfaced among voters and within all levels of government as the Court began to change direction. In *Dandrige v. Williams* (1970), the Court refused to force states to match welfare grants to living needs. In *Wyman v. Tames* (1971), the Court agreed that states could terminate public assistance benefits if a client denied a caseworker access to her home, and in 1973, in *New York State Department of Social Services v. Dublino*, the Court upheld state work requirements more restrictive than those in federal law.[100] Welfare backlash—played out as an attack on AFDC—continued to mount, culminating in 1996 in its abolition and replacement with Temporary Assistance for Needy Families (TANF), a development discussed in Chapter 4.

Legal philosophers buttressed the welfare rights movement by redefining the concepts of property, rights, and entitlements. By far the most important and influential of these redefinitions was law professor Charles Reich's article, "The New Property," which appeared in the *Yale Law Journal* in April 1964. Property, stressed Reich, is not a natural right but a deliberate construction of society. Because it is created by law, property is not limited to land, possessions, or other forms of material wealth. Property, rather, "represents a relationship between wealth and its 'owner'" sanctioned by law. Therefore, a person with property "has certain legal rights with respect to an item of wealth." In the modern state, governments have created myriad new forms of wealth: income and benefits, job, occupational licenses, franchises, contracts, subsidies, use of public resources, and services. Together, these compose what Reich called new forms of "government largesse." "The valuables dispensed by government take many forms, but all share one characteristic. They are steadily taking the place of traditional forms of wealth—forms which are held as private property." Changes in the forms of private wealth enhanced the significance of government largesse, because "today more and more of our wealth takes the form of rights or status rather than of intangible goods." Thus, a profession or a job is frequently far more valuable than a house or bank account. As for the jobless, "their status as governmentally assisted or insured persons may be the main source of assistance."[101]

For Reich, the new forms of government largesse had significant costs: They eroded conventional boundaries between public and private, enhanced the power of the state, and threatened individual liberty.

Only new procedural safeguards, he argued, could both protect individual liberty and guard individuals' access to this "largesse." "Eventually," he wrote, "those forms of largesse which are closely linked to status must be deemed to be held as of right." And he saw the concept of right most urgently needed with respect to benefits like unemployment compensation, public assistance, and old age insurance. These forms of largesse, he emphasized, rest on a recognition that "misfortune and deprivation are often caused by forces far beyond the control of the individual." Their goal is "to preserve the self-sufficiency of the individual, to rehabilitate him where necessary, and to allow him to be a valuable member of a family and a community; in theory they represent part of the individual's rightful share in the commonwealth."[102]

The conservative judicial retreat of the 1970s circumscribed the influence of Reich's elegant redefinition of property, although his article set off a debate among scholars. William Simon, writing from a political position to the left of Reich, pointed out that "The New Property" offered no criteria for distribution and reified individual rights and state power as "distinct and opposed entities." Reich's portrayal of welfare benefits as matters of right obscured their role in the transfer of wealth "from one group of right-holders to another." Rights for Simon reflect power; they do not guard against it. For this reason, he found Reich's argument unintentionally conservative. When all wealth is translated into rights, its forced redistribution by government becomes impossible. This was one paradox; the other was the contradiction between Reich's intended legitimation of the welfare state and his portrait of the state as a menace. Simon's final verdict on Reich's new property was harsh: "[Its] view of welfare rights is incoherent as jurisprudence and exhausted as politics. It is irrelevant to what ought to be the two principal concerns of liberal welfare jurisprudence." These were theories and programs based on need as a distinctive principle and an approach to public administration that recognized "the values of a responsible state as well as the dangers of an irresponsible one."

Moral as well as legal philosophers also reconsidered distributive justice in the 1960s. Most important among them was John Rawls of Harvard. First in a series of articles, then in his immensely influential *A Theory of Justice*, Rawls challenged the utilitarian basis of liberalism and, by implication, its translation into the opportunity-based strategy of the War on Poverty and Great Society. Rawls argued for a concept of justice based neither on utilitarianism, which stressed efficiency, nor on its leading philosophic criticism, intuitionism. Instead, starting with social contract theory, he returned to first principles: "The principles of justice," he wrote, "are the object of the original agreement," or social contract. "They are the principles that free and rational persons concerned to further their own interests would accept in an initial position of equality as defining the fundamental terms of their association." These principles regulated "all further agreements," specifying permissible forms of "social cooperation" and "government." Rawls called this way of regarding the principles of justice "justice as fairness."[103]

Justice as fairness depended on liberty and social justice. "First: each person is to have an equal right to the most extensive basic liberty compatible with a similar liberty for others. Second: social and economic inequalities are to be arranged so that they are both (a) reasonably expected to be to everyone's advantage, and (b) attached to positions and offices open to all." Rawls's emphasis on social justice led to the criterion he then applied to social policies and institutions: They are to be judged by the degree to which they improved the circumstances of "the least advantaged members of society."[104]

This criterion led Rawls to criticize a concept he labeled "liberal equality," which, although he did not draw the connection, underpinned the War on Poverty and Great Society. For Rawls, liberal equality intuitively appeared "defective" because its stress on removing barriers to opportunity still permitted "the distribution of wealth and income to be determined by the natural distribution of abilities and talents," leaving distributive shares to be "decided by the outcome of the natural lottery," an outcome "arbitrary from a moral perspective." Because of the practical impossibility of securing "equal chances of achievement and culture for the similarly endowed," he continued, "we may want to adopt a principle which recognizes this fact and also mitigates the arbitrary effects of the natural lottery."

His "difference principle," that is, the primary claims of the least advantaged, drew Rawls to an alternative conception of equal opportunity: "To treat all persons equally, to provide genuine equality of opportunity, society must give more attention to those with fewer native assets and to those born into the less favorable social positions." The difference principle rested on values at variance with those at the core of liberal equality. "It transforms the aims of the basic structure so that the total scheme of institutions no longer emphasizes social efficiency and technocratic values." The difference principle was, instead, "an agreement to regard the distribution of natural talents as a common asset and to share in the benefits of this distribution whatever it turns out to be."[105]

A "properly organized democratic state," according to Rawls, differed little from other social democratic blueprints for a welfare state. Besides guarantees of liberty, freedom of thought, equal citizenship, and a just, open political process, the government should ensure "fair (as opposed to formal) equality of opportunity," and guarantee "a social minimum either by family allowances and special payments for sickness and employment, or more systematically by such devices as a graded income supplement (a so-called negative income tax)." Rawls offered liberals what they badly needed: a fresh, cogent legitimation of the welfare state. But it came too late, and it veered too sharply from the utilitarianism that now underlay social policy. Within a year after *A Theory of Justice* appeared, the initiative had passed to conservatives, and the War on Poverty, for all practical purposes, was over.[106] The formal abolition of the Office of Economic Opportunity happened in 1975. The newly created Community Services Administration—housed in the Department of Health and Human Services—picked up its oversight of community action agencies—until it, too, was ended by President Ronald Reagan in 1981. The Department of Health and Human Service's Office of Community Affairs now supervised community services block grants, the important but defanged remnant of the Community Action Program.[107]

The value of AFDC benefits in real dollars is a reasonable, if rough, index of national generosity. It peaked in 1972 and then declined precipitously. Until AFDC's abolition in 1996, welfare rights activists expended more energy protecting earlier gains than on extending them, and they lost their battle. What had been won in the War on Poverty and by the Great Society? And of these victories, which ones proved lasting? How should we think about the War on Poverty and Great Society as a moment in intellectual history?

Unheralded Results

The War on Poverty, Great Society, and extension of public social benefits reinforced the historic distinction among the three tracks of the public branch of the American welfare state: social insurance, public assistance, and taxation.[108] In the social insurance track, Social Security benefits increased and were indexed. In the public assistance track, SSI folded programs into new forms of means tested relief. Congress added a broadened and liberalized food stamp program to public assistance, whose benefits were lower than Social Security's. Health insurance also divided into two programs, one, Medicare, part of the social insurance apparatus was offered universally to all Americans age sixty-five and over, the other, Medicaid, which included payments for nursing home care for individuals with extremely low incomes and no assets, was part of the public assistance track. The benefits they provided and the reimbursement they paid providers differed sharply. At the same time, the preference for delivering benefits through the tax code increased, most notably through the Earned Income Tax Credit, which hardened the line between the employed and nonemployed poor, solidifying the place of the latter as the preeminent undeserving poor. Statistics of government expenditure tell the story. Social insurance received by far the greatest share of public funds and provided the highest benefits. In 1970 Social Security payments to the elderly, $3.3 billion, already exceeded AFDC payments by about ten times. In 2012 Social Security payments, which were indexed to inflation, had mushroomed to $116 billion. TANF's costs, which were not indexed, amounted to about $18 billion while spending on the EITC grew from $5 billion in 1975 to $60 billion in 2010.[109]

Nonetheless, despite their limitations, Medicare and Medicaid resulted in vast increases in the availability of medical care for the elderly and indigent. By May 31, 1966, enrollment in the optional Part B of Medicare had become nearly universal, and the use of medical care by the elderly soared: between 1964 and 1973, hospital discharges of the elderly rose three-and-one-half times. At the same time, the share of Americans visiting a physician rose, and the proportion never examined by a doctor plummeted from one-fifth to 8 percent as poor people started to visit doctors at the same rate as everyone else. Prenatal visits by poor women to doctors also increased dramatically between 1965 and 1972, while, among blacks, infant mortality dropped by half and the gap in life expectancy between blacks and whites contracted from about eight to five years.[110]

The achievements of a number of service-based programs also deserve recognition. Operation Head Start helped significant numbers of poor children prepare for school; Upward Bound prepared large numbers of adolescents for college; and financial assistance permitted thousands of young people from families with low or modest incomes to take advantage of higher education while the funds provided by the Elementary and Secondary Education Act channeled unprecedented dollars to local schools, allowing them to hire staff and develop programs for students from impoverished families. As Legal Services opened access to litigation by poor people for the first time, lawyers used class action suits to expand the rights of the poor in several key areas: medical aid, landlord-tenant relations, state housing laws, consumer credit, and welfare administration. However, despite the success of some Job Corps centers, manpower training and employment programs remained disappointing, although the jobs provided by the Comprehensive Employment and Training Act (CETA) were an important form of work relief to many individuals and a source of staff to many public and private service sector programs.[111]

Community action, the most controversial part of the War on Poverty, for all its problems, nourished a growing citizen's movement, reshaped local politics, and launched a new generation of minority leaders, many of them women, into public life.[112]

The intersection of the Community Action Program with the Civil Rights Movement and affirmative action opened up vast numbers of jobs to African Americans. Indeed, public and quasi-public sector jobs (jobs located in the private sector but funded in whole or part by public money) became the distinctive occupational niche of African Americans. The percentage of working African American women in them escalated from 13 percent in 1950 to 43 percent in 2000. These jobs formed the backbone of a fragile but growing African American middle class. The public and service sector job cuts that resulted from the Great Recession that began in 2008 dealt this new African American middle class a savage blow.[113]

Legacies for the Intellectual History of Public Policy and Social Science

The War on Poverty and Great Society could have left a profound intellectual legacy. On one side was the new stream of legal and philosophic scholarship represented by Reich, Simon, Rawls, and others, which formulated new approaches to the legitimacy of the welfare state and distributive justice. On the other was a debate about strategies of social change and welfare reform led by Frances Fox Piven and Richard Cloward primarily in two influential books, *Regulating the Poor* and *Poor People's Movements*, which recast the history of public welfare and challenged liberal approaches to reform through legislation, organization, and reliance on disinterested elites.[114] In fact, the intellectual legacy left by the War on Poverty and Great Society turned out to be a lot less than its promise. As American politics moved rightward after the mid-1970s, entitlements came under increasingly fierce attack. The 1996 "welfare reform" legislation buried the idea of a right to welfare. Aligning social welfare policy more closely with the market—not with distributive justice—became the lodestone of social policy, as Chapter 4 explains. The Heineman Commission's preference for throwing social welfare to the market, not Charles Reich's or John Rawls's calls for active government, won the intellectual day and, increasingly, the policy day as well.

A new bureaucratic definition of poverty constituted another intellectual legacy of the War on Poverty and Great Society. The War on Poverty began without an official definition of poverty—the United States only started collecting income statistics in 1940. The Office of Economic Opportunity, which needed a defensible standard as a yardstick for diagnosing poverty and measuring progress against it, drew on the work of economist Mollie Orshansky in the Social Security Administration's Office of Research and Statistics. The Orshansky index, as it was called, assumed that poor families spent about one-third of their income on food, so it pegged the poverty line at three times the cost of the Department of Agriculture's low-cost budget for food, adjusted for family composition and rural-urban differences. Reliance on the Department of Agriculture's food budget found precedents in both public and private sectors. "Food plans prepared by the Department of Agriculture," observed Orshansky, "have for more than

30 years served as a guide for estimating costs of food needed by families of different compositions." Indeed, for many years, welfare agencies had used the low-cost plan to keep down the cost of food allotments to needy families.[115]

Orshansky never harbored illusions about the adequacy of the low-cost food budget. It assumed, she pointed out, "that the housewife will be a careful shopper, a skillful cook, and a good manager who will prepare all the family's meals at home." It included no "additional allowance for snacks or the higher cost of meals away from home or meals served to guests." It established, at best, a "crude criterion of income adequacy." In fact, Orshansky developed the index as a research tool, not an instrument of policy or a criterion for determining eligibility for anti-poverty programs. She wanted to determine the demography of the poverty population and to identify groups at risk. The index, she wrote, "is not designed to be applied directly to an individual family with a specific problem. Nor even as a screening device can it be expected to stand unchallenged as an exact count of the poor in absolute numbers. But it can delineate broadly the relative incidence of poverty among discrete population groups and in this way outline targets for action." The poverty line, she said, identifies "groups most vulnerable to risk of poverty" even though it cannot measure poverty precisely. "The best that can be said of the measure," she wrote, "is that at a time when it seemed useful, it was there."[116]

Contrary to Orshansky's intentions, the Office of Economic Opportunity adopted her index as its standard, only it utilized estimates based on the Department of Agriculture's economy food plan, which was about 25 percent lower than the low-cost plan used by Orshansky. In 1968 the Social Security Administration, concerned about the index's adequacy, proposed adjusting it "to conform to the higher general level of living," but the Bureau of the Budget's Office of Statistical Standards overruled the proposal. Instead, a Federal Interagency Committee, created in October 1968, reconsidered the poverty line. The committee decided to retain 1963 as the base year but to "switch to the Consumer Price Index as the price inflates for annual updating." As Orshansky pointed out: "This meant, of course, that the food-income relationship which was the basis for the original poverty measure no longer was the current rationale." Another important alteration to the poverty index had taken place two years earlier, when the Census Bureau "quietly dropped its method of estimation of unreported incomes" and, as a consequence, reduced the number of persons in poverty by about 1.5 million.[117] As many critics have observed, the official poverty index remains far too low. It rests on unrealistic assumptions about the relation of food to income; it does not include noncash benefits; it does not vary with regional differences in the cost of living; and it ignores changing standards of consumption. But it established a new way of looking at poverty. For the purposes of government policy, poverty is not deprivation; it is bureaucratic category.

If nothing else, the history of the poverty line illustrates the politics of numbers. Federal administrators waged a quiet but persistent campaign against increased poverty thresholds and, at every junction, chose the lowest plausible figure. In this way, they both checked the expansion of benefits, which a higher threshold would have triggered, and minimized the problem of poverty in America, thereby avoiding embarrassment. Had the Census Bureau updated its thresholds to account for "more recent nutrition standards and consumption practices," asserted Orshansky, the number of poor people in America in 1975 would have risen "from 26 million to 36 million, or from 24 million to 37 million, depending on which census survey you use."[118]

The days of the old poverty standard finally are numbered. Criticism of it mounted from many sources, culminating in a 1995 National Academy of Sciences report calling for a revamped poverty line. In 2009, responding to the NAS report, the Census Bureau established an interagency technical working group, which in 2012 published a Supplemental Poverty Measure. In New York City, a blue ribbon commission on poverty appointed by mayor Michael Bloomberg in 2006 attacked the existing poverty line, calling for New York's nascent anti-poverty program to adopt a more realistic standard, which, it showed, would substantially boost the number of New Yorkers living in poverty. The major issue addressed by the new poverty line is noncash benefits. For US poverty-line reformers, this became the nub of the issue. Poor Americans receive a number of noncash benefits such as food stamps and housing vouchers, which, the critics argue, need to be incorporated into a more realistic measure. At the same time, the measurement of income should deduct expenses, such as those related to child care, employment, or medical care. The net result increases the number of elderly who fall below the poverty line and decreases the number of children, but the proportion of all Americans in poverty goes up. This shift in the measurement of poverty does not represent an intellectual revolution or paradigm shift. It still measures poverty by an absolute standard, when much of the rest of the world uses a relative standard—generally, relation to median income. With poverty measured as an income less than half the median income, a standard common among other nations, the number of Americans in poverty rises still further.[119] The official US poverty rate for 2010 was 15.3 percent, but an authoritative study by the Luxembourg Income Study found 18 percent of the US population with incomes below half the median income in 2010, compared to 8 percent in Germany and 12 percent in Canada in 2007. Among the countries in the study, only in Mexico, India, and Guatemala did more people live on incomes this low.[120]

In the 1960s public policy reconceived poverty not only by adopting an official poverty standard, but also by its appetite for research. Indeed, the distinguished economist Robert Haveman, former director of the University of Wisconsin's Institute for Research on Poverty, the semiofficial poverty think tank of the US government, argues that between 1965 and 1980, social science transformed American public policy.[121]

In the early 1960s anthropologists and sociologists took the lead in applying modern social science to contemporary poverty. However, the core concept—the culture of poverty—drew devastating criticism, and their ethnographic methods did not help policymakers in need of systematic data. The angry protest following Daniel Patrick Moynihan's 1965 report, *The Negro Family: The Case for National Action*, as we have seen, helped bury both the culture of poverty and the black family as acceptable topics in liberal social science and to pass the leadership in poverty research to economists. Economists met government's need for systematic data, predictive models, and program evaluation. From its "outset," writes Haveman, "the War on Poverty was conceived as an economic war; the designs, the debates, and the evaluations were all conducted in economic terms. Economics was the central discipline in both the action and the research components of the war."[122]

Massive new government spending on poverty and social welfare prompted new research, most of it funded by the federal government. In part, the government stressed research for reasons of political convenience. The "politics of federal antipoverty policy," writes Haveman, "made research spending an attractive option. Research support was clearly less controversial and risky than, say, community action or a guaranteed income program." However, the emphasis on research had other sources as well. From the earliest planning for the War on Poverty, claims Haveman, "the presumption that research and evaluation should guide policy decisions was a principal tenet." This emphasis reflected "the movement to place government on a more rational and analytic basis" stimulated by Robert McNamara, President Kennedy's secretary of defense, who in turn had been influenced by his experience at the Ford Motor Company. McNamara urged the application of systems analysis techniques to war planning and staffed the Defense Department's new and influential Office of the Assistant Secretary for Planning and Evaluation with military analysts from the Rand Corporation. The federal government's chief poverty warrior, Sargent Shriver, first director of OEO, appointed key staff with Defense Department and Rand Corporation backgrounds. As a result, OEO's Office of Planning, Research, and Evaluation "embodied the philosophy of PPBS [planning-programming-budget system]" pioneered at Defense.[123] PPBS tightened the links between the Cold War, the war in Vietnam, and War on Poverty.[124]

OEO, which turned to agencies outside the government for most of its research, established the Institute for Research on Poverty at the University of Wisconsin and funded a great deal of other poverty-related research as well. Between 1965 and 1980, in current dollars, annual federal spending on poverty-related research increased from $2.5 to $160 million or from 0.64 percent to 30.12 percent of all federal research and development spending. This increased government spending changed research priorities in the social sciences. Between 1962 and 1964, five leading economics journals published only three articles on poverty-related research; by 1971–1973, the number had increased to fifty-nine. For five leading sociology journals, the increase in the same period was from fifteen to forty-five.[125]

Poverty researchers' first task was descriptive: how to assess and measure changes in economic well-being, poverty, and inequality, and how to incorporate noncash transfers into measures of economic status. Because academic literature on these topics in the early 1960s was nearly nonexistent, the adoption of an official government poverty line became an early priority. This is why OEO seized on Orshansky's index so eagerly and put it to uses for which it was not intended. The unplanned expansion of the nation's income support system also posed urgent research questions: did welfare programs and income transfer policies cause people to work less? Although research showed only very modest work disincentives, it did highlight the inequities that resulted from administrative discretion and benefit variations among states. As a result, most poverty researchers began to advocate a unitary, uniform, and national income maintenance program.

Only the creation of data sets that followed individuals and families over longer periods of time could provide the answer to another question: Was poverty primarily permanent or transitory? OEO funded the Panel Study of Income Dynamics at the University of Michigan, which in 1968 began to trace a representative sample of the American population. The analysis showed the great differences that emerged from longitudinal, as contrasted with cross-sectional, methods. Sociologists also used new longitudinal data sets for increasingly detailed and sophisticated studies of mobility. (Mobility studies, claims Haveman, had a great influence on sociology but little impact on policy.) Research on a variety of other topics also shaped thinking about poverty. Studies of the relations among education, income, and social mobility called into question not only human capital models, but also the entire educational strategy of the War on Poverty. In the same years, dual labor market hypotheses forced modifications in neoclassical economic theories—modifications that proved to be temporary.[126]

Poverty research also influenced social science methods. First, and to Haveman most important, poverty researchers pioneered large-scale social experiments. Indeed, randomized experiments became the gold-standard in public policy research. Although the implications of poverty research supported a guaranteed national income program, no one could predict its impact. As a result, OEO sponsored income maintenance experiments designed to test the effect of income guarantees on work incentives. These enormously complicated and costly experiments proved ambiguous. Nonetheless, Haveman feels, the "social policy experiments stand as the clearest example of a breakthrough in the methodology of social science attributable to the War on Poverty." Other breakthroughs were the development of new methods for correcting bias selectivity (dealing with samples that are not representative), and the creation of microdata simulation models to estimate the effects of policies on large populations.[127]

Together with PPBS, poverty research fostered the creation of public policy analysis as a discipline. New schools within universities trained policy analysts who found work in higher education, government, private research centers, and a burgeoning evaluation research industry. In the process, poverty became a technical subject to be discussed only by experts.[128]

Haveman, like many others, recognized the limited impact of research on policy: the path between the results of empirical research and policy, even when they are clear, which often is not the case, never runs straight. Politics always intervenes. In this situation, Haveman advocated a modest but crucial role for research as a brake on ideology and an arbiter of public debate.[129] In recent years, even this unimpeachable goal has grown more evanescent.

Great Society poverty research proved to be the last hurrah of twentieth-century liberalism. It rested on an expectation with roots in the Progressive era that reason, science, and expertise could inform public policy and persuade a benevolent state to engineer social progress. By placing government policy on a scientific basis, poverty researchers hoped to transcend politics and ideology. In the end, although they won several battles, they lost the intellectual war. They developed new measures with which to chart the contours of poverty; invented dazzling methods with which to experiment, evaluate, and predict; and created a new discipline. But they remained unable to agree on a definitive answer to the most ancient question about poverty and welfare.

For more than two centuries, reformers, critics, and administrators all have asked: Does social welfare leave the poor less willing to work? The economists who dominated poverty research also remained obsessed with this question, even though they disagreed on its answer. Rarely did economists consider the role of politics or capitalism in the production of poverty or examine their assumptions about the role of market incentives or the limits of market models as the basis for public social obligations, and they either ignored or belittled the few alternative frameworks proposed. It is telling that nowhere in his intelligent, even-handed analysis does Haveman mention the heuristic connection (discussed in Chapter 2) between American poverty and the dependency theory advanced by black scholars in the late 1960s early 1970s. As a consequence, research failed to shore up the intellectual foundation of the welfare state. Almost no one noticed that it had crumbled, until it was too late.

4

Interpretations of Poverty in the Conservative Ascendance

AFTER THE MID-1970S PROGRESS against poverty stalled. The 1973 oil crisis ushered in an era of growing inequality interrupted only briefly by the years of prosperity during the 1990s. Productivity increased, but, for the first time in American history, its gains were not shared by ordinary workers, whose real incomes declined even as the wealth of the rich soared. Poverty concentrated as never before in inner city districts scarred by chronic joblessness and racial segregation. America led western democracies in the proportion of its children living in poverty. It led the world in rates of incarceration. Trade union membership plummeted under an assault by big business abetted by the federal government. Policy responded by allowing the real value of the minimum wage, welfare benefits, and other social protections to erode. The dominant interpretation of America's troubles blamed the War on Poverty and Great Society and constructed a rationale for responding to misery by retrenching on social spending. A bipartisan consensus emerged for solving the nation's social and economic problems through a war on dependence, the devolution of authority, and the redesign of public policy along market models.

Urban Transformation

The years after the mid-1970s witnessed a confrontation between massive urban structural transformation and rightward moving social policy that registered in a reconfigured and intensified American poverty in the nation's cities. It is no easy task to define an American city in the early twenty-first century. Fast-growing cities in the post-war Sun Belt differ dramatically from the old cities of the Northeast and Midwest as any drive through, for example, Los Angeles and Philadelphia makes clear. Nonetheless, all the nation's central cities and their surrounding metropolitan areas experienced transformations of economy, demography, and space that resulted in urban forms without precedent in history. These transformations hold profound implications for poverty as both fact and idea, and they underscore the need to understand poverty as a problem of place as well as persons. A long tradition of social criticism—from nineteenth-century advocates of slum clearance through the "Chicago school" of the 1920s to the most cutting-edge urban theory of the twenty-first century (discussed in Chapter 5)—presents poverty as a problem of place. In one version, which has dominated discussions, conditions *in* places—most notably, substandard housing—produce, reinforce, or augment poverty. In an alternate version, poverty is a product of place itself, reproduced independent of the individuals who pass through it. Both versions help explain the link between poverty and the multisided transformation of metropolitan America.

The first transformation was economic: the death of the great industrial city that flourished from the late nineteenth century until the end of World War II. The decimation of manufacturing evident in Rust Belt cities resulted from both the growth of foreign industries, notably electronics and automobiles, and the corporate search for cheaper labor. Cities with economic sectors other than manufacturing (such as banking, commerce, medicine, government, and education) withstood deindustrialization most successfully. Those with no alternatives collapsed, while others struggled with mixed success. Some cities such as Las Vegas built economies on entertainment, hospitality, and retirement. With manufacturing withered, anchor institutions, "eds and meds," increasingly sustained the economies of cities lucky enough to house them; they became, in fact, the principal employers. In the late twentieth century, in the nation's twenty largest cities, "eds and meds" provided almost 35 percent of jobs.[1] As services replaced manufacturing everywhere, office towers emerged as the late twentieth century's urban factories. Services include a huge array of activities and jobs, from the production of financial services to restaurants, from high paid professional work to unskilled jobs delivering pizza or cleaning offices.

Reflecting this division, economic inequality within cities increased, accentuating both wealth and poverty.

The second kind of urban transformation was demographic. First was the migration of African Americans and white southerners to northern, midwestern, and western cities. Between World War I and 1970, about seven million African Americans moved north. The results, of course, transformed the cities into which they moved. Between 1940 and 1970, for example, San Francisco's black population multiplied twenty-five times and Chicago's grew five times. The movement of whites out of central cities to suburbs played counterpoint. Between 1950 and 1970, the population of American cities increased by ten million people while the suburbs exploded with eighty-five million.[2]

The idea that the white exodus to the suburbs represented "flight" from blacks oversimplifies a process with other roots as well. A shortage of housing; urban congestion; mass-produced suburban homes made affordable with low interest, long-term, federally insured loans; and a new highway system all pulled Americans out of central cities to suburbs. At the same time, through "blockbusting" tactics, unscrupulous real estate brokers fanned racial fears, which accelerated out-migration. In the North and Midwest, the number of departing whites exceeded the incoming African Americans, resulting in population loss and the return of swaths of inner cities to empty, weed-filled lots that replaced working-class housing and factories—a process captured by the great photographer Camilo Jose Vergara with the label "green ghetto." By contrast, population in Sun Belt cities such as Los Angeles moved in the opposite direction. Between 1957 and 1990, the combination of economic opportunity, a warm climate, annexation, and in-migration boosted the Sun Belt's urban population from 8.5 to 23 million.[3]

A massive new immigration also changed the nation and its cities. As a result of the nationality based quotas enacted in the 1920s, the Great Depression, and World War II, immigration to the United States plummeted. The foreign-born population reached its nadir in 1970. The lifting of the quotas in 1965 began to reverse immigration's decline. Immigrants, however, now arrived from new sources, primarily Latin America and Asia. More immigrants entered the United States in the 1990s than during any other decade in its history. These new immigrants fueled population growth in both cities and suburbs. Unlike the immigrants of the early twentieth century, they often bypassed central cities to move directly to suburbs and spread out across the nation. In 1910, for example, 84 percent of the foreign born in metropolitan Philadelphia lived in the central city. By 2006 the proportion had dropped to 35 percent. New immigrants have spread beyond the older gateway states to the Midwest and South, areas from which prior to 1990 immigrants largely were absent.[4] Thanks to labor market networks in agriculture, construction, landscaping, construction, and domestic service, Hispanics spread out of central cities and across the nation faster than any other ethnic group in American history. This new immigration has proved essential to labor market growth and urban revitalization. Again in metropolitan Philadelphia, between 2000 and 2006, the foreign born accounted for 75 percent of labor force growth. A New York City research report "concluded that immigrant entrepreneurs have become an increasingly powerful economic engine for New York City...foreign-born entrepreneurs are starting a greater share of new businesses than native-born residents, stimulating growth in sectors from food manufacturing to health care, creating loads of new jobs and transforming once-sleepy neighborhoods into thriving commercial centers." Similar reports came in from around the nation from small as well as large cities and from suburbs.[5]

Suburbanization became the first major force in the spatial transformation of urban America. Although suburbanization extends well back in American history, it exploded after World War II as population, retail, industry, services, and entertainment all suburbanized. In the 1950s, suburbs grew ten times as fast as central cities. Even though the Supreme Court had outlawed officially mandated racial segregation in 1917 and racial exclusions in real estate deeds in 1948, suburbs found ways to use zoning and informal pressures to remain largely white until late in the twentieth century, when African Americans began to suburbanize.[6] Even in suburbs, however, they clustered in segregated towns and neighborhoods. Suburbs, it should be stressed, never were as uniform as their image. In the post-war era, they came closer than ever before to the popular meaning of "suburb" as a bedroom community for families with children. But that meaning had shattered completely by the end of the twentieth century, as a variety of suburban types populated metropolitan landscapes, rendering distinctions between city and suburb increasingly obsolete. The collapse of the distinction emerged especially in older inner ring suburbs where the loss of industry, racial transformation, immigration, and white out-migration registered in shrinking tax bases, eroding infrastructure, and increased poverty.[7]

Gentrification and a new domestic landscape furthered the spatial transformation of urban America. Gentrification may be redefined as the rehabilitation of working-class housing for use by a wealthier class. Outside of select neighborhoods, gentrification by itself could not reverse the economic and population decline of cities, but it did transform center city neighborhoods with renovated architecture and new amenities demanded by young white professionals and empty-nesters who had moved in. At the same time, it often displaced existing residents, adding to a crisis of affordable housing that helped fuel homelessness and other hardships.

The new domestic landscape resulted from the revolutionary rebalancing of family types that accelerated after 1970. In 1900 married couples with children made up 55 percent of all households, single-mother families 28 percent, empty-nesters 6 percent, and nonfamily households (mainly young people living together) 10 percent, with a small residue living in other arrangements. By 2000 the shift was astonishing. Married couple households now made up only 25 percent of all households, single-mother families 30 percent, empty-nesters 16 percent, and nonfamily households 25 percent. (The small increase in single-mother families masked a huge change. Earlier in the century they were mostly widows; by century's end they were primarily never married, divorced, or separated.) What is stunning is how after 1970 these trends characterized suburbs as well as central cities, eroding distinctions between them. Between 1970 and 2000, for example, the proportion of census tracts where married couples with children comprised more than half of all households plummeted from 59 percent to 12 percent and in central cities from 12 percent to 3 percent. In the same years, the proportion of suburban census tracts where single mothers composed at least 25 percent of households jumped an astonishing 440 percent—from 5 percent to 27 percent—while in central cities it grew from 32 percent to 59 percent. The share of census tracts with at least 30 percent nonfamily households leaped from 8 to 35 percent in suburbs and from 28 to 57 percent in cities. These changes took place across America, in

Sun Belt as well as Rust Belt. Truly, a new domestic landscape eroding distinctions between city and suburb had emerged within metropolitan America. Its consequences were immense. The rise in single-mother families living in poverty shaped new districts of concentrated poverty and fueled the rise in suburban poverty. Immigration brought young, working-class families to many cities and sparked revitalization in neighborhoods largely untouched by the growth and change brought about by gentrification.[8]

Racial segregation also transformed urban space. The first important point about urban racial segregation is that it was much lower early rather than late in the twentieth century. In 1930 the neighborhood in which the average African American lived was 31.7 percent black; in 1970 it was 73.5 percent. No ethnic group in American history ever experienced comparable segregation. Sociologists Douglas Massey and Nancy Denton, with good reason, described the situation as "American apartheid." In sixteen metropolitan areas in 1980, one of three African Americans lived in areas so segregated along multiple dimensions that Massey and Denton labeled them "hypersegregation." Even affluent African Americans were more likely to live near poor African Americans than affluent whites. Racial segregation, argued Massey and Denton, by itself produced poverty.[9] Areas of concentrated poverty, in turn, existed largely outside of markets—any semblance of functioning housing markets had dissolved, financial and retail services had decamped, jobs in the regular market had disappeared.[10] Concentrated poverty and chronic joblessness went hand in hand. Public infrastructure and institutions decayed, leaving them epicenters of homelessness, crime, and despair. Even though segregation declined slightly in the 1990s, at the end of the century, the average African American lived in a neighborhood 51 percent black, many thousands in districts marked by a toxic combination of poverty and racial concentration. This progress reversed in the first decade of the twentieth century. "After declining in the 1990s," reported a Brookings Institution study, "the population in extreme-poverty neighborhoods—where at least 40 percent of individuals lived below the poverty line—rose by one-third from 2000 to 2005–09."[11]

Despite continued African American segregation, a "new regime of residential segregation" began to appear in American cities, according to Massey and his colleagues. The new immigration did not increase ethnic segregation; measures of immigrant segregation remained "low to moderate" while black segregation declined modestly. However, as racial segregation declined, economic segregation increased, separating the poor from the affluent and the college educated from high school graduates. Spatial isolation marked people "at the top and bottom of the socioeconomic scale." The growth of economic inequality joined increased economic segregation to further transform urban space. America, wrote three noted urban scholars, "is breaking down into economically homogeneous enclaves." This rise in economic segregation afflicted suburbs as well as inner cities, notably sharpening distinctions between old inner ring suburbs and more well-to-do suburbs and exurbs. Early in the twenty-first century, as many poor people lived in suburbs as in cities, and poverty within suburbs was growing faster within them.[12]

In the post-war decades, urban redevelopment also fueled urban spatial transformation. Urban renewal focused on downtown land use, clearing out working-class housing, small businesses, and other unprofitable uses, and replacing them with high-rise office buildings, anchor institutions, and expensive residences. The 1949 Housing Act kicked off the process by facilitating city governments' aspirations to assemble large tracts of land through eminent domain and sell them cheaply to developers. The Act authorized 810,000 units of housing to re-house displaced residents; by 1960, only 320,000 had been constructed. These new units of public housing remained by and large confined to racially segregated districts and never were sufficient in number to meet existing needs. "Between 1956 and 1972," report Peter Dreier and his colleagues, experts in urban policy, "urban renewal and urban freeway construction displaced an estimated 3.8 million persons from their homes" but rehoused only a small fraction. The costs of urban renewal to the social fabric of cities and the well-being of their residents were huge. Urban renewal "certainly changed the skyline of some big cities by subsidizing the construction of large office buildings that housed corporate headquarters, law firms, and other corporate activities" but at the price of destroying far more "low-cost housing than it built" and failing "to stem the movement of people and businesses to suburbs or to improve the economic and living conditions of inner-city neighborhoods. On the contrary, it destabilized many of them, promoting chaotic racial transition and flight."[13]

Neither the War on Poverty nor Great Society slowed or reversed the impact of urban redevelopment and racial segregation on the nation's cities. President John F. Kennedy finally honored a campaign pledge in 1962 with a federal regulation prohibiting discrimination in federally supported housing—an action that "turned out to be more symbolic than real" on account of weak enforcement.[14] In the 1968 Fair Housing Act, President Lyndon Johnson extended the ban on discrimination, and the practices that produced it, to the private housing market. Unfortunately, weak enforcement mechanisms left it, too, inadequate to the task throughout the 1970s and 1980s.[15]

For the most part, the War on Poverty and Great Society rested on an understanding of poverty as a problem of persons, or, in the case of community action, of power, but less often of place. Opportunity-based programs addressed the deficiencies of individuals, not the pathologies of the places in which they lived. This hobbled their capacity from the outset. The conservatives who seized on the persistence of poverty to underscore and exaggerate the limits of the poverty war and Great Society retained this individual-centered understanding of poverty as they developed a critique of past efforts and a program for the future, neither of which was adequate to the task at hand.

The coincidence of America's urban slide into deep urban racial segregation, concentrated poverty, deindustrialization, physical decay, and near-bankruptcy coincided with the manifest failures of public policy, notably in urban renewal, and in the efforts of government to wage war on poverty. No matter that the story as popularly told was riddled with distortions and omissions. This narrative of catastrophic decline and public incompetence produced the trope of the "urban crisis," which, in turn, handed conservatives a gift: a ready-made tale—a living example—to use as evidence for the bundle of ideas they had been nurturing for decades and which emerged triumphant by the late 1970s.

The Conservative Ascendance

The growth of urban poverty did not rekindle compassion or renew the faltering energy of the Great Society. Instead, a war on welfare accompanied the conservative revival of the 1980s. City governments, teetering on the edge of bankruptcy, cut social services; state governments trimmed welfare rolls with more restrictive rules for General Assistance (state outdoor relief); and the federal government attacked social programs. As President Ronald Reagan famously remarked, government was the problem, not the solution. The result of these activities reduced the availability of help from each level of government during the years when profound structural transformations in American society increased poverty and its attendant hardships.[16]

Several sources fed the conservative restoration symbolized by Ronald Reagan's election as president in 1980. Business interests, unable to compete in an increasingly international market, wanted to lower wages by reducing the influence of unions and cutting social programs that not only raised taxes but offered an alternative to poorly paid jobs. The energy crisis of 1973 ushered in an era of stagflation in which public psychology shifted away from its relatively relaxed attitude toward the expansion of social welfare. Increasingly worried about downward mobility and their children's future, many Americans returned to an older psychology of scarcity. As they examined the sources of their distress, looking for both villains and ways to cut public spending, ordinary Americans and their elected representatives focused on welfare and its beneficiaries, deflecting attention from the declining profits and returns on investments that, since the mid-1970s, should have alerted them to the end of unlimited growth and abundance.[17]

Desegregation and affirmative action fueled resentments. Many whites protested court-ordered busing as a remedy for racial segregation in education, and they objected to civil rights laws, housing subsidies, and public assistance support for blacks who wanted to move into their neighborhoods while they struggled to pay their own mortgages and grocery bills. White workers often believed they lost jobs and promotions to less qualified blacks. Government programs associated with Democrats and liberal politics became the villains in these interpretations, driving blue-collar workers decisively to the right and displacing anger away from the source of their deteriorating economic conditions onto government, minorities, and the undeserving poor.

Suburbanization, the increased influence of the South on electoral politics and the politicization of conservative Protestantism, also fueled the conservative ascendance. "Suburbia," political commentator Kevin Phillips asserted, "did not take kindly to rent subsidies, school balance schemes, growing Negro migration or rising welfare costs.... The great majority of middle-class suburbanites opposed racial or welfare innovation." Together, the Sun Belt and suburbs, after 1970 the home to a majority of voters, constituted the demographic base of the new conservatism, assuring the rightward movement of politics among Democrats as well as Republicans and reinforcing hostility toward public social programs that served the poor—especially those who were black or Hispanic. The "middle class" became the lodestone of American politics, the poor its third rail.

Prior to the 1970s, conservative Christians (a term encompassing evangelicals and fundamentalists) largely distrusted electoral politics and avoided political involvement. This stance reversed in the 1970s when conservative Christians entered politics to protect their families and stem the moral corruption of the nation. Among the objects of their attack was welfare, which they believed weakened families by encouraging out-of-wedlock births, sex outside of marriage, and the ability of men to escape the responsibilities of fatherhood. Conservative Christians composed a powerful political force, about a third of the white electorate in the South and a little more than a tenth in the North. By the 1990s they constituted the largest and most powerful grassroots movement in American politics. In the 1994 elections, for the first time a majority of evangelicals identified themselves as Republicans. Although the inspiration for the Christian Right grew out of social and moral issues, it forged links with free-market conservatives. Fiscal conservatism appealed to conservative Christians whose "economic fortunes depend more on keeping tax rates low by reducing government spending than on social welfare programs that poor fundamentalists might desire," asserted sociologists Robert Wuthnow and Matthew P. Lawson. The conservative politics that resulted fused opposition to government social programs and permissive legislation and court decisions (abortion, school prayer, gay civil rights, the Equal Rights Amendment, teaching evolution) with "support of economic policies favorable to the middle-class"—a powerful combination crucial for constructing the electoral and financial base of conservative politics.[18]

Two financial sources bankrolled the rightward movement of American politics. Political action committees mobilized cash contributions from grassroots supporters while conservative foundations, corporations, and wealthy individuals supported individual candidates, organized opposition to public programs, and developed a network of think tanks—including the American Enterprise Institute, the Heritage Foundation, and the libertarian Cato Institute—designed to counter liberalism, disseminate conservative ideas, and promote conservative public policy. Within a year of its founding in 1973, the Heritage Foundation had received grants from eighty-seven corporations and six or seven other major foundations. In 1992 to 1994 alone, twelve conservative foundations holding assets worth $1.1 billion awarded grants totaling $300 million. In 1995 the top five conservative foundations enjoyed revenues of $77 million compared to only $18.6 million for "their eight political equivalents on the left."[19]

As well as producing ideas, conservative think tanks marketed them aggressively. Historian James Smith writes that, "marketing and promotion" did "more to change the think tanks' definition of their role (and the public's perception of them)" than did anything else. Their conservative funders paid "meticulous attention to the entire 'knowledge production process,'" represented as a "conveyor belt" extending from "academic research to marketing and mobilization, from scholars to activists." Their "sophisticated and effective outreach strategies" included policy papers, media appearances, advertising campaigns, op ed articles, and direct mail. In 1989 the Heritage Foundation spent 36 percent of its budget on marketing and 15 percent on fundraising. At the same time, wealthy donors countered the liberal politics of most leading social scientists with "lavish amounts of support on scholars willing to orient their research" toward conservative outcomes and a "grow-your-own approach" that funded "law students, student editors, and campus leaders with scholarships, leadership training, and law and economics classes aimed at ensuring the next generation of academic leaders has an even more conservative cast than the current one."[20]

Conservative politics fused three strands: economic, social, and nationalist. The economic strand stressed free markets and minimal government regulation. The social emphasized the protection of families and the restoration of social order and private morality. Where the state intervened in the right to pray or in religiously sanctioned gender relations, it opposed federal legislation and the intrusion of the courts. Where the state sanctioned or encouraged family breakdown and immoral behavior, as in abortion or welfare, it favored authoritarian public policies. Militant anti-communism composed the core of conservatism's nationalist strand, fusing the other two in opposition to a common enemy. It favored heavy public spending on the military and focused on both the external enemy—the Soviet Union—and the internal foe—anyone or anything threatening the socialist takeover of America. With the collapse of the Soviet Union, the bond holding together the social and economic strands of conservatism weakened, replaced at last by a new enemy, militant Islam embodied in Iraq and Iran and in the Taliban and Al Qaeda.

Conservatives triumphed intellectually in the 1980s because they offered ordinary Americans a convincing narrative that explained their manifold worries. In this narrative, welfare, the undeserving poor, and the cities they inhabited became centerpieces of an explanation for economic stagnation and moral decay. Welfare was an easy target, first because its rolls and expense had swollen so greatly in the preceding several years and, second, because so many of its clients were the quintessential undeserving poor—unmarried black women. Welfare, it appeared, encouraged young black women to have children out of wedlock; discouraged them from marrying; and, along with generous unemployment and disability insurance, fostered indolence and a reluctance to work. Clearly, it appeared, however praiseworthy the intentions, the impact of the War on Poverty and the Great Society had been perverse. By destroying families, diffusing immorality, pushing taxes unendurably high, maintaining crippling wage levels, lowering productivity, and destroying cities they had worsened the very problems they set out to solve.

Even though these arguments were wrong, liberals failed to produce a convincing counter-narrative that wove together a fresh defense of the welfare state from new definitions of rights and entitlements, emergent conceptions of distributive justice, ethnographic data about poor people, and revised historical and political interpretations of the welfare state. This inability to synthesize the elements needed to construct a new narrative and compelling case for the extension of the welfare state was one price paid for the capture of poverty by economists and the new profession of public policy analysis. It resulted, as well, from a lack of empathy: an inability to forge a plausible and sympathetic response to the intuitive and interconnected problems troubling ordinary Americans: stagflation; declining opportunity; increased taxes and welfare spending; crime and violence on the streets; and the alleged erosion of families and moral standards.

Conservatives Confront Welfare and Poverty

The conservative criticism of federal anti-poverty programs updated the oldest and most coherent tradition in the political economy of welfare. In *An End to Poverty?*, the historian Gareth Stedman Jones excavates the origins of this tradition. The "moment of convergence between the late Enlightenment and the ideals of a republican and democratic revolution," writes Stedman Jones, "was a fundamental historical turning point. However brief its appearance, however vigorously it was thereafter repressed, it marks the beginning of all modern thought about *poverty*." The "first practicable proposals to end poverty," found in the writings of Condorcet and Thomas Paine, "date back to the 1790s, and were a direct product of the American and French revolutions." In their aftermath, attacks on the institutions of state and church in Britain and France provoked a fierce reaction fueled by Paine's wild popularity in Britain. "The effort to thwart this revolutionary subversion of beliefs demanded the mobilization of unprecedented numbers of the population and engaged the energies of every organ of church and state in every locality." The result "stamped upon the still protean features of political economy...a deeply anti-utopian cast of mind, transforming future enquiry in the area into a gloomy and tirelessly repeated catechism." The "ambition to combat poverty," writes Stedman Jones, "was henceforward conceived as a bleakly individual battle against the temptations of the flesh."[21]

The most enduring tradition in the political economy of poverty in the United States as well as Britain is a product of this history. The poor constitute the unfortunate casualties of a dynamic, competitive economy in which they fail to grasp or hold onto the levers of opportunity. The widowed, the sick, and a few others remain exceptions, but for the most part the poor are losers, too incompetent or ill-disciplined to reap the bounty of increased productivity. Aiding them with charity or relief only interferes with the natural working of markets, retards growth, and, in the end, does more harm than good. From the social Darwinists of the nineteenth century through the work of contemporary political economists on the Right, this idea, dressed often with quantitative sophistication and theoretical skill, has retained an amazing purchase on popular thought and on politics as well.[22]

The modern conservative assault on the welfare state, which echoed this ancient interpretation, began in the 1970s with an attempt to deny that poverty remained a major problem. In 1978 Martin Anderson, who had been a domestic policy advisor to Richard Nixon, argued that poverty was no longer a serious problem in America. His book, *Welfare: The Political Economy of Welfare Reform in the United States*, attacked the concept of a guaranteed income (he had staunchly opposed the Family Assistance Plan from within the Nixon administration) and tried to show that the combination of in-kind benefits (food stamps, Medicare, housing) with public assistance and social insurance had eliminated all but residual pockets of poverty. He recommended a scaled-back, more efficiently administered version of the existing welfare state, whose political economy, he believed, left it impervious to fundamental reform.[23]

As he reflected on the claim of Anderson and others that poverty remained only a small, residual problem, Michael Harrington wryly observed: the "most astounding conservative discovery of the 1970s" was that poverty had "disappeared and no one noticed." Within only a few years, he continued, "the statistical abolition of poverty had turned into an academic cottage industry in the United States." The Reagan administration welcomed this new industry's product as scientific support for its proposed reduction of social benefits, and the media publicized the good news.[24]

Almost all academic and political attention, Harrington observed, focused on possible ways the poor had been overcounted—largely through the failure to include in-kind benefits in the definition of poverty. In fact, official poverty statistics regularly undercounted the poor in two ways. First, manipulations of the official poverty line, as we have seen, excluded several million people from the ranks of the poor. Second, the Census Bureau count did not include undocumented workers, most of whom do not earn enough to escape poverty. Harrington estimated that in 1984 as many as thirty million more people—roughly double the Census Bureau's count—could be labeled poor by the original official standards.[25] Contrary to Anderson and other proponents of the poverty reduction thesis, poverty did not trend downward. After the mid-1970s, the real value of public assistance decreased, and it represented an increasingly smaller proportion of median income. Although the cash value of Medicaid grew, its rise reflected the increased cost of health care, not a wider or improved delivery of services. In fact, poverty rates had started to climb. Reading the poverty reduction literature, one writer observed, it seemed as though a social problem had disappeared "like magic." Nonetheless, the growth and persistence of poverty mocked accounts of its disappearance, and soon even conservatives could no longer base policy on the assumption that in-kind benefits had combined with public assistance to eliminate want.

By the early 1980s, the impact of in-kind benefits on poverty-level incomes was beside the point. Whatever statisticians might conclude, their arguments seemed distracting quibbles beside the mounting evidence of hunger, homelessness, and destitution. Because conservatives could not redefine poverty out of existence, they needed a fresh set of reasons for cutting social benefits. In 1981 a best-selling Book-of-the-Month Club selection, *Wealth and Poverty* by George Gilder, gave the new administration the intellectual ammunition it needed to justify an ambitious attempt to cut social spending on the poor and reduce taxes on the rich.

Wealth and Poverty received lavish praise from Jack Kemp, David Stockman, *Barron's*, and *The New York Times* and became, according to one reviewer, the "Bible of the Reagan administration."[26] In 1984, as Gilder's influence waned, Charles Murray's more sober and conventional *Losing Ground* provided conservatives with an allegedly authoritative argument against direct government spending to combat the undeniable growth of poverty. In the same years, those who needed a more sophisticated philosophic justification for reducing the role of government could turn to *Anarchy, the State, and Utopia*, by Harvard philosopher Robert Nozick.[27]

More a moralist than a social scientist, Gilder exalted capitalism as he mounted the barricades to defend it against its enemies, which included redistributive taxation, the welfare state, and feminism. As he rummaged through intellectual history, choosing bits of conservative anthropology, economics, and theology, Gilder played on the anti-intellectualism never far from the surface of American culture. Although he often drew on their conclusions for support, social scientists emerged as the most dangerous foes—muddleheaded, arrogant, self-aggrandizing technocrats whose narrow, amoral approach to policy had very nearly destroyed America.

Above all, *Wealth and Poverty* was a paean to capitalism. According to Gilder, the essence of capitalism is altruism, not self-interest. "Capitalism begins with giving. Not from greed, avarice, or even self-love can one expect the rewards of commerce but from a spirit closely akin to altruism, a regard for the needs of others, a benevolent, outgoing, and courageous temper of mind." Capitalism takes the universal "gift impulse" and transforms it into a "disciplined process of creative investment based on a continuing analysis of the needs of others." Not surprisingly, Gilder's hero is the small entrepreneur, the daring risk-taker, agent of change, foundation of Schumpeter's "creative destruction."[28]

Gilder celebrated both great wealth and inequality because they embody not only the just rewards of success, but more important, the leaven for raising the living standards of all, including the poor. Poverty results from indolence, cynicism, and the demoralizing impact of public policy. "The only dependable route from poverty," asserted Gilder, "is always work, family, and faith. The first principle is that in order to move up, the poor must not only work, they must worker harder than the classes above them.... But the current poor, white even more than black, are refusing to work hard." The demoralization of the poor was the consequence of a perverse welfare system, which eroded "work and family" and thus kept "poor people poor."[29]

Gilder's second principle of upward mobility is the maintenance of monogamous marriage. Married men, "spurred by the claims of family," channel their "otherwise disruptive male aggressions" into providing for wives and children. The increase in female-headed families therefore perpetuates the poverty of women and children and unleashes the primitive impulses of men. "The key to lowerclass life in contemporary America," he asserted, was that "unrelated individuals" had become so "numerous and conspicuous" that they set the tone for the entire community." Neither "matriarchy" nor race constituted the core problem. Instead, it was "familial anarchy among the concentrated poor of the inner city, in which flamboyant and impulsive youths rather than responsible men provide the themes of aspiration."[30]

Wealth and Poverty is riddled with inconsistencies and contradictions. Gilder's glorification of great wealth sits uneasily besides his heroic portrait of small entrepreneurs or attack on the bailout of the Chrysler Corporation. Nor was Gilder's equation of capitalism with disinterested public love consistent with his stress on sober self-interest as a guide to how tax policy and economic incentives actually work. Nonetheless, his relentless assault on any public policy that retarded the individual pursuit of wealth did not swerve as he ranged across taxation, environmental regulation, affirmative action, and welfare. Most of his arguments were not new. His concrete criticisms of welfare, for instance, restated the classic arguments against the dole, which, as always, were couched in the best interests of the poor.[31] But two themes set Gilder's attack on welfare policy apart. One was the harshness of his assault on affirmative action. The other was his belief in the biological basis of sex roles. Affirmative action, he maintained, had aggravated the demoralizing effects of welfare by perpetuating "false theories of discrimination and spurious claims of racism and sexism as the dominant forces in the lives of the poor." The fact of the matter was that "it would seem genuinely difficult to sustain the idea that America is still oppressive and discriminatory." As for gender, based on his reading of anthropology, Gilder asserted that "female sexuality, as it evolved over the millennia, is psychologically rooted in the bearing and nurturing of children." Civilization therefore depends on "the submission of the short-term sexuality of the young to the extended maternal horizons of women." Welfare destroys constructive male values by appropriating the role of provider from husbands and fathers and giving it to the state. As a result, men are "cuckolded by the compassionate state."[32]

Gilder played fast and loose with his sources and often relied on proof by haphazard anecdote. Overwhelming evidence refuted most of his claims about poverty and welfare, for instance. However, whether the data supported his theories did not matter all that much. For Gilder was primarily a moralist and theologian who rested his case on faith and courage in the face of a wild, unpredictable universe. More to the point, Gilder, more than careful and responsible social scientists, spoke to the interlaced economic, personal, and moral anxieties that fueled conservatism's triumph in the era of Ronald Reagan.[33]

Gilder's paean to capitalism attacked the social and economic policies of the War on Poverty and Great Society, but it did not engage John Rawls's philosophic defense of redistributive government or the concept of distributive justice on which it rested. Instead, the major challenge to Rawls came from his Harvard colleague Robert Nozick. Nozick's *Anarchy, the State, and Utopia* (1974) and Rawls's *Theory of Justice*, noted one reviewer in a judgment from which few would dissent, were the "two most important books in political ethics since World War II." Together, observed another reviewer, Rawls and Nozick were "inaugurating a needed renaissance in political philosophy." Nozick, who also found a more popular audience, attracted a growing number of followers. Indeed, *Anarchy, the State, and Utopia*, observed *The New York Times Book Review*, was "welcomed by American business journals as a ringing defense of private enterprise and a devastating critique of the welfare state."[34]

It was ironic that conservatives praised Nozick, for he did not consider himself one of them. He intended *Anarchy, the State, and Utopia* to give comfort to no political party and identified himself most closely with the libertarian position. Indeed, his argument runs directly counter to the moral authoritarian strand within contemporary conservatism. Nonetheless, readers often appropriate books for purposes other than those their author intended. Given Nozick's summary statement of his thesis, little mystery exists about the attraction of *Anarchy, the State, and Utopia* for the political Right:

> Our main conclusions about the state are that a minimal state, limited to the narrow functions of protection against force, theft, fraud, enforcement of contracts, and so on, is justified; that any more extensive state will violate persons' rights not to be forced to do certain things, and is unjustified; and that the minimal state is inspiring as well as right. Two noteworthy implications are that the state may

not use its coercive apparatus for the purpose of getting some citizens to aid others, or in order to prohibit activities to people for their own good or protection.[35]

Anarchy, the State, and Utopia rests on the assumption that "individuals are ends and not merely means; they may not be sacrificed or used for achieving of other ends without their consent. Individuals are inviolable." Two major arguments follow from this radical individualist premise. The first defends the existence of the state with a hypothetical account of its origins. The second attempts to show why arguments in favor of extending the scope of the state are wrong. A final brief section delineates a libertarian utopia whose possibility, for Nozick, makes the minimal state inspiring as well as just.[36]

Like Rawls, Nozick began with a state of nature; only, its inhabitants did not make decisions behind a Rawlsian "veil of ignorance." Instead, they shrewdly confronted dangers by creating protective associations that, over time and without prior intent, they merged into a monopoly with the essential characteristics of a state. Because it arose from a process that did not violate individual rights, the monopoly or minimal state was both necessary and legitimate. Nonetheless, with one important exception, any extensions of its scope impermissibly violated individual rights. All major theories that attempted to legitimate these extensions were, for Nozick, fatally flawed.

Nozick concentrated most on Rawls and Marxism. Beyond their individual failings as theories, both shared the weakness of almost all theories of distributive justice: They were "end-state" theories, in that they advocated some optimal distribution of resources and evaluated societies on the basis of how closely they approximated it. They showed little concern, however, with how distribution decisions were reached, especially with the inescapable conclusion that they were attainable only through the violation of inviolable individual rights. Nozick proposed, to the contrary, to evaluate distributions according to three criteria: "the principle of acquisition of holdings, the principle of transfer of holdings, and the principle of rectification of violations of the first two principles." Individual holdings acquired and transferred through morally permissible means are entitlements. Individuals deserve them; the state may not take them away. "Taxation of earnings from labor is on a par with forced labor." The state may not appropriate the wealth of one individual for the benefit of another. It has no moral right to coerce any person to share resources. It has no obligation to assist the poor through the public purse, nor may it intervene to prohibit behavior that does not violate the inviolable rights of others.[37]

Through the principle of rectification of violations, Nozick provided a back door for an activist, redistributive state: "Although to introduce socialism as the punishment for our sins would be to go too far," he observed, "past injustices might be so great as to make necessary in the short run a more extensive state in order to rectify them." In fact, distribution patterns might be taken as "rough rules of thumb" for identifying the result of historic injustices, and "a rough rule of thumb for rectifying injustice" might be to "organize society so as to maximize the position of whatever group ends up least well-off in society." Nozick therefore did not rule out ending up with the same practical politics as Rawls, even though he would reach them by an entirely different route.[38]

That route entailed a radical and curious disjunction of method. His account of the origins of the state rested on a wholly hypothetical state of nature, whose lack of concrete historical foundation he vigorously defended. Yet he criticized most theories of distributive justice for their ahistorical basis. As end-state theories, they remained unconcerned with how societies reached desired distributions and were thus insensitive to violations of individual rights. Only through historical accounts of the acquisition and transfer of holdings, he countered, may individuals' entitlements to their possessions be sanctioned as legitimate, or condemned as its opposition.

Despite his stress on historical process, Nozick offered no evidence that contemporary distributions of wealth were outcomes of just processes of acquisition and transfer. Nor did he provide any but the most general guide for assessing them. Indeed, using his principles, few historians would have difficulty reaching a conclusion opposite to that which he implied—namely, the entitlement of contemporary Americans to the undisturbed enjoyment of all their wealth. For evidence of fraud, collusion, violence, and the violation of individual rights abound in the nation's past.

To Nozick, property was wholly a matter of things. He entered the debate about distributive justice among philosophers and political theorists but ignored its counterpart among legal scholars, thereby avoiding questions about the definition of property such as those raised by Charles Reich. Could he agree that property represents a relationship sanctioned by, and not antecedent to, the state? How would acknowledgment of changing forms of property affect his argument?

However Nozick intended his arguments to be used, they lent themselves easily to the retrenchment of social benefits and the exaltation of greed fashionable in the early 1980s. It is a greatly oversimplified, distorted, and vulgar, but nonetheless comprehensible, step from Nozick's dazzling scholarship to Reagan's Director of the Office of Management and Budget, David Stockman's, assertion that no one is entitled to claim any social benefits from government. It is an even less precipitous step to Charles Murray's attack on the welfare state.

In *Losing Ground* (1984), Charles Murray quoted Robert Nozick only once. His chapter on the purposes of social welfare ("What Do We Want to Accomplish?") started with Nozick's observation that "The legitimacy of altering social institutions to achieve greater equality of material condition is, though often assumed, rarely argued for." Like Nozick and Gilder, Murray is not an egalitarian. His slogan is, "Billions for equal opportunity, not one cent for equal outcome." The legitimacy of social inequality underpinned his attack on social welfare, just as it did Gilder's defense of wealth and Nozick's concept of entitlement.[39] Together, Gilder and Murray provided the perfect social theories for an age of expanding inequality.

Another assumption, not wholly consistent with the first, lurked just beneath the surface of Murray's argument. The first assumption justified inequality with equal opportunity. The second assumed a harsh world of limited possibilities in which reward mirrored merit. "The tangible incentives that any society can realistically hold out to the poor youth of average abilities and average industriousness are mostly penalties, mostly disincentives." With public support stripped away, as Murray wanted, most people could look forward only to hard work and limited gains. Social policy, therefore, must emphasize the stick rather than the carrot.[40]

Murray's contention that social welfare harmed the poor updated an old position in the endless debates about poor laws, and his stance on the classification of poor people also echoed ancient arguments. "Some people," he wrote, "are better than others. They deserve more of society's rewards, of which money is only one small part." Despite centuries of failed attempts to draw the line between the deserving and undeserving poor, for Murray the distinction between them emerged clearly enough to serve as the basis of social policy.

One reason for the spectacular success and influence of *Losing Ground* was Murray's concentration on the core preoccupations within poverty discourse. Another was his style. Murray wrote clearly and in the manner of a social scientist. *Losing Ground* bristles with graphs and quantitative data. It has none of the bizarre flights of fancy or overt misogamy of Gilder's work. A third was its marketing by the Manhattan Institute, which funded Murray to write it. Murray's success illustrates the role of big money in the marketplace of ideas. William Hammett, president of the conservative Manhattan Institute, read a pamphlet Murray had written and invited him to the institute, where he was supported for the two years during which he wrote *Losing Ground*.[41] Hammett invested in the production and in the promotion of Murray's book. He spent about $15,000 to send more than 700 free copies to influential politicians, academics, and journalists, and he paid for a public relations specialist, Joan Taylor Kennedy, to manage the "Murray campaign." Kennedy aggressively booked Murray on TV shows and the lecture circuit; arranged conferences with editors and academics; and contacted newspapers and magazines. The institute even organized a seminar on *Losing Ground* with intellectuals and journalists influential in policy circles. Participants were paid honoraria of $500 to $1,500 and housed at an expensive New York hotel. As one observer commented, "the quality of Murray's intellectual goods" was not the only reason for his success.[42]

Murray's argument fit the Reagan agenda perfectly. At precisely the appropriate moment, it provided what appeared to be an authoritative rationale for reducing social benefits and dismantling affirmative action. Nearly every reviewer commented on Murray's influence. In March 1985, policy expert Robert Greenstein observed: "Congress will soon engage in bitter battles over where to cut the federal budget, and *Losing Ground* is already being used as ammunition by those who would direct more reductions at programs for the poor." Murray's name, pointed out the prominent sociologist Christopher Jencks, "has been invoked repeatedly in Washington's current debates over the budget—not because he has provided new evidence of the effects of particular government programs, but because he is widely presumed to have proven that federal social policy as a whole made the poor worse off over the past twenty years." *Losing Ground*, others pointed out, was the Reagan administration's new bible.[43]

The core of Murray's thesis may be restated in the form of several propositions:

- Despite massively swollen spending on social welfare after 1965, the incidence of both poverty and antisocial behavior increased.
- Neither the growth of poverty nor antisocial behavior resulted from economic conditions, which were improving.
- Black unemployment increased during the period because young blacks voluntarily withdrew from the labor market.
- Female-headed black families increased because young men and women saw less reason to marry.
- Labor market and family behavior (also criminal behavior) reflected rational short-term responses to economic incentives.
- These incentives were the perverse result of federal social policy after 1965.

All these propositions, as one commentator after another showed, were wrong. For one thing, welfare did not cause the rise in black out-of-wedlock births, and Murray had the facts about incentives backward. Welfare benefits, in constant dollars, fell steeply after 1972, during the same period in which Murray claimed their generosity acted as a perverse incentive. (Murray nowhere mentioned this large decline in AFDC benefits.) The number of black children supported by AFDC declined by 5 percent from 1972 to 1980. No correlations existed between state-level benefits and the size of AFDC rolls. Out-of-wedlock births also rose sharply among women who did not receive welfare.

Similarly, Murray confused the relation between the growth of the economy and poverty. Poverty increased because the economy worsened after 1973. The Gross National Product, on which Murray relied, was an inadequate measure of either opportunity or individual well-being. Real wages declined, productivity dropped, inflation soared, and unemployment increased in part because the economy did not grow fast enough to absorb the large number of entering workers.

Christopher Jencks's reworking of Census Bureau statistics showed that the share of the population living below the official poverty line was almost twice as high in 1965 as in 1980, and almost three times as high in 1950 as in 1980. The reduction in poverty appeared remarkable when set against the unemployment rate, which doubled between 1968 and 1980.[44] As for the rationality of behavior, the relative advantage of work versus welfare increased during the 1970s, in contrast to Murray's claim that it decreased. Murray's assertion rested on the hypothetical example of a couple, Harold and Phyllis, who must choose whether or not to marry when Phyllis becomes pregnant. By 1980, claimed Murray, it made less economic sense for them to marry than ever before. As Robert Greenstein showed, Murray's argument was flat wrong. First, it was based not on the nation but on Pennsylvania, where welfare benefits grew twice as fast during the 1970s as in the country as a whole. It also miscalculated income by incorrectly assuming that the family would have lost food stamp benefits had Harold worked. (Murray, however, included foods stamps in calculating the family income.)

With accurate computation, work at a minimum-wage job was more profitable than welfare throughout most of the country; in the South, minimum-wage jobs often paid twice as much. Murray failed to provide a 1980 budget for Harold and Phyllis. Had he done so, it would have shown that the value of all welfare benefits packaged together had dropped by 20 percent during the 1970s. Conversely, after 1975 the Earned Income Tax Credit increased the advantages of working. As Greenstein pointed out: "in 1980—even in Pennsylvania—Harold and Phyllis would have one-third more income if Harold worked than if he remained unemployed and Phyllis collected welfare."[45]

Murray distorted or ignored the accomplishments of social programs. He did not recognize the decline in poverty among the elderly, increased access to medical care and legal assistance, the drop in infant mortality rates, or the near abolition of hunger prior to the Reagan administration's policies. He did not observe the irony that without

federal affirmative action programs and other anti-discrimination measures, the black economic progress that he had lauded could not have
occurred.

Murray was also mostly wrong concerning the history of poverty
and social welfare in America, including social policy since 1965. Only
because he told the story in a contextual vacuum was he able to argue
that the federal government stumbled into a set of misguided policies that worsened the condition of the poor—which, without massive
public intervention, had started to "improve." For instance, he pointed
to rising black unemployment in the 1960s but did not connect it to
the mechanization of southern agriculture in the 1950s that drove so
many from the land and toward northern cities. His book remained
innocent of any discussion of the transformations within American cities described in this chapter. Murray had nothing to say about the role
of shifting occupational structures and spatial patterns in promoting
poverty. Only by adding these omissions to his neglect of declining real
wages, rising unemployment, and faulty economic and social history
was Murray able to assert the unmediated and demoralizing impact of
federal social policy on the poor during a period of growing prosperity
and opportunity.

Because social policy is usually either futile or perverse, Murray recommended draconian cuts: the elimination of virtually all social benefits except Social Security (the reasons for whose stay of execution
he did not explain) and reconstituted, limited unemployment insurance. In his view, only by cutting the cord that bound them to the
government could federal policy truly help the poor. However, even
the Reagan administration could not persuade Congress to dismantle
the welfare state. Sophisticated conservatives in the 1980s still accepted
the inevitability of big government in modern America. Their problem
was to make it work for their ends and to set it on a plausible theoretical and moral base. This was the task begun by Lawrence Mead as he
helped launch a new stage in the conservative ascendance.

By the mid-1980s, few conservatives still urged dismantling the welfare state. One reason was the intractable nature of poverty, especially
among minorities in inner cities. As homelessness and children's poverty became national issues, only the most stubborn conservative could
argue that cutting social benefits would improve the condition of poor

people by prodding them toward independence. A second reason was moral. Conservatives objected not only to government intervention in the economy, liberal foreign policy, and decreased military spending, but to trends they believed threatened family life and violated moral values. As the Reagan revolution failed to check abortion, divorce, out-of-wedlock pregnancy, and drug use, social conservatives reasserted the importance of authority in public life. Because only government had the power to prohibit or enforce behavior, the future of conservatism necessitated its reconciliation with the state. In social policy, the first major book to justify big government in conservative terms was Lawrence Mead's *Beyond Entitlement: The Social Obligations of Citizenship*, published in 1986.

Mead did not quote Adam Smith; his preferred philosophers were Hobbes, Burke, and Tocqueville. His concern was society, not the individual, and he worried more about order than liberty. His target was permissive social policy, and his solution, enforced work obligations for the poor.

"My question," wrote Mead, "is why federal programs since 1960 have coped so poorly with the various social problems that have come to afflict American society." Although his question echoed Murray, Mead's answer was different. The major problem with the welfare state, he claimed, was "its *permissiveness*, not its size." By permissiveness, Mead meant that federal programs "award their benefits essentially as entitlements, expecting next to nothing from the beneficiaries in return." These permissive federal social programs resulted partly from the structure of American government and partly from an intellectually flabby liberalism grounded in sociological explanations of poverty that denied the importance of authority and obligation.[46]

Mead believed that "functioning" in American society had declined during the previous two decades. By functioning, he meant competence as reflected in the proportion of the population on welfare, the unemployment rate, the amount of serious crime, and SAT scores. Americans, he concluded, not only were rejecting their social obligations to one another; they were losing their ability to cope with the ordinary tasks of everyday life. The fault, Mead was clear, did not lie with social structure or economic conditions. Its source was individual will conditioned by government programs that "shield their clients from the threats and rewards that stem from private society—particularly from the market place." Instead of "blaming people as they deviate," government must persuade them to *blame themselves.*" As for the poor, Mead asserts, "the main barrier to acceptance is no longer unfair social structures, but their own difficulties in coping."[47]

With Gilder, Nozick, and Murray, Mead shared a dark view of human nature. Gilder's unbridled male aggression, Nozick's warlike state of nature, Murray's natural indolence and amorality, and Mead's inability to resist the snares of permissiveness all circumscribed the limits of reform and mandated public coercion. Gilder, Murray, and Mead assumed that many people would always have to work hard at badly paid, dull jobs they detest. Workplace reform, high wages, the constructive use of automation to increase leisure and decrease alienation played no role in their visions of the future. Instead, they believed public policy should help Americans adapt to their gloomy prospects by lowering their expectations. Gilder, Murray, and Mead therefore rejected equality of condition as a dangerous and illusory social goal. The American definition of equality, asserted Mead, did not rest on income or status. Rather, equality meant "the enjoyment of equal citizenship, meaning the same rights *and* obligations as others." Mead defended his definition of equality by expedience rather than on constitutional or philosophical grounds: "The great virtue of equal citizenship as a social goal is that it is much more widely achievable than status."[48]

Mead assumed that anyone who wanted a job could find one. Deindustrialization and structural unemployment played no larger a role in his argument than in Murray's. "Unemployment has more to do with functioning problems of the jobless themselves than with economic conditions." The lack of child care, for example, did not excuse unemployment among women AFDC beneficiaries. A "lack of *government* child care," he claimed, "seems seldom to be a barrier; most prefer to arrange care with friends or relatives." Others remained unemployed because they were unwilling to relocate, accept or remain at unpleasant and badly paid jobs, or commute more than twenty miles to work. The point was simple: "disadvantaged workers are unlikely to labor regularly unless they are required to as a condition of support of society."[49]

The quality and material rewards of work remained irrelevant for Mead. "There are good grounds to think," he asserted, "that work at least in 'dirty,' low-wage jobs, can no longer be left solely to the initiative of those who labor." For them, "employment must become a duty, enforced by public authority, rather than an expression of self interest." Low-wage work "apparently must be mandated," he wrote, "just as a draft has sometimes been necessary to staff the military." Government "need not make the desired behavior worthwhile to people. It simply threatens punishment." What is more, the refusal to work was a grave act against the state. "Nonwork," asserted Mead, "is a political act" that underlines the "need for authority... In an open political system rebellious actions, even if not overtly political, tend to provoke countervailing forces." With plenty of jobs available, continued unemployment reflected more than indolence; it was subversion.[50]

The primary responsibility of government is not to raise living standards, increase personal satisfaction, or even to facilitate markets. "Government is really a mechanism by which people force themselves to serve and obey *each other* in necessary ways." Obedience necessitates the enforcement of shared values. "Federal policymakers must start to ask how programs can affirm the norms for functioning on which social order depends." Because social order demanded the public creation of norms, government "must take over the socializing role."[51]

Mead used the condition of blacks to show how permissive social policy had backfired. Before the civil rights movement, he claimed, black society was more "coherent" than after; "at least racism did not exempt blacks from normal social demands as recent federal policy has done." With no supporting evidence, Mead asserted that the lack of accountability built into federal social programs was "among the reasons why nonwork, crime, family breakup, and other problems are much commoner among recipients [of government benefits] than Americans generally." The remedy is an "authoritative social policy" that enforces social obligations. Mead called for an enhanced, intrusive state to recapture social policy from the soft, muddled liberal intellectuals whose influence had moved government away from the values and desires of the vast majority of Americans.[52]

Mead nonetheless remained ambivalent about the scope of the state. He would assign it a key role in socialization but deny it one in employment. He redefined employment in public works projects as just another form of dependence. Great Society training programs offered "what amounted to welfare through the allowances and other benefits." Indeed, by effectively relaxing the work obligation for many men, "the employment programs probably increased joblessness rather than reducing it."[53] The word "probably" was the key: Mead had no hard evidence for his speculation because none existed. Similarly, his brief, inaccurate, and derogatory comments on the community action programs ignored the grassroots origins of the civil rights movement, its role as a catalyst of the War on Poverty, and the pivotal ideological and administrative position of community action. Instead, Mead treated the War on Poverty as a conspiracy by the elite to advance its own power and position by trapping the disadvantaged in a web of dependence.[54]

Mead read the history of American political reform from 1900 to 1965 as a progressive tradition directed toward "the elimination of barriers to competent citizens." These reforms assumed the competence of ordinary Americans, who made "good use of new opportunities with little further help from government." Because Mead assumed these movements met their goals, he believed no major structural barriers to advancement now blocked the path toward prosperity or social justice.[55] Mead's reading of history distorted the past to support his interpretation of the present. A more accurate way to read the same events is this: Minorities and working people, no matter how competent, could not—and cannot—reduce discrimination, improve wages and working conditions, or escape periodic unemployment without the intervention of an active state operating on their behalf to legitimate and protect collective bargaining, set the minimum wage and hours of work, provide a social safety net, and enforce civil rights, among other crucial functions.

Mead's account of the past also missed the authoritarian strand in the history of American social reform. Since the early nineteenth century, reformers had tried to regulate behavior and use government as an agent of socialization through, for example, compulsory public education, the temperance movement, and breaking up poor families. This history is important because it illustrates that the intrusive, authoritarian moments in the history of American reform usually failed to meet their goals. Prohibition provoked law-breaking, adulterated whiskey, and violence. Compulsory education did remove some poor children from the streets, but it had had little impact on crime, poverty, or public morality, as its advocates had promised. Child protection agencies did not stop child abuse, and within two decades family breakup had been discredited as an object of social policy. Juvenile courts failed to stem delinquency and disappointed their founders. Welfare regulations did not change the sexual behavior of poor women.[56] Given this history, Mead's stress on authority as the foundation of social policy appeared neither novel nor promising.

Mead was right about one key piece of history: throughout the nation's past, Americans have held the work ethic sacred, and they have defined the undeserving poor by its absence. Whether alcoholics, tramps, unwed mothers, or young black men, the undeserving poor have remained outside the regular labor market by reason of their own personal deficiencies, not because of the difficulty of finding work. On examination, this harsh implication of work's deification always has collapsed. In Mead's case the claim that labor demand exceeded supply constituted the empirical centerpiece of his argument. But his evidence was unconvincing.[57]

Even if forced to concede a job shortage, Mead almost certainly would have staged only a tactical retreat. For his case had a moral rather than an empirical core. It rested, that is, on his concept of citizenship and its obligations—one of the core concerns in the history of poverty and welfare. To Mead, citizenship demanded the successful discharge of social and political obligations. "The capacities to learn, work, support one's family, and respect the right of others," wrote Mead, "amount to a set of *social* obligations alongside the political ones [such as voting, paying taxes, serving in the military]." He defined a "civic society" as one in which "people are competent in all these senses, as citizens and as workers." In the social realm, government programs defined social expectations, as did the Constitution in the political realm. As a result, the structure of program benefits and requirements constituted "an *operational definition of citizenship*." Except in the narrow legal definition, citizenship is not an entitlement of birth; it must be earned daily through competent and responsible behavior.[58] As Mead used the term, "competence" became the badge of the deserving poor. Low SAT scores, unemployment, criminal convictions, and welfare dependence became interchangeable signals of incompetence—hallmarks of the undeserving poor whom Mead wrote out of citizenship.

Mead tried to be clear about what poor people owe other Americans. However, obligation implies mutual responsibilities, and Mead failed to ask what we, in our organized capacity as government or philanthropy, owe in return. Is it merely survival, or something more generous? Are obligations graduated? Should longer and harder work bring more benefits? There can be no legal or moral justification for asking people in need to sign a contract whose terms remain undisclosed. Unless it provides the prerequisites of competence, society (another of Mead's ill-defined abstractions) lacks a moral title to obligation. Potential citizens should expect the resources essential for learning, work, and family life. These include adequate schools, affordable housing, reasonably priced child care, first-class health care, and decent jobs. In America, poor people can count on none of these.[59]

All the poor may know is that they are obliged to work. *Why* is less clear. In places, Mead implied that work is necessary for self-esteem and mental health. Any work is preferable to dependent idleness. More often, Mead assigned work a different purpose: oiling the gears of productivity. Whether individuals like their work is beside the point. Society needs their labor, and the needs of society always trump the preferences of individuals. If necessary, Mead would subsidize the wages of poorly paid workers rather than force their employers to pay them more. Mead did not explain why he was willing to underwrite private profits with public subsidies. In fact, the harder one pushes, the more Mead's concept of social obligation collapses into a new strategy for preserving a pool of cheap, docile labor, an updated version of "regulating the poor," one of welfare's historic functions.[60] As such it is a euphemism. For without mutuality, obligation becomes coercion.[61]

Beyond Entitlement may have failed as moral philosophy and social science, but it succeeded as politics. Mead tapped the widespread hostility toward the dependent poor that underlay the ferocious assault on welfare, as embodied in AFDC, which culminated in the 1996 "welfare reform" legislation. As he read political trends in his 1992 book, *The New Politics of Poverty: The Non-Working Poor in America*, a new politics of dependency had replaced the old politics of class.[62] His argument had five parts:

1. "Nonwork" is the major cause of a new form of poverty. Young African American men and single mothers constitute the overwhelming number of the new poor.

2. Neither economic trends, racism, segregation, inadequate child care, nor other tangible obstacles explain the emergence of the new poverty.

3. Instead, the new poverty's roots lie in psychology, culture, and human nature.

4. As a response to the new poverty, a new politics of dependence based on "social and personal" issues has emerged to replace the old redistributive politics of class.

5. At its most constructive, the new politics of dependence realizes that only public policy that utilizes the authority of the state to enforce acceptable behavior can alleviate the new poverty.

Mead was correct about the link between nonwork and poverty in the 1990s, although with the further erosion of wages, intensifying inequality, and Great Recession, his focus on nonworking African American mothers and young African American men seems increasingly anachronistic. His dismissal of "tangible obstacles" in favor of "psychology, culture, and human nature" is contradicted by virtually all credible historical and social science research and suffused with a racial animus, which Chapter 5 will explore in its discussion of African American poverty and progress. But his identification of a new politics of dependency based on social and personal issues was right on the money, and his recognition that the new politics led straight to an authoritarian role for the state as enforcer of acceptable behavior found confirmation in the Republican Party's 1994 *Contract with America* and then in 1996 in the successful and ultimately bipartisan campaign to abolish the entitlement to welfare by replacing AFDC with Temporary Assistance for Needy Families.

The Liberal Retreat from Inequality

Liberals failed to block the bipartisan assault on the welfare state. No liberal supporters of vigorous anti-poverty programs seized public attention with the force of George Gilder, Charles Murray, or Lawrence Mead. In fact, either implicitly or explicitly, the relatively few scholars defending the expansion of social welfare ceded vital terrain to the conservatives.

That terrain was equality. Most liberals rejected greater equality as the ground on which to attack poverty or defend the welfare state. Instead, they stressed either the immorality of deprivation, the threat to community, or a combination of the two. Some argued that severe deprivation violated moral and even constitutional obligations. Others contended that poverty inhibited participation in civic life and eroded the basis of community. As they formulated their case, however, nearly all liberal writers on poverty and welfare criticized exclusive reliance on market models as the basis for social policy. (The major exceptions to this general neglect of inequality were the work of Ronald Dworkin, whose writings defended greater equality as the goal of liberal social and political policy, and Amartya Sen, who offered a technically and philosophically sophisticated defense of "needs" rather than "desert" as the metric of inequality for distributional judgments and a definition of poverty as "capability deprivation.")[63]

Writing in the *Harvard Law Review* in 1969, Frank Michelman first developed his case for the constitutional basis of welfare in the Fourteenth Amendment. The "judicial 'equality' explosion of recent times," he observed, "has been largely ignited by reawakened sensitivity, not to equality, but to a quite different sort of value or claim which might better be called 'minimum welfare.'" Welfare's purpose, he was very clear, was not the promotion of economic equality, but "minimum protection against social hazard." The "injury" resulting from poverty, he claimed, "consists more essentially of deprivation than of discrimination," and "the cure accordingly lies more in provision than in equalization."

A decade later, Michelman added provision of the conditions for political participation to his brief on behalf of the constitutional foundation of welfare rights. Welfare rights, he asserted, are "part of constitutionally guaranteed democratic representation." Poverty, he stressed, not only disadvantaged individuals politically; it identified them as members of a group whose interests, despite their numbers, were "systematically subordinated" in the formation of political coalitions and the routine exercise of political influence. The relation between poverty and political deprivation remained especially severe for blacks. For them, meeting their "basic welfare interests" remained crucial to eliminating "vestiges of slavery from the system of democratic representation."[64]

In contrast to Michelman, the contributors to *Democracy and the Welfare State*, edited by Amy Gutmann, based their arguments more on considerations of community and civic participation than on deprivation or vulnerability. "The primary focus of many of the papers in this volume," wrote Gutmann, "is not individual virtue, equality, or self-realization, but democratic citizenship. The pivotal questions are: What social institutions are necessary to encourage and protect citizenship? What rights do citizens have, and what duties are required of them?" Emphasis on the responsibilities of citizens, however, is a slippery idea that can lead toward a harsh and authoritarian state—to Lawrence Mead—unless it is accompanied by an inclusive definition of citizenship and an appreciation of the conditions that make possible the full exercise of citizenship. A definition of citizenship that rests on obligations and contributions, as the political theorist T. H. Marshall recognized, runs the risk of marginalizing those who do not work in the regular labor market, and creating second-class citizens. At the same time, poverty and deprivation undermine democracy by eroding the capacity to participate fully in civic life.[65] "Unless everybody can live a life free of elementary fears," warned political theorist Ralf Dahrendorf, "constitutional rights can be empty promises and worse, a cynical pretense of liberties that in fact stabilize privilege." A welfare state, as many of its theorists have recognized, is a precondition for modern democracy.[66]

In his contribution to *Democracy and the Welfare State,* J. Donald Moon responded to Gutmann's questions by linking criticism of exclusive reliance on market models—the major trend in social policy—to the basis of civic participation. "[The] justification for organizing economic life through the market," observed Moon, rests on "a conception of the individual as agent, capable of choice and deliberation, and entitled to certain rights and to be treated with respect." Consequently, the "justification of the market" weakens when its normal operation "deprives some people—through no fault of their own—of the very means of survival, not to mention the possibility of maintaining their well-being and dignity." Poverty's significance extends beyond suffering to "an undeserved exile from society." Moon found "something deeply and undeniably unjust about a social order that necessarily frustrates fulfillment of the promises it makes."[67]

For Michael Walzer as well, poverty violates the basis of community. His argument derived from his concept of complex equality, developed in *Spheres of Justice*, the first major theoretical work on distributive justice to follow Rawls and Nozick. To Walzer, the primary enemy of justice is domination rather than the inegalitarian distribution of goods. Justice is "the opposite of tyranny," and the recognition of complex equality the guarantor of democracy. Complex equality assumed the division of goods into multiple distributive spheres, each guided by its own rules, each relatively autonomous. "Every social good or set of goods," he wrote, "constitutes as it were, a distributive sphere within which only certain criteria and arrangements are appropriate." Protecting the relative autonomy of spheres requires constant policing of their boundaries.

The greatest danger of violation usually comes from the market sphere. Powerful men and women most often use the resources accrued there to invade other spheres; "market power," which tends to "overspill the boundaries" turns into a form of tyranny, "distorting distributions in other spheres." Only democracy has the capacity to protect the autonomy of spheres. "Once we have located ownership, expertise, religious knowledge, and so on in their proper places and established their autonomy, there is no alternative to democracy in the political sphere," wrote Walzer.

Because citizenship is active and participatory, public policy, according to Walzer, should have as one goal empowerment, or widespread "participation in communal activities, the concrete realization of membership." Membership, he contended, is "the primary social good that we distribute to one another," and the "denial of membership is always the first of a long train of abuses." Walzer's emphasis on membership raises two important questions. What rights do individuals possess as members of communities, and what circumstances deprive them of full membership?[68]

Poverty and prolonged unemployment deprive people of membership because they represent a "kind of economic exile, a punishment
that we are loath to say that anyone deserves." Poverty creates exiles by
stripping people of self-respect, which requires some substantial connection to the group; it thereby dilutes the meaning of citizenship, and
turns neighbors into strangers.[69]

For Walzer, the public response to poverty should reflect three
principles that together demand an extensive welfare state. Political
communities should meet the needs of their members as they are
collectively understood, distribute goods in proportion to need, and
honor the "underlying equality of membership." By their arrogance
and the dependence they breed, public relief programs too often adopt
the worst practices of private charity. "The old patterns survive; the
poor are still deferential, passive, and humble, while public officials
take on the arrogance of their private predecessors." Public programs,
therefore, should "aim at setting up the poor on their own" through
"rehabilitation, retraining, subsidizing small businesses, and so on."
Because participation is so central to citizenship, the participation of
the poor in the life of the community should not await the abolition of
poverty; "rather, the struggle against poverty (and against every other
sort of neediness) is one of those activities in which many citizens, poor
and not so poor and well-to-do alike, ought to participate."[70]

Walzer's inclusive model of community and participatory definition
of citizenship rest on a presumption of human dignity. Only an irre-
ducible commitment to individual human worth justifies his horror of
domination and emphasis on self-respect. Similar assumptions under-
pin the most comprehensive explanation of the injustice of poverty
written in the 1980s—the 1986 *Economic Justice for All*, the Catholic
bishops' pastoral letter on the US economy.

Poverty, asserted the pastoral letter, "is not merely the lack of financial resources. It entails a profound kind of deprivation, a denial of full
participation in the economic, social, and political life of society and an
inability to influence decisions that affect one's life." For the bishops, as
for Walzer, poverty represents a violation of community, a deprivation
of citizenship, and an essential powerlessness that "assaults not only
one's pocketbook but also one's fundamental human dignity."[71]

The bishops' definition of poverty reflected their search for a language of inclusion capable of appealing to non-Catholic audiences and broadly shared American social values. Their "option for the poor," they stressed, should "not mean pitting one group against another, but rather, strengthening the whole community by assisting those who are most vulnerable." Their reluctance to use divisive or provocative language, however, did not prevent the bishops from voicing unambiguous outrage at the persistence of poverty in America. "That so many people are poor in a nation as rich as ours," they wrote, "is a social and moral scandal that we cannot ignore."[72]

The letter's brief against poverty was moral, its starting point human dignity, which, "realized in community with others and with the whole of God's creation, is the norm against which every social institution should be measured." Human dignity derives from the creation of humans in God's image. Because it comes from God, it inheres in everyone, independent of "nationality, race, sex, economic status, or any accomplishment." Dignity manifests itself "in the ability to reason and understand"; in "freedom to shape their own lives and the life of their communities, and in the capacity for love and friendship."[73]

The recommendations in the pastoral letter rested on important assumptions about human rights, the conditions of human dignity, the nature of social obligations, and the quality of work. They assumed, first, that human rights encompass economic as well as civil and political rights. In this, they reflected the most controversial premise of contemporary poverty law, now generally rejected by federal courts but resurgent within the human rights community (as discussed in Chapter 5). They also assumed the social basis of human dignity, which cannot be realized apart from community. By implication, therefore, they rejected the individualism inherent in classical liberalism, advocated by free-market conservatives or libertarians such as Nozick.

Commitment to community leads to an emphasis on social obligations, which the latter, unlike Mead, based on reciprocity. "Social justice implies that persons have an obligation to be active and productive participants in the life of society and that society has a duty to enable them to participate in this way." Forcing people to work at unrewarding, deadening, or degrading work, as Mead would permit, clearly violates both human dignity and the reciprocity essential to the realization of community, because social justice requires organizing "economic and social institutions so that people can contribute to society in ways that respect their freedom and the dignity of their labor." Work is necessary for human fulfillment, but it "should enable the working person to become 'more a human being,' more capable of acting intelligently, freely, and in ways that lead to self-realization." (Ronald Dworkin made a similar point. "Treating people as equals requires a more active conception of membership. If people are asked to sacrifice for their community, they must be offered some reason why the community which benefits from that sacrifice is their community.")[74]

Although the letter considered inequality in contemporary America too severe, its main goals remained the realization of community and the protection of human dignity. Indeed, in keeping with Catholic teaching, the bishops not only accepted but celebrated "the private ownership of productive property." At the same time, the Church's teaching rejected the notion that a free market "automatically" produces justice. Instead, the bishops, like Walzer, argued that there are some goods that money cannot buy. Markets, they asserted, are "limited by fundamental human rights. Some things are never to be bought and sold. This conviction has prompted positive steps to modify the operation of the market when it harms vulnerable members of society."

Nor did they prefer government as the primary agent of social justice. Rather, they advanced the principle of subsidiarity, that "in order to protect basic justice, government should undertake only those initiatives which exceed the capacity of individuals or private groups acting independently." Subsidiarity, much like Walzer's separate spheres, protects freedom through "institutional pluralism" and links individuals to society through "mediating structures" composed of "small-and-intermediate-sized communities or institutions." Subsidiarity also implies the diffusion of moral responsibility for the poor through society and all its institutions.[75]

Despite its anchor in Catholic theology, the pastoral letter embodied most of the major themes in the liberal attempt to reconstruct the intellectual basis of the welfare state. Like a variety of secular sources, it grounded its advocacy of expanded social benefits more in deprivation (or vulnerability) and the conditions of community than in inequality; incorporated both public and private action in the quest for social justice; relied on institutional pluralism to protect liberty; and, though it assumed the legitimacy of private property, resisted the intrusion of the market beyond its appropriate sphere. Nonetheless, even *Economic Justice for All* reflected the retreat from equality that underpinned liberal writing on poverty and welfare.

The retreat from equality appeared to make good strategic sense in an era when "liberal" had become a pejorative label. But events proved this avenue a dead end. It led, first, away from a confrontation with the economic inequality spreading like wildfire through American society and exacerbating the problem of poverty. And, second, the reconstructed defense of the welfare state utterly failed to rehabilitate the idea of welfare or to penetrate public policy, which pivoted around a bipartisan attempt to redesign the American welfare state on completely different principles.

Ending Welfare

In the 1980s public policy coalesced around three major goals. "The first was the war to end dependence—not only the dependence of young unmarried mothers on welfare, but all forms of dependence on public and private support and on the paternalism of employers. The second was to devolve authority, that is, to transfer power from the federal government to the states, from state to counties, and from the public to the private sector. The third was the application of market models to social policy. Everywhere the market...triumphed as the template for a redesigned welfare state."[76] The design of "welfare reform" in 1996 reflected the interweaving of these three goals. It also reflected the triumph of Mead's call to replace entitlement with obligation based on work and to make full citizenship depend on participation in the regular labor market. The irony is that Mead's vision was implemented by Democratic president Bill Clinton.

The Welfare Reform Bill of 1996 represented the endpoint of a long, largely bipartisan effort to tie welfare to work. Known since the 1960s as workfare, this was in fact a very old idea. Since the workhouses of the eighteenth century, welfare reformers, to use the modern term, had tried unsuccessfully to make claimants work for benefits. "Twenty years ago," wrote Jamie Peck in his 2001 *Workfare States*, "the issue of 'workfare,' which at the time signified a particular type of U.S. work program requiring participants to 'work off' their welfare checks, was pretty much a marginal concern for anything other than a specialist audience.... a rather perverse preoccupation of a small but influential cadre of intellectuals and social visionaries on the U.S. right." By the 1990s, the picture had changed. "While the keyword *workfare* retains many of its pejorative connotations, its various generics such as 'welfare-to-work,' 'labor-force attachment,' 'active-benefit systems,' and 'work-first welfare reform' now trip off the tongues of politicians and policymakers across the political spectrum."[77] Peck's survey of *The New York Times, Washington Post*, and *Wall Street Journal* found more references to workfare in 1995 alone than in the entire period from 1971 to 1980.[78] Workfare, Peck argues, represented more than a policy innovation designed to punish poor people, frighten them away from welfare, or lower the cost of public assistance. Rather, it played a central role in the "attempt to restructure the 'boundary institutions' of the labor market"—to manage the transition away from what he calls a "welfarist" regime to a post-welfare regime marked by flexible labor markets and contingent workers where the former "discourses of needs, decency, compassion, and entitlement have been discredited" and replaced by new, "reworked discourses of work, responsibility, self-sufficiency and empowerment."[79]

In 1967, with the Work Incentive Program (WIN), popularly known as workfare, the federal government, using a mix of sanctions and incentives, tried to revive the idea that employable welfare recipients should work for their benefits. Like all earlier programs, WIN failed—in the program's first twenty months, only 10.6 percent of the 1.6 million cases referred for work were considered employable and the AFDC rolls continued to grow. WIN was caught in its own contradictions and the divergent priorities of its sponsors, who offered varied definitions of the problem welfare reform was supposed to solve. Was workfare to be the first phase of a broad attack on poverty? Was it a long-term strategy for reducing the cost of AFDC and enforcing a universal obligation to work? Was it a strategy designed primarily to restore family structure? Was it a means of solving the labor force problems of the low-wage service sector? How many of these purposes could workfare serve simultaneously? Were they consistent with each other? These were questions scarcely debated in the heady days when workfare appeared to be the hitherto elusive means with which to reform America's welfare system.

Workfare represented a new social policy synthesis that rejected the Great Society's emphasis on compassion, empowerment, and entitlement. Instead, its key concept revealed an increased belief by both liberals and conservatives that welfare recipients should earn their benefits through work and good behavior. In the 1970s workfare was defined narrowly to mean that people should work off their welfare grants—that is, welfare recipients should be required to work, even in make-work jobs, in exchange for receiving their benefits. However, this punitive conception of workfare failed in the few places where it was tried.[80]

In its 1981 budget act, Congress allowed states to test "new employment approaches to welfare reform, officially called CWEP (Community Work Experience Programs)." This, claimed social policy expert Richard Nathan, stimulated "new-style workfare":

> New-style workfare embodies both the caring commitment of liberals and the themes identified with conservative writers such as Charles Murray, George Gilder, and Lawrence Mead. It involves a strong commitment to reducing welfare dependency on the premise that dependency is bad for people, that it undermines their motivation to support themselves, and isolates and stigmatizes welfare recipients in a way that over a long period feeds into and accentuates the underclass mindset and conditions.[81]

As Fred Block and John Noakes argue, the two other events that moved new-style workfare high on the national agenda were its bipartisan support by the National Governors Association in 1985 and the introduction of welfare reform bills in both the Senate and House in 1987. New-style workfare, they contend, proved especially appealing to congressional Democrats who could use it to show their leadership in forging a bipartisan solution uniting compassion with efficiency and thereby solving a heretofore intractable problem.[82] New-style workfare consisted of obligational state programs encompassing a variety of employment and training services and activities: job search, job training, education programs, and also community work experience. By the mid-1980s, more than two-thirds of the states, asserted Nathan, had experimented with new-style workfare, and an intensive study of eight by MDRC, the policy evaluation firm, showed "promising", if not "large and dramatic", effects on increased earnings and reduced welfare dependency.[83] Workfare advocates pounced on the results as justification for further reform tying welfare to work. However, a hard look at the data by Block and Noakes raised serious doubts about the outcome of new-style workfare. At best, they found, the programs helped state governments save some money by churning their rolls. They did not move participants into permanent self-sufficiency or even temporarily lift them out of poverty.[84] Nonetheless, the MDRC results helped fuel the passage of the flawed Family Support Act of 1988, which commanded strong bipartisan support, passing the House 347 to 53 and the Senate 96 to 1.

Hailed in the national press, in reality the Family Support Act offered little hope of reforming welfare. It made unrealistic assumptions about the availability of good jobs for AFDC clients. In fact, few jobs open to them paid enough to lift a family out of poverty and were often unstable, did not offer benefits, and lacked prospects for upward mobility. Nor did working off welfare payments open up routes to unsubsidized jobs and independence. Workfare carried a stigma that made jobs in the regular labor market harder to land. The Family Support Act did enhance child support mechanisms by forcing women to identify the fathers of their children as a condition of support, and it required employers to withhold child support payments from absent fathers' paychecks. Nonetheless, the rise in out-of-wedlock births outpaced the increase in collections from unmarried fathers. The Act also extended AFDC to two-parent families in several states, helped a small number of clients leave AFDC, and encouraged state experimentation with welfare reform. Severely underfunded, however, the Family Support Act did not live up to its heady promise and as a practical source of welfare reform died a quiet death. Its greatest achievement was paving the way for the harsher, more punitive version of welfare reform of 1996.[85]

In 1992 Bill Clinton ran for president with a pledge to "end welfare as we know it." As a slogan, it was sufficiently ambiguous to avoid a major confrontation with his supporters on the political left. After all, everyone hated welfare. Liberals found it mean-spirited, demeaning, and inadequate. Conservatives, following Murray and Mead, believed it eroded the work ethic, fostered dependency, and rewarded the undeserving poor. The Heritage Foundation's Robert Rector and William Lauber added to the sense of urgency around welfare "reform" by manufacturing a crisis of cost in their preposterous but widely cited *America's Failed $5.4 Trillion War on Poverty.*[86]

In his perceptive *Why Americans Hate Welfare*, political scientist Martin Gilens found the most important component of Americans' hostility to welfare to be the "widespread belief that most welfare recipients would rather sit home and collect benefits than work hard to support themselves."[87] Working mothers, now the majority, resented the free ride provided by welfare that excused beneficiaries from juggling the burdens of home, work, and child care that confronted them every day. Welfare also was coded black. In 1994 63 percent of AFDC recipients nationwide—a number much higher in anti-welfare southern states and some older cities—were African American. In Alabama it was 75 percent and in Washington, DC, 97 percent.[88] Its racial hue helped drive a wedge between AFDC supporters and the white working poor.

As it happened, none of the arguments advanced against welfare by conservatives found support in empirical data. AFDC was not an expensive program—indeed, its real secret lay in its cheapness. It was hard to imagine a less expensive way to keep millions of nonworking people alive. Nor was it the source of the rise in out-of-wedlock births or family instability. In fact, AFDC rolls increased as both the real value of benefits and the number of children born to AFDC beneficiaries declined. As with Murray and Mead, conservative critics ignored or downplayed the factors that forced women onto welfare rolls, where most—contrary to common belief—remained only for short periods. A lack of jobs, declining wages, parental poverty, poor schools, the influence of neighborhood, racial and gender discrimination—none of these played any role in the conservative assault on welfare. In truth, it was the structure of AFDC that caused most of the program's weaknesses. Rules for eligibility undermined attempts to build modest savings or keep a car reliable enough to drive to work. The Reagan administration had virtually eliminated rules allowing welfare beneficiaries to keep some of the money they earned through work, thereby removing incentives to supplement AFDC benefits. In fact, without subsidies for child care, employment often remained impossible, and, perhaps worst of all, exchanging AFDC for low-wage work in most cases meant giving up medical insurance. Faced with these irrational impediments to improving welfare, many governors sought and won waivers from the federal requirements, and welfare rolls started to go down before the draconian 1996 legislation.

On August 22, 1996, President Clinton signed The Personal Responsibility and Work Opportunity Reconciliation Act after a long, tortuous legislative struggle. It had passed the House by a vote of 256 to 170 and the Senate by 74 to 24. In one poll, 82 percent of Americans approved.[89] Its passage signaled the triumph of Mead's "new politics of poverty." The new legislation replaced AFDC with TANF, a time-limited program. In place of AFDC, TANF provided states with two block grants, one giving "cash and other benefits to help needy families support their children while simultaneously requiring families to make verifiable efforts to leave welfare for work and to avoid births outside marriage." Lifetime benefits were limited to a maximum of five years, although states could set lower limits. The second block grant combined four major child care programs for low income families. Under the new law, legal immigrants lost benefits—they were dropped from Supplemental Security Income and food stamps, and barred from most means-tested programs. In its philosophy and provisions, the new legislation embodied the three goals driving the redesign of social policy. It was, of course, a frontal assault on dependency. At the same time, it devolved significant authority to state governments—a new hallmark of federal policy became setting goals while allowing state and local governments to choose the means with which to implement them, and with the new bill, market models suffused the goals, administration, and philosophy of welfare. Market logic drove the abolition of the entitlement to public assistance. Entitlement, which, contradicted the market imperative, swiftly became one of the most negative terms in the public policy lexicon. Even more, the new legislation reoriented welfare around the transition to work in the private labor market, and it left states free to contract with private providers to administer its provisions. For profit corporations, which seized the opportunity, decided whether American citizens would receive funds essential for their survival. Nina Bernstein at *The New York Times* reported that Lockheed

Martin, "the $30 billion giant of the weapons industry," was bidding against Electronic Data Systems (Ross Perot's $12.3 billion information technology company) and Anderson Consulting to administer the $563 million Texas welfare program. Lockheed planned "to market even more comprehensive welfare contracts to states and counties in what is potentially a new multibillion-dollar industry to overhaul and run welfare programs."[90]

The new legislation offended some high-level Clinton administration officials, who resigned in protest. One of them, poverty expert Peter Edelman, called it "the worst thing Bill Clinton has done," and offered a stinging critique predicting that in five years, when the first time limits were reached, many beneficiaries would "fall into the abyss all at once." The Congressional Budget Office found the legislation badly underfunded, without enough money to reach its goals. Others worried that TANF would prove unable to cope with a serious recession—a prediction fulfilled in the recession that began in 2008. Critics on the political Left, who had found themselves in the ironic position of defending the AFDC program that for years they had excoriated, were outraged and projected dire consequences. At first, the bill's critics appeared wrong. Welfare rolls dropped farther and faster than anyone had expected. Both Republicans and Democrats touted the legislation as a huge success. A more careful look at the data—at the reasons why the rolls went down and at the consequences of the legislation for poor people—presents a far more ambiguous and unsettling picture. But for ideas about poverty, the triumphalist interpretation had an unexpected consequence. It transformed the uniform image of single mothers of color: no longer lazy and dependent, many of them became plucky moms trying hard to make it on their own with minimal help from the state—an image that proved temporary when social scientists and popular commentators in the early twenty-first century rediscovered family pathology and poor single mothers as culprits in the growth and persistence of urban poverty (as discussed in Chapter 5).[91]

The conservative narrative of poverty and welfare triumphed with the 1996 Welfare Bill. Poverty and welfare had become so intertwined in public debate that it was perhaps easy to forget that, although related, they were separate issues and that fixing welfare did not touch the structural origins of poverty. In practical terms, the 1996 legislation put into place a new federal public assistance program that met the goals of Murray, Mead, the Heritage Foundation, and others who had been pounding on AFDC from the political Right. At the same time, it pulled in the center Left, which had been largely if not entirely won over by the main lines of the conservative story about welfare, poverty, and dependence. Even more, it set the terms for debate about poverty and welfare, narrowing the scope of discussions of poverty by the political Left largely to the question of whether TANF worked as advertised or harmed current and potential beneficiaries. The major question became whether women forced into paid employment earned enough to escape poverty. The first best-selling book on poverty in many years, social critic Barbara Ehrenreich's 2001 *Nickeled and Dimed*, which recounted the struggles of women trying to get by on low pay from miserable jobs, focused on this question. "Welfare reform" intensified attention on making work pay and on the working poor, who became the primary beneficiaries of poverty policy and public sympathy. After Ehrenreich, the next widely heralded book on poverty was Pulitzer Prize-winning journalist David Shipler's 2007 *The Working Poor*.[92]

The fact that even a full-time job did not guarantee escape from poverty was a huge and growing problem, and one that gave the lie to conservative claims like Mead's that virtually all poverty resulted from nonwork. But exclusive concentration on the working poor deflected attention from poor people who remained out of the regular labor market, largely abandoned by their presumptive political allies, and from large questions about the political economy of poverty. In fact, without realizing it, fixation on the working poor led even those writers and policy officials sympathetic to poverty issues into the oldest trap in the framing of poverty: the reification of the distinction between the able bodied and impotent poor, to use the language of the eighteenth and early nineteenth century, or the deserving and undeserving poor of poverty discourse from the second quarter of the nineteenth century through today. No one, to reiterate a fundamental point of this book, ever has been able to draw the lines between categories with precision. One reason is that poverty is a fluid and usually temporary state. Social welfare scholar Mark Rank, in his powerful, *One Nation, Underprivileged: Why American Poverty Affects Us All*, showed first that the majority of "Americans who encounter poverty experience a short-term spell of impoverishment, while only a small minority experience poverty for an extended period," and, second, "rather than being an event occurring among a small minority of the U.S. population, poverty is an experience that touches a clear majority of Americans at some point during their adult lifetimes."[93] Drawing a sharp line between the working and nonworking poor ignores the temporary, fluid, ubiquitous character of poverty, creating fictive distinctions that reinforce the politics of moral condemnation and neglect.

Women remaining on the TANF rolls became a shrinking residuum—the undeserving poor, to be sure—but not a serious public problem. By its victory, the new politics of poverty had dissolved the need for its own continued existence. Aside from the problem of the working poor, poverty and dependence slipped into the background, no longer problems worth political capital, slippery, potentially explosive issues best left unmentioned.

5

The Rise and Fall of the "Underclass"

CONSERVATIVES PRODUCED AN INTUITIVELY compelling narrative to explain poverty in transformed American cities, and they offered a harsh answer to the question of social obligation in tune with the social Darwinist core of the new politics of dependence. A new image— "underclass"—reinforced the contempt and loathing that underpinned the conservative narrative. With astonishing speed, the "underclass" narrative became the new bipartisan consensus and dominated discussions of urban poverty. The eminent sociologist William Julius Wilson attempted to wrest "underclass" from its conservative moorings by anchoring it in the structural conditions that generated poverty. In the process, he produced the most powerful and widely disseminated counter-narrative to the conservative story. The Rockefeller Foundation also adopted "underclass" as the basis for an activist anti-poverty strategy and funded the Social Science Research Council to implement a program of research planning and support for graduate education designed to produce both a body of knowledge and a cadre of well-trained researchers on poverty. Wilson's theory served as the leading hypothesis for the SSRC work.

Within a few years, Wilson acknowledged his failure to rescue "underclass" from its derogatory popular meaning and advocated abandoning the term. Not long after, the Rockefeller Foundation ended its support for the SSRC committee. But the fall of "underclass" did not signify that the problem of urban poverty had gone away. Indeed, explaining and responding to African American poverty remained a major concern, spawning fierce debates about personal responsibility, culture, incentives, obligations, and black history. Research and controversy focused once more on the black family and on African American men, while homelessness remained a tangible reminder of poverty's stubborn persistence and devastating consequences as well as of the nation's inability to solve its perennial crisis of low-income housing.

Major foundations had not placed all their bets on the "underclass" and academic research, however. They also had funded comprehensive community initiatives led by community activists. These, too, did not fulfill their promise, leading many researchers and policy officials to stress moving poor people out of depressed neighborhoods instead of investing yet more money in the reclamation of inner cities. Others took a wholly different tack, rejecting the pathological image of the urban poor and turning to the market for a new set of technologies with which to confront poverty. Almost all players in this history of the rise and fall of the "underclass" focused on categorizing the poor, explaining the reasons for their poverty, and finding the mix of incentives, sanctions, and training that would ease their disadvantage. But they largely avoided poverty as a problem in political economy, embedded, that is, in capitalist development itself. At the same time, a new, loosely coupled body of scholarship used history, theory, empirical research, and ethnography to link political economy with geography in a radical politics of space. As it excavated and plotted new forms of urban poverty around the world, this scholarship provided a theoretical counterpart to the new programmatic linkages between technologies of poverty work that moved from South Asia and Latin America to the United States.

Conventional poverty research, new market-based technologies of poverty work, the emergent spatially based political economy: none of these paid much attention to the question of why poverty matters and what we owe each other—the ethical issues raised by Reich, Rawls, and Nozick. Conventional research and market-based anti-poverty strategies ignored or rejected greater equality as a goal of public policy. These normative questions, however, remained alive in the writing of a few eloquent, if isolated, voices and in the Human Rights Movement's inclusion of absence from want as a fundamental human right.

The "Underclass"

In August 1977 *Time* frightened Americans by proclaiming its discovery of a menacing new class lurking in the mysterious wilderness of the nation's cities. "Behind the [ghetto's] crumbling walls lives a large group of people who are more intractable, more socially alien and more hostile than almost anyone had imagined. They are the unreachables; the American underclass." "Underclass" was more a metaphor than a theory.[1] It bound together three elements: novelty, complexity, and danger. The nation's urban ghettos were unprecedented urban forms; they could not be characterized by a single factor; and the social pathologies within them threatened to spill beyond their borders, threatening everyone. "Their bleak environment," *Time* continued, "nurtures values that are often at odds with those of the majority—even a majority of the poor." From the underclass came "a highly disproportionate number of the nation's juvenile delinquents, school dropouts, drug addicts, and welfare mothers, and much of the adult crime, family disruption, urban decay, and demand for social expenditures."[2] Ten years later *The New York Times* reported that the underclass had captured the attention of social scientists as well as of the media. "*Social scientists have focused new energies on an 'underclass' of Americans who live in near total isolation from mainstream society, and scholars are trying to learn more about the deteriorating inner-city areas where not working is the norm, crime is a commonplace and welfare is a way of life* [italics in original]."[3]

"Underclass" evoked a territory full of violence and despair; a group beyond mainstream politics and society. It also offered a gendered image of urban poverty, frightening Americans with the menace posed by black men and alarming them with the passivity of black women who avoided work, birthed illegitimate children, and lived on the charity of the welfare state, creating a morally corrosive epidemic of dependence and draining the public treasury. Two groups—black teenage mothers and black jobless youths—dominated the images of the underclass. The former received the most attention, and—as Chapter 4 showed—anti-poverty policy, redefined as welfare reform, came to mean intervening in the alleged cycle of dependency in which young, unmarried black women and their children had become trapped. Black males became less a problem for social welfare and more of one for criminal justice. Instead of training and employment, public policy responded by putting more of them in prison. Rates of incarceration in the United States soared above those in every other nation.

Commentaries on the underclass revived the oldest tropes in the literature on poverty. They echoed the nineteenth-century behavioral and cultural descriptions of the undeserving poor and picked up on the culture of poverty theme, discussed in Chapter 1. Their emphasis on the emergence of mysterious, menacing, pathogenic, and isolated districts at the core of American cities evoked the central images in the writing of nineteenth-century urban reformers and advocates of slum clearance. In the underclass literature—as in so much of the writing about urban poverty throughout American history—poverty was both a problem of persons—individual bad behavior and cultural deficiency—and of place—toxic environments that bred criminality and dependence.

The central problem confronted by writers on the underclass was defining exactly what they meant. For underclass eluded clear and consistent definition. Writers described it not only by behavioral pathology and deviant values, but also by its relation to the process of social mobility. "Underclass" referred to people "stuck at the bottom, removed from the American dream," and therefore left unclear just who composed the underclass, whether its members represented a population disadvantaged by lack of mobility, in which case their numbers would include many poor people untainted by drugs, promiscuity, or criminality, or whether the term should be reserved as a label for behavior. *Time* stressed that the underclass differed from the rest of America. They were aliens, outcasts, alarming strangers in our midst. A confluence of factors—"the weakness of family structure, the presence of competing street values, and the lack of hope amid affluence" had created an American "underclass unique among the world's poor people."[4]

During the next decade, mass media interpretation of the underclass changed very little. In 1986 a *U.S. News and World Report* cover story, "A Nation Apart," reinforced the image of poor people of color in America's inner cities as strangers, aliens in their own land, defined primarily by their deviant values. A "second nation" had emerged within black America, "a nation outside the economic mainstream—a separate culture of have-nots drifting further apart from the basic values of the haves. Its growth is now the central issue in the country's urban centers." Little more than a year later, an article in *Fortune* reinforced the same interpretation. It defined "underclass communities" as "urban knots that threaten to become enclaves of permanent poverty and vice" and impose severe social and economic costs on the rest of American society, leaving business without a workforce sufficiently skilled for twenty-first century jobs. Not so much their poverty or race as their "behavior—their chronic lawlessness, drug use, out-of-wedlock birth, non-work, welfare dependence, and school failure" defined the underclass. "Underclass describes a state of mind and a way of life. It is at least as much a cultural as an economic condition."[5]

Social scientists did relatively little to modify the popular image of a menacing underclass defined by behavior rather than poverty. Indeed, when American social science discovered the underclass, it paid more attention to its behavior than to its origins in the transformations that intensified poverty within the nation's cities. As early as 1969, the eminent sociologist Lee Rainwater criticized this constricted vision. Social scientists, he wrote, had neglected to analyze "the central fact about the American underclass—that it is created by, and its existence is maintained by, the operation of what is in other ways the most successful economic system known to man."[6]

Douglas Glasgow's *Black Underclass* tried to direct debate along the path later urged by Wilson. Glasgow used underclass to frame his research on the young men who had participated in the Watts riot of 1965 in Los Angeles. The emergence of an underclass as a "permanent fixture of our nation's social structure," he wrote, represented "one of the most significant class developments in the past two decades." By underclass, he meant "a permanently entrapped population of poor persons, unused and unwanted, accumulated in various parts of the country." Blacks, disproportionately represented among the poor, remained particularly vulnerable to the magnetic force of the underclass. "Structural factors found in market dynamics and institutional practices, as well as the legacy of racism, produce and then reinforce the cycle of poverty and, in turn, work as a pressure exerting a downward pull toward underclass status."[7]

Glasgow's interpretation of the underclass excluded two themes that would dominate most subsequent discussion and pull interpretations of the underclass away from the structural forces in which he tried to anchor it. First, he wrote only about men. Second, he scarcely mentioned black family structure. In 1980 discussions of black family structure still remained tainted by discredited notions of the culture of poverty and the debacle of the Moynihan report. But in the years that followed, the embargo on writing about the black family quickly gave way to a renewed criticism. As we saw in Chapter 4, writers on poverty associated with the conservative political ascendance reestablished culture and family structure on the agenda of social science and public policy. Confronted with the growth of concentrated poverty, out-of-wedlock births, and alleged welfare dependency, even politically centrist and liberal poverty discourse refocused on family and culture. One result was wide consensus on a narrative explaining the transformation of inner-city social structure and its implications for the growth of a new poverty embodied in the underclass.

In an influential, widely cited 1982 book, *The Underclass*, journalist Ken Auletta drew on the new narrative to broadcast the discovery of the underclass. Auletta defined the underclass as a relatively permanent minority of the poor with "four distinct categories": "(a) the *passive poor*, usually long-term welfare recipients; (b) the *hostile* street criminals who terrorize most cities, and who are often school dropouts and drug addicts; (c) the *hustlers*, who, like street criminals, may not be poor and who earn their livelihood in an underground economy, but rarely commit violent crimes; (d) the *traumatized* drunks, drifters, homeless shopping-bag ladies and released mental patients who frequently roam or collapse on city streets."[8] Auletta remained more concerned with the behavior of the underclass than its origins and focused on strategies that taught its members how to enter the mainstream working world.

Auletta's account fit within the historic tradition of American poverty discourse. Like those who wrote on poverty two centuries before him, Auletta began by separating poor people into two categories and identifying one of them primarily by its deviant behavior. Economic and occupational criteria did not determine class membership. In his definition, the source of stratification lay elsewhere. The underclass was a moral, not a sociological, category. Its members were the new undeserving poor. In the tradition of nineteenth-century social critics who fused crime, poverty, and ignorance into interchangeable eruptions of moral pathology, Auletta linked disparate groups into one class. His definition subsumed women on welfare, street criminals, hustlers, and homeless drunks, drifters, and bag ladies into one interchangeable unit identified not by income or dependence, but by behavior.[9]

Auletta based his book on observations of an experimental work program funded by the Manpower Demonstration Research Corporation of New York City (now officially renamed MDRC). Despite this focus on a work training program, his discussion of poverty subordinated employment and redirected attention to family and behavior. "The struggle to overcome poverty," he wrote, "has entered a new phase, and one of the most significant problems that has emerged is family structure." Auletta traced the role of family structure in the work of E. Franklin Frazier, Kenneth Clark, and Daniel Patrick Moynihan, and recounted the events that drove it from the agendas of social science and public policy. Increasingly, he reported, the black family had begun to reappear as a major topic in discussions about poverty, and even "some leading black officials" had "become less inhibited on the subject." Therefore, when Auletta presented thirteen "facts on poverty and the underclass" that were "undebatable and unavoidable," women and family headed the list. His first fact was, "Poverty has become feminized," and his second, "Whether family dissolution is a cause or an effect of poverty, it unquestionably cannot be overlooked." *None* of his facts identified joblessness as a source of poverty. Rather, his discussion ended by observing that "the face of poverty has been altered" and that Moynihan—whose stress on joblessness he ignored—in his emphasis on the family "was prescient about the changing structure of American poverty."[10]

Most subsequent commentaries on the underclass also used imprecise definitions that stressed family and behavior and rested on implicitly moral conceptions of class structure. Consider the two long and widely read 1986 articles in *The Atlantic* by Nicholas Lemann, who became dean of the Columbia University Graduate School of Journalism in 2003. In "The Origins of the Underclass," Lemann described life in the ghettos as "utterly different" from the American mainstream. Lemann lamented "the bifurcation of black America in which blacks are splitting into a middle class and an underclass that seems likely never to make it. The clearest line between the two groups is family structure." The result was the isolation of the underclass. "As apart as all of black life is, ghetto life is a thousand times more so, with a different language, economy, educational system, and social ethic." The statistic that most accurately captured the distinction was the rise in out-of-wedlock birth, "by far the greatest contributor to the perpetuation of the misery of ghetto life." Lemann revived the culture of poverty thesis to explain underclass behavior because he viewed its "distinctive culture" rather than unemployment or welfare, as "the greatest barrier to progress by the black underclass." His argument, he stressed, "is anthropological, not economic; it emphasizes the power over people's behavior that culture, as opposed to economic incentives, can have."[11] By the early twenty-first century, as we shall see later in this chapter, cutting-edge anti-poverty strategies had turned this interpretation on its head by replacing individually and culturally based theories with a view of poor people as rational actors as responsive to economic incentives as anyone else.

Lemann's idea of *underclass* remained even less precisely defined than Auletta's, but he shared Auletta's behavioral approach. Membership in Chicago's underclass, which contained between 200,000 and 420,000 of the city's 1.2 million blacks, was not simply a function of poverty or blocked mobility. Rather, it resulted from behavior that should not be sanctioned by the well-meaning relativism of liberals or the misplaced racial pride of black militants. Underclass behavior had crystallized into a pathological and self-perpetuating culture on which public policy should launch a major assault.[12]

Lemann misidentified the origins of the underclass as a result of southern blacks' migration into northern cities and of northern middle-class movement to suburbs. "Every aspect of the underclass culture in the ghettos," asserted Lemann, "is directly traceable to roots in the South—and not the South of slavery but the South of a generation ago. In fact, there seems to be a strong correlation between underclass status in the North and a family background in the nascent underclass of the sharecropper South."[13] Unfortunately for Lemann's thesis, all the available data contradicted it. Southern black migrants to northern cities enjoyed higher employment rates, better wages, and less dependency on welfare than northern-born blacks. In the 1960s northern-born blacks, in fact, accounted for increased welfare rates.[14] Women, according to economist Gerald Jaynes, headed fewer than 10 percent of households in the rural south because sharecropping *presupposed* a family labor system. Southern-born blacks did not import an underclass culture to northern cities. Rather, the harsh experiences they encountered—of which the most serious was lack of employment—broke down their culture. Indeed, Jaynes argues, developments within black communities in the 1960s represented a sustained acceleration of trends rather than a new departure.[15] (In contrast to the South, the ability of black women in northern cities to support themselves fueled the increase in female household heads among them, just as improving employment opportunities had a similar effect among white women.)[16]

Along with Auletta, Lemann reinforced the identification of a menacing underclass with unmarried black women. The coincidence of their views with popular stereotypes distracted casual readers from their imprecision, contradictions, and weak evidence, and "underclass" swiftly became the most fashionable term in poverty discourse. Marian Wright Edelman, president of the Children's Defense Fund, highlighted the dangers of an imprecise definition of underclass:

> References to the underclass will add nothing to our understanding of poverty, but will erode public confidence in our ability to do something about it. If applied too loosely to all who have remained persistently poor, the term underclass may reinforce the misguided belief that poverty is the product solely or primarily of individual pathology, ignoring the institutional forces in our society which help perpetuate deprivation. By implying that there are major differences in the character of the poor vis-à-vis the nonpoor, the term undermines our confidence and desire to try to help.[17]

The underclass emerged no more clearly from social science than from journalism. As they summarized their review of the social science literature on the urban underclass, Martha Gephart and Robert Pearson, Social Science Research Council staff associates to the council's urban underclass committee, concluded that definitional and conceptual problems would "undoubtedly continue to confront scholars because there are unlikely to be easily agreed-upon definitions of the underclass available to those who seek to understand it."[18]

Drastically different estimates of the size of the underclass by researchers reflected its imprecise definition. Erol R. Ricketts and Isabel V. Sawhill, using 1980 census data, estimated the underclass at about 500,000. Peter Gottschalk and Sheldon Danziger, two economists who specialized in poverty research, using different types of measures, reached an estimate of less than 1 million in 1984. By contrast, the estimate offered by two other researchers, Patricia Ruggles and William P. Marton, was 8 million for 1985. Two estimates for 1979 by other experts varied between 1.8 million and 4.1 million people.[19]

William Julius Wilson, the Social Science Research Council, and the Underclass

Sociologist William Julius Wilson supplied the major alternative to the narrative account of the growth and persistence of urban poverty based on cultural defect and individual bad behavior. The 1987 publication of his *The Truly Disadvantaged* focused national attention on persistent and concentrated urban poverty and brought more sophistication to the debate over its origins and intensification.[20] Wilson accepted the usefulness of the term *underclass* but redirected its meaning away from culture and toward the economy. He rejected explanations that traced the origins of an underclass to female-headed families and a culture of poverty and tried to point debate toward its roots in black male joblessness.

In 1978 in *The Declining Significance of Race*, Wilson had stressed the emergence of class stratification among blacks. With the constraints of discrimination removed, a black middle class had moved into both better jobs and neighborhoods, its upward mobility no longer hampered by race. The situation of blacks left behind in inner cities, however, had worsened. Wilson's thesis provoked a controversy that centered on his description of improvements in the circumstances of the black middle class and neglected his argument about "the deteriorating conditions of the black underclass."[21]

Wilson had entered an emotionally charged debate about African American progress dominated by two extreme views, one of which claimed the continued dominance of racial discrimination in black experience and the other which proclaimed lessened discrimination accompanied by social and economic progress. In 1992, in *Two Nations: Black and White, Separate, Hostile, Unequal,* political scientist Andrew Hacker claimed that despite the achievements of the civil rights movement, racism remained a powerful force in American life, circumscribing the life chances and defiling the everyday experiences of African Americans. In 1997 historian Stephan Thernstrom and political scientist Abigail Thernstrom answered Hacker with *America in Black and White: One Nation, Indivisible,* which told a story of black progress on several fronts. The attempt to force black social experience into a dichotomous frame took the story in a misleading direction. What, in fact, had happened was that the historic pattern of black inequality rooted in overlapping social, economic, and political oppression and exclusion had shattered during the last half of the twentieth century, replaced by a new configuration of inequality. Inequality now resulted from a cumulative process rather than from a massive and mutually reinforcing, legal and extralegal, public and private pattern of oppression. Instead, it had become subtler, working its way through a series of screens that from childhood onward filtered African Americans into more or less promising situations. The process resulted in a new African American social structure with distinct properties. First was differentiation: the production of individual social mobility and the formation of a black middle class and, at the same time, of entrenched black poverty and joblessness. The second feature of this new social structure was a growing gender gap. Black women fared far better than black men. By 2000, with education held constant, black women had erased their earnings gap with white women, and they had received more education and entered better jobs than black men. Third, a huge share of black men remained outside the regular labor force, many chronically jobless, while a disproportionate share were incarcerated. Fourth, public and quasi-public employment (service sector jobs in private programs and agencies funded with public money) provided the backbone of the emergent black middle class. They had become the distinctive African American occupational niche, in 2000, for instance, employing 43 percent of African American women. This reliance on the public sector built African American progress on a fragile foundation, vulnerable to cutbacks in public sector spending, as happened with the Great Recession that began in 2008 and resulted in huge public sector job losses.[22]

Incorrectly labeled a conservative, Wilson, who thought himself a Social Democrat, had been trapped by the misleading either/or debate over black progress. As a result, he decided to focus on the ghetto underclass and spell out the policy implications of his thesis. The first result was *The Truly Disadvantaged*, followed by other books developing his argument about the origins and importance of joblessness and accompanied by a major research project.[23] Wilson argued that neutral terms, such as lower class or working class, failed to address the recent transformations within American cities that resulted in dramatic increases in concentrated poverty. The exodus of the black middle and working class left neighborhoods to the most disadvantaged, a "heterogeneous grouping of families and individuals who are outside the mainstream of the American occupational system." These included "individuals who lack training and skills and either experience long-term unemployment or are not members of the labor force, individuals who are engaged in street crime and other forms of aberrant behavior, and families that experience long-term spells of poverty and/or welfare dependency." This, for Wilson, was the underclass. As he used it, underclass referred to "the groups that have been left behind" and were as a consequence "collectively different from those that lived in these neighborhoods in earlier years."[24]

Wilson's definition of the underclass incorporated geography, occupation, behavior, and history. As such, it was an alternative to the conservative narrative of urban poverty. It was geographical because it assigned a key role to social concentration within a distinct territory. It identified members of the underclass by their existence outside the mainstream of the "American occupational system." It stressed the development of behaviors at variance with "mainstream patterns and norms," and it rested on a version of recent history that viewed the underclass as unprecedented.[25] As Wilson realized, *The Truly Disadvantaged* should be read as a hypothesis about inner-city poverty based on the incomplete evidence available for its analysis. Indeed, he mounted a major research project, The Chicago Urban Poverty and Family Life Project, to gather data with which to test his ideas.[26]

To Wilson, the sources of the underclass were both demographic and economic. Drawing on the work of Harvard sociologist Stanley Lieberson, he argued that vast migrations of blacks to cities aroused latent racial consciousness and spurred the creation of barriers to housing and employment. This growing black central city population was "relatively young," and "youth is not only a factor in crime; it is also associated with out-of-wedlock births, female-headed homes, and welfare dependency." Thus, the increase in the number of young people by itself explains much of what is "awry in the inner city."[27] However, changes in urban economic structure that reduced the demand for unskilled labor contributed more than demography to the creation of the underclass. Earlier immigrants entered cities when manufacturing was expanding and the demand for skilled and semiskilled labor was growing. Blacks now confronted the shift away from a manufacturing to a service economy. As blue-collar jobs dwindled, the service jobs that replaced them demanded high educational qualifications, or, at the other extreme, paid little and offered minimal career opportunity. On almost every measure of the labor market, Wilson pointed out, the economic position of blacks had deteriorated. So serious had joblessness among black youths become that "Only a minority of noninstitutionalized black youth are employed."[28]

Poverty concentration further exacerbated the impact of age structure and joblessness. From 1970 to 1980, population in the nation's fifty largest cities rose by 12 percent while the number of persons living in poverty areas increased by more than 20 percent and the black population in "extreme-poverty" neighborhoods soared by 148 percent compared to a 24-percent rise among whites. This "growth of the high- and extreme-poverty areas," observed Wilson, "epitomizes the social transformation of the inner city."[29]

The migration of middle- and working-class families out of many ghetto neighborhoods removed a key "social buffer" that might have deflected the full impact of prolonged and increasing joblessness on behavior. When inner city neighborhoods were more socially diverse, their basic institutions (churches, schools, stores, recreational facilities) remained viable, and, by their presence, mainstream role models nurtured "the perception that education is meaningful, that steady employment is a viable alternative to welfare, that family stability is the norm, not the exception."[30] Without them, social isolation—that is, "the lack of contact or sustained interaction with individuals and institutions that represent mainstream society"—has increased, with serious consequences. Because it left people outside job networks and failed to develop behavior essential for successful work experience, it exacerbated the difficulty of finding jobs. Due to its relation to attitudes and behavior, social isolation led Wilson to emphasize culture. But unlike earlier writers on the culture of poverty, he defined culture as "a response to social structural constraints and opportunities."[31]

Wilson pointed out that American poverty discourse, both liberal and conservative, had neglected jobs, which were the key to unlocking opportunities and freeing the underclass from ghetto neighborhoods. Debate had focused, instead, on ameliorating the condition of disadvantaged people with income supports and social services and on eradicating the cultural traits that retard their economic progress. As a result, female-headed families remained more central to the poverty debate than good jobs. Indeed, at the time, little poverty discourse focused on the working poor or on the poverty rate among white adult males, which had increased dramatically, in contrast to the rate among female household heads, which had remained nearly static.

How should we explain the neglect of so transparently critical a factor as jobs? Although conservatives had misread and made selected use of economic data, liberals also had been negligent. Part of the reason was historic. Poverty debate followed well-worn grooves, focusing on the three historic preoccupations (classifying poor people, debating the effects of welfare on their behavior, and defining the limits of social obligation) that pulled attention away from the forces that generated poverty. By slighting the unavailability of work, poverty discourse reinforced the hostility to working-age men almost always reflected in relief policy. The assumption that any able-bodied man could find work underlay the vicious war against tramps in the late nineteenth century, the consignment of men to poorhouses, and the reluctance of welfare administrators and reformers to grant them outdoor relief. Except for the Great Depression of the 1930s, even abundant evidence of job scarcity failed to shake the belief that men were unemployed because they were lazy or incompetent. Poverty discourse that focused on behavior echoed and reinforced these old stereotypes and nourished popular perceptions about poor people that influenced policy directions chosen by politicians. Behavioral and cultural explanations of poverty also are least threatening. They disturb fewest interests because they do not require income redistribution or sharing power or other resources.

In 1987 the Rockefeller Foundation asked the Social Science Research Council to consider creating a Committee on the Urban Underclass. The new committee tried to stimulate research through a five-year $6 million program of fellowships and scholarships (undergraduate, graduate, and postdoctoral) and a set of research planning activities. The activities of the SSRC Committee on the Urban Underclass helped stimulate interest in underclass issues among social scientists and revive research on urban poverty, which had languished since the mid-1970s. The key issues generated by Wilson's work, largely, though not wholly, dominated the committee's early deliberations.[32] "The SSRC project," reports historian Alice O'Connor, "underwrote interdisciplinary working groups, conferences, volumes, and more than one hundred undergraduate, pre- and postdoctoral fellows, all under the direction of a committee of well-known poverty researchers and a professional staff."[33]

Despite its title, the SSRC Committee on the Urban Underclass did not adopt an official definition of *underclass*. Rather, it defined its working focus as "persistent and concentrated urban poverty." Nor did other urban researchers adopt a standard definition. Indeed, many, including some members of the committee, "much to the dismay of the Rockefeller Foundation," objected to the term. Debate over the term "underclass" constituted only one of the tensions running through the committee's five-year life. Other tensions included the content and method of underclass research. The SSRC committee had proposed avoiding an exclusive commitment to either quantitative research or neoclassical economic models and had promised to encourage new entrants to the poverty research field. "Nevertheless, tensions quickly arose over perceptions of what one participant called a 'pecking order' in Committee appointments, leadership, and funding decisions that favored 'quantitative, analytic, ideally economistic rational choice models' over qualitative, contextual, or structural research." Critics asked pointed and embarrassing questions. "Where... was the research on urban politics and policy? Why the continued emphasis on 'social isolation,' 'disorganization,' and 'family dysfunction' when ethnographic research had shown far more diversity and agency in 'underclass' neighborhoods than that? Why not focus research on changes in neighborhood and labor market institutions rather than so exclusively on the individual outcomes they produced? Why neglect education, housing, and homelessness, even though all had been hotspots in recent debates?"[34]

Two other tensions ran through the Committee's history. One focused on gender and race. To some extent, these were concerns about the Committee's membership and governance, but, even more, they focused "on the failure to make gender and race central issues for substantive research." Only late in the Committee's history "did gender and racial segmentation begin to get more explicit recognition." Instead, for the most part, gender and race differences were treated as variables accounted for by "such supposedly 'neutral' measures of disadvantage as skill, education, family background, and space—as if these disadvantages were somehow independent of the structural restrictions experienced by women and nonwhites." Nonetheless, an external evaluation concluded that the Committee had reduced "the risk of studying the black family and deviance of blacks" even as it deemphasized race as a structural barrier.[35] As O'Connor concluded, in the post-civil rights 1980s, this "was in itself a statement of considerable ideological and political significance."[36]

The Committee focused most directly on race in its fellowship and workshop programs, which were its most successful activities. The summer dissertation workshops for minority graduate students constructed professional networks and built peer and mentoring relationships of lasting value. The dissertation fellowship program introduced a wider array of disciplines, theoretical perspectives, and topics to urban poverty research. The sponsorship of undergraduate courses on poverty—while a small program—provided an exciting, high-quality induction into poverty research. The Committee also broadened its focus by spinning off relatively autonomous workshops and its sponsorship of the Multi-City Study of Urban Inequality, "an interdisciplinary study of labor markets, residential segregation, and racial attitudes that moved research beyond boundaries of poor neighborhoods to the metropolitan area while making the intersection between economic, geographic, and racial barriers an explicit focus of empirical research."[37]

The second tension concerned the relation between research and policy, or the "kind of knowledge that mattered most in understanding, and changing, the plight of the urban poor." Essentially, there were three groups of players: academic researchers, guardians of "basic" or "scientific" knowledge; policy shops like MDRC and the Urban Institute, practitioners of "applied" or "policy-relevant" research; and "ground-level practitioners" who ran local action programs also funded by the Rockefeller Foundation in its Community Planning and Action Program and whose research questions grew out of experience living and working in urban communities.[38] These three sets of players by and large spoke past each other, and the Rockefeller Foundation's attempts to bring them into dialogue largely failed—much to the Foundation's frustration. This failure undoubtedly contributed to the Foundation's decision to terminate the Committee earlier than expected. In January 1991, recounts O'Connor, the Rockefeller Foundation "expressed its dissatisfaction" by telling the SSRC's Underclass Committee "that funding would be terminated sooner than expected—after five-years, rather than what had earlier been held out as a possible ten-year span of annual grants."[39]

In his August 1990 presidential address to the American Sociological Association, Wilson, who had advocated the usefulness and objective foundation of *underclass*, recommended its abandonment by researchers.[40] Wilson observed the "spate of studies highly critical of the use of the term 'underclass' [that had] accompanied the increased research activity on the inner-city ghetto. The general view is that the term ought to be rejected because it has become a code word for inner-city blacks, has enabled journalists to focus on unflattering behavior in the ghetto, and has no scientific usefulness." Herbert Gans, continued Wilson, had offered "the most important, powerful, and representative critique of the concept" as "a value-laden, increasingly pejorative term that seems to be becoming the newest buzzword for the *undeserving* poor." Wilson worried that the controversy swirling around the use of underclass would distract attention from the important issues in poverty research. "In order to keep us focused on research issues, I will substitute the term 'ghetto poor' for the term 'underclass'...."[41]

Even Charles Murray confirmed the death of the underclass. Murray, reported a national news service, "somberly summed up his views on why media concern over single parenthood seems to have declined even while it hits a record level nationally, saying it is because the 'underclass has dropped out of sight—because it's no longer in our face. They don't bother us like they used to.' "[42]

The underclass era had ended.

Urban Poverty After the Underclass: African American Families, Black Men, and the Homeless

The fall of "underclass" did not mean that urban poverty had gone away. Indeed, explaining and responding to the poverty of African Americans and, increasingly, of new immigrants in the nation's cities, remained topics of fierce debate and controversy. Only, no key organizing concept for discussions of poverty replaced "underclass." Instead, the language of debate often marginalized discussions of poverty itself, instead translating poverty into other issues. The three major problem areas were the African American family, now restored as a legitimate object for social science, policy, and public criticism; African American men suffering high rates of chronic joblessness, excoriated as absent fathers, and locked up as criminals; and the homeless, visible reminders of poverty's stubborn persistence, the nation's failure to solve its perennial low-income housing crisis, and its inability to completely sanitize the streets of revitalized city centers. By the way in which they were treated—if not in so many words—nonworking single minority mothers, out of work black men, and the homeless constituted the core of the undeserving poor now supplemented by undocumented immigrants who drained the public fisc, raised crime rates, and undermined American culture—never mind that these were illusions that ignored how the presence of immigrants usually lowered crime rates, frequently revived faltering municipal economies, and facilitated the performance of essential work.

The rehabilitation of Daniel Patrick Moynihan signified the phoenix-like rise of the black family as an object of study and criticism. Moynihan's inflammatory language in his infamous 1965 report *The Negro Family: The Case for National Action*, as we have seen in Chapter 1, helped drive discussion of black families off the agenda of public discussion. The work of the SSRC underclass committee, the conservative ascendance with its focus on the culture and behavior of the poor, the panic over welfare dependence, the growing disconnect between marriage and parenthood: all fueled and legitimated renewed attention directed to black and other minority families for their failures at socialization and contributions to low educational achievement, crime, lagging work ethic, and welfare dependence. The mantra became "Moynihan was right." By this, commentators meant that his identification of out-of-wedlock births as an escalating and dangerous phenomenon had been prescient, but they omitted his excoriation of the impact of black matriarchy on the emasculation of black men, an idea still too hot to handle. For example, distinguished historian of poverty and public policy James Patterson, in his 2010 *Freedom Is Not Enough*, claimed:

> ... by the late 1970s, widespread rejection by liberal scholars of *The Negro Family* had not only perpetuated the great silence Moynihan had lamented in the late 1960s, it had also hardened into an orthodoxy that virtually excused lower-class black people from much if any responsibility for their own difficulties and that discouraged white scholars, fearing to be pilloried as racists, from raising the subject of black family problems.[43]

"Though savaged by many liberal academics at the time," reported a *New York Times* obituary, Moynihan's report "is now generally regarded as 'an important and prophetic document,' in the words of Prof. William Julius Wilson of Harvard." Recounting the furor following Moynihan's report, the conservative *Washington Times* observed, "It was not until the 1990s that elite opinion accepted Mr. Moynihan's conclusions, influencing the 1996 Welfare Reform Act although the New York senator voted against that bill."[44] Political commentator George Will observed, "For calling attention, four decades ago, to the crisis of the African-American family—26 percent of children were being born out of wedlock—he was denounced as a racist by lesser liberals. Today the percentage among all Americans is 33, among African-Americans 69, and family disintegration, meaning absent fathers, is recognized as the most powerful predictor of most social pathologies."[45]

Criticism of African American families reflected more general anxieties about marriage and family in America based on the growth of out-of-wedlock births. Peter Edelman summarizes the statistics:

> Between 1970 and 2009, the percentage of families headed by women with children under eighteen doubled—from 12.7 to 25.4 percent. The percentage of African American families with children of that same age that were headed by women went from 37.1 percent in 1971...to 52.7 percent in 2009. Most of these increases occurred during the 1970s, simultaneously with the wave of changes in the economy.[46]

Although the figures for out-of-wedlock births have historically been higher among African Americans, the "unmarried birth rate among African American women," Edelman points out, "has actually decreased since 1970" while the white and Hispanic rates increased, meaning that the "growth in the rate of unmarried births in the United States over the past thirty years is almost entirely attributable to changes among whites and Hispanics."[47] The teenage birth rate also has gone down, most steeply among African Americans—"from one hundred per thousand African American teens to fifty-four per thousand in 2010," an astounding decline in just twenty years.[48] This sharp decline likely results from the educational and occupational gains of African American women in the same period.[49]

What worries observers of family trends most is the disassociation of marriage and parenthood. Between 1950 and 2000, for example, the proportion of black twenty-five-year-old women who had married plummeted from 82 percent to 28 percent, but in both years half of them had children living at home. Trends among white women went in the same direction, although less dramatically.[50] In 2009, Edelman reports, "72.3 percent of African American children were born outside of marriage, compared to 24 percent in 1965. The trend among Hispanics was from 37 percent to 42 percent over the same period, and among whites was from 6 percent to 24 percent."[51] Social scientists worry that these trends will lead to the reproduction of inequality while conservative social critics predict that they signify the accelerating moral unraveling of American society and culture. "Regardless of the reasons," writes Edelman, "the growth in the number of female-headed families with children is a significant cause of the increase in child poverty....The percentage of poor children under eighteen who lived in female-headed families rose from 24.1 in 1959 to 55 in 2010."[52] Researchers Sara McLanahan and Christine Percheski point out that a substantial body of research shows that "living apart from a biological parent (typically the father) is associated with a host of negative outcomes that are expected to affect children's future life chances or ability to move up the income ladder." These children "score lower on standardized tests, report poorer grades, and view themselves as having less academic potential than children who grow up with both biological parents. Most importantly, they are also more likely to drop out of high school, less likely to attend college, and less likely to graduate from college." They also "experience a higher prevalence of behavioral and psychological problems.... [and] are more likely to have sex at an early age" and more likely to live in poverty as adults.[53] The conservative Heritage Foundation's Charles A. Donovan stressed the menace to the nation. He warned that current family trends are leading to the Europeanization of America. "Buffeted by changing sexual mores, fraying family ties, and burgeoning welfare states that discourage family formation, marriage is in retreat in American culture and following a European pattern." The situation, according to Donovan, is dire. "As stark as the record of out-of-wedlock birthrate and cohabitation figures are for the United States, European statistics suggest that marital breakdown could increase by up to 50 percent over the next decade. No nation can afford to be neutral about the substantial impact that such dislocation imposes on the well-being of future generations and the resulting effects of spurring the growth of government and slowing the economy."[54]

Even though critics paid obeisance to trends that cut across classes, they focused most sharply on poor people, including African Americans and, to some extent, Hispanics, who occupied the far end of the continuum. However, in his 2012 book *Coming Apart*, Charles Murray returned to the theme of family disintegration as a source of social pathology, only this time concentrating exclusively on whites. Murray divided white America into two classes, a "New Upper Class" and a "New Lower Class," represented, respectively, by affluent Belmont,

Massachusetts, and poor Fishtown, a Philadelphia neighborhood. Although he satirized the alleged cultural pretensions of the new upper class, he based his Cassandra-like prophecies about the imminent cultural and social unraveling of America on the new lower class, with its rejection of the "founding virtues" of marriage, industriousness, honesty, and religiosity. "Over the last century," he lamented, "marriage has become the fault line dividing American classes." This decline of marriage among the lower class underlay the erosion of the other founding virtues and fueled the disintegration of the nation. Deeply pessimistic, *Coming Apart* purports to open a window on America's class-defined dystopian future from which there is scant hope of escape.[55]

The concern with promoting marriage among the poor, which crossed political boundaries, found its way into national policy in provisions of the 1996 Welfare Reform Bill and its reauthorization by the Deficit Reduction Act of 2005, signed into law by President Bush in February 2006. The reauthorization extended and expanded the original legislation, which, point out McLanahan and Percheski, "allowed states to use part of their block grants to promote marriage and two-parent families." Included in the 2005 bill was $100 million a year for programs to increase "healthy marriage." This "'new marriage initiative' is based on the assumptions that (1) children would be better off if they were raised by two, married, biological parents; (2) we know how to increase healthy marriage among low-income parents; and (3) government has a legitimate role in trying to influence parents' marital behavior." All three of these assumptions, McLanahan and Percheski observe, remain "controversial among researchers as well as advocates."[56] They are testimony to ideology more than research.

Nonscholarly writers like Murray seized on demographic trends and the results of social science research to revive cultural explanations of poverty and refurbish images of the undeserving poor rooted in feckless, immoral behaviors. They ignored the roots of inner-city poverty in the economic, demographic, and spatial transformations, described in Chapter 4, which accentuated inequality, poverty, and isolation. They also ignored a body of ethnographic and qualitative research that showed the importance of marriage as an ideal among poor women and the heroic efforts they make to raise families with almost no money. Kathryn Edin and Maria Kefalas interviewed 162 low-income single mothers in eight Philadelphia and Camden, NJ, marginal neighbor-hoods. They found that, "While the poor women we interviewed saw marriage as a luxury, something they aspired to but feared they might never achieve, they judged children to be a necessity, an absolutely essential part of a young woman's life, the chief source of identity and meaning."[57] Family critics evaded, as well, the research that traced low marriage rates among black women to the lack of marriageable men[58]—a situation with roots in the joblessness and incarceration to be discussed later in this chapter. They also missed the educational aspirations evident in responses to lotteries for admission to selective and charter schools.[59] In short, conservative writers on family twisted demography to fit a politics of fear and contempt that supported cut-backs in public support and the application of punitive sanctions.

Trends in family structure represent points on a continuum, not a sharp break between classes or ethnicity. They show that, like it or not, the meaning of family has been changing. Between 1960 and 2000, traditional families—married couples with children—dropped from about 45 to 25 percent of all households. They were replaced, as we have seen, by increases in nonfamily households (young unmarried people without relatives living alone or together); female-headed families with children; and empty-nesters.[60] How to respond to this changed fam-ily landscape—characteristic of suburbs as well as cities—is the ques-tion. One way is through paternalistic policies that punish unwelcome behavior and try to force a return to an older idea of normative family patterns through sanctions and legislation. Another is to recognize that new meanings and configurations of family have emerged and will be around for a long time and to figure out ways to help all people—regardless of the structure of the families in which they live—realize comfortable and productive lives.

The conflation of gender, race, and welfare dependence transformed young black women living by themselves with their children into the iconic face of urban poverty. They remain the primary objects of pov-erty research, legislation, and both sympathy and opprobrium. Young black men remain shadowy figures, less well known, more menacing, shut out from most welfare benefits, falling behind black women in education and work, discussed more often in terms of crime than pov-erty. "Strongly identified with violent criminality by skin color alone," observes sociologist Elijah Anderson, "the anonymous young black male in public is often viewed first and foremost with fear and suspicion, his counter-claims to propriety, decency, and law-abidingness notwithstanding."[61] "The current view of black men," writes Cornel West, "has something to do with the fact that we have been living for forty years in an ice age where it is fashionable to be indifferent to poor people suffering, the most vulnerable citizens suffering. Young black men are a significant slice of the most vulnerable, so they are rendered invisible."[62] Although the linked problems of joblessness and discrimination have a long history, recognized by writers from W. E. B. Du Bois to Daniel Patrick Moynihan to William Julius Wilson, the situation of black men has failed to break through the wall of isolation, fear, and contempt that has separated them from constructive public responses to the structural sources of their joblessness and poverty. So invisible have black men become, continues West, "that the dilapidated housing, the disgraceful school systems, the lack of access to jobs that pay a living wage, the underemployment and lack of employment that afflict young men in the inner city—all these have now become part of the norm."[63]

Once again, it was the work of William Julius Wilson, as have seen, that forced the situation of black men onto the public agenda where a common trope has become the "crisis" of the black male, a figure of speech compounding danger and sympathy. After Wilson, the most important writer on black males has been sociologist Elijah Anderson. "Living in areas of concentrated ghetto poverty, still shadowed by the legacy of slavery and second-class citizenship, too many black men," writes Anderson, "are trapped in a horrific cycle that includes active discrimination, unemployment, poverty, crime, prison, and early death." In a bid for respect, argues Anderson, young black men react to the stereotypes they confront by adopting a "consciously offputting, or 'thuggish'" self-presentation whose unintended consequence gives "potential employers reason to discriminate in favor of less threatening workers—often from the pool of recent immigrants, who appear clean-cut, hard-working, and willing to work for less and without the benefits and protections expected by the ghetto male."[64] Anderson roots the contemporary situation of black males in the intersection of economic and urban transformation with racial discrimination, which left the inner-city black community sunk "into entrenched structural poverty," turning, of necessity, to a "thriving, irregular, and often illegal economy" for survival. One result was the trade in crack cocaine and the "violent crimes perpetrated by desperate addicts and greedy dealers," which "reinforced deeply negative images of the black urban ghetto." This history set the stage for the current scene. "The social costs of impoverishment fell particularly hard on the heads of the young black men who were feared by the rest of society and left to fend for themselves by white authorities. In his alienation and use of violence, the contemporary poor young black male is a new social type peculiar to postindustrial urban America. This young man is in profound crisis." From childhood onward, he walks a path "from the community to prison or cemetery, or at least to a life of trouble characterized by unemployment, discrimination, and participation in . . . an oppositional culture."[65] For many black men, the "reality of daily life . . . in areas of concentrated poverty revolves around simply meeting the challenge of 'staying alive.' "[66]

Unfortunately, Anderson did not exaggerate the perilous state of young black men in inner cities. Economist Harry J. Holzer, for one, laid out the steady deterioration in the employment situation of young black men since Moynihan made it the centerpiece of his 1965 report on the black family.[67] The statistics are terrible. The proportion of twenty-one- to twenty-five-year-old African American men not in the labor force escalated from 9 percent in 1940 to 27 percent in 1990 and 34 percent in 2000.[68] The downward trend in employment, Holzer points out, even worsened in the 1990s, when the economy was strong and when the employment situation of young black women improved dramatically.[69] The downward employment trend occurred among older black men as well. In 2000 more than one in four aged forty-one to fifty remained out of the labor force. As a result, more than twice as many black as white men in their prime working years remained out of the regular labor force. One reason so many black men were out of the labor force is that they were in prison. The number of inmates in federal and state prisons increased 82 percent in just the decade between 1990 and 2000—reaching 1,355,748 on June 30, 2002. Most of this increase—57 percent—reflected mandatory sentences for drug offenders; it bore no relation whatsoever to actual crime rates. America's rate of incarceration was the highest in the world. Incarceration bore down hard on African American men. In the last decade of the twentieth century, the proportion of imprisoned black twenty-six- to thirty-year-olds, for example, increased by a third, from 9 to 12 percent, while 49 percent of prisoners compared to 13 percent of the overall population was black. Every day one of three black men in their twenties "is under some form of criminal justice supervision....either in prison or jail or on probation or parole." By and large, they exit prison lacking job skills, unattractive to employers, and headed for poverty, the irregular labor market, and, too often, crime and repeat incarceration.[70] Employers, surveys show, remain reluctant to hire young black men, who face discrimination in a labor market where they also often lack the requisite skills. To make matters worse, Holzer argues, their wages have deteriorated more than the wages of other groups. The "deterioration of wage opportunities for black men occurred on top of a lengthy list of continuing disadvantages in the labor market"—discrimination, lack of skills, employer hostility to the formerly incarcerated—that pushed them beyond the point where the limited jobs available seemed worth taking.[71]

Black men in America's inner cities also died young. A famous article by two researchers "estimated that in 1980 Black male youths in Harlem, New York City, were less likely to survive to age 65 than were male youths in Bangladesh." In Harlem, mortality rates in 1980 for women between the ages of twenty-five and thirty-four, and for men aged thirty-five to forty-four, were *six* times higher than for white women and men nationally. Between 1980 and 1990, this situation grew worse, until it began to improve in the century's last decade. Still, urban blacks died younger. "For example," write researcher Arline Geronimus and her colleagues in the conclusion to an update of the 1980 mortality study, "16-year-old Black males residing in urban locales in 2000 had only a 50 percent to 62 percent chance of surviving to the age of 65 years" compared to a nationwide probability of 80 percent for whites. Black mortality declined in the 1990s primarily on account of a drop in homicides. Death rates from circulatory disease and cancer, the other two main causes of death, remained about the same, failing to follow a decline among whites and signaling the enduring black deficit in health.[72]

Joblessness, incarceration, poor health and early death: all go a long way toward explaining the persistence of poverty among inner-city black men and the dearth of "marriageable" men for young black women. Another line of criticism, however, takes a harsher view. Critics—largely from within the black community—excoriate black men for a lack of responsibility as husbands and fathers. For them, the twin crises of black males and black families intertwine. They have little patience with explanations that excuse or explain the failure of black men to marry and support the mothers of their children. The most famous—and to some, notorious—exhortation to black men to step up and accept responsibility was actor Bill Cosby's May 17, 2004, speech commemorating the fiftieth anniversary of the Supreme Court's *Brown v. Board of Education* decision declaring racial segregation in schools unconstitutional. A heroic generation had opened hitherto closed doors to African Americans, but "in our cities and public schools, we have 50 percent drop out. In our own neighborhood, we have men in prison. No longer is a person embarrassed because they're pregnant without a husband. No longer is a boy considered an embarrassment if he tries to run away from being the father of the unmarried child...."[73]

Not surprisingly, Cosby encountered sharp criticism. Political scientist Michael Eric Dyson, for instance, responded with a book, *Is Bill Cosby Right (Or Has The Black Middle Class Lost Its Mind?)*. "Cosby's beliefs," according to Dyson, "are most notably espoused by the *Afristocracy*: upper-middle-class blacks and the black elite who rain down fire and brimstone upon poor blacks for their deviance and pathology, and for their lack of couth and culture.... I will dissect Cosby's flawed logic, reveal the thin descriptive web he weaves to characterize the poor, and address the complex dimensions of the problems he bitterly broaches."[74] Still, the theme that black men need to accept more family responsibility remains a strong current within the black community—argued most notably by President Barack Obama. Obama inaugurated a Father's Day weekend with a series of events aimed at beginning "a national conversation on responsible fatherhoods and healthy families," reported the White House. A reporter writing about the event pointed out Obama's "fixation on responsible fatherhood" throughout his political career. Obama made fatherhood "one of the four major, coequal priorities of [his] revamped Office of Faith-based and Neighborhood Partnerships." As a candidate "who had only just won the Democratic nomination for president," Obama "delivered an admonishing, scripture-laded, pro-parenting Sunday sermon at the Apostolic Church of God in Chicago." He told parishioners: "If we are honest with ourselves, we'll admit that...too many fathers are also missing—missing from too many lives and too many homes. They have abandoned their responsibilities, acting like boys instead of men. And the foundations of our families are weaker because of it." Obama, observed the reporter, stood in a long line of black leaders who had "been urging responsible fatherhood and stand-up-straight living for as long as there have been black pulpits to preach from." But his status as "first father" gave the message unprecedented prominence—with results that remained to be seen.[75] Although no one can argue with responsible fatherhood as a goal, the danger is that without action to change the conditions that result in black joblessness and excessive incarceration, exhortations can end up nothing more than empty rhetoric or, at worst, words that blame the victim and divert attention from the political economy of poverty to the deficiencies of poor people.

After the end of the "underclass" era, nonworking single minority mothers and out-of-work black men made up two groups at the core of the undeserving poor—identifiable by their treatment in public policy as much as by public rhetoric. A third group within the urban poor, often overlapping with the other two, was the homeless, who became a public problem in the 1980s. The homeless embody the clash between urban transformation and rightward moving public policies. Huddled over steam vents, in doorways, on the benches of subway and train stations, they remind us of the enduring presence of poverty and inequality. They bear the most visible cost of the transformation of American cities by urban renewal, gentrification, and downtown revitalization; of the dismantling of the old industrial economy; and of the government war on dependence. They show that the richest and most powerful nation in the world cannot provide all its citizens with a decent and secure place in which to live. The large number of families among them drive home the awful fact that among industrialized countries, only in America is childhood the age of greatest poverty.

The emergence of homelessness as a public problem reflected, first, its visibility. Homelessness did not take place in private, nor did it confine itself to ghetto areas where affluent persons rarely traveled. On the contrary, it is defined by its public nature. Because homelessness manifests itself in public spaces, its spectacular increase altered urban topography. As they appropriated spaces in railroad stations, subways, lobbies, and doorways, homeless people redefined urban space. They might not be helped, but they could not be ignored.

For historian Mark J. Stern, it was the 1981 consent decree in New York City's Callahan case that initially turned homelessness into a public problem. "The decree committed the city to provide clean and safe shelter for every homeless man and woman who sought it and set standards against overcrowding in shelters." National political action reinforced events in New York City, as a coalition formed at the Democratic Convention organized demonstrations; two books, *Shopping Bag Ladies* by Ann Marie Rousseau and *Private Lives, Public Spaces* by Ellen Baxter and Kim Hopper, focused the attention of the public on the issue, and the harsh winter of 1981–1982 finally forced it to the forefront of public consciousness.[76]

In its response to homelessness, however, the administration of President Ronald Reagan proved slow off the mark. The first major federal legislation, The Stewart B. McKinney Homeless Assistance Act, passed by Congress only in 1987, defines a homeless person as "one who lacks a fixed nighttime residence or whose nighttime residence is a temporary shelter, welfare hotel, transitional housing for the mentally ill, or any public and private place not designed as a sleeping accommodation for human beings." HUD has tried to fill in the definition's ambiguities; in 2011 it issued a new definition dividing the homeless into four categories.[77] At the boundaries, even the new definition inevitably required interpretation because, as we have seen with other issues, the lines between categories never are wholly clear. Three types of homeless persons pose distinct challenges for policy. The chronically homeless constitute about 11 percent of the population of homeless shelters, which they use as long-term housing, and occupy half the beds. Transitional homeless persons stay in shelters only for a day or two. They make up about 80 percent of the individuals who will use a shelter at some point but account for only about a third of shelter days. Between the two, blurring category boundaries, are the episodic homeless, representing about 9 percent of persons using shelters and

17 percent of total shelter days. Among shelter residents, families tend to stay about twice as long as homeless individuals.[78]

The discovery of homelessness illustrates an important theme in writing about poverty in America—what sociologist Michele Dauber labels *aggregation* and *iconization*, subsuming individual heterogeneity into a mass whose suffering results from a "single, overarching cause" and "rendering individuals as representatives of a type—victims of circumstance—rather than as individuals with personal biographies."[79] When they first came into public view, the homeless, as Stern argued, were for a short time the new deserving poor. He located their appeal in the capacity of homelessness to reestablish the "gift relationship" as the basis of public and private charity. Charity's historic role extended beyond the alleviation of poverty; it served to bind classes together and to reinforce social relations based on deference and obligation. In his great study of poverty in late nineteenth-century London, Gareth Stedman Jones wrote: "To give, from whatever motives, generally imposes an obligation upon the receiver. In order to receive one must behave in an acceptable manner, if only by expressing gratitude and humiliation." Responses to homelessness reflected the appeal of the gift relationship.[80] Plans for fighting homelessness, as Stern notes, initially tried to reestablish "the bond between giver and recipient" through voluntary rather than state action. Discourse on the homeless stressed "their almost saintlike spirits" and "docility and gratitude," rather than "anger and suspicion."[81]

The framing of homelessness as a problem for charity posed dilemmas for policy. First, it frustrated solutions to long-term problems because voluntarism could not abolish homelessness. Not only did the appropriation of homelessness as a charity deflect attention away from its potential to energize a broader attack on poverty, it also inhibited direct, aggressive action by poor people on their own behalf. As the homeless organized unions, pressed their demands in demonstrations, and formed coalitions with other poor people, their special appeal faded, and single homeless men, if not families, slipped again into the ranks of the undeserving poor.[82] Homelessness, according to sociologist Teresa Gowan, became subdivided into three specific discourses: "*sin-talk, sick-talk,* and *system-talk,*" each of which reflected a particular construction of poverty: "*moral, therapeutic, and systemic.*"

Each discourse on homelessness shares with its related construction of poverty the same fundamental strategies for managing the disruly poor. The moral construction and sin-talk are primarily tied into strategies of *exclusion* and *punishment* (although there is also the possibility of *redemption* for the more deserving); the therapeutic construction and sick-talk look to *treatment*; and the systemic construction and system talk urge *social regulation* or even *transformation*.[83]

Homelessness illustrates what legal scholar Martha Minow has called the dilemma of difference. For it is a social category, not a defining quality of persons. Those poor people with nowhere to live vary greatly in their characteristics. To collapse them into one category by abstracting one aspect of their lives is to subordinate their individuality; to mark them as different, and because they need help, as inferior to the rest of us; and to leave them with a label that can turn as quickly into a stigma as into a plea for help. Yet without the creation of this category, public sympathy on behalf of those poor people included within it would not have swelled, many fewer volunteers would have responded, and poor people would have suffered even more.[84] This dilemma of difference cuts across many areas of public life—not just homelessness—where the aggregation of unlike individuals into one category captures public attention. The question is whether, in the long run, it does more harm than good because, as with homelessness, sympathy can turn into contempt as the part comes to stand for the whole and aggregation obscures the discriminations necessary for effective policy.

Homelessness is not a new problem in America. But the homelessness that surfaced as a public problem in the 1980s and escalated in the following decades differed from older patterns of homelessness in important ways. "This contemporary version of homelessness," write homelessness experts Dennis Culhane and Stephen Metraux, "is distinctly different from the earlier 'skid row' homelessness that was documented by sociologists in the 1950s and 1960s. The 'skid row' homeless population was defined primarily by their residence in transient housing, usually confined to a particular area of central cities. In contrast, the new homelessness has had no fixed spatial dimensions, and is defined by an outright lack of private accommodations. Put simply, the contemporary homeless have faced much more dispersed and starker sleeping conditions, relying on public spaces, makeshift arrangements, and open barracks-style shelters." The new homeless were much younger as well. Researchers reported that almost all homeless persons in the 1950s and 1960s were older, single white men—three of four older than forty-five. By contrast, a 1989 survey of Philadelphia's homeless population found three of four under the age of forty-five, 88 percent African American, and 18 percent children under the age of eighteen—signifying the emergence of homelessness among families, who now compose about a third of the homeless population.[85] Unlike young men on the road in search of work a century ago, most of the homeless are relatively long-term residents of the cities in which they live. Today's homeless probably work less than their counterparts in the nineteenth century. Often, they are not between jobs; instead, they are more or less permanently unemployed, and a majority of them, now, are not white.[86] A substantial subset—about 40 percent—are mentally ill or suffer from other disabilities.[87]

Since the 1989 survey, the age structure of the homeless population has changed. Culhane and his colleagues discovered a "cohort" effect in single adult homelessness—a disproportionate number were born between 1954 and 1966 and came of age during the hard economic times of the 1980s and amid the crack epidemic. In 2012 their average age was fifty-two and their average life-expectancy only sixty-four. This cohort effect was one reason why the population of single homeless men declined between 2007—the first year for which there is reliable age data—and 2011.[88] Whether homelessness will rise among the age cohort who reached early adulthood during the Great Recession that began in 2008 remains an open question.

The federal government's 2010 "Strategic Plan to Prevent and End Homelessness" accounts for the increase in homelessness after 1980 as "the result of a convergence of three factors: the loss of affordable housing and foreclosures; wages and public assistance that have not kept pace with the cost of living, rising housing costs, job loss and underemployment, and resulting debt; and the closing of state psychiatric institutions without the concomitant creation of community-based housing and services."[89] Initially, because the federal government did not appreciate homelessness's deep roots and viewed it as a "short-term crisis," its main response was to help fund emergency shelters. As public shelters became "institutionalized," they drew in "vulnerable and marginally housed people," and welfare agencies turned to the shelter system "as a regular and ongoing destination" for clients they discharged. As a result, the number of residential programs for homeless single adults and families nearly tripled between 1984 and 1988 and then almost doubled between 1988 and 1996. Underfunded, often foul and dangerous, shelters became the new poorhouses of the twentieth century. Over time, emergency shelters accounted for fewer and fewer of all shelter beds as "transitional housing programs (featuring longer stays and expanded availability of services)" increased. The upshot was a homeless system unable to "reduce the prevalence of homelessness because through institutionalization it [had] increased the number of people who, for lack of better alternatives" turned "to it for assistance" and remained "in the system for increasing lengths of time." As it became clear that homelessness was growing worse and would not disappear anytime soon, the federal government turned to an approach known as "a continuum of care" based on the "theory...that people experiencing homelessness would progress through a set of interventions, from outreach to shelter, into programs to help address underlying problems, and ultimately be ready for housing."[90] Its unintended consequences soon pointed to the weaknesses in the continuum of care policy. By coordinating the "patchwork" of services, point out Culhane and his colleagues, continuum of care created a "parallel social welfare system...for a select population eligible only by virtue of their temporary housing status, and typically only at the time of their residence in a facility for the homeless." This allowed mainstream social welfare services "to largely ignore their clients' housing problems."[91]

With the failures and limitations of earlier and existing homeless policies in mind, the Obama administration shifted the emphasis away from shelters toward preventing homelessness and moving as many people as possible rapidly into housing. Both of these policy thrusts followed a conceptual shift in the understanding of homelessness based on the research of Dennis Culhane. In 1994 Culhane, using shelter registers from Philadelphia and New York, showed that the number of people homeless at some point during the year was about three times higher than the number of people homeless at any one time. This meant that most people were homeless only for brief periods and needed radically different kinds of assistance than the chronically homeless. Other research has since confirmed his findings. In 2011, on a single night in January, 636,017 people were homeless in the United States, but in the period between October 1, 2010 and September 30, 2011, about 1,502,196 people used an emergency shelter or a transitional housing program. (About 60 percent of the homeless live in shelters and 40 percent are "unsheltered."[92]) Culhane also showed that most homelessness originated in well-defined neighborhoods. By focusing on places that produced homelessness, policy could be turned toward prevention.[93] Reflecting this research, the centerpiece of the Obama administration's first homelessness policy was the three-year, $1.5 billion "Homelessness Prevention and Rapid Rehousing Program (HPRRP)" included in the American Recovery and Reinvestment Act of 2009 (otherwise known as the economic stimulus program). By all accounts, the program was both popular with state governments and successful. State governments used program funds to provide individuals and families with a variety of forms of help that allowed them to stay in their homes and, when homeless, to move quickly to alternative accommodations rather than into shelters. Because of the HPRRP, along with the "cohort effect," homelessness did not increase nearly as much as feared during the recession that began in 2008—indeed, among single men, two-thirds of the homeless population, it decreased, while among families the increase was modest. HUD reported that "overall the level of homelessness remained essentially the same from 2011 to 2012, with the number of homeless individuals falling slightly and the number of homeless families increasing slightly.... The number of chronically homeless people...fell about 7 percent in 2011 and more than 19 percent since 2007. Homelessness among veterans declined more than 7 percent in 2011 and 17 percent since 2009."[94]

With the end of HPRRP and flat HUD budgets, however, homelessness and its attendant miseries was poised to increase again. Requests for emergency food assistance rose forty-one percent in Philadelphia during 2012 while "one-third of the demand for shelter among the homeless went unmet." The. U.S. Conference of Mayors' survey of 25 cities reported increases in requests for emergency food in all but 4 with three of four expecting requests to increase over the next year. On

average, the number of homeless persons increased 7 percent and families 8 percent; 60 percent of the mayors expected the number to rise
during the next year while 58 percent expected their emergency shelter
resources to decrease.[95]

Below the radar, another, disturbing subset of the homeless emerged.
In December 2012 *The New York Times* reported that, "Across the
country, tens of thousands of underemployed and jobless young people, many with college credits or work histories, are struggling to house
themselves in the wake of the recession, which has left workers between
the ages of 18 and 24 with the highest unemployment rate of all adults."
These young adults composed the "new face of a national homeless
population," which both researchers and case workers claim is increasing. "Yet the problem is mostly invisible." Cities and states that direct
their efforts toward homeless families have not reached out to them
while young adults "tend to shy away from ordinary shelters out of fear
of being victimized by an older, chronically homeless population."[96]

The homeless pose a special problem for shiny, redeveloped center cities. They annoy passersby with their begging, tarnish the streets
with their unsightliness, and provide living reminders of the persistent poverty that many would like to ignore or forget. Consequently,
they are prime objects in a larger effort to sanitize urban space. This
attempt to render the poor invisible has introduced a schizophrenic
character into homelessness policy. The progressive thrust of federal
policy is countered by more inconsistent policies at the local level—
on the one hand supporting programs to assist the homeless, while
on the other, trying to keep them away from public spaces. One such
conflict arose in Philadelphia in 2012, when the city government tried
to prohibit volunteers from providing food for the homeless on the
city's signature cultural space, the Benjamin Franklin Parkway, home
to the Philadelphia Museum of Art, the new Barnes Foundation, and
other city icons. The city offered a variety of reasons for why it was
against the best interests of the homeless to receive food on the Parkway
and pointed to available alternatives, but the bottom line was clear, if
unspoken: they were unsightly additions to the landscape on which
the city counted for promoting the tourism essential to its economic
future. The city's arguments did not convince the judge who heard
homeless advocates' challenge to its ordinance, and outdoor programs

for feeding the homeless won at least a temporary reprieve.[97] In one way or another, similar conflicts were played out with varying results around the country. "With the downturn in the economy," reported *The New York Times* in October 2012, "cities across the country have been cracking down on an apparent rise in aggressive panhandling, while advocates for the homeless and civil liberties groups contend that sweeping bans go too far." A civil rights lawyer with the National Law Center on Homelessness and Poverty observed that, "Rather than addressing the issue of homelessness," cities "are adapting measures that move homeless people out of downtowns, tourist areas or even out of a city."[98] The determination to drive the homeless from public space and relegate them to shelters with unspeakable conditions testifies to their membership within the undeserving poor.[99]

As with the homeless, the harsh treatment of immigrants under welfare law speaks to their place within the undeserving poor. Before 1996, legal permanent residents enjoyed eligibility for federal benefits on the same basis as citizens. Undocumented immigrants did not, with the exception of children, who, as a result of the Supreme Court's 1982 ruling in *Pyler v. Doe*, could not be excluded from public schools. This situation changed with two pieces of federal legislation in 1996. The Illegal Immigration and Immigrant Responsibility Act toughened border policing, increased interior enforcement, ramped up grounds for deportation, raised penalties for employing or assisting "illegal aliens," and placed restrictions on immigrant eligibility for federal benefits. The Personal Responsibility and Work Reconciliation Act (otherwise known as "welfare reform") sharply curtailed the eligibility of legal immigrants, denying them access to most federal benefits for the first five years of their residence in the United States. SSI and some other benefits eventually were restored for immigrants already in the country legally before 1996, and food stamp benefits were restored for the children of immigrants entering legally after 1996, but for other newcomers the restrictions remained in place. State governments faced a difficult choice: whether to continue using federal dollars for TANF and Medicaid to assist eligible immigrants who had arrived before 1996—every state extended TANF and only Wyoming denied Medicaid—and whether to create their own programs for immigrants ineligible for federal assistance, which some states did. Tellingly, points out immigration expert Audrey Singer, "the Act explicitly limited state and local governments' authority to provide any benefits to undocumented immigrants. Doing so meant they had to enact a state law after August 2, 1996, that 'affirmatively provides for such eligibility.' In other words, state governments must declare that they are making a choice to provide undocumented immigrants with benefits." With sentiment against undocumented immigrants running high, most states proved unwilling to take this step, thereby affirming the relegation of undocumented immigrants to the ranks of the undeserving poor.[100]

Restrictions on public benefits posed serious problems for immigrants because so many of them, both documented and undocumented, were poor. In 2010 23 percent of the 40 million documented and undocumented immigrants and their US-born children, compared to 13.5 percent of the native born and their children, lived in poverty. Immigrants made up a quarter of all US residents and their children a third of all children living in poverty. Poverty varied among immigrant groups, with the highest rate—35 percent for adult immigrants and their children—occurring among immigrants from Mexico. Although immigrants made economic progress over time, after twenty years of living in the United States their poverty rate remained 50 percent higher than the rate of the adult native-born. Nearly three of ten immigrants and their children, more than twice the percentage of the native-born, lacked health insurance. They lived in overcrowded housing more than six times as often, and 36 percent used at least one major welfare program, compared to 23 percent of the native-born.[101]

Immigrant poverty and welfare use did not reflect unwillingness to work. The share of the working-age holding a job, 68 percent, was identical among immigrants and the native born. In fact, work rates were higher among immigrant than among native-born men and lower among women.[102] In Metropolitan Philadelphia, between 2001 and 2006, the foreign-born accounted for 75 percent of labor force growth.[103] Immigration did not hurt America's economy or increase crime. Quite the contrary, in fact. Two scholars, John M. MacDonald and Robert Sampson, commissioned articles investigating the impact of immigration for the *Annals of the American Academy of Political and Social Science*. In a *New York Times* op ed, they summed up their findings. The scholars contributing to the volume agreed that "while new immigrants are poorer than the general population and face considerable hardship, there is no evidence that they have reshaped the social fabric in harmful ways." To the contrary, the nation is "neither less safe because of immigration nor is it worse off economically. In fact, in the regions where immigrants have settled in the past two decades, crime has gone down, cities have grown, poor urban neighborhoods have been rebuilt, and small towns that were once on life support are springing back." The disconnection between the sentiment driving the backlash against immigrants and the reality of their impact on local communities surfaced all over the country, as in Hazelton, Pennsylvania, which led the nation in passing ordinances designed to drive undocumented immigrants from the town. In truth, immigrants had "bolstered" the declining population and "helped to reverse economic decline."[104]

The rise of anti-immigrant sentiment should not surprise anyone acquainted with America's long history of xenophobic nativism. The mid-nineteenth century famine Irish, the Southern and Eastern Europeans who entered in the late nineteenth and early twentieth centuries, Asians arriving before the mid-twentieth century, Mexicans as early as the 1920s and 1930s: all met racially-based hostility that resulted in legislation designed to deny them entry or push them out of the country—for instance, the Chinese Exclusion Act of 1882, the nationality-based quotas of the 1920s, the denial of welfare benefits to Mexicans in the 1930s, and Japanese internment during World War II. Despite its image as a nation of immigrants with the Statue of Liberty holding aloft a welcoming beacon, America has proved profoundly uneasy when confronted with linguistic and cultural difference, and over the course of its history, politicians, scientists, journalists, and others have constructed an array of rationalizations—usually at variance with the facts—to explain their hostile and punitive responses, which time and again relegate some immigrants—by no means all, for the deserving/undeserving dichotomy applies here, too—to the ranks of the undeserving poor.[105]

Urban Poverty as a Problem of Places and Markets

With only a few exceptions, research and policy focused on African American families, black men, and the homeless approached poverty as a problem of persons, of fixing or responding to the characteristics and needs of individuals. Another strand in research and policy concentrated on poverty as a problem of place, either comprehensively remaking the urban places that reproduced poverty or, alternatively, moving poor people out of them. A third and newer approach diagnosed poverty as a problem of failed markets and underpinned an array of efforts to put markets to work for the benefit of the poor. The first was represented best by several foundation-sponsored "comprehensive community initiatives"; the second by the federal Moving-to-Opportunity Program; and the third by four new technologies of poverty work: recreating markets in inner cities, microfinance, asset building, and conditional cash transfers.

Thinking about poverty as a problem of place has a long history. The famous late nineteenth-century journalist and social reformer Jacob Riis, for instance, writes historian Max Page, "believed that people's behavior would improve exactly as much as did their living conditions. Tenement dwellers are 'shiftless, destructive and stupid,'" wrote Riis. "In a word, they are what the tenements have made them.'"[106] As a problem of place, poverty exhibits two sides. In one side, which has dominated discussions, conditions *in* places, most notably, substandard housing—Riis's slums and their successors—produce, reinforce, or augment poverty. In the other version, poverty is a product of place itself, reproduced independent of the individuals who pass through it. Nineteenth-century reformers assumed the importance of place. No one doubted what came to be called, in the language of late twentieth-century social science, "neighborhood effects." Many reformers responded to the consequences of pathogenic places by advocating solutions based on housing reform but including, as well, education, public health, improved recreational facilities, and city planning.

The Chicago school of urban sociology, which flourished especially in the 1920s, originated a powerful current in American urban studies that stresses the independent influence of place on the production of poverty. In his 1929 classic *The Gold Coast and the Slum*, Chicago school sociologist Harvey Warren Zorbaugh observed that, "The slum sets its mark upon those who dwell in it, gives them attitudes and behavior problems peculiar to itself."[107] Subsequent scholarship has modified or rejected the Chicago school's ecological model of succession and concentric circles. But its larger emphasis on the role of place in the patterning of social experience—on the need for the close study of neighborhoods as wholes and the intersection of context with lived experience—has endured. Nonetheless, in the 1980s, social scientists began to question whether neighborhoods had independent impacts on individual behavior. Indeed, a review of the complex literature on the subject by Christopher Jencks and Susan Mayer concluded that the emphasis on neighborhood effects was misplaced.[108] However, the older emphasis on the importance of place resurfaced, also in the late 1980s, in the identification of areas of concentrated poverty that allegedly produced an array of social pathologies.

The most famous book was sociologist William Julius Wilson's 1987 *The Truly Disadvantaged*, which identified the "growth of the high- and extreme-poverty" areas as "epitomizing the social transformation of the inner city." The term that best captured "the differences in the experiences of low-income families who live in inner-cities," wrote Wilson, was "*concentration effects*." From this concentration of poverty flowed "massive joblessness, flagrant and open lawlessness, and low achieving schools." With these places shunned by outsiders, their residents, "whether women and children of welfare families or aggressive street criminals, have become increasingly socially isolated from mainstream patterns of behavior."[109] Sociologists Douglas Massey and Nancy Denton, on the other hand, in their 1993 *American Apartheid* explained the reproduction and intensification of inner-city poverty with a model grounded in racial segregation. "Segregation, not middle-class out-migration, is the key factor responsible for the creation of communities characterized by persistent and spatially concentrated poverty," they wrote. "When a highly segregated group experiences a high or rising rate of poverty, geographically concentrated poverty is the inevitable result, and from the geographic concentration of poverty follows a variety of other deleterious conditions."[110] In their emphasis on the independent role of racial segregation, Massey and Denton differed from Wilson, who stressed the role of middle-class out-migration and joblessness in the production of spatially concentrated poverty as a problem of place. But both rekindled an understanding of poverty as a problem of place—an understanding powerfully reinforced by sociologist Robert Sampson's 2012 *Great American City: Chicago and the Enduring Neighborhood Effect* (with a foreword by William Julius Wilson). In the "broadest sense," writes Sampson, "the present study is an effort to show that neighborhoods are not merely settings in which individuals act out the dramas produced by autonomous and preset scripts, or empty vessels determined by 'bigger' external forces, but are important determinants of the quantity and quality of human behavior in their own right." As for poverty, "Neighborhood social disadvantage has durable properties and tends to repeat itself, and because of racial segregation is most pronounced in the black community."[111]

In the 1990s, even as it was funding underclass research, the Rockefeller Foundation acted on an understanding of poverty as a problem of place by initiating six "comprehensive community initiatives" (CPAPs) directed by leaders of community-based agencies and community activists, not by academic researchers. All the CPAPs, reports historian Alice O'Connor, "rejected 'underclass' as a label."[112] The CPAPs were one of several foundation and community-sponsored comprehensive community initiatives active at the same time. The others included the Ford Foundation's Neighborhood and Family Initiative, the Annie E. Casey Foundation's New Futures Initiative, the Surdna Foundation's Comprehensive Community Revitalization Project, The Atlanta Project, The Chicago Initiative, and the Austin Project, Sandtown-Winchester in Baltimore, Dudley Street Neighborhood Initiative in Boston, Target Area Demonstration Program in Portland, Oregon, and Core City Neighborhoods in Detroit.[113] These programs drew on the legacy of the Ford Foundation's 1961 Gray Areas program, the Community Action component of the War on Poverty, and the Great Society's Model Cities program as well as on an understanding of poverty as partially a problem of place.

These new initiatives attempted "to address the inter-related issues that affect today's inner cities with comprehensive, long-term strategies."[114] They were built on "an emerging consensus that long-term community change requires at least two elements: (1) the participation of residents and other stakeholders in the articulation of community change goals; and (2) a comprehensive lens that promotes an integrated, cross-sector approach to community change."[115]

Despite the variety among them, the 1990s Comprehensive Community Initiatives shared common features: the participation of citizens in planning, implementation, and evaluation; a focus on small inner-city neighborhoods; a "holistic approach" that addressed "issues such as poverty, inequality, disinvestment, and unemployment as a web of inter-related problems;" a collaboration between public and private sectors, including corporations, foundations, local government, and residents; and a commitment to the "idea that relationships between all the stakeholders must be based on consensus rather than confrontation."[116] These relationships frequently were fraught. A review of foundations and comprehensive community initiatives concluded, "A 'space' or distance frequently exists between foundations and the comprehensive community initiatives that they support.... this space is too often characterized by lack of understanding and trust, dishonest communications, and struggles over power and accountability."[117]

By and large, the comprehensive community initiatives did not meet the hopes of their founders. Their track records, at best mixed, discouraged attempts to revive them, until the idea staged an unanticipated comeback in a new form, revived by Geoffrey Canada and his Harlem Children's Zone (HCZ). Canada grew up one of four brothers in a single-parent family in the Bronx. His academic ability won him a scholarship to Bowdoin College in Maine. Later, he earned a graduate degree from the Harvard Graduate School of Education. In 1983 he became director of the Rheedlen Foundation, dedicated to reducing truancy in Harlem. At the foundation, he conceived the idea for a web of cradle-to-college social services, which became the HCZ. In 1997 he expanded the Zone to include two new charter schools, called Promise Academies. The HCZ included ninety-seven square blocks of Harlem, an area home to about 17,000 people, with a budget that grew from approximately $6 million in 1994 to $74 million in 2008. The Zone's revenue derived from a variety of sources, including foundations, wealthy donors, and the city government. CEOs of major national corporations played a prominent role on its board.[118]

Canada used two concepts to explain the HCZ. First, was the "pipeline," a metaphor for the integrated social and educational programs that would move young people from cradle to college. Indeed, children entered the pipeline when their expectant parents enrolled in the "baby college," a prenatal education program. The "tipping point" was the other concept. Canada predicts that when the HCZ succeeds with

65 percent of the zone's residents, the rest will be pulled upward by osmosis. No theory or data supports this prediction; it is an article of faith,[119] and Canada does not expect to reach full success for several years—twenty years was the time he projected for the HCZ to fully attain its goals. It is hard to know just how well the HCZ is succeeding. Test results from the Promise Academies are mixed; by New York City standards they are good, but other schools do better, despite the Promise Academies' relentless focus on test-taking.[120] As of 2012 no measures of success were available for the social services. Employment data for the Zone, for instance, showed little change.[121] Enthusiasm in the Zone, however, remained high, and Canada exuded optimism. "This is a science we're creating," he told an audience in another city as he enumerated a litany of urban problems. "All of these problems are solvable. We had a plan at the Harlem Children's Zone, and it worked."[122]

The Harlem Children's Zone might have remained an inspiring local New York story, even after it was discovered and canonized by the national media. But its promise attracted presidential candidate Barack Obama, who made its replication part of his campaign platform. As president, Obama and his education secretary, Arne Duncan, adopted the Harlem Children's Zone as their key poverty-fighting strategy. They proposed to take it national by creating twenty Promise Neighborhoods based on the HCZ model. At the same time, other cities, notably Newark and Camden, New Jersey, announced they would use the HCZ template to revitalize their schools and neighborhoods. Whether the HCZ model can be replicated successfully, whether it can flourish without Geoffrey Canada's charisma and New York City's philanthropy, remains unknown. But the HCZ model, with its high expectations and optimism, stands as a powerful alternative to the pathological image of inner-city poverty reinforced by the culture of poverty and underclass ideas. It is, without question, the most powerful current-day response to an understanding of poverty as a problem of place.

An understanding of poverty as a problem of place led in two other directions as well—toward Community Development Corporations and, then, to programs designed to move poor people out of places of poverty. Across the nation, thousands of Community Development

Corporations (CDCs) work to revitalize low-income communities and build affordable housing. They emphasize the importance of citizen control of economic development and the role of local institutions. For the most part, they operate on a small scale in single, bounded communities and serve low-income people. Collectively, they have lent millions of dollars to businesses and produced hundreds of thousands of units of affordable housing, millions of square feet of commercial and industrial space, tens of thousands of jobs. CDCs emerged first in the 1960s. The catalytic moment in their early history occurred in 1966, when Senator Robert Kennedy, determined to push for a more comprehensive anti-poverty strategy than offered by current Office of Economic Opportunity programs, walked through a poor section of Bedford Stuyvesant in Brooklyn. Together with New York Congressman James Scheur and Senator Jacob Javits, he sponsored an amendment to the Economic Opportunity Act that created the Special Impact Program designed to accelerate economic development in poor neighborhoods. SIP, as the program was known, along with other federal agencies funded hundreds of CDCs, which also received support from national advocacy and technical assistance organizations. Foundations, notably the Ford Foundation, provided the other early source of support and took the lead in funding the new Local Initiatives Support Corporation (LISC), which became the major national intermediary for loans, grants, and equity investments. The Enterprise Foundation, founded by developer James Rouse in 1982, also became a major national intermediary. Another source of funding came from the 1975 Community Reinvestment Act, which forced merging banks to prove they were serving the needs of poor as well as affluent neighborhoods. With this legislation behind them, advocates turned the bank mergers of the 1980s into a major source of money for CDCs. Despite Reagan-era budget cuts, the number of CDCs increased dramatically, bundling federal money with income from a variety of other sources such as banks, corporations, churches, and state and city governments.[123]

Their new funding sources tilted CDCs increasingly toward housing and away from comprehensive economic development. They also blunted the CDC movement's radical edge, pushing them away from advocacy or militancy and into partnerships with the market and state they originally had approached with caution or opposed.[124] Still,

CDCs remained the heart of what housing policy specialist David J. Erickson calls the housing policy revolution, a "decentralized housing network" composed of "CDCs, new government entities at the state and local levels, capacity-building intermediaries, new private sector participants, and other institutions such as foundations and the government-sponsored enterprises, Fannie Mae and Freddie Mac" producing affordable rental housing of unprecedented quality. The network's importance extended beyond its concrete accomplishments because, according to Erickson, it exemplified a new model "providing an inspiration for policy areas as diverse as economic development, education, health, and the environment."[125]

But what had CDCs done for the problem of urban poverty? Jeremy Nowak, executive director of a successful, Philadelphia-based intermediary, offered a skeptical answer that pointed to the third direction in thinking about poverty as a problem of place. Nowak remarked that for more than a decade his fund had invested millions of dollars in low-income neighborhoods "increasingly isolated from the mainstream economy" in the hope of reversing "the outflow of jobs, capital, and people from the inner city." His fund worked on the assumption that the appropriate agents of revitalization were local. What had these investments accomplished? Despite dozens of CDCs in every city, "the persistence and acceleration of poverty" scarred "the very areas where so much community development activity" had taken place. CDCs, concluded Nowak, were too small for the scale of the problem, and they ignored "the requirements of social mobility." That is, they paid too little heed to "household poverty defined by access to good jobs and the accumulation of wealth." To Nowak, the interpretation of poverty as a problem of place confused the links between neighborhood revitalization and "poverty alleviation." "Neighborhood development strategies" could "reinforce the segregation of the poor by building housing in the worst employment markets." Nowak wanted to reorient community development toward poverty alleviation by linking inner cities to regional economies through strategies that promoted opportunities and helped families build assets. In part, this meant helping people reach jobs rather than expecting jobs to locate in significant numbers in the inner cities where they lived.[126]

Others wanted to move the people themselves out of segregated, high-poverty neighborhoods. The first experiment, known as the Gautreaux Project, originated in metropolitan Chicago. In 1966 the American Civil Liberties Union initiated a law suit, *Dorothy Gautreaux v. Chicago Housing Authority* (CHA), which alleged that the CHA had violated the Civil Rights Act of 1964 by building public housing exclusively in racially segregated, high-poverty neighborhoods. HUD joined the lawsuit, which wound up in the US Supreme Court in 1976 as *Hills v. Gautreaux*. A consent decree ordered the CHA to provide scattered-site housing for public housing residents in areas of concentrated poverty. The CHA used Section 8 housing vouchers—federally funded vouchers given to eligible low-income people to rent housing in the private market—to allow 7,500 African American families supported by public assistance to move to low-poverty areas in the city or suburbs. For the most part, the program, which ended in 1998 after sponsoring moves by 7,100 families, appeared a success. In their analysis of the program, Leonard S. Rubinowitz and James E. Rosenbaum stressed its many dimensions and outcomes. "The story of the Gautreaux program," they emphasized, "is too complex to capture in a single bottom line." Still, all in all, the story was remarkably positive. "Many of the families who moved to the suburbs," despite difficulties they experienced there, "were rewarded for their efforts." Their experiences "supported the basic premise of the concept of 'geography of opportunity'—people who move to better areas can improve their opportunities and attainments." Equally heartening was the way in which these families contradicted the "pessimistic predictions of 'culture of poverty' models that depicted low-income Black families as dysfunctional" by showing "substantial ability to adapt to the middle-class environments where they relocated." The experiences of children, in fact, indicated that "many of the benefits are intergenerational."[127] These successes made Gautreaux a model for similar programs in other metropolitan areas and inspired the federal Moving to Opportunity (MTO) program.

"MTO set out to test the idea that where you can live in America matters for our well-being and life prospects—and also to test *how* it might matter. . . . If 'bad' neighborhoods are truly bad for children and families, especially the minority poor, can moving to better neighborhoods lead to better lives? Might these families have a better quality of life if they continued to be poor?" An $80 million experiment funded by HUD in 1994, MTO "enrolled 5,000 very low-income, mostly black and Hispanic families, many of them on welfare, who were living in public housing in the inner-city ghettos of Baltimore, Boston, Los Angeles, and New York." The program gave participants housing vouchers with which to locate subsidized housing in low-poverty areas and compared their experiences with security, education, jobs, and community with a control group that remained in the inner city.[128]

The history of the first fifteen years of MTO is told in *Moving to Opportunity: The Story of an American Experiment to Fight Ghetto Poverty* by Xavier de Souza Briggs, Susan J. Popkin, and John Goering. They report successes, failures, and everything in between. It is not possible to offer an unqualified answer to the question, did the program "work"? The most they can say is that MTO was a "strong-idea-weakly implemented." A number of improvements in program design, such as counseling families on education, jobs, and other issues after they had moved, would overcome some of the worst of the program's weak spots. They argue persuasively that without a massive increase in the supply of affordable rental housing, MTO-like programs will not reach their potential and the lives of the inner-city poor will not improve. Assisted mobility programs like MTO, moreover, comprise only half of what is needed: "initiatives to expand housing opportunity for the inner-city poor should not be substituted for investing in the revitalization of distressed neighborhoods. Both place-based and people-based policies should be pursued in smart ways; both are central to creating a more equitable geography of opportunity."[129] Despite MTO's mixed record with respect to improvements in education, employment, and income, a follow-up study reported that in comparison to the control group, program participants were in better health and were notably happier—their subjective well-being matched that of individuals with incomes $13,000 higher, a remarkable difference because the average control group income was only $20,000. Importantly, neighborhood economic disadvantage proved much more important than racial segregation, a finding with alarming implications at a time when income segregation was increasing.[130]

The third strand in recent responses to urban poverty did not focus on poverty as either a problem of people or places. Nor did it try to split the difference. Instead, it approached poverty as a problem of markets. Beginning in the 1980s, market-oriented models reshaped public policy in housing, health care, education, welfare, and elsewhere. They also reconfigured ideas about poor people and anti-poverty policy. No longer an underclass, poor people became entrepreneurs. In the new market-based approach to poverty policy, initiative passed from a reduced state to the private sector, which offered innovations at once less demeaning and more effective—as well as less expensive. Advocates of market-based anti-poverty policies rejected pathological descriptions of poor people. Instead, in the writing of market theorists poor people emerged as rational actors—consumers, savers, and entrepreneurs. Four overlapping but distinct strategies dominated these new technologies of poverty work: place-based approaches intended to rebuild markets in inner cities; micro-finance programs to transform poor people into entrepreneurs; asset-building strategies designed to give poor people the means to accumulate capital; and conditional cash transfers that deployed monetary incentives to encourage poor people to change their behavior.[131]

Zones of concentrated poverty at the core of older American cities drifted outside legitimate markets. Prices plummeted so low, supply so outstripped demand, that no housing market remained.[132] Supermarkets, banks, and manufacturing as well as other institutions of commerce had fled. In this situation, urban planners reasonably concluded that inner-city revitalization required the recreation of markets. Two widely heralded policies—Ronald Reagan's Enterprise Zones and Bill Clinton's Empowerment Zones—proved disappointments, falling short of expectations. Enterprise and Empowerment Zones started with deficit models. They intended to supply poor inner-city neighborhoods with missing assets. In his famous 1995 *Harvard Business Review* article, "The Competitive Advantage of the Inner City," Harvard Business School professor Michael Porter took a radically different tack, portraying inner cities as full of untapped strengths that capitalism, free of the clumsy and bureaucratic interference of governments, could tap to revitalize cities and reduce poverty. Porter influenced both the federal Small Business Administration and President Bill Clinton's New

Markets Initiative, which attempted to mobilize tax incentives and private capital to revitalize poor urban and rural areas. On its website, the Initiative for a Competitive Inner City (ICIC), Porter's national nonprofit, highlights successes in mobilizing money with which to support the creation of small businesses and tens of thousands of jobs. Impressive as the numbers are, however, nowhere on its website does the ICIC assess the bottom line: poverty and employment rates in inner cities and joblessness among African American men. Would its efforts prove isolated instances of success or transformative? The jury remained out.[133]

Of the four market-based anti-poverty strategies, only the first—rebuilding markets in inner cities—concentrated on regenerating places. The other three focused on individuals. Microfinance, the most famous of these, started in Bangladesh and spread with breathtaking speed around the world, to developed as well as developing countries. Microfinance began in January 1977, when Muhammad Yunus, an economics professor in Bangladesh, started to lend poor women small amounts of money with which to start their own businesses.[134] In 1993 he founded the Grameen Bank (*Grameen* means "village"). The Grameen program offered poor women, unable to tap the formal banking system, an alternative to the informal economy of loan sharks and money lenders who exploited them. Yunus lent money to women rather than men because he believed women were more likely to use it for the well-being of their families and because he hoped it would empower them. Borrowers repaid their loans in one year at an interest rate of 20 percent. Yunus claimed a repayment rate of 98 percent. Conventional poverty programs, which assumed poor people lacked the skills with which to find and hold paid work, began with training programs. Yunus turned this idea on its head by starting with cash. What the poor lacked, he believed, was access to credit—a fundamental right. Inspired by Grameen, a great many organizations around the world developed microcredit programs. The number of organizations affiliated with Grameen exploded. In 2008, throughout the world, 112 million people participated in microcredit programs. In 2006 Muhammad Yunus received the Nobel Peace Prize.[135]

Grameen reached even the United States—the first anti-poverty program to spread from an East Asian country to the developed

West—with Grameen America opening its first branch in New York City in Queens in January 2008. The second opened in Omaha, Nebraska, in 2009. Experienced managers were imported from Bangladesh to run them. Even the US federal government adopted microfinance programs. With its own national organization, the Association for Enterprise Opportunity, microlending in fact became an industry. Eventually, sharp philosophical differences divided microlenders into two camps. To Yunus, the purpose of microlending was poverty alleviation. To the Consultative Group to Assist the Poor (CGAP), sponsored by the World Bank, the first priority was economic development. In practice, this resulted in the entrance of for-profit firms into microlending. Appalled at this transformation of microfinance, Yunus told listeners at the United Nations, "we didn't create microcredit to encourage loan sharks. . . . Microcredit should be seen as an opportunity to help people get out of poverty in a business way, but not as an opportunity to make money out of poor people." Microfinance has not lacked for critics, and in recent years scandals have rocked programs.[136] In the end, the bottom line about the results of microfinance remain unclear. Defining a metric of success, designing research programs, agreeing on a methodology for evaluation: all remain elusive. What is clear is that Muhammad Yunus and Grameen have replaced pathological stereotypes of the poor with images of competent entrepreneurs. In the history of poverty policy, this is a signal achievement.

In its second phase, Yunus and other leaders of the microfinance movement began to recognize the importance of financial services to poor people and the importance of savings.[137] Reframed as asset-building, saving became the core of an asset-building movement started in the United States—stimulated notably by Michael Sherraden's 1991 *Assets and the Poor*.[138] Asset-building quickly became an anti-poverty strategy of choice throughout the world of social policy. A 2010 report by the New American Foundation, one of the principal advocates of asset-building as social policy, explained: "Asset building refers to public policy and private sector efforts to enable individuals to accumulate and preserve long-term, productive assets—savings, investments, a home, post-secondary education and training, a small business, and a nest-egg for retirement." Like Yunus, the asset-based movement rejects pathological, moral, or culturally based theories of poverty. In the United States federal, state, and local governments have promoted the importance of individual assets. Through the tax-code, for example, the federal government has supported home ownership and retirement savings. Almost all federal asset-based policy, however, goes to steadily employed homeowners, not the poor. According to one authoritative analysis, in 2005, less than 3 percent of tax-based subsidies went to the three-fifths of families with the lowest incomes. The situation is especially bleak among African Americans. The gap separating black from white wealth is much greater than the income gap. Between 1984 and 2009, report Thomas Shapiro and his colleagues, the gap between black and white assets skyrocketed from $84,000 to $236,500. At $265,000, median white household assets dwarfed the $28,500 figure among blacks.[139]

To direct asset-building toward helping poor people leave poverty, Michael Sherraden proposed Individual Development Accounts (IDAs). These are subsidized savings accounts targeted at poor people through matching grants rather than tax breaks. Sherraden sees IDAs as the vanguard of a revolution that will shift the emphasis of social policy from income support to asset accumulation. In fact, hundreds of IDA programs are spread across the country. Most states have some sort of IDA-enabling policy while "federal legislation....provided a legal structure and funding mechanism for IDAs." Many community-based organizations implemented IDAs in the 1990s, most often with foundation funds. Major sponsorship has come from the Ford Foundation, the New American Foundation, the Bill and Melinda Gates Foundation, and several others. The Assets@21 conference sponsored by the New America Foundation in May 2012 clearly illustrated how asset-building has become a national social movement. Two major research projects—the American Dream Demonstration (ADD) and Savings for Education, Entrepreneurship, and Downpayment (SEED)- have tested asset-building as policy. The results, although pointing to useful directions for future policy, fell short of unequivocal evidence of success. Research on IDA programs raises many questions, as the researchers themselves admit. Some are practical; others are more philosophical. Indeed, the reorientation of the welfare state around asset-building would hasten its redesign on market principles. Still, it is undeniable that the lack of assets traps people in poverty and that many promising asset-building programs are underway throughout the country.[140]

In New York City, Mayor Michael Bloomberg launched an ambitious anti-poverty program that also rejected pathological images of the poor. The program included Conditional Cash Transfers (CCTs), the fourth new strategy of anti-poverty work, which Bloomberg imported from Mexico. CCTs did not constitute the most important part of his anti-poverty agenda, but they became the most controversial. After eighteen months, they proved the most visible failure. Conditional Cash Transfer programs transfer cash to poor households on the condition that they make specific investments in the human capital of their children: periodic medical checkups, growth monitoring, vaccinations, prenatal care for mothers, mothers' attendance at periodic health information talks, and school-related behavior—enrollment, regular attendance, and, occasionally, academic achievement. Most CCT programs transfer money directly to mothers, or, in some circumstances, to students. Details of CCT programs vary—there are huge programs in Brazil and Mexico—but all of them, a World Bank specialist points out, provide poor families with cash "on the condition that they make investments in human capital such as sending children to school or bringing them to health centers on a regular basis." CCTs represent a "new generation of social programmes" that rely "on market principles."[141]

Bloomberg, who traveled with staff to Mexico to observe its Oportunidades program, formed a public-private partnership, Opportunity NYC, to implement the first full CCT program in the United States. A cross-section of elite American philanthropy put up $50 million to fund a three-year trial. After eighteen months, a mid-course evaluation by the firm MDRC, hired to design and evaluate the program, turned in a mixed report, and Bloomberg announced the abrupt termination of the program, although not the evaluation. Neither the political Left nor Right liked Opportunity NYC. To the Right, it rewarded the undeserving poor—why reward parents who had failed to send their children to school regularly or take them for medical checkups? The Left found CCTs paternalistic and offensive. Lacking a solid constituency, Bloomberg could not scale up CCTs with city funds. Perhaps it was less embarrassing to pull the plug than to lose a bruising fight with city council. The other components of Bloomberg's anti-poverty program appeared more promising, although it failed to stop the rise in the city's poverty rate, which reached 21 percent in 2010. In fact, Bloomberg deserves great credit for mounting a major anti-poverty program with poverty off the national political agenda. No other mayor within memory had tried anything remotely similar.[142]

Bloomberg created the perfect anti-poverty program for a twenty-first century American city because it did not rely on federal initiatives or funding, combined public and private resources, reflected market-based principles, and was resolutely pragmatic and nonideological. It also fit the twenty-first century because it focused on the deserving or working poor, eschewed redistribution, and paid no attention to the dependent poor. In this, Bloomberg's anti-poverty initiative tracked national policy, which since the 1990s has developed an array of programs to help the working poor while neglecting the nonworking poor, whose situation stagnated or deteriorated.

Market-based technologies of poverty work do not assault the rigidities of social structure or the citadels of power. They elide the political economy of power. They propose to solve poverty on the cheap, with relatively little public money, and without growing the size of government very much. They reduce the role of government to impresario organizing, partially funding, and coordinating a new show rather than creating and managing new programs. That said, they have the potential to improve the lives of a great many people while smoothing the rough edges of capitalism. Is this the best for which we can hope?

Poverty as a Problem in Political Economy and Social Justice

Neither mainstream poverty research nor the new market-based technologies of poverty work attempted a deep excavation of the roots of the new urban poverty or paid much attention to the question of why poverty matters and what we owe each other—the ethical issues raised by Reich, Rawls, and Nozick—and they ignored greater equality as a goal of public policy, at least until the Great Recession made it inescapable. Work by sociologists, anthropologists, geographers, historians, religious leaders, philosophers, and legal scholars, however, kept these questions alive. Even if the answers did not form a unified narrative or ethics, they offered a powerful and sometimes deeply moving basis for rekindling scholarship and action.

For the most part, poverty research and policy focused on categorizing the poor, explaining the reasons for their poverty, and finding the mix of incentives, sanctions, and training that would ease their disadvantage. They did not dig deeply into the origins and transformation of poverty in the process of capitalist development itself and the actions of the state. However, an exciting new body of scholarship—some of it by geographers, some by sociologists—linked political economy to a radical politics of space. The most important of the radical political geographers has been David Harvey, whose many books include *Social Justice and the City, A Brief History of Neoliberalsm,* and *Rebel Cities: From the Right to the City to the Urban Revolution.*[143] A towering presence in the intellectual history of urban studies, Harvey's application of Marxist political economy to urban geography inspired much of the contemporary scholarship that roots poverty in the capitalist transformation of urban space.

The excavation of new, spatially rooted forms of global poverty provided a theoretical counterpoint to the new programmatic linkages between technologies of poverty work, which moved from the Global South to the United States and Western Europe.[144] With his books exploring the origins, characteristics, and implications of what he calls "advanced marginality," Loïc Wacquant, a former student of both Pierre Bourdieu in France and of William Julius Wilson at Chicago, stands out as the most prominent theoretician of this new political geography of poverty. Wacquant breaks "with the trope of 'disorganization' that has guided mainstream research on poverty in America since the early works of the Chicago School" and replaces it with an "institutionalist conception of the ghetto" that combines "mechanisms of ethnoracial control founded on the history and materialized in the geography of the city." In his 2008 *Urban Outcasts: A Comparative Sociology of Advanced Marginality*, Wacquant retraces "the historic shift from the *communal ghetto* of the mid-twentieth century," a "compact and sharply circumscribed" place where "blacks of all classes were consigned and bound together by a broad complement of institutions, specific to the group and its reserved space," to the "*hyperghetto*" of the late twentieth century. The hyperghetto is a new kind of place characterized by segregation based on the combination "of race *and* class in the context" of labor market collapse and the retrenchment of the welfare state in inner cities, "necessitating and eliciting the corresponding deployment of an intrusive and omnipresent police and penal apparatus." For him, the decline of the welfare state and the rise of the carceral state form twinned processes reshaping inner-city ghettos. Wacquant distinguishes his interpretation from Wilson's—which stresses the economy—and Massey's—which emphasizes segregation. In their place, he underscores the role of the state: "*the collapse of public institutions,* resulting from state policies of urban abandonment and leading to the punitive containment" of poor African Americans. This, he argues, is the most potent and distinctive cause of entrenched marginality in the American metropolis. These "racially skewed and market-oriented state policies...have aggravated, packed, and trapped poor blacks at the bottom of the spatial order of the polarizing city."[145] The result is a "modernized misery" whose "distinctive structural properties," which he finds operative in France as well as the United States, are less apparent than its "concrete manifestations."[146]

These six structural properties—increased insecurity in the wage-labor relation; the disconnection of spaces of advanced marginality from macroeconomic trends like economic growth and increased productivity; the stigmas attached to "bounded territories increasingly perceived by outsiders and insiders as social purgatories"; the transformation of "communal 'places'" full of "joint meanings" and established institutions into "indifferent 'spaces' of mere survival and relentless contest"; the disappearance of a "hinterland" where "individuals...excluded from paid employment" could "readily rely on collective informal support while they wait for new work" that now may never arrive; and the decomposition of the working-class or proletariat into a series of fragments that undermine efforts "to forge a sense of common condition and purpose"—constitute the condition of advanced marginality. They merit the adjective "advanced" because "these forms of marginality are not *behind* us." To the contrary, "they stand *ahead of us;* they are etched on the horizon of contemporary societies." They do not, however, imply that advanced marginality plays out identically in different countries. Indeed, one of Wacquant's goals is to undermine the popular idea of a growing convergence between American ghettos and French *banlieus*. Each of the six properties "expresses itself differently in different countries and/or types of urban environment" as a result of their "social and political history." They are, in fact, ideal-types that require "empirical investigation" and a research agenda different from the one that dominates mainstream poverty research.[147]

In part, the research agenda implied by Wacquant is, of necessity, historical. Only precise, detailed historical analysis will explain the expression of advanced marginality in different settings. Its absence, in fact, leads understanding astray. Researchers, for instance, often assume, without evidence, that deindustrialization destroyed the decently paid, stable, semi-skilled jobs on which African American men depended.[148]

However, except for a few cities like Chicago and Detroit, most African American men did not work in manufacturing or construction because racial discrimination frequently excluded them. They worked, instead, in low-skilled service and laboring jobs. Their most important road to modest prosperity led not through manufacturing but through jobs in the public sector. Indeed, research by Mark J. Stern has shown that in a representative sample of American cities, poverty rates were positively correlated with African American manufacturing employment and negatively correlated with employment in the public sector.[149] The systematic and detailed history of the distinct African American employment niche in the public sector remains to be written, but enough is known to highlight the implications of the collapse of public sector jobs and the downsizing of government and the welfare state for African American poverty.

Historians, by and large, have been slow to trace the emergence of America's territories of advanced marginality. Arnold Hirsch and Thomas J. Sugrue constitute the two major exceptions, Hirsch in his 1983 *Making of the Second Ghetto* and Sugrue in his 1996 *Origins of the Urban Crisis*. Both provide hard evidence for Wacquant's view of the role of politics and state action in the production of advanced marginality. Hirsch differentiates Chicago's second, or post–World War II ghetto, from the first ghetto by the involvement of federal, state, and local governments in its production through urban renewal, the location of public housing, and zoning. In his dramatic account of the emergence of modern urban poverty in Detroit, Sugrue traces similar forces, along with manufacturing collapse and the emergence of white homeowner groups supported by city government.[150] In another example, the chapter authors of *The "Underclass" Debate: The View From History* (1993) collectively show the crucial role of history in explaining urban poverty.[151]

Advanced marginality, as Wacquant points out, is not an abstract concept. It is a condition expressed in the circumstances within places and the lives of individuals. Economic transformation, the withdrawal of the welfare state and the rise of the carceral state, the decay of inner-city fabric, the stigmatization of place: all these come together in the stories of individuals struggling to get by and survive. Ethnographic observation offers the only method for bringing those stories to light and grasping their implications. Despite the visibility and predictability of "the impact of devolution, fiscal austerity, and interurban competition...at the level of government," point out ethnographers Robert P. Fairbanks II and Richard Lloyd, "we are only beginning to understand the shifting impacts of these forces on the everyday life of urban subjects." To grasp how these processes work "at the community, neighborhood, and urban scales—quite often at the edges of formal institutions and legality"—ethnographic methods are essential.[152] In *How It Works: Recovering Citizens in Post-Welfare Philadelphia* (2009), Fairbanks exemplifies the "critical ethnography" that he and Lloyd advocate. He sets his ethnographic observations inside one of the city's "recovery houses"—derelict row houses repurposed by street-level entrepreneurs—to accommodate recovering addicts sent to them by the criminal justice and welfare systems. Fairbanks shows how poverty is actually managed in the context of austerity and the application of market models to public policy and the ways in which the state (in this case primarily local government) achieves its goals by operating through nominally private actors. He lays out in granular detail how one aspect of the informal economy actually works in an American city and how the recovery houses function as a component of a crucial but unheralded informal welfare state. Fairbanks shows as well the ways in which they help maintain social order by servicing a part of the large population that is outside the regular labor market but not incarcerated, and how through them the state achieves regulation without formal legal or institutional structures, indeed through their absence.

At the same time, Fairbanks strikes a serious blow at lingering ideas of the culture of poverty or at the notion that the ethic of individualism is absent from poor people in inner cities. His ethnographic observations show how the operators and managers of the recovery houses, themselves poor and recovering addicts, exemplify an entrepreneurial spirit in the best American tradition. At the most general level, the book shows how trends in the history of cities have resulted in new forms of poverty and new modes of regulation. That is, it successfully performs the difficult task of linking the domestic and global forces of urban transformation to both new forms of poverty and new modes of regulation or governance.[153]

In *Righteous Dopefiend*, to take another example of the power of urban ethnography, anthropologist Philippe Bourgois and photographer Jeff Schonberg unveil the results of ten years of ethnographic work among homeless heroin addicts who set up camp in an abandoned corner of San Francisco. Like Fairbanks, they restore face, agency, and humanity to an invisible, despised population and trace the subtle and complicated relationships that characterize their interactions. The "central goal" of their "photo-ethnography of indigent poverty, social exclusion, and drug use," they tell readers, "is to clarify the relationships between large-scale powerful forces and intimate ways of being in order to explain why the United States, the wealthiest nation in the world, has emerged as a pressure cooker for producing destitute addicts embroiled in everyday violence." "The suffering of homeless heroin injectors," they argue, "is chronic and cumulative and is best understood as a politically structured phenomenon that encompasses multiple abusive relationships, both structural and personal," including "the restructuring of the labor market, the 'War on Drugs,' the gentrification of San Francisco's housing market, the gutting of social services, the administration of bureaucracies, racism, sexuality, gender power relations, and stigma."[154]

Historians and ethnographers make a few minor dents in the hard shell that encases Wacquant's conception of advanced marginality by pointing to the agency exercised by individuals caught within it and restoring their dignity. But so tightly is it constructed, so intricately connected its parts, that readers of Wacquant's work are left without any clear idea of how it may be cracked open, barring a revolution that is not about to happen. It is an intellectually perfect system that produces despair. Even the best ethnographers, like Fairbanks and Bourgois, while they crush stereotypes, undermine the concept of the undeserving poor, and restore dignity, remain unable to point to ways to crack open the shell of advanced marginality. It is difficult to put down their deeply researched, empathetic, and engrossing books and be hopeful. Here lies a great challenge: how to find the spaces unacknowledged by Wacquant from which forces for constructive progressive change can emerge and begin to cause cracks in the shell—if, in fact, such spaces exist. The architect Teddy Cruz, who looks at marginalized neighborhoods as sites of production rather than despair, finds hopeful examples in Latin America. "While the attention of the world had been focused on...enclaves of abundance, the most radical ideas advancing new models of urban development," he writes, "were produced on sites of scarcity across Latin American cities." He points to "visionary mayors" in Porto Alegre, Curitiba, Bogota, and Medellin who fostered "rethinking the very meaning of infrastructure, housing, and density, and mediating top-down development and bottom-up social organization." There is no other "continental region of the world where we can find this type of collective effort led by municipal and federal governments seeking a new brand of progressive politics to produce an urbanism of inclusion." This urbanism of inclusion rejects conventional planning "from above" and "stand-alone experimental architectural gestures supported by large capital and corporate branding." Instead, its practitioners experiment "by reconfiguring socioeconomic relations first, uncovering the potential of informal systems and social networks to rethink urbanization, negotiating formal and informal economies and large and small scales of development." Cruz offers exciting, inspiring cases histories.

> These experiments ranged, for example, from the decision by the municipality of Porto Alegre in Brazil to enact 'participatory budgets,' enabling communities to decide the distribution of municipal budgets; to Brazilian president Ignacio de Lula's economic policy awarding property titles to thousands of slum dwellers in Rio de Janeiro and declaring the intervention into slums as a vital part of his urban development agenda, not by erasure but by retrofit; to the

announcement by President Evo Morales that he would insert illegal coca production into the Bolivian national economy to subsidize social housing; to Bogota's ex-mayor Antanas Mockus' mobilization of a civic culture founded on a massive urban pedagogical project that paved the way for one of the most successful public transportation systems in the world, Colombia's TransMilenio project; to Mayor Sergio Fajardo's decision that he would transform his violence-ridden city by building an infrastructure of public library parks in the slums of Medellin; and also even to Venezuelan Hugo Chavez's demagogic proclamations promising to give huge oil revenues to the poor of his country toward the formation of the new socialist city. All have become paradigmatic gestures during recent years.

In his research, Cruz seeks to uncover these projects' "operative procedures" in order to "enable public policy and activism in the US." Already, he has identified principles of knowledge exchange; "a committed investment in education at the scale of the metropolitan"—that is, "an urban pedagogy that would close the gap between institutions and publics" and capitalize on "the creative intelligence of communities and activists, mobilizing mutual support and volunteerism in the shape of citizen-led collaborations to face the most pressing urban problems in the contemporary city." Massive citizen mobilization leads to a visionary goal, unthinkable from Wacquant's portrait of territories of advanced marginality: the belief that "communities themselves can, in fact, be participants in the shaping of the city of the future; and that the identity of this city is based not on the dominance of private development alone and its exorbitant budgets to sponsor the image of progress, but...can also emerge from the value of social capital and incremental layering of urban development, enabling a more inclusive idea of ownership." In his architectural practice on both sides of the US-Mexican border, Cruz tries to activate these principles with projects of extraordinary imagination. This Latin American urban progressivism offers an alternative based on real-world examples to the narrative of pessimism that portrays the history of modern American cities as a march toward the desolate and intractable spread of advanced marginality.[155]

As a trope for characterizing districts of concentrated poverty within American cities, advanced marginality has much to recommend it over "underclass." It is precise, theoretically-driven, rooted in the actions of the state and the operation of the global economy – not in the behavior and personality of individuals. Yet, like "underclass" it carries dangers. While Wacquant intends it to refer to places rather than persons, it is easy to slip from one to the other, unintentionally characterizing poor persons as marginal, a term they may appreciate no more than underclass. "Advanced" too is not without ambiguity. Wacquant intends it to refer to the future – the direction in which these districts are headed, but, again, "advanced" could be read by a reader who does not pay careful attention to the text as a condition, a disease rotting away the capacity for efficacy and mobilization.[156]

The question remains, though, why should we care about advanced marginality, the inequality upon which it rests, and the poverty that it reproduces? The question might seem banal, the answer self-evident. But when in 2012 a major party candidate for president of the United States could write off nearly half the American population as freeloaders who saw themselves as "entitled to health care, to food, to housing, to you name it" and disclaim responsibility for their well-being, the issue of why we should care about poverty and what we owe to each in our collective capacity as citizens remains alive.[157] Indeed, the difficulty goes beyond apathy. Poverty is a toxic issue, avoided by national political candidates, unable to rouse widespread passion or outrage. In the summer of 2012, philosopher Cornel West and journalist Tavis Smiley organized a "poverty tour" across America. "Smiley & West are going on a road trip," explains the tour's website, "to highlight the plight of the poor people of all races, colors, and creeds so they will not be forgotten, ignored, or rendered invisible during this difficult and dangerous time of economic deprivation and political cowardice."[158] Mainstream media paid them almost no attention, even as newspapers reported new census bureau figures showing shocking increases in poverty and declines in income.[159]

Occasional books tried to keep poverty as an issue alive and front and center. Among the most important were Mark Robert Rank's 2004 *One Nation Underprivileged: Why American Poverty Affects Us All* and Peter Edelman's 2012 *So Rich, So Poor: Why It's So Hard to End Poverty in America*. Rank, a professor of social welfare, combined empirical analysis of poverty data with a strong normative argument about the damage that poverty does to the nation. By using longitudinal rather than cross-sectional data, he showed that "a majority of Americans experience poverty during their adult lifetimes," a startling revelation that should break down stereotypes and justify putting poverty high on the national agenda. Rank argued against the common idea "that poverty is the result of individual inadequacies" and "lies outside the mainstream of American experience." Poverty, rather, "is the result of systemic failings within the U.S. economic and social structures…and…an issue of vital national concern."[160]

Edelman, a law professor, top advisor to Senator Robert F. Kennedy, and senior official in the Clinton administration who resigned in protest after Clinton signed the 1996 "welfare reform" legislation, long has been the conscience of the nation on poverty issues. *So Rich, So Poor* offers a powerful, concise overview of the contours of poverty in contemporary America. Edelman frames his analysis with a ringing defense of government's successes at reducing poverty. "We need to be clear that public policy had indeed made a huge different in the lives of poor people," he correctly observes. "To suggest dismissively—as so many conservatives do—that 'we waged a war on poverty and poverty won' simply because there is still poverty is like saying the Clean Air and Clean Water Acts failed because there is still pollution." Edelman structures his book around four large points. First is the question of why, despite past achievements, so much poverty remains. The most important reason is "the fundamental change that occurred in the American economy" with the loss of well-paid, low-skill jobs and the increase of low-wage work with no future. Added to this is the "substantial increase in the number of families headed by a single parent" at a time when one income rarely can sustain a family, and the enduring influence of race and gender. Second is that the problem is not just poverty, but the increase in the number of people in extreme poverty, that is, living below half the poverty line. "An astonishing 20.5 million people lived in extreme poverty in 2010, up by nearly 8 million in just ten years, and 6 million had no income other than food stamps." Third is the massive increase in inequality. "The economic and political power of those at the top is not only eroding our democracy but also making it virtually impossible to find resources to do more at the bottom." Finally, "progress on poverty" demands "bold action…on many fronts: public policy and private action, national and local initiatives, and steps across many fields of endeavor—income from work, work supports like child care, safety-net measures, health, housing, criminal justice reform, human services of all kinds, and investments in education and child development."[161]

Rank and Edelman and a few others brought passion, data, and clarity to debates about poverty and the role of government. They were, however, lone voices, not part of a movement, unable to jump-start a national discussion. Under the radar, poverty lawyers remained unsung heroes. Even with federal programs slashed, they continued a vigorous defense of poor people, battling public bureaucracies, working for the extension of civil rights from politics to economics, and representing the homeless. Nonetheless, the body of scholarship on which poverty lawyers could draw remained fairly thin. The flurry of debate stimulated by Charles Reich petered out, despite the notable work of a few scholars such as Frank Michelman of Harvard, William Simon of Stanford, the late Edward Sparer of the University of Pennsylvania, and Ronald Dworkin of NYU and Oxford. In fact, poverty law, which had entered law schools with astonishing speed in the last half of the 1960s, retreated in importance in law school curricula, until it was revived in the 1990s in the context of teaching about human rights. At the same time, poverty assumed an increasingly important place in the international human rights movement.[162]

The 1948 Universal Declaration of Human Rights adopted by the United Nations General Assembly anchors the link between human rights and poverty. Article 25 reads, "(1) Everyone has the right to a standard of living adequate for the health and well-being of himself and of his family, including food, clothing, housing, and medical care and necessary social services, and the right to security in the event of unemployment, sickness, disability, widowhood, old age or lack of livelihood in circumstances beyond his control. (2) Motherhood and childhood are entitled to special care and assistance. All children, whether born in or out of wedlock, shall enjoy the same social protection."

With its 2000 Millennium Declaration, the United Nations reaffirmed and strengthened its commitment to eradicating poverty and extending social protection. The Declaration was adopted at an unprecedented gathering of world leaders in the Millennium Assembly, which took place at the United Nations in September 2000. The subsequent Millennium Development Goals (MDG) set out a plan for implementing the declaration with "a series of quantified and time-bound goals to reduce extreme poverty, disease, and deprivation." President George W. Bush responded to the MDG by pledging "that the United States would increase its foreign assistance to countries that demonstrated the will and the capacity to use that increased funding effectively." In the end, however, the promise proved greater than the delivery. "The aid," reported economist Jeffrey Sachs, who directs the U.N. Millennium Project, "is not only very small compared to U.S. GNP and foreign needs, but is given in a form that offers little long-term help."[163]

In 2002 UNESCO responded to the MDG by launching the first cycle of workshops on poverty. They focused "on the conceptual analysis of poverty within the framework of human rights." The challenge, wrote Mark Shino, team leader of the UNESCO project, was "to see how an organization such as UNESCO might galvanize the commitment of the world community by addressing the moral obligation to take action to eradicate poverty and to contribute to the full realization of the fundamental basic rights of all peoples." Poverty, Shino argued, "is not simply a matter of material deprivation. It is a matter of human dignity, justice, fundamental freedoms, and basic human rights."[164]

The sharp increase in concentration on human rights within US law schools reflects both this worldwide focus on poverty eradication and a wider and growing interest in human rights among lawyers, advocacy organizations, and foundations. This "domestic practitioner focus on human rights," reports legal historian Martha Davis, "is not limited to civil and political rights." Rather, it parallels the history of the civil rights movement, which extended its reach from civil and political to economic and social rights. The National Law Center on Homelessness and Poverty, for example, "employs a human rights attorney to augment the other aspects of its work toward a right to housing." A poverty law journal serving legal services and other poverty law practitioners has decided "to expand its coverage of legal issues through a human rights lens." Human rights clinics in law schools also have taken up economic rights issues. Human Rights Watch includes US worker rights in its project on labor and human rights. Other advocacy organizations emphasizing the link between poverty and human rights include the

Center for Economic and Social Rights, Southern Poverty Law Center, Amnesty International USA, and The Poor People's Economic and Human Rights Campaign. "Further, the same foundations that played such an important role in the poverty movement of the 1960s have demonstrated an increased interest not only in human rights abroad but in human rights at home." The Ford Foundation played a central role in establishing the US Human Rights Fund in 2002 to "support human rights advocacy within the United States." Other foundations supporting US-based human rights advocacy include Atlantic Philanthropies, the Open Society Institute, the JEHT Foundation, the Public Welfare Foundation, and Mertz Gilmore.[165]

From the underclass to poverty as the denial of a human right: the distance was vast. In the underclass idea, poverty resulted from antisocial and pathological behavior. As a human right, poverty violated the dignity inherent in every human being. The underclass poor had no inherent rights to material well-being or inherent dignity: they were the undeserving poor. In human rights, no human being was inherently undeserving. The underclass and human rights: these ideas lead to radically different answers to the ancient questions: What are the limits of social obligation? What do we owe to each other? The response to these questions requires taking a step back to answer an antecedent one: Just what kind of a problem is poverty? Some reflection on this question will be a fitting conclusion to this book.

EPILOGUE

What Kind of a Problem Is Poverty?

WHAT KIND OF A problem is poverty? This book has shown that the question is important because the answer is fundamental to both research and public policy. It bears weightily on how we study poverty and where we look for methods to reduce it. There is an ethical dimension to the answer as well because it allocates responsibility and obligation. Who is to blame for poverty as a condition of individuals or groups? Where does obligation for ameliorating or eliminating poverty lie?

Three profound questions, we have seen, frame debates about poverty's origins and run through the history of debates over poverty since the late eighteenth century. They are, first, how to draw the boundaries between who does and who does not deserve to be helped; second, how can we provide help without increasing dependence or creating moral hazard; and third, what are the limits of social responsibility? What do we owe the poor and each other?

How we answer the question about poverty's sources bears directly on each of these enduring concerns. The answer in this book is that poverty largely has been talked about and acted on as one of six kinds of problems. They represent an archeology of poverty rather than a typology because they are layered, each of the first five digging deeper into the question, and the sixth and newest going off at an orthogonal angle. These six are:

. *Persons. Poverty is the outcome of the failings of individuals.*
. *Places. Poverty results from toxic conditions within geographic areas.*
. *Resources. Poverty is the absence of money and other key resources.*
. *Political economy. Poverty is a by-product of capitalist economies.*

268

. *Power. Poverty is a consequence of political powerlessness.*
. *Markets. Poverty reflects the absence of functioning markets or the failure to utilize the potential of markets to improve human lives.*

This book has argued that of these six definitions, the idea that poverty is a problem of persons—that it results from personal moral, cultural, or biological inadequacies—has dominated discussions of poverty for well over two hundred years and given us the enduring idea of the undeserving poor. Although the idea that some poor people are undeserving is old, we have seen that the identity of those who fall within the category has changed with time and circumstance. We have discovered the identity of the undeserving poor by looking both at what was said and written about them and about how classes of individuals were treated in legislation, administrative regulations, and on-the-ground practice.

The obverse of the undeserving also has a history at which we have looked. There always has been some concession to those people—widows, children, the sick and disabled—who cannot help themselves. They are the deserving poor. Today, they include workers whose wages are too low to keep them out of poverty. They have received what limited sympathy public policy can muster toward people in poverty, and a great many have been helped to climb just above the poverty line. The condition of the nonworking, or undeserving, poor, meanwhile, has been treated with neglect and contempt. At the same time, neuroscience and epigenetics have fostered the emergence of a new version of poverty as a result of individual biology. It has aroused excitement because it parses the difference between the conservative believers in the hereditarian basis of economic achievement and the liberal champions of environmental causation. It is difficult for anyone versed in the historical application of biological thought to human society and individual merit to view this resurgence of biology without trepidation.

In mainstream poverty research, the role of culture in the production and perpetuation of poverty, as we have observed, is enjoying a revival. Although its practitioners take great pains to distinguish themselves from the old culture of poverty, their work remains implicitly animated by the questions, in what ways are poor people different (the answer is not because they lack money) and what should be done about

these differences? The questions often lead to technically sophisticated research and useful policy suggestions. But they are not the most
important questions to ask about poverty today.

Another tradition—almost as old—views poverty as a problem of
place. From the dominant perspective, conditions *in* places—most
notably substandard housing or, more colloquially, slums—produce,
reinforce, or augment poverty. From the other perspective, poverty is
a product of place itself, reproduced independently of the individuals who pass through it. From both perspectives, America, like other
nations, has always had its territories of poverty. There is a major book
waiting to be written about their history. One of its principal themes
will have to be invisibility. Poverty has concentrated in urban slums
and rural backwaters, easy to miss on a day-to-day basis. But its invisibility is not accidental. It has been constructed through real estate
markets, city planning, and public policy. A cynical historian would
say that it has been easier to push poverty out of sight than to deal
with it.

Efforts to deal with poverty as a problem of place, as this book has
observed, have a remarkably poor record of success. Slum clearance and
public housing shuffled poor people around; they did not make much
of a dent in poverty. Model Cities, the Comprehensive Community
Initiatives of the 1990s, Ronald Reagan's Enterprise Zones, Bill Clinton's
Empowerment Zones: these place-based programs did not meet their
objectives. Responses have taken two divergent paths. One, represented
by the Harlem Children's Zone, is to do place-based anti-poverty better; the other, represented by the federal Moving to Opportunity program is to move people out of high poverty neighborhoods. The jury
on the long-term results of each of these strategies remains out.

No strategies, however, build on the insights of the short life of
internal colonialism—a radically different place-based strategy—perhaps because following its logic would lead in such difficult and politically unpalatable directions. There is, however, promise in the work
of geographers who have revived their discipline with theories of the
political economy of spatial development and in that of scholars who
have taken up the old question of why some nations remain poor with
new theories that reject conventional development and modernization
models.[1]

One of the odd aspects of the history of writing about poverty is the avoidance of the simple view that people are poor because they lack money. Again, a cynical historian could see much of the writing on poverty as an elaborate dance choreographed to stay away from the point. But the idea has never lacked advocates. Some critics have focused on the poverty that resulted from low wages— the impossibility of escaping poverty through work—while others have focused more on those who lacked wages altogether—call them the nonworking or dependent poor. Economists by and large have given the idea that poverty represents a lack of money the most attention. It was, in fact, as we have noted, Milton Friedman who in the 1960s first advocated a negative income tax. Today, an international organization keeps advocacy of a guaranteed income alive while the Living Wage Movement counts victories in a host of cities. In Wisconsin, in 2012 a public policy institute produced a poverty-reduction plan with 4 income-based components which an independent evaluation by the Urban Institute concluded could reduce poverty by up to sixty-six percent.[2]

Poverty as a problem of resources also receives attention because it is the official or bureaucratic view. In the 1960s, as we have seen, with the launch of the War on Poverty, the federal administration required a standard against which to measure the impact of its programs. The work of a young government economist, Mollie Orshansky, became the basis of the federal poverty line, which, despite its grave deficiencies, has endured to this day, when it is finally being edged toward replacement.

The question of the poverty line is a deep political and philosophic as well technical issue. Successive federal administrations avoided implementing a new line that would increase the official poverty rate while the history of the official poverty rate has been used to justify both optimistic and pessimistic accounts of the capacity of government to respond effectively to economic need. Recently, two scholars have developed a sophisticated measure of "consumption" as contrasted with "income" poverty and used it to argue that federal policy since the early 1970s reduced poverty far more effectively than we have realized.[3] The derivation of a poverty line also requires taking a position on the essence of disadvantage. Is it only money? The Nobel laureate Amartya Sen and the political philosopher Martha Nussbaum have been arguing for a metric that replaces money with "capabilities," a measure identifying what is necessary for an individual to realize her human potential and lead a full and productive life as a citizen. The list of capabilities is fluid, but the idea holds the promise of directing the question of the resource deficit implied by poverty in more expansive, humanly rich, and politically heuristic directions. It links as well with the growing attention to poverty in the human rights movement—represented by the United Nations' Millennial Goals—joining the conceptualization of poverty to the preconditions for the realization of human dignity; racial and gender equality; and the exercise of full citizenship.[4] The human rights movement, in turn, as it arcs back to the United States, holds out the promise of remaking poverty a moral issue—a result needed to overcome an ethical lapse in American politics and public discourse.

Whether we think of poverty as a problem of persons, places, or resources, we are left with the question of why so much of it exists in the first place. That leads straight to political economy, to the understanding that modern, that is post-late-eighteenth century, poverty emerges from the routine intersection of politics with economics. The oldest and most coherent tradition in the political economy of poverty in the United States as well as in Europe, as we have observed, views the poor as the unfortunate casualties of a dynamic, competitive economy, unable to gain a secure foothold on the ladder of opportunity and too incompetent or ill-disciplined to reap the bounty of increasing productivity. Aiding them with charity or relief only interferes with the natural working of markets, retards growth, and, in the end, does more harm than good. Often dressed with quantitative sophistication and theoretical skill, this idea has retained an amazing purchase on popular thought as well as on politics. The widowed, the sick, and a few others remain exceptions, but for the most part the poor are losers.

There is, of course, a long tradition of writing about the political economy of poverty from the perspective of the political Left. These include economists responding to the consequences of the Industrial Revolution; Gilded Age, Progressive-era, and 1930s radicals; black theorists of internal colonialism and black feminists; and current-day urban ethnographers, radical sociologists, and urban geographers. As the work of these scholars shows, the United States has not lacked for social critics and political spokespersons who have traced poverty to its roots in a capitalist economy and politics. But the political Left has lacked an intellectual tradition—a powerful counter-narrative—comparable to the reasonably coherent and powerful conservative political economy of the right that has persisted for more than two centuries. It might be worth thinking about why this is the case and from where a compelling and unifying progressive political economy of poverty might emerge.

The most promising direction is in the overlap of a revitalized geography and political economy with urban ethnography. There is, however, a tension in this literature between structure and agency. Ethnographies, for the most part, celebrate agency by showing the resilience, capability, and intelligence of their subjects who find the interstices in the seemingly monolithic situations that entrap them. But for all their cleverness at finding ways to survive and manipulate systems, they do not overthrow them. They live within them. This is no surprise given the deeply embedded forces excavated by the political sociology of urban space, as we have seen, in the work of sociologist Loïc Wacquant who explores the conditions of advanced marginality. For the potential to break out of this iron cage, we need to learn from the examples of transformative urban change in some of Latin American cities, as described by the architect Teddy Cruz in Chapter 5. Undaunted by the iron cage of urban marginality, Cruz and other practitioners of the architecture of social engagement use a participatory, bottom up process of urban design to revitalize urban spaces and open the lives of their residents to new possibilities.

The question of transforming the condition of advanced marginality brings us straight to politics. Suppose we construct a new political economy of poverty—what happens next? As the political Right has known all along, the gap between theory and implementation is filled by power. Poverty is more than a problem of political economy; it is also, as this book has argued, a problem of power. In theory, in a democracy poor people should be able to gain purchase on the levers of power by electing representatives who champion their interests. In America, this has happened briefly and episodically as in the New Deal, the War on Poverty and Great Society, and in the occasional state and local election. But for the most part electoral politics has not proved an effective route to power for poor Americans, or those who hope to serve their interests. With the unchecked influence of wealth on politics, this may be more true today than at any point since the first Gilded Age. The trade union movement, legitimated by the Wagner Act in 1935, emerged as a counterweight to the power of capital. It played a huge, if indeterminate, role in the decline in working-class poverty after World War II, and undoubtedly many fewer workers would be in poverty today had the rate of unionization not sunk under the onslaught of corporate interests abetted by the state. Periodic "poor people's movements," in the words of Frances Fox Piven and Richard Cloward, also have tilted the balance of power, as have the remarkable successes of some community organizing networks and the grassroots programs initiated as part of the Community Action program of the War on Poverty.

There are a few central points to remember about power. The first is that the political economy of poverty needs a theory of power if it is to move from insight to action. The second point is that effective responses to poverty have originated outside the electoral system. Ultimately, the redress of poverty requires legislation and policy. But the engine of change starts beyond the formal political arena. Third, significant changes will not come about as a result of elite goodwill. Real change requires countervailing centers of power. The trade union movement, decimated by decades of attack, still remains vital, if weakened. Community organizing networks provide a second center. Building from the grassroots to players on the national policy scene, they have mounted some of the most effective challenges to entrenched interests and institutions. Fourth, attempts to leverage countervailing power provoke powerful backlash. A meaningful assault on poverty will not happen easily or quietly, or without great skill and effort. The December 2012 passage of anti-union legislation in Michigan, where modern trade unionism was born, provides one example of the forces arrayed against the maintenance, let alone revival, of union power. Other instances are the assault on public sector unions in Wisconsin and Ohio and the national attack on teacher unions. On the other side of the ledger, however, has been the successful organizing among home health-care workers, described in Chapter 2, the Justice-for-Janitors movement, and less nationally visible achievements such as the

December 2012 organizing of security guards in Philadelphia. There were, as well, in the 2012 elections, glimmers of a potential if loose coalition whose agenda will include more effective responses to poverty. PICO, the national, congregationally based community organization network, read the election as an affirmation of its success in mobilizing around specific issues such as increased funding for education in California.

There is, however, as Chapter 5 explains, a new strategy of anti-poverty work that does not threaten existing configurations of power or pose uncomfortable questions about capitalism. It is, in fact, of a piece with the hegemony of markets as models for American public policy, and in a short span of time it has become the cutting-edge technology of anti-poverty work.

Beginning in the 1980s, market-oriented models reshaped public policy in housing, health care, education, welfare, and elsewhere. They also reconfigured ideas about poor people and anti-poverty policy. No longer an underclass, poor people became entrepreneurs, and initiative passed from a reduced and weakened state to the private sector, which offered innovations at once less demeaning and more effective—as well as less expensive. Advocates of market-based anti-poverty policies rejected pathological descriptions of poor people. Instead, they approached them as rational actors—consumers, savers, and entrepreneurs. Four overlapping but distinct strategies dominate these new technologies of poverty work: place-based approaches intended to rebuild markets in inner cities; micro-finance programs to transform poor people into entrepreneurs; asset-building strategies designed to give poor people the means to accumulate capital; and conditional cash transfers that deploy monetary incentives to encourage poor people to change their behavior. Even though these market-based technologies of poverty work do not take aim at the foundations of social structure, attack the mal-distribution of power, or excavate the political economy of poverty, they just may help many people escape poverty, or survive it with less hardship. In an age of diminished expectations, do they mark the outer limits of realistic aspirations?

The literature on market-based technologies of power for the most part ignores the markets that matter most to poor people around the world. These are the informal economies that provide employment, services, and goods for much of the world's population. They are at once mechanisms of exploitation and means of survival. A rich literature on informal economies has emerged in studies of the Global South. But it remains massively understudied by students of poverty in the United States, outside the boundaries of mainstream poverty research. Informal economies, nonetheless, flourish in American cities, performing much the same functions as they do in the Global South.[5] How does the informal economy intersect the new market-based technologies of poverty work? Is there a way to use informal economies as the basis on which to build anti-poverty strategies?

One strand runs through all six answers to the question, what kind of a problem is poverty? That is the question of work. Indeed, so central have concerns about work remained to poverty discourse over the centuries that I considered highlighting it as a seventh answer. But in one way or another it penetrates all the others. In the eighteenth century, the capacity to work defined the boundary between types of poor people—the able bodied and the impotent. Today, it polices the border of social policy, separating the working and non-working poor and rewarding only the former with anything approaching adequate benefits. Chronic joblessness marks the areas of concentrated poverty in America's cities where the lack of work distinguishes the territories of poverty. At the same time, another way to talk about the political economy of poverty is through the unemployment produced by the routine workings of capitalism. This was true in the nineteenth and early twentieth centuries when work remained irregular and seasonal. It remains the case today when so many have been laid off on account of deindustrialization followed by the contraction of service sector jobs, especially in the public sector. The rewards of work, moreover, have depended on power, notably on the capacity of organized workers to extract a living wage without which work becomes exploitation, not the means to a decent life. Work, of course, also has been closely tied to labor markets. Tight labor markets always have proved effective anti-poverty strategies, as in World War II or during the early 1990s.

In practical terms where does that take us? At the risk of intellectual incoherence, we should support whatever works, taking advantage of successful ideas and programs that flow from each definition of poverty. But we need to pay special attention to those strands that mainstream poverty policy treats most lightly: resources, political economy, and power.

This means we need to risk inconsistency. Inconsistency is the price progressives have to pay in a world marked by contradiction. In the early twentieth century, Progressive-era reformers and social scientists wrote about poverty at a moment when poverty suddenly appeared unnecessary and the possibility of its near disappearance was a sustaining faith. Some of them even rejected the idea of the undeserving poor. One of the most experienced early poverty researchers, Lilian Brandt, wrote in 1908 that in the preceding two or three years the heretical idea that "poorly paid employment" constituted one of the prime causes of poverty had taken root among some researchers. "And we are coming, therefore, to think of 'insufficient income,' when it means inadequate compensation, not as a joke, but as one of the causes of dependence." In the end, most poverty, Brandt concluded, resulted from "some form of exploitation...some defect in governmental efficiency." Poverty, in short, was at the heart of the problem of political economy: exploitation without, in modern terms, an adequate safety net. To be sure, some "natural depravity" and "moral defects" resulted in dependence, but they "may not be large enough to constitute a serious problem."[6] Brandt's boss, Edward T. Devine, the longtime director of New York's Charity Organization Society, wrote in his widely read book *Misery and Its Causes* that misery, including poverty, "is economic, accidental and transfigured by the abiding presence of hope."[7] For Devine, Brandt, and others, poverty was also a seventh kind of problem—a problem of pessimism, which they were determined to overcome. To make real progress, we need to recapture their energy and their faith.

ACKNOWLEDGMENTS

THE FIRST INCARNATION OF *The Undeserving Poor* grew out of an invitation in the late 1980s from André Schiffrin and Sara Bershtel, then of Pantheon Books, to write a short book on poverty for a new series on the politics of knowledge. I remain grateful for the invitation and for their support and help during the process. I will not repeat the acknowledgments in the book's initial version. But my thanks to the individuals listed there remain as strong as ever.

This is essentially a new book, longer, updated, and with significant revisions in interpretation. There are descriptive sections that have changed little—although there are at least minor editorial changes to almost every paragraph. In a separate essay, I will try to explain the differences between editions and the reasons for them. The impetus to write the new version came from the realization that the book was still assigned to students even though parts were badly outdated. Because of its name recognition, it seemed to make more sense to capitalize on the title than to write a competing book. I received special encouragement from the students in my then-colleague Eric Michael Dyson's class on poverty; my good friend, the great writer, Mike Rose, who, as so often before, helped me out of a writing jam; and my friend and colleague Tom Sugrue, whose work and knowledge are a continuing inspiration.

Thanks to my agent, Geri Thoma, for immediately seeing the importance of the project and to Dave McBride at Oxford University Press for his enthusiasm from the first moment it was proposed. Special thanks to Autumn Hope McGrath for meticulous assistance with footnotes and proofreading.

This book draws on my writing on poverty and the welfare state in the years since the publication of the first version. In those books I have tried to thank the many people who helped me along the way and will not repeat the long list here. But, again, know that I remember your help with gratitude.

For this new version I do need to single out some colleagues and friends. When it became apparent that I had to add biology to the discussion of the undeserving poor, Merlin Chowkwanyun became my unofficial guide to literature and respondent as I shaped ideas; his assistance proved indispensable. Neuroscientist Joshua Jacobs read the section and offered reassurance. Remaining errors are, of course, my responsibility. Dennis Culhane and Mark Stern helped me to become up-to-date on homelessness. Over many years I have learned a great deal from Alice O'Connor and have leaned heavily on her work, most notably her magisterial *Poverty Knowledge*. My other debts to the outstanding recent scholarship on poverty should be apparent in the book's footnotes.

Critics of the first version made it clear that the book's treatment of gender was its weakest part. I have tried to do better this time. Thanks to Viviana Zelizer for helping me with the task. Herb Gans pointed out that the first version lacked a definition of liberalism, which this one supplies and tries to use consistently. Herb's written work and private comments have been a beacon of engaged scholarship for decades.

In May 2012 Ananya Roy invited me to a September conference, "Territories of Poverty," at Berkeley. For the conference, I wrote a long paper, "What Kind of a Problem is Poverty?," which became the intellectual spine of this book. The conference came at just the right moment to push my thinking and provoke new ideas. I have been inspired, too, by Ananya's writing, especially *Poverty Capital*.

My personal debts to my friends in Clioquossia remain large, as do my debts to my wife Edda and children who have given me, as always, unfailing support.

NOTES

Preface

1. Michael Harrington, *The Other America: Poverty in the United States* (New York: Simon and Schuster, 1962), 1–2.

2. Daniel M. Fox, *The Discovery of Abundance: Simon Patten and the Transformation of Social Theory* (Ithaca, N.Y.: Cornell University Press, 1967).

Chapter 1

1. Daniel M. Fox, *The Discovery of Abundance: Simon Patten and the Transformation of Social Theory* (Ithaca, N.Y.: Cornell University Press, 1967), 88.

2. For a meditation on social obligations to strangers, see Michael Ignatieff, *The Needs of Strangers: An Essay on Privacy, Solidarity, and the Politics of Being Human* (New York: Penguin Books, 1984). On the early history of social welfare policies in America, see Walter I. Trattner, *From Poor Law to Welfare State: A History of Social Welfare in America*, 3rd ed. (New York: Free Press, 1984), 1–46; David J. Rothman, *The Discovery of the Asylum: Social Order and Disorder in the Early Republic* (Boston: Little, Brown, 1971); Benjamin J. Klebaner, "Public Poor Relief in America, 1790-1860," Ph.D. diss., Columbia University, 1952; and Michael B. Katz, *In the Shadow of the Poorhouse: A Social History of Welfare in America* (New York: Basic Books, 1986), 3–35.

3. For examples of criticism of settlement practices, see "Report of the Secretary of State [of New York], 1824, on the Relief and Settlement of the Poor," reprinted in David J. Rothman, ed., *The Almshouse*

Experience: Collected Reports (New York: Arno Press and New York Times, 1971), 967, 952. For contemporary evidence that there is little relation between the generosity of welfare benefits and the size of AFDC roles, see Kirsten A. Gronbjerg, *Mass Society and the Extension of Welfare 1960-1970* (Chicago: University of Chicago Press, 1977), 51–54. Cybelle Fox, *Three Worlds of Relief: Race, Immigration, and the American Welfare State from the Progressive Era to the New Deal* (Princeton: Princeton University Press, 2012) documents the reluctance to provide assistance to Mexican immigrants.

4. [Josiah Quincy] "Report on the Committee on the Pauper Laws of this Commonwealth [1821]," in Rothman, *Almshouse Experience*, 4.

5. Philadelphia Board of Guardians, "Report of the Committee Appointed by the Board of Guardians of the Poor of the City and Districts of Philadelphia and Salem [1827]," in Rothman, *Almshouse Experience*, 26.

6. Charles Burroughs, "A Discourse Delivered in the Chapel of the New Alms-House, in Portsmouth, N.H . . ." (Portsmouth, N.H.: J.W. Foster, 1835), in David J. Rothman, ed., *The Jacksonians on the Poor* (New York: Arno Press, 1971), 9.

7. Walter Channing, "An Address on the Prevention of Pauperism" (Boston: Office of the Christian World, 1843), in Rothman, *Jacksonians*, 20.

8. On the relation between concepts of poverty, welfare, and the labor market, see Frances Fox Piven and Richard A. Cloward, *Regulating the Poor: The Functions of Public Welfare* (New York: Vintage, 1971); on the history of the work ethic in America, see Daniel Rodgers, *The Work Ethic in Industrial America, 1850–1920* (Chicago: University of Chicago Press, 1978). For an example of the connections between poverty and the structure of social existence in antebellum America, see Christine Stansell, *City of Women: Sex and Class in New York, 1789–1869* (New York: Knopf, 1986). Stansell also emphasizes the moralization of poverty in the early nineteenth century. See also, Billy G. Smith, *The "Lower Sort": Philadelphia's Laboring People, 1750–1900* (Ithaca, N.Y.: Cornell University Press, 1990). On the link between the development of capitalism, wage labor, poverty, and poor relief in early America, see, Seth Rockman, *Scraping By: Wage Labor, Slavery, and Survival in Early Baltimore* (Baltimore: The Johns Hopkins University Press, 2009).

9. For reanalysis of data collected in the nineteenth century, see Michael B. Katz, *Poverty and Policy in American History* (New York: Academic Press, 1983), 55–182.

10. Robert Hunter, *Poverty* (Harper and Row, 1965, first published, New York: Macmillan, 1904), 3, 63. On scientific charity, see Katz, *Shadow*, 58–84, and Paul Boyer, *Urban Masses and Moral Order in America, 1820–1920* (Cambridge: Harvard University Press, 1978). Also relevant are James T. Patterson, *America's Struggle against Poverty, 1900–1980* (Cambridge: Harvard University Press, 1981), and Daniel

Kevles, *In the Name of Eugenics: Genetics and the Uses of Human Heredity* (New York: Knopf, 1985).

11. Lilian Brandt, "The Causes of Poverty," *Political Science Quarterly* 23, no.4 (December 1908): 642–645.

12. E. Wight Bakke, *The Unemployed Worker: A Study of the Task of Making a Living Without a Job* (New Haven: Yale University Press, 1940); Bonnie Fox Schwartz, *The Civil Works Administration: The Business of Emergency Employment in the New Deal* (Princeton: Princeton University Press, 1984), 227–228; Josephine Chapin Brown, *Public Relief 1929–1939* (New York: Henry Holt, 1941), 317.

13. Cybelle Fox, *Three Worlds of Relief: Race.*

14. Winifred Bell, *Aid to Dependent Children* (New York: Columbia University Press, 1965). On how the Social Security Administration preserved the distinction between social insurance and public assistance, see Jerry R. Cates, *Insuring Inequality: Administrative Leadership in Social Security, 1935–1954* (Ann Arbor: University of Michigan Press, 1983).

15. Michael B. Katz, *The Price of Citizenship: Redefining the American Welfare State*, Updated Edition (Philadelphia: University of Pennsylvania Press, 2008), 1–8.

16. Michael B. Katz, *Poverty and Policy in American History* (New York: Academic Press, 1983), 120–125; Michelle Alexander, *The New Jim Crow: Mass Incarceration in an Age of Colorblindness* (New York: New Press, 2010).

17. Michael Harrington, *The Other America* (New York: Macmillan, 1962; republished by Penguin Books, 1963), 9.

18. Alice O'Connor, *Poverty Knowledge: Social Science, Social Policy, and the Poor in Twentieth-Century U.S. History* (Princeton: Princeton University Press, 2001), 102–107.

19. O'Connor, *Poverty Knowledge*, 113–117.

20. Oscar Lewis, *The Children of Sanchez* (New York: Random House, 1961); *La Vida: A Puerto Rican Family in the Culture of Poverty—San Juan and New York* (New York: Random House, 1966); "The Culture of Poverty," *Scientific American* 215 (1966): 19–25; "The Culture of Poverty," in Daniel P. Moynihan, ed., *On Understanding Poverty: Perspectives from the Social Sciences* (New York: Basic Books, 1969), 187–220. For useful comments on the origins of the culture of poverty concept in American social science, see Lee Rainwater, "The Problem of Lower Class Culture," *Journal of Social Issues* 26 (1970): 133–137. Rainwater points to the growing emphasis on lower-class culture as one stream in social science since the 1930s. Oscar Lewis, he contends, developed his definition "somewhat independently."

21. O'Connor, *Poverty Knowledge*, 117.

22. Lewis, *La Vida*, xliii.

23. Lewis, *La Vida*, xliii–xlv.

24. Lewis, *La Vida*, xlv.

25. Lewis, *La Vida*, xxlv–xlvii.
26. Lewis, *La Vida*, xlvii–xlviii.
27. Lewis, *La Vida*, xlviii–xlix.
28. Lewis, *La Vida*, li–lii.
29. Lewis, *La Vida*, xiii.
30. Lewis, *La Vida*, xlviii, lii.
31. Lewis, *La Vida*, xlii. For biographical background on Harrington, see Maurice Isserman, *The Other American: The Life of Michael Harrington* (New York: Public Affairs, 2000).
32. Harrington, *The Other America*, 22–23.
33. Harold Meyerson, "Seeing What No One Else Could See," *American Prospect*, July/August 2012, 68.
34. Frank Riessman, *The Culturally Deprived Child* (New York: Harper and Row, 1962), 2–3. For criticisms of cultural deprivation as a concept in education, see Murray L. Wax and Rosalie H. Wax, "Cultural Deprivation as an Educational Ideology," and Mildred Dickeman, "The Integrity of the Cherokee Student," in Eleanor Burke Leacock, *The Culture of Poverty: A Critique* (New York: Simon and Schuster, 1971), 127–139 and 140–179. For an extension of the culture of poverty to cultural deprivation and its application to social work, see Jerome Cohen, "Social Work and the Culture of Poverty," *Social Work* 9 (January 1964): 3–11.
35. Riessman, *Culturally Deprived Child*, 30–35.
36. Oscar Handlin, *Boston's Immigrants: A Study in Acculturation*, rev. and enlarged ed. (Cambridge: Harvard University Press, 1959), 51, 120–212; 125.
37. John W. Cell, *The Highest Stage of White Supremacy: The Origins of Segregation in South Africa and the American South* (New York: Cambridge University Press, 1982), 236; Stanley M. Elkins, *Slavery: A Problem in American Institutional Life*, 3rd ed. (Chicago: University of Chicago Press, 1976).
38. Alyosha Goldstein, *Poverty in Common: The Politics of Community Action in the American Century* (Durham: Duke University Press, 2012).
39. I am indebted to a conversation with Ivar Berg for the hypothesis that the popularity of the culture of poverty rested in part on liberal dissatisfaction with the concept of false consciousness.
40. "Remarks of the President at Howard University, June 4, 1965," in Lee Rainwater and William L. Yancey, *The Moynihan Report and the Politics of Controversy* (Cambridge: The M.I.T. Press, 1967), 127–128.
41. For the history of the report and the controversy following its preparation, the definitive source is James T. Patterson, *Freedom is Not Enough: The Moynihan Report and America's Struggle Over Black Family Life from LBJ to Obama* (New York: Basic Books, 2010).
42. The full text of the report is included in Rainwater and Yancey, *The Moynihan Report*, 39–125.

43. Rainwater and Yancey, *Moynihan Report*, 6–7; Kenneth B. Clark, *Dark Ghetto: Dilemmas of Social Power* (New York: Harper and Row, 1965); E. Franklin Frazier, *The Negro in the United States* (New York: Macmillan, rev. ed., 1957), esp. 636–637.

44. Eleanor Burke Leacock drew the connection among nineteenth-century ideas about poverty, Lewis's version of the culture of poverty, and Moynihan's report in the introduction to her edited volume, *The Culture of Poverty*, 11.

45. Rainwater and Yancey, *Moynihan Report*, 27, 29. Rainwater and Yancey analyze the principal criticisms of the Moynihan report in detail and show precisely where distortions existed. See, for instance, *Moynihan Report*, 220–244.

46. Patterson, *Freedom Is Not Enough*, 19.

47. "The Negro Family: The Case for National Action," in Rainwater and Yancey, *Moynihan Report*, 43.

48. Rainwater and Yancey, *Moynihan Report*, 45.

49. Rainwater and Yancey, *Moynihan Report*, 20.

50. Rainwater and Yancey, *Moynihan Report*, 51.

51. Rainwater and Yancey, *Moynihan Report*, 75.

52. Rainwater and Yancey, *Moynihan Report*, 62.

53. Rainwater and Yancey, *Moynihan Report*, 17.

54. Rainwater and Yancey, *Moynihan Report*, 66–67. Emphasis in original.

55. Rainwater and Yancey, *Moynihan Report*, 67 and 71.

56. Rainwater and Yancey, *Moynihan Report*, 74–75.

57. Rainwater and Yancey, *Moynihan Report*, 76–78.

58. Rainwater and Yancey, *Moynihan Report*, 75.

59. Rainwater and Yancey, *Moynihan Report*, 80–90.

60. Rainwater and Yancey, *Moynihan Report*, 93–94.

61. Rainwater and Yancey, *Moynihan Report*, 31.

62. Rainwater and Yancey, *Moynihan Report*, 142, 22–244.

63. Rainwater and Yancey, *Moynihan Report*, 238.

64. See the major attacks on the report by Benjamin F. Payton and William Ryan. Rainwater and Yancey, *Moynihan Report*, 396, 463.

65. Edward C. Banfield, with the assistance of Laura Fasano Banfield, *The Moral Basis of a Backward Society* (New York: Free Press, 1958). Lewis introduced the culture of poverty in *The Children of Sanchez*, published in 1961.

66. Banfield, *Moral Basis*, 83.

67. Banfield, *Moral Basis*, 8, 18–32, 40–41, 115.

68. Banfield, *Moral Basis*, 155; 66.

69. Edward C. Banfield, *The Unheavenly City* (Boston: Little, Brown, 1970), and *The Unheavenly City Revisited* (Boston: Little, Brown, 1974).

70. Banfield, *The Unheavenly City Revisited*, 2–3.

71. Banfield, *The Unheavenly City Revisited*, 53.

72. Banfield, *The Unheavenly City Revisited*, 56.

73. Banfield, *The Unheavenly City Revisited*, 54.
74. Banfield, *The Unheavenly City Revisited*, 78.
75. Banfield, *The Unheavenly City Revisited*, 84, 96.
76. Banfield, *The Unheavenly City Revisited*, 47–48.
77. Banfield, *The Unheavenly City Revisited*, 128–131.
78. Banfield, *The Unheavenly City Revisited*, 135. Emphasis in original.
79. Banfield, *The Unheavenly City Revisited*, 141.
80. Banfield, *The Unheavenly City Revisited*, 143.
81. Banfield, *The Unheavenly City Revisited*, 235.
82. Banfield, *The Unheavenly City Revisited*, 240–259.
83. Banfield, *The Unheavenly City Revisited*, 281.
84. Charles E. Lindblom and David K. Cohen, *Usable Knowledge: Social Science and Social Problem Solving* (New Haven: Yale University Press, 1979), 58.
85. *Second Annual Report of the [Massachusetts] Board of State Charities to which are added the Reports of the Secretary and the General Agent of the Board, Public Document 19*, January 1866, xxii–xxiii.
86. Michael B. Katz, *The Irony of Early School Reform: Educational Innovation in Mid-Nineteenth Century Massachusetts* (Cambridge: Harvard University Press, 1968; reissued with a new introduction New York: Teachers College Press, 2001), 115–160, 170–185.
87. Harold Schwartz, *Samuel Gridley Howe, Social Reformer, 1801–1876* (Cambridge: Harvard University Press, 1956), 271–272, 275–276.
88. Norm Dain, *Concepts of Insanity in the United States, 1987–1865* (New Brunswick: Rutgers University Press, 1964), 110; W. David Lewis, *From Newgate to Dannemora: the Rise of the Penitentiary in New York, 1796-1848* (Ithaca: Cornell University Press, 1965), 231; David Brion Davis, *Homicide in American Fiction, 1978-1860: A Study in Social Values* (Ithaca: Cornell University Press, 1957), 43–44; State Board of Charities, *Second Annual Report*, xxii–xxxvii.
89. Daniel J. Kevles, *In the Name of Genetics: Genetics and the Uses of Human Heredity* (New York: Knopf, 1985), ix, 14.
90. Kevles, *In the Name of Genetics*, 20; Richard Hofstadter, *Social Darwinism in American Thought*, revised edition (Boston: Beacon Press, 1955).
91. Quoted in Bender, *American Abyss: Savagery and Civilization in the Age of Industry* (Ithaca: Cornell University Press, 2009), 202.
92. Daniel E. Bender, *American Abyss,* 6–7.
93. Kevles, *In the Name of Eugenics*, 3.
94. Kevles, *In the Name of Eugenics*, 72.
95. Bender, *American Abyss*, 8.
96. Quoted in Bender, *American Abyss*, 9.
97. Bender, *American Abyss*, 194–195.
98. Quoted in Bender, *American Abyss*, 179.
99. Kevles, *In the Name of Eugenics*, 45–47, 54–55.
100. Kevles, *In the Name of Eugenics*, 78–79. Quotations in Kevles.

101. Stephen J. Gould, *The Panda's Thumb: More Reflections on Natural History* (New York: W. W. Norton, 1980), 162.

102. Paula S. Fass, *Outside In: Minorities and the Transformation of American Education* (New York: Oxford University Press, 1989), 46.

103. Kevles, *In the Name of Eugenics*, 82–83.

104. Fass, *Outside In*, 50.

105. Terman's remarks were reprinted in *School and Society*, XIX, No. 483 (March 29, 1924): 359–364 and excerpted in Clarence J. Karier, ed., *Shaping the American Educational State: 1900 to the Present* (New York: Free Press, 1975, quotation, 188).

106. Kevles, *In the Name of Eugenics*, 110–111.

107. Bender, *American Abyss*, 178, 198–199.

108. Kevles, *In the Name of Eugenics*, 117–118, 251; Bender, *American Abyss*, 235, 251.

109. Keveles, *In the Name of Eugenics*, 269; "Arthur R. Jensen Dies at 89; Set Off Debate Around IQ," *New York Times*, November 2, 2012 [http://www.nytimes.com/2012/11/02/science/arthur-r-jensen-who-set-off-debate-on-iq-dies].

110. Arthur R. Jensen, "How Much Can We Boost IQ and Scholastic Achievement," *Harvard Educational Review*, 39, No. 1 (1969): 2, 3.

111. Jensen, "How Much Can We Boost IQ and Scholastic Achievement," 5, 19, 28, 51; Kevles, *In the Name of Eugenics*, 281.

112. Richard J. Herrnstein and Charles Murray, *The Bell Curve: Intelligence and Class Structure in American Life* (New York: Free Press, 1994), 9.

113. Richard Herrnstein, "I.Q.," *The Atlantic*, 228 (September 1971): 63–64; Shockley quoted in Kevles, *In the Name of Eugenics*, 271.

114. Edward O. Wilson, "Human Decency is Animal," *The New York Times Magazine*, October 12, 1975, 39.

115. Herrnstein and Murray, *Bell Curve*, 22–23.

116. Herrnstein and Murray, *Bell Curve*, 118, 127, 270, 371.

117. Herrnstein and Murray, *Bell Curve*, 341, 509, 518 (quotation page 518).

118. Fischer et al., *Inequality by Design*, 11–12.

119. Fischer et al., *Inequality by Design*, 32, 75–75, 85–86, 125.

120. http://www.pioneerfund.org/ [accessed October 29, 2012].

121. Edward M. Stricker, "2009 Survey of Neuroscience Graduate, Postdoctoral, and Undergraduate Programs." http://www.sfn.org/Careers-and-Training/Higher-Education-and-Training/~/media/SfN/Documents/Survey%20Reports/2009%20Survey%20Report%20FINAL/2009%20Survey%20Report%20FINAL.ashx], accessed April 7, 2013.

122. Barbara Wolfe, William Evans, and Teresa E. Seeman, editors, *The Biological Consequences of Socioeconomic Inequalities* (New York: Russell Sage Foundation, 2012).

123. See, for instance, Jamie Hanson, Nicole Hair, Amitabh Chandra, Ed Moss, Jay Bhattacharya, Seth D. Polk, and Barbara Wolfe, "Brain

Development and Poverty: A First Look," in Wolfe, et al., *Biological Consequences*, 208.

124. Michael Rutter, "Achievements and Challenges in the Biology of Environmental Effects," PNAS, 109, Supplement 2, 17151.

125. Carey, *The Epigenetics Revolution: How Modern Biology is Rewriting Our Understanding of Genetics, Disease, and Inheritance* (New York: Columbia University Press, 2012), 7.

126. These numbers are based on the result of a search in the Thomson Reuters "Web of Knowledge" database for "achievement gap" performed on November 1, 2012. My thanks to Nick Okrent of the University of Pennsylvania library staff.

127. For two important interpretations of the achievement gap, see Heather Ann Thompson, "Criminalizing Kids: The Overlooked Reason for Failing Schools" and Pedro Nogeura, "The Achievement Gap and The Schools We Need: Creating the Conditions Where Race and Class No Longer Predict Student Achievement" in Michael B. Katz and Mike Rose, *Public Education Under Siege* (Philadelphia: University of Pennsylvania Press, 2013).

128. Carey, *Epigenetics Revolution*, 250.

129. W. Thomas Boyce, Maria B. Sokolowski, and Gene E. Robinson, "Toward a New Biology of Social Adversity," PNAS 109, Supplement 2, 17143.

130. Rutter, "Achievement and Challenges," 17152.

131. James J. Heckman, "Schools, Skills, and Synapses," *Econ. Inq.* 46, No.3 (June 2008): 289. See also, James Heckman, "Promoting Social Mobility," *Boston Review*, September/October 2012 [http://www.bostonreview.net/BR37.5/ndf_james_heckman_social_mobility.php].

132. Jack P. Shonkoff, "Leveraging the Biology of Adversity To Address the Roots of Disparities in Health and Development," PNAS, 109, suppl. 2 (October 16, 2012): 17302.

133. Rutter, "Achievements and Challenges," 17150.

134. Michelle C. Carlson, Christoher L. Seplaki, and Teresa E. Seeman, "Reversing the Impact of Disparities in Socioeconomic Status over the Life Course on Cognitive and Brain Aging," in Wolfe et al., *Biological Consequences*, 233–234.

135. Dorothy Roberts, *Fatal Invention: How Science, Politics, and Big Business Re-create Race in the Twenty-first Century* (New York: New Press, 2011), 91.

136. Jesse J. Prinz, *Beyond Human Nature: How Culture and Experience Shape the Human Mind* (New York: W. W. Norton, 2012), 4.

Chapter 2

1. For a general criticism of the politics of the culture of poverty, see Hylan Lewis, "Culture of Poverty? What Does It Matter?" in Eleanor Burke

Leacock, *The Culture of Poverty: A Critique* (New York: Simon and Schuster, 1971), 345–363.

2. Randolf S. David, "The Sociology of Poverty or the Poverty of Sociology? A Brief Note on Urban Poverty Research," *Philippine Sociological Review* 25 (1977): 145–146, 149. Emphasis in original.

3. Alessio Colombis, "Amoral Familism and Social Organisation in Montegrano: A Critique of Banfield's Thesis," *Domination et Dependance: Situations Peuples Mediterraneans* 25 (1983): 24.

4. Alejandro Portes, "Rationality in the Slum: An Essay on Interpretive Sociology," *Comparative Studies in Society and History* 14 (1972): 269.

5. Portes, "Rationality in the Slum," 274, 272. In *Marketing Democracy: Power and Social Movements in Post-Dictatorship Chile* (Berkeley and Los Angeles: University of California Press, 2001), Julia Paley shows how poor residents of a Chilean shantytown developed an indigenous social science that formed the basis of local political mobilization.

6. Colombis, "Amoral Familism," 33.

7. David, "The Sociology of Poverty," 148–149.

8. Walter B. Miller, "Subculture, Social Reform, and the 'Culture of Poverty,'" *Human Organization* 30 (1971): 112.

9. Chandler C. Davidson, "On the 'Culture of Shiftlessness,'" *Dissent* 23 (1976): 355.

10. Eleanor Leacock, "Distortions of Working-Class Reality in American Social Science," *Science and Society* 31 (1967): 3–4.

11. See, for example, Audrey James Schwartz, "A Further Look at 'Culture of Poverty:' Ten Caracas Barrios," *Sociology and Social Research* 59 (July 1975): 362–386.

12. Leonard Davidson and David Krackhardt, "Structural Change and the Disadvantaged: An Empirical Test of Culture of Poverty/Situational Theories of Hard-Core Work Behavior," *Human Organization* 36 (1977): 308.

13. Frederick S. Jaffe and Steven Polgar, "Family Planning and Public Policy: Is the 'Culture of Poverty' the New Cop-Out?" *Journal of Marriage and the Family* 30 (1968): 228–235.

14. Harland Padfield, "New Industrial Systems and Cultural Concepts of Poverty," *Human Organization* 29 (1970): 33. Some other examples of empirical studies are: Victor S. D'souza, "Socio-Cultural Marginality: A Theory of Urban Slums and Poverty in India," *Sociological Bulletin* 28 (1979): 9–23; Seymour Parker and Robert J. Kleiner, "The Culture of Poverty: An Adjustive Dimension," *American Anthropologist* 72 (1970): 516–527; David B. Miller, "A Partial Test of Oscar Lewis's Culture of Poverty in Rural America," *Current Anthropology* 17 (1976): 720–723; Hyman Rodman, *Lower-Class Families: The Culture of Poverty in Negro Trinidad* (London: Oxford University Press, 1971), Schwartz, "A Further Look";

Gordon Ternowetsky, "Work Orientations of the Poor and Income Maintenance," *Australian Journal of Sociology* 12 (1977): 266–279; and Sonia R. Wright and James D. Wright, "Income Maintenance and Work Behavior," *Social Policy* 6 (1975): 24–32.

15. Rodman, *Lower-Class Families*, 195. Rodman developed his concept from his field work in Trinidad.

16. Elliot Liebow, *Tally's Corner: A Study of Negro Streetcorner Men* (Boston: Little, Brown, 1967), 213, 208, 209, 222.

17. The discussion that follows draws on the following sources: Davidson and Krackhardt, "Structural Change;" Davidson, " 'Culture of Shiftlessness;' " David Elesh, "Poverty Theories and Income Maintenance: Validity and Policy Relevance," *Social Science Quarterly* 54 (1973): 359–373; Lola M. Irean, Oliver C. Moles, and Robert M. O'Shea, "Ethnicity, Poverty, and Selected Attitudes: A Test of the 'Culture of Poverty' Hypothesis," *Social Forces* 47 (June 1969): 405–413; Miller, "Subculture"; Padfield, "New Industrial Systems"; Jack L. Roach and Orville R. Gursslin, "An Evaluation of the Concept of 'Culture of Poverty,' " *Social Forces* 45 (March 1967): 383–393; Hyman Rodman, "Culture of Poverty: The Rise and Fall of a Concept," *The Sociological Review* 25, new series (1977): 867–876; Charles A. Valentine, *Culture and Poverty: Critique and Counter-Proposals* (Chicago and London: University of Chicago Press, 1968), and "Models and Muddles Concerning Culture and Inequality: A Reply to Critics," *Harvard Educational Review* 42 (1972): 97–108; Lee Rainwater, "The Problem of Lower Class Culture," *Journal of Social Issues* 26 (1970): 133–148; J. Allen Winter, ed., *The Poor: A Culture of Poverty or a Poverty of Culture?* (Grand Rapids, Mich.: William B. Eerdmans, 1971); Leacock, *Culture of Poverty*.

18. Orlando Patterson, "A Poverty of the Mind," *New York Times*, March 26, 2006.

19. William Julius Wilson, *More Than Just Race: Being Black and Poor in the Inner City* (New York: Norton, 2009), 3.

20. Wilson, *More Than Just Race*, 4.

21. Mario Luis Small, David J. Harding, and Michèle Lamont, "Reconsidering Culture and Poverty," *Annals of the American Academy of Political and Social Science* 629 (May 2010): 6–8. Emphasis in original.

22. Small, Harding, and Lamont, "Reconsidering," 9–12.

23. Small, Harding, and Lamont, "Reconsidering," 14, 20.

24. Small, Harding, and Lamont, "Reconsidering," 19.

25. For a history of response to the report, see James T. Patterson, *Freedom is Not Enough: The Moynihan Report and America's Struggle Over Black Family Life from LBJ to Obama* (New York: Basic Books, 2010).

26. Lee Rainwater and William Yancey, *The Moynihan Report and the Politics of Controversy* (Cambridge: MIT Press, 1967), 217–218.

27. Quoted in Rainwater and Yancey, *Moynihan Report*, 130.

28. Quoted in Rainwater and Yancey, *Moynihan Report*, 200.

29. Rainwater and Yancey, *Moynihan Report*, 202.
30. Rainwater and Yancey, *Moynihan Report*, 16.
31. Rainwater and Yancey, *Moynihan Report*, 271.
32. Rainwater and Yancey, *Moynihan Report*, 175–176.
33. Rainwater and Yancey, *Moynihan Report*, 177–178; 133–135.
34. Elizabeth Herzog, "Is There a 'Breakdown' of the Negro Family?" reprinted in Rainwater and Yancey, *Moynihan Report*, 347.
35. William Ryan, "Savage Discovery: 'The Moynihan Report,'" reprinted in Rainwater and Yancey, *Moynihan Report*, 459–464.
36. Office of Policy Planning and Research, United States Department of Labor, *The Negro Family: The Case for National Action*, March 1965, 13, 14. One partial exception among critics was Laura Carper, "The Negro Family and the Moynihan Report," reprinted in Rainwater and Yancey, *Moynihan Report*, 469. On the rise in AFDC rolls, see Frances Fox Piven and Richard Cloward, *Regulating the Poor: The Functions of Public Welfare* (New York: Vintage, 1971), 183–199, and *Poor People's Movements: Why They Succeed, How They Fail* (New York: Pantheon, 1982), 264–362. See also James T. Patterson, *America's Struggle Against Poverty, 1900-1980* (Cambridge: Harvard University Press, 1981), 171–184.
37. Herbert J. Gans, "The Negro Family: Reflections on the Moynihan Report," reprinted in Rainwater and Yancey, *Moynihan Report*, 455–456.
38. Christopher Jencks, "The Moynihan Report," reprinted in Rainwater and Yancey, *Moynihan Report*, 444.
39. Kathryn Edin and Maria Kefalas, *Promises I Can Keep: Why Poor Women Put Motherhood Before Marriage*, 3d revised edition (Berkeley and Los Angeles: University of California Press, 2011).
40. Carol Stack, *All Our Kin: Strategies for Survival in a Black Community* (New York: Harper and Row, 1974), 28, 30, 31, 90.
41. Benjamin F. Payton, "New Trends in Civil Rights," in Rainwater and Yancey, *Moynihan Report*, 399 and 401.
42. Jacqueline Jones, *Labor of Love, Labor of Sorrow: Black Women, Work, and the Family from Slavery to the Present* (New York: Basic Books, 1985); Herbert G. Gutman, *The Black Family in Slavery and Freedom, 1750-1925* (New York: Vintage Books, 1976); Theodore Hershberg, ed., *Philadelphia: Work, Space, Family, and Group Experience: Essays Toward an Interdisciplinary History of the City* (New York: Oxford University Press, 1981); Stewart E. Tolnay, *The Bottom Rung: African American Family Life on Southern Farms* (Urbana and Chicago: University of Illinois Press, 1999).
43. Herbert G. Gutman, *The Black Family in Slavery and Freedom, 1750-1925* (New York: Vintage Books, 1976); Frank F. Furstenberg, Jr., Theodore Hershberg, and John Modell, "The Origins of the Female-Headed Black Family: The Impact of the Urban Experience," in Theodore Hershberg, ed., *Philadelphia: Work, Space, Family, and Group Experience in the Nineteenth Century* (New York: Oxford University Press, 1981), 435–454;

Olivier Zunz, *The Changing Face of Inequality: Urbanization, Industrial Development, and Immigrants in Detroit, 1880-1920* (Chicago: University of Chicago Press, 1982); Kenneth L. Kusmer, *A Ghetto Takes Shape: Black Cleveland, 1870-1930* (Urbana: University of Illinois Press, 1976); Stanley Lieberson, *A Piece of the Pie: Blacks and White Immigrants since 1880* (Berkeley: University of California Press, 1980); Cybelle Fox, *Three Worlds of Relief: Race, Immigration, and the American Welfare State from the Progressive Era to the New Deal* (Princeton: Princeton University Press, 2012); Jacqueline Jones, *The Dispossessed: America's Underclasses from the Civil War to the Present* (New York: Basic Books, 1992); James N. Gregory, *Southern Diaspora: How the Great Migrations of Black and White Southerners Transformed America* (Chapel Hill: University of North Carolina Press, 2007).

44. *Annals of the American Academy of Political and Social Sciences* 621 (January 2009).

45. Thomas Sowell, "Racial Censorship; 'PC' Atmosphere Paralyzes? Sincerity," *Human Events Online*, October 13, 2003.

46. Maris Vinovskis, *An "Epidemic" of Adolescent Pregnancy? Some Historical and Policy Considerations* (New York: Oxford University Press, 1988).

47. Stokely Carmichael and Charles V. Hamilton, *Black Power: The Politics of Liberation in America* (New York: Random House, 1967), 167.

48. Conventional historiography places the origins of the civil rights movement in the South, with the movement spreading north. Recent historical writing, however, has shown that an active and parallel movement dates from an early point in the North as well. The definitive study is Thomas J. Sugrue, *Sweet Land of Liberty: The Forgotten Struggle for Civil Rights in the North* (New York: Random House, 2008).

49. On the early civil rights movement, see Aldon D. Morris, *The Origins of the Civil Rights Movement: Black Communities Organizing for Change* (New York: Free Press, 1984).

50. Peniel E. Joseph, "Introduction: Toward a Historiography of the Black Power Movement," in Peniel E. Joseph, ed., *The Black Power Movement: Rethinking the Civil-Rights-Black Power Era* (New York and London: Routledge, 2006), 8.

51. Robert L. Allen, *Black Awakening in Capitalist America: An Analytic History* (Garden City: Doubleday, 1969), 27-28; see also Carmichael and Hamilton, *Black Power*, 50; and Jack M. Bloom, *Class, Race, and the Civil Rights Movement* (Bloomington: University of Indiana Press, 1987), 164-179. For contrasting comments on Allen, see Martin Kilson, "Militant Rhetoric and the Bourgeoisie," *New York Times Book Review*, February 22, 1971, 28, and Anne Kelley, [review], *Black Scholar* 3 (1971): 50-54.

52. Thomas H. Jackson, *From Civil Rights to Human Rights: Martin Luther King and the Struggle for Economic Justice* (Philadelphia: University of Pennsylvania Press, 2009).

53. Martin Luther King, Jr., "President's Address to the Tenth Anniversary Convention of the Southern Christian Leadership Conference, Atlanta, Georgia, August 16, 1967," in Robert L. Scott and Wayne Brockriede, eds., *The Rhetoric of Black Power* (New York: Harper and Row, 1969), 147–148.

54. King, "President's Address," 155–158.

55. Martin Luther King, Jr., *Where Do We Go From Here: Chaos or Community?* (Boston: Beacon Press, 1968), 169, 177–178.

56. Robin D. G. Kelley, *Freedom Dreams: The Black Radical Imagination* (Boston: Beacon Press, 2002), 62–63.

57. King, "President's Address," 159–160. On the riots, see Robert M. Fogelson, *Violence as Protest: A Study of Riots and Ghettos* (Garden City: Anchor Books, 1971).

58. Cleveland Sellers, *The River of No Return: The Autobiography of a Black Militant and the Life and Death of SNCC* (New York: Morrow, 1965), 166; and Bloom, *Class, Race, and the Civil Rights Movement*, 208–209. On the history of SNCC, see also Clayborne Carson, *In Struggle: SNCC and the Black Awakening of the 1960s* (Cambridge: Harvard University Press, 1981).

59. Donna Jean Murch, *Living for the City: Migration, Education, and the Rise of the Black Panther Party in Oakland, California* (Chapel Hill: University of North Carolina Press, 2010), 72. See, also, Jeanne Theoharis and Komozi Woodard, eds., *Groundwork: Local Black Freedom Movements in America* (New York: New York University Press, 2005), 12.

60. Robert O. Self, *American Babylon: Race and the Struggle for Postwar Oakland* (Princeton: Princeton University Press, 2003), 218.

61. Harold Cruse, "Revolutionary Nationalism and the Afro-American," *Studies on the Left* 2, no. 3 (1962).

62. Especially important were: Harold Cruse, Kenneth Clark, and Malcolm X. Allen, *Black Awakening*, 6; Carmichael and Hamilton, *Black Power*, 2.

63. Carmichael and Hamilton, *Black Power*, 16–31. For an insightful analysis of the lack of political power in cities, its implications, and its relation to urban political programs, see Joyce Ladner and Walter W. Stafford, "Black Repression in the Cities," *Black Scholar* 1 (April 1970): 39–52.

64. Frank G. Davis, *The Economics of Black Community Development: An Analysis and Program for Autonomous Growth and Development* (Chicago: Markham, 1972): 6–7; Guy C. Z. Mhone, "Structural Oppression and the Persistence of Black Poverty," *Journal of Afro-American Issues* 3 (1975): 406; Charles Sackrey, "The Economics of Black Poverty," *The Review of Black Political Economy* 1 (1971): 48, 50; Wilfred L. David, "Black America in Development Perspective, Part I," *The Review of Black Political Economy* 3 (1973): 99–100; Ron Bailey, "Economic Aspects of the Black Internal Economy," *Review of Black Political Economy* 6 (1973): 62–63; Robert Heilbroner, "Introduction," in Thomas Vietorisz and Bennett Harrison, *The Economic Development*

of Harlem (New York: Praeger, 1970): xxiii; and on growth as an idea underlying post-World War II domestic and foreign policy, Alan Wolfe, *America's Impasse: The Rise and Fall of the Politics of Growth* (Boston: South End Press, 1981). For a useful comment on Davis, see the review by Carolyn Shaw Bell, *Journal of Negro History* 57 (1972): 437–439.

65. Andre Gunder Frank, "The Development of Underdevelopment," in Charles K. Wilbur, comp., *The Political Economy of Development and Underdevelopment* (New York: Random House, 1973), 94–95; Bailey, "Economic Aspects," 60; Wilfred L. David, "Black America in Developmental Perspective," *Review of Black Political Economy* 3 (1973): 87; Donald J. Harris, "The Black Ghetto as Colony: A Theoretical Critique and Alternative Formulation," *Review of Black Political Economy* 2 (1972): 26; Joseph N. Seward, "Developmental Economics and Black America: A Reply to Professor David," *Review of Black Political Economy* 5 (1975): 11–12; Thaddeus H. Spratlen, "Ghetto Economic Development," *Review of Black Political Economy* 1 (1971): 43–71, is a useful review of the literature.

66. Bailey, "Economic Aspects," 44; Paul A. Baran and Paul M. Sweezy, *Monopoly Capital: An Essay on the American Economic and Social Order* (New York: Monthly Review Press), 285–287. Baran and Sweezy's book generated considerable comment and controversy. See, for instance, Karl de Schweinitz, Jr., "Who Decides?—Economics and Politics," *Public Administration Review* 28 (1968): 84–90; James O'Connor, "Marxist Heavyweight Division," *Nation* 202 (1966): 749–750; Howard J. Sherman, "Economic Systems: Planning and Reform; Cooperation," *American Economic Review* 55 (1966): 919–921; Henry Pachter, "The Political Economy of Fidelism," *Dissent* 14 (1967): 358–361; Harvey Magdoff, [review], *Economic Development and Cultural Change* 16 (1967): 145–149; and Myron E. Sharpe, Maurice Dobb, Joseph M. Gillman, Theodore Praeger, and Otto Nathan, "Marxism and Monopoly Capital: A Symposium," *Science and Society* 30 (1966): 461–496.

67. David, "Black America...Part II," 82; Bailey, "Economic Aspects," 59–64; Robert Allen, "A Historical Synthesis: Black Liberation and World Revolution," *The Black Scholar* 3 (1972): 8; William K. Tabb, *The Political Economy of the Black Ghetto* (New York: Norton, 1970), 21–24. For comments on Tabb's book, see the reviews by Joseph L. Arnold, *Journal of Negro History* 56 (1971): 294–296, and Morris Levitt, *American Political Science Review* 65 (1971): 1176–1178.

68. Davis, *Economics of Black Community Development*, 5–8; Kenneth H. Parsons, "Poverty as an Issue in Development Policy: A Comparison of United States and Undeveloped Countries," *Land Economics* 45 (February 1969): 60–61; David, "Black America...Part II," 85–86.

69. Bailey, "Economic Aspects," 64–66; Allen, "A Historical Synthesis," 11–12; Baran and Sweezy, *Monopoly Capital*, 273; Tabb, *Political Economy*,

27; Seward, "Developmental Economics," 11; Joyce Ladner and Walter W. Stafford, "Black Repression in the Cities." James Turner, "Blacks in the Cities: Land and Self-Determination," *The Black Scholar* 1 (1970): 11, argues that the movement toward metropolitan government had as its purpose depriving blacks of effective political power.

70. Ralph H. Metcalf, Jr., "Chicago Model Cities and Neocolonization," *The Black Scholar* 1 (April 1970): 23; David, "Black America...Part I," 91; Turner, "Blacks in the Cities," 10; Allen, "A Historical Synthesis," 8; Bailey, "Economic Aspects," 4–6; Tabb, *Political Economy*, 23.

71. Michael Omni and Howard Winant, *Racial Formation in the United States: From the 1960s to the 1990s*, second edition (New York and London: Routledge, 1994), 110.

72. J. H. O'Dell, "Colonialism and the Negro American Experience," *Freedomways* 6 (1966): 300; David, "Black America...Part II," 98; Bailey, "Economic Aspects," 47; Allen, "A Historical Synthesis," 9–10.

73. Bailey, "Economic Aspects," 55–56; James Turner, "Blacks in the Cities: Land and Self-Determination," *The Black Scholar* 1 (1970): 25; Kwame Nkrumah, "The Mechanics of Neocolonialism," chapter 18 in Nkrumah, *Colonialism, the Last Stage of Imperialism*, reprinted in *Freedomways* 6 (1966): 139.

74. Bailey, "Economic Aspects," 45–46, 57–58; Harris, "The Black Ghetto as Colony," 11–12.

75. Thomas Sowell, "Economics and Black People," *Review of Black Political Economy* 1 (1971): 16–17.

76. Seward, "Developmental Economics," 198–199.

77. Sowell, "Economics and Black People," 16.

78. Davis, *Economics of Black Community Development*, 19; Guy C. Z. Mhone, "Structural Oppression and the Persistence of Black Poverty," *Journal of Afro-American Issues* 3 (1975): 417–418.

79. Turner, "Blacks in the Cities," 12–13; Sackrey, "Economics and Black Poverty," 59.

80. Sugrue, *Sweet Land of Liberty*, 512; H. Paul Friesema, "Black Control of Central Cities: The Hollow Prize," *Journal of the American Institute of Planners* (March 1969): 75.

81. Omi and Winant, *Racial Formation*, 108.

82. Murch, *Living for the City*, 193. On intercommunalism see also, Self, *Babylon*, 301.

83. There are many accounts of law enforcement agencies' assaults on civil rights leaders and on black power, especially the Black Panthers. See, for example, Yohuru Williams, " 'A Red, Black and Green Liberation Jumpsuit': Roy Wilkins, the Black Panthers, and the Conundrum of Black Power" in Joseph, ed., *The Black Power Movement*, 175–180.

84. Kelley, *Freedom Dreams*, 95.

85. For a trenchant critique of internal colonialism from a politically Left perspective, see Omi and Winant, *Racial Formation*, 44–47.

86. http://www.urpe.org.

87. See the journal's home page on the Sage Publications website.

88. My definition of cultural authority is taken from Paul Starr, *The Social Transformation of American Medicine* (New York: Basic Books, 1982), 13: "the probability that particular definitions of reality and judgments of meaning and value will prevail as valid and true."

89. Katznelson, *City Trenches: Urban Politics and the Patterning of Class in the United States* (New York: Pantheon, 1981), esp. 179–180.

90. One discussion of the decline in household manufacture is Nancy Cott, *The Bonds of Womanhood: "Woman's Sphere" in New England, 1780-1835* (New Haven: Yale University Press, 1977).

91. A good statistical overview of women's employment is Lynn Y. Weiner, *From Working Girl to Working Mother: The Female Labor Force in the United States, 1820-1900* (Chapel Hill: University of North Carolina Press, 1985), which has a very useful bibliography. See also Michael B. Katz, Michael J. Doucet, and Mark J. Stern, *The Social Organization of Early Industrial Capitalism* (Cambridge: Harvard University Press, 1981), 97–101 and Seth Rockman, *Scraping By: Wage Labor, Slavery, and Survival in Early Baltimore* (Baltimore: Johns Hopkins University Press, 2009), 132–157.

92. For examples of women's poverty, see Stansell, *City of Women*, and Katz, *Poverty and Policy*, 17–54. Michael B. Katz, "Surviving Poverty in Early Twentieth-Century New York City," in Arnold Hirsch and Raymond Mohl, eds., *Urban Policy in Twentieth-Century America* (New Brunswick: Rutgers University Press, 1973), 46–62.

93. Michael B. Katz, *In the Shadow of the Poorhouse: A Social History of Welfare in America* (New York: Basic Books, 1986), 58–109, and *Poverty and Policy*, 57–89.

94. The most immediate political consequence of granting suffrage to women in 1920 was the Sheppard-Towner Act, which created federally sponsored free medical clinics for mothers and children. Despite the program's success, the hostility of the organized medical profession killed it late in the decade. On the Sheppard-Towner Act, see Sheila M. Rothman, *Woman's Proper Place: A History of Changing Ideas and Practices, 1870 to the Present* (New York: Basic Books, 1978), 136–141; on veterans' pensions, see Ann Shola Orloff and Theda Skocpol, "Why Not Equal Protection? Explaining the Politics of Public Social Welfare in Britain and the United States, 1880s-1920s," paper presented at the annual meeting of the American Sociological Association, Detroit, Michigan, September 2, 1983, 49–55, and Ann Shola Orloff, "The Politics of Pensions: A Comparative Analysis of the Origins of Pensions and Old Age Insurance in Canada, Britain, and the United States, 1880s-1930s," Ph.D. diss., Princeton University, 1985; a useful survey of Progressive-era policies for children is Susan Tiffin, *In Whose Best Interest? Child Welfare Reform in the Progressive Era* (Westport, Conn.: Greenwood Press, 1982); a good

discussion of mothers' pensions is Roy Lubove, *The Struggle for Social Security 1900-1935* (Cambridge: Harvard University Press, 1968), 91–112; see also Katz, *Shadow*, 113–145.

95. Fox, *Three Worlds of Relief*; Winifred Bell, *Aid to Dependent Children* (New York: Columbia University Press, 1965).

96. On AFDC, see Piven and Cloward, *Regulating the Poor*; Bell, *AFCD*; Patterson, *America's Struggle*; on the NWRO, see Guida West, *The National Welfare Rights Movement: The Social Protest of Poor Women* (New York: Praeger, 1981); Larry R. Jackson and William A. Johnson, *Protest by the Poor: The Welfare Rights Movement in New York City* (Lexington, Mass.: Heath, 1974), and Piven and Cloward, *Poor People's Movements*, 264–361; an extremely useful source on trends in spending for social welfare programs is Committee on Ways and Means, U.S. House of Representatives, Background Material and Data on Programs Within the Jurisdiction of the Committee on Ways and Means (Washington, DC: GPO, 1985). See also Michael B. Katz and Lorrin R. Thomas, "The Invention of Welfare in America," *Journal of Policy History* 10, no. 4 (1998): 399–418.

97. On the expansion of social welfare, see Patterson, *America's Struggle*, 157–209, and Katz, *Shadow*, 261–272. On the EITC, see Christopher Howard, *The Hidden Welfare State: Tax Expenditures and Social Policy in the United States* (Princeton: Princeton University Press, 1997), 64–74, 139–160. On the child tax care credit, see, IRS, "Ten Things to Know About the Child and Dependent Care Credit," IRS Tax Tip 20-46, March 7, 2011 [http://www.irs.gov/uac/Ten-Things-to-Know-About-the-Child-and-Dependent-Care-Credit].

98. Michael B. Katz, Mark J. Stern, and Jamie J. Fader, "Women and the Paradox of Economic Inequality in the Twentieth-century," *Journal of Social History* 39, no. 1 (2005): 65–88.

99. Michael B. Katz and Mark J. Stern, "1940s to Present," in Gwendolyn Mink and Alice O'Connor eds., *Poverty in the United States: An Encyclopedia of History, Policy and Politics*, v. 1, (Santa Barbara: ABC-CLIO, 2004), 33–48.

100. Harrell R. Rodgers, Jr., *Poor Women, Poor Families: The Economic Plight of America's Female-Headed Households* (Armonk, N.Y. and London: M. E. Sharpe, 1986), 16–36; Irwin Garfinkle and Sara S. McLanahan, *Single Mothers and Their Children: A New American Dilemma* (Washington, DC: The Urban Institute Press, 1986), 45–85; Robert Pear, "Poverty Rate Dips," *New York Times*, July 31, 1987, A12; Frances Fox Piven and Richard A. Cloward, "The Contemporary Relief Debate," in Fred Block et al., *The Mean Season: The Attack on the Welfare State* (New York: Pantheon, 1987), 55–57.

101. Sar A. Levitan and Isaac Shapiro, *Working But Poor: America's Contradiction* (Baltimore: Johns Hopkins University Press, 1987); Community Service Society of New York, *Poverty in New York City*;

Marian Wright Edelman, *Families in Peril: An Agenda for Social Change* (Cambridge: Harvard University Press, 1987), 48; see also 25-29. Edelman is director of the Children's Defense Fund, which has played a major role in publicizing children's poverty.

102. For examples of the literature describing the feminization of poverty, see Rodgers, *Poor Women*, and Mary Corcoran, Greg J. Duncan, and Martha S. Hill, "The Economic Fortunes of Women and Children: Lessons from the Panel Study of Income Dynamics;" Roslyn L. Feldberg, "Comparable Worth: Toward Theory and Practice in the United States;" and Sheila B. Kammerman, "Women, Children, and Poverty: Public Policies and Female-Headed Families in Industrialized Countries," in Barbara C. Gelpi, Nancy C. M. Hartsock, Clare C. Novak, and Myra H. Strober, eds., *Women and Poverty* (Chicago: University of Chicago Press, 1986), 1–24, 163–180, 41–64; and Diane Pearce, "The Feminization of Poverty: Women, Work and Welfare," *Urban and Social Change Review* 10 (1978): 28–36. The latter is the article that introduced the phrase "feminization of poverty." For a criticism of the feminization of poverty literature from the political Left, see Wendy Savasy and Judith van Allen, "Fighting the Feminization of Poverty: Socialist-Feminist Analysis and Strategy," *Review of Radical Political Economics* 16, no. 4 (1984): 89–110.

103. Diana M. Pearce, "Toil and Trouble: Women Workers and Unemployment Compensation," in Gelpi et al., *Women and Poverty*, 146. On the institutionalization of the split between public assistance and social insurance in the 1930s, see Katz, *Shadow*, 234–245. On the origins of the split between social insurance and public assistance, see Margaret Weir, Ann Shola Orloff, and Theda Skocpol, eds., *The Politics of Social Policy in the United States* (Princeton: Princeton University Press, 1988). See also Linda Gordon, *Pitied But Not Entitled: Single Mothers and the History of Welfare, 1890-1935* (New York: The Free Press, 1994).

104. "History of the Organization," *Triple Jeopardy*, no. 1, September 1971. See also, Stephen Ward, "The Third World Women's Alliance: Black Feminist Radicalism and Black Power Politics," in Joseph, ed., *The Black Power Movement*, 119–144; Kimberly Springer, *Living For The Revolution: Black Feminist Organizations, 1968-1980* (Durham, NC: Duke University Press, 2005), 47–50.

105. *Triple Jeopardy*, September 1971, unpaginated.

106. "Sterilization of BLACK Women Is Common in the U.S.," *Triple Jeopardy* 3, no. 1 (Sept.-Oct. 1973).

107. Dorothy Roberts, *Killing the Black Body: Race, Reproduction, and the Meaning of Liberty* (New York: Pantheon Books, 1997), 90.

108. Patricia Hill Collins, *Black Feminist Thought: Knowledge, Consciousness, and the Politics of Empowerment*, second edition (New York and London: Routledge, 2000), 241.

109. Beverly Guy-Sheftall, "Introduction: The Evolution of Feminist Consciousness Among African American Women," in Guy-Sheftall, ed., *Words of Fire: An Anthology of African-American Feminist Thought*, 15.

110. Gordon, *Pitied But Not Entitled*, 113.

111. Ruth Rosen, *The World Split Open: How the Modern Women's Movement Changed America* (New York and London: Penguin, 2000), 282.

112. Guy-Sheftall, 2.

113. See, e.g., Guy-Sheftall, "Introduction," 2–14; Springer, *Living for the Revolution*, 8–9.

114. Linda La Rue, "The Black Women's Liberation Movement," in Guy-Sheftall, ed., *Words of Fire*, 71; Collins, *Black Feminist Thought*, 75–76.

115. Furstenberg et al., "The Origins of the Female-Headed Black Family: The Impact of the Urban Experience." Hershberg, ed., *Philadelphia*.

116. Louis R. Harlan, *Separate and Unequal: Public School Campaigns and Racism in the Southern Seaboard States, 1901-1915* (Chapel Hill: University of North Carolina Press, 1958).

117. Jones, *Labor of Love*.

118. Fox, *Three Worlds of Relief*.

119. Collins, *Black Feminist Thought*, 241.

120. Pauli Murray, "The Liberation of Black Women," in Guy-Sheftall, ed., *Words of Fire*, 195.

121. Collins, *Black Feminist Thought*, 209.

122. Rosen, *The World Split Open*, 285.

123. Springer, *Living for the Revolution*, 92.

124. Jacqueline Jones, *Labor of Love, Labor of Sorrow: Black Women, Work, and the Family from Slavery to the Present* (New York: Basic Books, 1985), 315. Morrison quoted in Jones.

125. Felicia Kornbluh, *The Battle for Welfare Rights: Politics and Poverty in Modern America* (Philadelphia: University of Pennsylvania Press, 2007), 10.

126. Annelise Orleck, *Storming Caesar's Palace: How Black Mothers Fought Their Own War on Poverty* (Boston: Beacon Press, 2005), 308.

127. Orleck, *Storming Caesar's Palace*, 306.

128. Orleck, *Storming Caesar's Palace*, 174–175.

129. Orleck, *Storming Caesar's Palace*, 307.

130. Singer, *Living for the Revolution*, 50.

131. Singer, *Living for the Revolution*, 140.

132. Singer, *Living for the Revolution*, 156.

133. Collins, *Black Feminist Thought*, 3.

134. Springer, *Living for the Revolution*, 9–10.

135. "M.I.T. Conference: Final Resolutions," *Black Scholar* 24, no. 1 (Winter 1994): 6.

136. Kimberlé Crenshaw, "Mapping the Margins: Intersectionality, Identity Politics, and Violence against Women of Color," *Stanford Law Review* (1991): 1241–1299.

137. Quotations in Debra Henderson and Ann Tickamyer, "The Intersection of Poverty Discourses: Race, Class, Culture, and Gender," in Bonnie Thornton Dill and Ruth End Zambrana, eds., *Emerging Intersections: Race, Class, and Gender in Theory, Policy, and Practice* (New Brunswick: Rutgers University Press, 2009), 56.

138. Bonnie Thornton Dill and Ruth Enid Zambrana, "Critical Thinking About Inequality: An Emerging Lens," in Dill and Zambrana, eds., *Emerging Intersections*, 5.

139. Patricia Hill Collins, "Forward," in Dill and Zambrana, eds., *Emerging Intersections*, ix, xii.

140. Eileen Boris and Jennifer Klein, *Caring for America: Home Health Workers in the Shadow of the Welfare State* (New York: Oxford University Press, 2012), 11, 13, 22–23, 39, 69, 83, 125–126, 207 (quotation).

141. Michael B. Katz and Mark J. Stern, *One Nation Divisible: What America Was and What It Is Becoming* (New York: Russell Sage Foundation, 2006).

142. National Women's Law Center, "Poverty Among Women and Families," 2.

143. National Women's Law Center, "Poverty Among Women and Families, 2000-2010: Extreme Poverty Reaches Record Levels as Congress Faces Critical Choices," September 2011, 8. Daniel Trisi and La Donna Pavetti, "TANF Weakening as a Safety Net for Poor Families," Center on Budget and Policy Priorities, March 13, 2012, http://www.cbpp.org/cms/index.cfm?fa=view&id=3700, accessed December 8, 2012.

144. Rebecca Thiess, "The Future of Work: Trends and Challenges for Low-Wage Workers," *Economic Policy Institute*, April 27, 2012, Briefing Paper, #341, 2, 4.

145. Bureau of Labor Statistics, Table 14, Employed Persons by Detailed Industry and Sex, 2010, bls.gov/csp/wlf table 14-2010.pdf, accessed December 8, 2012.

146. Collins, *Black Feminist Thought*, 232.

147. Rhonda Y. Williams, "Black Women, Urban Politics, and Engendering Black Power," in Joseph, ed., *Black Power Movement*, 100.

Chapter 3

1. There are several useful books that deal with the War on Poverty and Great Society. They include: Henry J. Aaron, *Politics and the Professors: The Great Society in Perspective* (Washington, DC: Brookings Institution, 1978); Daniel Knapp and Kenneth Polk, *Scouting the War on Poverty: Social Reform in the Kennedy Administration* (Lexington, Mass.: Heath/Lexington Books, 1971); Daniel Moynihan, *Maximum Feasible Misunderstanding: Community Action in the War on Poverty*

(New York: Free Press, 1969); *The Politics of a Guaranteed Income: The Nixon Administration and the Family Assistance Plan* (New York: Random House, 1973); ed., *On Understanding Poverty: Perspectives from the Social Sciences* (New York: Basic Books, 1969); Robert A. Levine, *The Poor Ye Need Not Have With You: Lessons from the War on Poverty* (Cambridge: MIT Press, 1970); James L. Sundquist, ed., *On Fighting Poverty: Perspectives from Experience* (New York: Basic Books, 1969); Sar A. Levitan, *The Great Society's Poor Law: A New Approach to Poverty* (Baltimore: Johns Hopkins University Press, 1969).

2. Alyosha Goldstein, *Poverty in Common: The Politics of Community Action during the American Century* (Durham and London: Duke University Press, 2012), 108.

3. Henry Cohen in "Poverty and Urban Policy: Conference Transcript of 1973 Group Discussion of the Kennedy Administration Urban Poverty Programs and Policies," Kennedy Archives, 51. See also 46, 91, 93. Michael Harrington, *The Other America: Poverty in the United States* (New York: Macmillan, 1962); John Kenneth Galbraith, *The Affluent Society* (Boston: Houghton Mifflin, 1958); Dwight McDonald, "Our Invisible Poor," *New Yorker*, January 19, 1963, 82–132.

4. "Poverty and Urban Policy," 359.

5. Frederick Hayes, Richard Boone, and Adam Yarmolinsky, "Poverty and Public Policy," 164, 255, 242.

6. Interview with Paul Ylvisaker for the Ford Foundation Oral History Project, Cambridge, Massachusetts, September 27, 1973. Interviewer: Charles T. Morrissey, Session Number One, 54.

7. William Capron in "Poverty and Public Policy," 176; see also 139.

8. "Mobilization for Youth, Inc. General Support," in Ford Foundation, Grant No. 62-369, accepted proposals, docket excerpts, June 21-22, 1962, 1; Ylvisaker interview, Session Number Two, October 27, 1973, 58.

9. Adam Yarmolinsky in "Poverty and Urban Policy," 193.

10. Richard Cloward and William Capron in "Poverty and Urban Policy," 160–161.

11. Adam Yarmolinsky in "Poverty and Urban Policy," 162–163.

12. William Capron in "Poverty and Urban Policy," 167–168.

13. David Zarefsky, *President Johnson's War on Poverty: Rhetoric and History* (University, Ala.: University of Alabama Press, 1986), 43–44.

14. Frances Fox Piven and David Hackett in "Poverty and Urban Policy," 198 and 202; and Piven, "Great Society," 275–276, in Richard A. Cloward and Frances Fox Piven, eds., *The Politics of Turmoil: Essays on Poverty, Race, and the Urban Crisis* (New York: Pantheon, 1972).

15. Frances Fox Piven and Adam Yarmolinsky in "Poverty and Urban Policy," 392, 395.

16. Annelise Orleck and Lisa Gayle Hazirjian, eds., *The War on Poverty: A New Grassroots History, 1964-1980* (Athens, Ga.: University of Georgia Press, 2011), 15.

17. Orleck and Hazirjian, eds., *War on Poverty*, 3.
18. Amy Jordan, "Fighting for the Child Development Group of Mississippi: Poor People, Local Politics, and the Complicated Legacy of Head Start," in Orleck and Hazirjian, eds., *The War on Poverty*, 280.
19. Laurie B. Green, "Saving Babies in Memphis: The Politics of Race, Health, and Hunger during the War on Poverty," in Orleck and Hazirjian, eds., *The War on Poverty*, 133.
20. Robert Bauman, "Gender, Civil Rights Activism, and the War on Poverty in Los Angeles," in Orleck and Hazirjian, eds., *The War on Poverty*, 209.
21. David Austin in "Poverty and Urban Policy," 184.
22. The five-part PBS video series, *The War on Poverty*, by the great filmmaker Henry Hampton, provides a superb overview of the program that illustrates both grassroots mobilization and the local- and federal-level opposition that curbed the War on Poverty's impact. Unfortunately, this video series is impossible to obtain and must be sought in the relatively few libraries that have copies.
23. William Capron in "Poverty and Urban Policy," 170.
24. David Hackett in "Poverty and Urban Policy," 260–262.
25. Zarefsky, *President Johnson's War on Poverty*, 22–23.
26. Zarefsky, *President Johnson's War on Poverty*, 23–24.
27. [Council of Economic Advisors], "The Problem of Poverty in America," in *Economic Report of the* President, 55, 57, 76.
28. Robert Lampman quoted in Allen J. Matusow, *The Unraveling of America: A History of Liberalism in the 1960s* (New York: Harper and Row, 1984), 220; Zarefsky, *President Johnson's War on Poverty*, xi–xii.
29. David Austin in "Poverty and Urban Policy," 147.
30. [Lyndon Johnson], *Economic Report of the President Transmitted to the Congress January 1964 Together with the Annual Report of the Council of Economic Advisors* (Washington: GPO, 1964), 14–17; William Capron in "Poverty and Urban Policy," 140.
31. [Council of Economic Advisors], "The Problem of Poverty in America," in *Economic Report of the President*, 55, 57, 76.
32. "The Problem of Poverty in America," 62–69.
33. "The Problem of Poverty in America," 72–78.
34. Alice O'Connor, *Poverty Knowledge: Social Science, Social Policy, and the Poor in Twentieth-Century America* (Princeton: Princeton University Press, 2001), 148–149.
35. O'Connor, *Poverty Knowledge*, 149; Thomas H. Jackson, *From Civil Rights to Human Rights: Martin Luther King and the Struggle for Economic Justice* (Philadelphia: University of Pennsylvania Press, 2009).
36. O'Connor, *Poverty Knowledge*, 144.
37. O'Connor, *Poverty Knowledge*, 140–143.
38. Alan Wolfe, *America's Impasse: The Rise and Fall of the Politics of Growth* (Boston: South End Press, 1981), 10.

39. Andrew L. Yarrow, *Measuring America: How Economic Growth Came to Define American Greatness in the Late Twentieth Century* (Amherst and Boston: University of Massachusetts Press, 2010), 36–37.

40. Adam Yarmolinsky in "Poverty and Urban Policy," 286–288.

41. Richard A. Clowen and Lloyd Ohlin, *Delinquency and Opportunity: A Theory of Delinquent Gangs* (New York: Free Press, 1964), 194–211.

42. William Capron in "Poverty and Urban Policy," 149–150; W. Willard Wirtz, memorandum to Honorable Theodore Sorenson, January 23, 1964, Sorenson papers, Kennedy Library.

43. Adam Yarmolinsky in "Poverty and Urban Policy," 286–288. I discuss the outcome of the income maintenance plan (Heineman Commission) below.

44. David Austin, "Poverty and Urban Policy," 147.

45. Gretchen Aguiar, *"The Roots of Head Start: Defining the Public Purposes of Preschool,"* (Ph.D. diss., University of Pennsylvania, 2012), 105–163; Johnson quote, 157.

46. David Hackett in "Poverty and Urban Policy," 24; Frances Fox Piven, "The New Urban Programs: The Strategy of Federal Intervention," in Richard A. Cloward and Frances Fox Piven, eds., *The Politics of Turmoil*, 311, fn. 14; Alyosha Goldstein, *Poverty in Common: The Politics of Community Action during the American Century* (Durham and London: Duke University Press, 2012), 119–121.

47. Clowen and Ohlin, *Delinquency and Opportunity*, x. On the panic over juvenile delinquency in the 1950s, see James Gilbert, *A Cycle of Outrage: America's Reaction to the Juvenile Delinquent in the 1950s* (New York: Oxford University Press, 1986).

48. Clowen and Ohlin, *Delinquency and Opportunity*, 20–32.

49. Clowen and Ohlin, *Delinquency and Opportunity*, 33, 78, 86.

50. Clowen and Ohlin, *Delinquency and Opportunity*, 194–211.

51. Two case studies of how community action became a new form of social control are Ira Katznelson, *City Trenches: Urban Politics and the Patterning of Class in the United States* (New York: Pantheon, 1981), and Joseph H. Helfgot, *Professional Reforming: Mobilization for Youth and the Failure of Social Science* (Lexington, Mass.: Lexington Books, 1981).

52. Jane Addams, *Democracy and Social Ethics* (New York: Macmillan, 1907), 220.

53. Goldstein, *Poverty in Common*, 34.

54. Mobilization for Youth, "A Proposal for the Prevention and Control of Delinquency by Expanding Opportunities," June 10, 1962 (mimeo, Ford Foundation Archives, grant 62–369), 3–4.

55. O'Connor, 160.

56. O'Connor, 168.

57. O'Connor, 168.

58. Adam Yarmolinsky in "Poverty and Urban Policy," 284–285. See also 153–154 and 238–239.

59. William Cannon and William Capron in "Poverty and Urban Policy," 178, 146–147. See also 144 and 244–245.

60. Adam Yarmolinsky in "Poverty and Urban Policy," 285.

61. Lloyd Ohlin and Fred Hayes in "Poverty and Urban Policy," 270; see also 285.

62. Zarefsky, *President Johnson's War on Poverty*, 45–46; William Cannon in "Poverty and Urban Policy," 244.

63. William Capron in "Poverty and Urban Policy," 144 and 148.

64. Adam Yarmolinsky in "Poverty and Urban Policy," 248 and 260; see also 149, 218–219, 252–253, 275–278.

65. Piven, "The Great Society," 311.

66. Goldstein, *Poverty in Common*, 182.

67. Goldstein, *Poverty in Common*, 135.

68. Goldstein, *Poverty in Common*, 135.

69. Quoted in Office of Economic Opportunity, *As the Seed Is Sown: Fourth Annual Report* (Washington, 1969), 9 (italics in original).

70. *As the Seed Is Sown*, 11.

71. Goldstein, *Poverty in Common*, 153.

72. Orleck and Hazirjian, eds., *War on Poverty*, 18–19.

73. Felicia Kornbluh, *The Battle for Welfare Rights: Politics and Poverty in Modern America* (Philadelphia: University of Pennsylvania Press, 2007).

74. *As the Seed Is Sown*, 14.

75. Orleck and Hazirjian, eds., *War on Poverty*, 18–20.

76. Orleck and Hazirjian, eds., *War on Poverty*, 20.

77. Orleck and Hazirjian, eds., *War on Poverty*, 20.

78. Orleck and Hazirjian, eds., *War on Poverty*, 20.

79. Frances Fox Piven and Richard A. Cloward, *Poor People's Movements: Why They Succeed, How They Fail* (New York: Pantheon Books, 1977), 22, 29, 36.

80. Piven and Cloward, *Poor People's Movements*, 33, 34–35, 37.

81. John Atlas, *Seeds of Change: The Story of ACORN, America's Most Controversial Antipoverty Community Organizing Group* (Nashville: Vanderbilt University Press, 2010), 20.

82. Atlas, *Seeds of Change*, tells this story in detail.

83. PICO National Network, http://www.piconetwork.org.

84. William P. Quigley, *Ending Poverty as We Know It: Guaranteeing a Right to a Job at a Living Wage* (Philadelphia: Temple University Press, 2003), 117–136; Michael B. Katz, *The Price of Citizenship: Redefining the American Welfare State*, Updated Edition (Philadelphia: University of Pennsylvania Press, 2008), 391–395.

85. Ira Katznelson, *City Trenches: Urban Politics and the Patterning of Class in America* (New York: Pantheon Books, 1981).

86. Arnold Hirsch, *Making the Second Ghetto: Race and Housing in Chicago 1940-1960* (Chicago: University of Chicago Press, 2008); Thomas J. Sugrue, *The Origins of the Urban Crisis: Race and Inequality in Postwar Detroit* (Princeton: Princeton University Press, 1996).

87. See Robert Fisher, *Let the People Decide: Neighborhood Organizing in America* (New York: Twayne Publishers, 1944), for a sympathetic history of community organizing.

88. Scott W. Allard, *Out of Reach: Place, Poverty, and the New American Welfare State* (New Haven: Yale University Press, 2009), 3.

89. Brian Steensland, *The Failed Welfare Revolution: America's Struggle Over Guaranteed Income Policy* (Princeton: Princeton University Press, 2008), 3, 116.

90. Vincent J. Burke and Lee Burke, *Nixon's Good Deed: Welfare Reform* (New York: Columbia University Press, 1974), 14.

91. Robert H. Haveman, *Poverty Policy and Poverty Research: The Great Society and the Social Sciences* (Madison: University of Wisconsin Press, 1987), 82.

92. Ben W. Heineman, *Poverty Amid Plenty* (Washington, DC: U.S. Government Printing Office, 1969), 48.

93. Katz, *Price of Citizenship*, 292–298.

94. Heineman, *Poverty Amid Plenty*, 72, 52–55, 62–63.

95. Burke and Burke, *Nixon's Good Deed*, 92–93.

96. The debate continues to this day. For a view criticizing the NWRO for opposing the FAP, see Frances Fox Piven and Richard Cloward, *Poor People's Movements*; for a view supporting NWRO's opposition, see Felicia Kornbluh, *The Battle for Welfare Rights*. My own view is closer to Piven and Cloward's on this point.

97. Katz, *Price of Citizenship*, 260–261.

98. Frances Fox Piven and Richard Cloward, *Poor People's Movements*, 264–361; *Poverty amid Plenty*, 121–122; Guida West, *The National Welfare Rights Movement: The Social Protest of Poor Women* (New York: Praeger, 1981); Larry R. Jackson and William A. Johnson, *Protest by the Poor: The Welfare Rights Movement in New York City* (Lexington, Mass.: Heath, 1974); James T. Patterson, *America's Struggle Against Poverty, 1900-1980* (Cambridge, Mass.: Harvard University Press, 1981); Isaac Shapiro and Robert Greenstein, *Holes in the Safety Net: Poverty Programs and Policies in the States* (Washington, DC: Center on Budget and Policy Priorities, 1988); C. R. Winegarden, "The Welfare 'Explosion': Determinants of the Size and Recent Growth of the AFDC Population," *American Journal of Economic Sociology* 32 (1973): 244–256; R. Richard Ritti and Drew W. Hyman, "The Administration of Poverty: Lessons from the 'Welfare Explosion' 1967-1973," *Social Problems* 25 (December 1977): 158–175; Gilbert Y. Steiner, "Reform Follows Reality: The Growth of Welfare," *Public Interest* 34 (1974): 47–65.

99. Rand E. Rosenblatt, "Legal Entitlement and Welfare Benefits,"
    in David Kairys, ed., *The Politics of Law: A Progressive Critique*
    (New York: Pantheon, 1972), 263; Martha F. Davis, *Brutal Need: Lawyers
    and the Welfare Rights Movement, 1960-1973* (New Haven: Yale University
    Press, 1995).
100. Rosenblatt, "Legal Entitlement," 266, 269–270.
101. Charles Reich, "The New Property," *Yale Law Journal* 73 (April
    1964): 771, 738, 734–737, 733; William H. Simon, "The Invention and
    Reinvention of Welfare Rights," *Maryland Law Review* 44 (1985): 28.
102. Reich, "The New Property," 785–786.
103. John Rawls, *A Theory of Justice* (Cambridge: Harvard University Press,
    1971), 11.
104. Rawls, *A Theory of Justice*, 60 and 75.
105. Rawls, *A Theory of Justice*, 73–74, 100–101.
106. Rawls, *A Theory of Justice*, 275.
107. Goldstein, *Poverty in Common*, 249.
108. These are explained in Katz, *The Price of Citizenship*, chapter 1.
109. See John E. Schwarz, *America's Hidden Success: A Reassessment of
    Twenty Years of Public Policy* (New York: Norton, 1983); Social Security
    Administration, *2013 Budget Overview*, 4; Department of Health and
    Human Services Administration for Children and Families. Temporary
    Assistance for Needy Families *FY 2012* Budget, 3; Center for Budget
    and Policy Priorities, *Policy Basics: The Earned Income Tax Credit*,
    February 22, 2012; Nada Eissa and Hilary Haynes, *Redistribution and
    Tax Expenditures: The Earned Income Tax Credit*, National Bureau of
    Economic Research, Working Paper 14307, 2008.
110. Katz, *Price of Citizenship*, 261.
111. Peter Marris and Martin Rein, *Dilemmas of Social Reform: Poverty and
    Community Action in the United States* (London: Routledge and Kegan
    Paul, 1967); Allen J. Matusow, *The Unraveling of America: A History
    of Liberalism in the 1960s* (New York: Harper and Row, 1984); Sanford
    Kravitz, "The Community Action Program," in Sundquist, ed., *On
    Fighting Poverty*, 52–69; Sar A. Levitan and Robert Taggart, *The Promise
    of Greatness* (Cambridge: Harvard University Press, 1976), 169–187;
    Moynihan, *Maximum Feasible Misunderstanding*; Paul E. Peterson and
    J. David Greenstone, "Racial Change and Citizen Participation: The
    Mobilization of Low Income Communities through Community
    Action," in Robert Haveman, ed., *A Decade of Federal Antipoverty
    Programs: Achievements, Failures, and Lessons* (New York: Academic Press,
    1971), 263; West, *The National Welfare Rights Program*. On CETA, see
    Grace A. Franklin and Randall B. Ripley, *CETA: Politics and Policy,
    1973-1982* (Knoxville: University of Tennessee Press, 1984), 37; see also
    189-200 for their evaluation of CETA, which includes a favorable
    analysis of its economic impact on participants. William Mirengoff et al.,
    CETA: Assessment of Public Service Employment Programs (Washington,

DC: National Academy of Sciences, 1980), 4–5; Weir, *Politics and Jobs*, 100. For an overview of work and training programs in the late 1970s, see U.S. Department of Labor and Department of Health, Education, and Welfare, *Employment and Training Report of the President, 1978* (Washington, DC: GPO, 1978).

112. Orleck and Hazirijan, *War on Poverty*, 440–441.

113. Michael B. Katz and Mark J. Stern, *One Nation Divisible: What America Was and What It Is Becoming* (New York: Russell Sage Foundation, 2006).

114. France Fox Piven and Richard Cloward, *Regulating the Poor: The Functions of Public Welfare* (New York: Pantheon, 1971); *Poor People's Movements; The New Class War: Reagan's Attack on the Welfare State and Its Consequences* (New York: Pantheon, 1982); Patterson, *America's Struggle Against Poverty*, 180–184; Jack L. Roach and Janet K. Roach, "Mobilizing the Poor: Road to a Dead End," *Social Problems* 26 (December 1978): 160–167; Larry Isaac and William R. Kelly, "Racial Insurgency, the State and Welfare Expansion: Local and National Level Evidence from the Post-war United States," *American Journal of Sociology* 86 (May 1981): 1348–1386; Edward T. Jennings, "Racial Insurgency, the State, and Welfare Expansion: A Critical Comment and Reanalysis," *American Journal of Sociology* 88 (May 1983): 1220–1236; Joyce Gelb and Alice Sardell, "Strategies for the Powerless: The Welfare Rights Movement in New York City," *American Behavioral Scientist* 17 (March-April 1974): 507–530; Michael Betz, "Riots and Welfare: Are They Related?" *Social Problems* 21 (June 1974): 345–355. Peter Dreier, "Glen Beck's Attacks on Frances Fox Piven Trigger Death Threats," *Huff Post Media*, January 23, 2011.

115. Mollie Orshansky, "Counting the Poor: Another Look at the Poverty Profile," first published in the *Social Security Bulletin*, 1965, reprinted in Mollie Orshansky, *The Measure of Poverty: Technical Paper I Documentation of Background Information and Rationale for Current Poverty Matrix* (Washington, DC: GPO, 1977), 19–20.

116. Mollie Orshansky, "Children of the Poor," first published in the *Social Security Bulletin*, July 1963, reprinted in Orshansky, *The Measure of Poverty*, 10; Orshansky, "Memorandum for Dr. Daniel P. Moynihan Subject: History of the Poverty Line," July 1, 1970, 234; "Who's Who Among the Poor: A Demographic View of Poverty," first published in the *Social Security Bulletin*, July 1965, reprinted in *The Measure of Poverty*, 50, 68–69; "Perspectives on Poverty 2: How Poverty is Measured," *Monthly Labor Review* (February 1969), reprinted in *The Measure of Poverty*, 245.

117. Orshansky, "Counting the Poor," 24; "Who's Who Among the Poor," 50; "Perspectives on Poverty 2," 245; "Poverty Thresholds," in *The Measure of Poverty*, 276.

118. Mollie Orshansky, "Measuring Poverty: A Debate," *Public Welfare* (Spring 1978): 47. On the measurement of poverty, see Michael

Harrington, *The New American Poverty* (New York: Holt, Rinehart and Winston, 1984), 69–71 and 84–85; Harrell R. Rodgers, Jr., *The Cost of Human Neglect* (Armonk, N.Y.: M. E. Sharp, Inc., 1982), 15–30; Sidney E. Zimbalist, "Replacing Our Obsolete Poverty Line," *Public Welfare* 35 (Fall 1977): 36–41 and "Drawing the Poverty Line," *Social Work* 9 (July 1964): 19–26; John B. Williamson and Kathryn M. Hyer, "The Measurement and Meaning of Poverty," *Social Problems* 22 (June 1975): 652–663; Marie Withers Osmond and Mary Durkin, "Measuring Family Poverty," *Social Science Quarterly* 60 (June 1979): 87–95; James H. Hauver, John A. Goodman, and Marc A. Grainer, "The Federal Poverty Thresholds: Appearance and Reality," *Journal of Consumer Research* 8 (June 1981): 1–10; Theo Goehart, Victor Halberstadt, Arie Kapteyn, and Bernard Van Praag, "The Poverty Line: Concept and Measurement," *Journal of Human Resources* 12 (1977): 503–520; Sheldon Danziger and Peter Gottschalk, "The Measurement of Poverty: Implications for Antipoverty Policy," *American Behavioral Scientist* 26 (July-August 1983): 739–756; Donald E. Chambers, "Another Look at the Poverty Lines in England and the United States," *Social Service Review* 55 (September 1981): 472–483, and "The U.S. Poverty Line: A Time for Change," *Social Work* 27 (July 1982): 354–358; Leonard Beeghley, "Illusion and Reality in the Measurement of Poverty," *Social Problems* 31 (February 1984): 322–333; and Christopher Jencks, "The Politics of Income Measurement," in William Alonso and Paul Starr, eds., *The Politics of Numbers* (New York: Russell Sage Foundation, 1987), 83–131. The entire book is an excellent and authoritative source on the politics of numbers in contemporary American social science.

119. Patricia Ruggles, *Drawing the Line: Alternative Poverty Measures and Their Implications for Public Policy* (Washington, DC: Urban Institute Press, 1990); Constance F. Citro and Robert T. Michael, eds., *Measuring Poverty: A New Approach* (Washington, DC: National Academy Press, 1995); also National Academy of Sciences, "Summary and Recommendations [1995]" and U.S. Bureau of the Census, "Poverty – Experimental Measures," [March 2012] http://www.census.gov/hhes/povmeas. New York City Commission for Economic Opportunity, "Increasing Opportunity and Reducing Poverty in New York City" (report to Mayor Michael R. Bloomberg, September 2006; New York City Commission for Economic Opportunity, "Increasing Opportunity and Reducing Poverty in New York City" (report to Mayor Michael Bloomberg, September 2006), 8–9. For a brief, lucid overview of the poverty line, see Mark Levinson, "Mismeasuring—and its Consequences," *American Prospect*, July/August 2012, 42–43.

120. "Inequality and Poverty Key Figures," LIS Cross-National Data Center in Luxembourg, http://www.lisdatacenter.org/lis-ikf-webapp/app/search-ikf-figures, accessed October 1, 2012.

121. Haveman, *Poverty Policy*, 167.

122. Haveman, *Poverty Policy*, 51–52. For an excellent discussion of the use of research in the War on Poverty and the rising importance of economists, see O'Connor, *Poverty Knowledge*, 166–195.

123. Haveman, *Poverty Policy*, 32–34.

124. "Robert S. McNamara, January 21, 1961-February 1, 1968," Department of Defense, http://www.defense.gov/specials/secdef_histories/bios/mcnamara.htm.

125. Elizabeth Evanson, "A Brief History of the Institute for Research on Poverty," *Focus* 9 (Summer 1986): 2–7; [anon.], *A Description* (University of Wisconsin-Madison: Institute for Research on Poverty, 1986).

126. See Greg Duncan et al., *Years of Poverty, Years of Plenty: The Changing Economic Fortunes of American Workers and Families* (Ann Arbor: Institute for Social Research, University of Michigan, 1984).

127. Haveman, *Poverty Policy*, 192; Philip K. Robins et al., *A Guaranteed Annual Income: Evidence from a Social Experiment* (New York: Academic Press, 1980).

128. Haveman, *Poverty Policy*, 167.

129. Haveman, *Poverty Policy*, 236. See also Charles E. Lindblom and David K. Cohen, *Usable Knowledge: Social Science and Social Problem Solving* (New Haven, CT: Yale University Press, 1979).

Chapter 4

1. This discussion of urban transformation is based on chapter 1, "What is an American City?" in Michael B. Katz, *Why Don't American Cities Burn?* (Philadelphia: University of Pennsylvania Press, 2012), 19–46. For figures on "eds" and "meds," see 165, fn. 19, 47.

2. James N. Gregory, *The Southern Diaspora: How the Great Migrations of Black and White Southerners Transformed America* (Chapel Hill: University of North Carolina Press, 2005).

3. Kevin Fox Gotham, *Race, Real Estate, and Uneven Development: The Kansas City Experience, 1900-2000* (Albany: State University of New York Press, 2002), provides a vivid account of how realtors promoted racial segregation. Camilo J. Vergara, *The New American Ghetto* (New Brunswick, N.J.: Rutgers University Press, 1995). Laura J. Lawson, *City Bountiful: A Century of Community Gardening in America* (Berkeley: University of California Press, 2005) and Dominic Vitiello, "Growing Edible Cities," in Eugenie L. Birch and Susan L. Wachter, *Growing Greener Cities: Urban Sustainability in the Twenty-First Century* (Philadelphia: University of Pennsylvania Press, 2008), 259–78. Michael B. Katz, Mathew Creighton, Daniel Amsterdam, and Merlin Chowkwanyun, "Immigration and the New Metropolitan Geography," *Journal of Urban Affairs* 32, no. 5 (2010): 523–47.

4. Douglas S. Massey, *New Faces in New Places: The Changing Geography of Immigration* (New York: Russell Sage Foundation, 2008).

5. Testimony of Jonathan Bowles, director, Center for an Urban Future, Before City Council Committees on Small Business and Immigration, "Creating Greater Opportunities for Immigrant Entrepreneurs," December 14, 2007. See www.nycfuture.org. Mamie Marcuss with Ricardo Borgos, Federal Reserve Bank of Boston, "Who Are New England's Immigrants?" http://www.bostonfed.org/commdev/c&b/2004/fall/Immigrants.pdf.

6. Andrew Wiese, *Places of Their Own: African American Suburbanization in the Twentieth Century* (Chicago: University of Chicago Press, 2005); Thomas J. Sugrue, *Sweet Land of Liberty: The Forgotten Struggle for Civil Rights in the North* (New York: Random House, 2008); Carl H. Nightingale, *Segregation: A Global History of Divided Cities* (Chicago: University of Chicago Press, 2012), 295–322.

7. Kevin Fox Gotham, *Race, Real Estate, and Uneven Development: The Kansas City Experience, 1900-2000* (Albany: State University of New York Press, 2002); Douglas Massey and Nancy Denton, *American Apartheid: Segregation and the Making of the Underclass* (Cambridge, Mass.: Harvard University Press, 1993), 46–48, 64, 74, 85–87, 332–333; Dolores Hayden, *Building Suburbia: Green Fields and Urban Growth, 1820-2000* (New York: Pantheon, 2003), 14.

8. Michael B. Katz and Mark J. Stern, *One Nation Divisible: What America Was and What It Is Becoming* (New York: Russell Sage Foundation, 2006), 153-170.

9. Massey and Denton, *American Apartheid*.

10. David W. Bartelt, "Housing the Underclass," in *The "Underclass" Debate: Views from History*, ed. Michael B. Katz (Princeton: Princeton University Press, 1993), 118-157.

11. Brookings Institution, "The Re-Emergence of Concentrated Poverty: Metropolitan Trends in the 2000s," Metropolitan Opportunity Series, November 3, 2011, http://www.brookings.edu/research/papers/2011/11/03-poverty-kneebone-nadeau-berube.

12. Douglas Massey, Jonathan Rothwell, and Thurston Domina, "The Changing Bases of Segregation in the United States," *Annals AAPSS* 626 (November 2009): 74–90; Peter Dreier, John Mollenkopf, and Todd Swanstrom, *Place Matters: Metropolitics for the Twenty-First Century*, rev. 2nd ed. (Lawrence: University Press of Kansas, 2004), 18, 48.

13. Dreier et al., *Place Matters*, 130–132.

14. Massey and Denton, *American Apartheid*, 190.

15. Massey and Denton, *American Apartheid*, 195–199.

16. I have described the components of the war on welfare in *In the Shadow of the Poorhouse* (New York: Basic Books, 1986), ch. 10. There are now many books and articles on the rise of the political Right. A good overview is Kim Phillips-Fein, "Conservatism: a State of the Field," *Journal of American History* 98, no. 3 (December 2011): 723–743.

17. Katz, *Shadow*, 278; on the sources of conservatism, I have found useful: Barry Bluestone and Bennett Harrison, *The Deindustrialization of America* (New York: Basic Books, 1982); Ramesh Mishra, *The Welfare State in Crisis: Social Thought and Social Change* (New York: St. Martin's Press, 1984); Thomas Byrne Edsall, *The New Politics of Inequality* (New York: Norton, 1984); Thomas Ferguson and Joel Rogers, *Right Turn: The Decline of the Democrats and the Future of American Politics* (New York: Hill and Wang, 1986); Frances Fox Piven and Richard A. Cloward, *The New Class War: Reagan's Attack on the Welfare State and Its Consequences* (New York: Pantheon, 1982); Daniel Stedman Jones, *Masters of the Universe: Hayek, Friedman, and the Birth of Neoliberal Politics* (Princeton: Princeton University Press, 2012).

18. Robert Wuthnow and Matthew P. Lawson, "Sources of Christian Fundamentalism in the United States," in *Accounting for Fundamentalism*, ed. Martin E. Marty and R. Scott Appleby (Chicago: University of Chicago Press, 1994), 32; Godfrey Hodgson, *The World Turned Right Side Up: A History of the Conservative Ascendancy in America* (Boston: Houghton Mifflin, 1996), 175–184; Nancy T. Ammerman, "North American Fundamentalism," in *Fundamentalisms Observed*, ed. Martin E. Marty and R. Scott Appleby (Chicago: University of Chicago Press, 1991), 43–44; Sara Diamond, *Roads to Dominion: Right-Wing Movements and Political Power in the United States* (New York: Guilford Press, 1995), 311; Albert J. Menendez, *Evangelicals at the Ballot Box* (Amherst, N.Y.: Prometheus Books, 1996), 176–177.

19. Chuck Lane, "The Manhattan Project," *New Republic*, 25 March 1985, 14–15; James A. Smith, *The Idea Brokers: Think Tanks and the Rise of the New Policy Elite* (New York: Free Press, 1991), 192, 194; Hodgson, *The World Turned Right Side Up*, 282; Jean Stefancic and Richard Delgado, *No Mercy* (Philadelphia: Temple University Press, 1996), 89–90, app. tables 1, 2, 3; Vince Stehle, "Righting Philanthropy," *Nation*, June 30, 1997, 16; David M. Ricci, *The Transformation of American Politics* (New Haven: Yale University Press, 1993), 166; Karen M. Paget, "Lessons of Right-Wing Philanthropy," *American Prospect* 40 (September-October 1998): 91; National Committee for a Responsive Philanthropy, "Moving a Public Policy Agenda: The Strategic Philanthropy of Conservative Foundations," July 1997; and "Conservative Foundations Prevail in Shaping Public Policies" [http://www.ncrp.org/publications].

20. Stefancic and Delgado, *No Mercy*, 140–146; Smith, *Idea Brokers*, 203.

21. Gareth Stedman Jones, *An End to Poverty? A Historical Debate* (London: Profile Books, 2004), 9-10, 225-226.

22. Lilian Brandt, "The Causes of Poverty," *Political Science Quarterly*, 23, No. 4 (December, 1908): 643.

23. Martin Anderson, *Welfare: The Political Economy of Welfare Reform in the United States* (Stanford, Calif.: Hoover Institution Press, 1978).

24. Michael Harrington, *The New American Poverty* (New York: Holt, Rinehart, and Winston, 1984), 77, 79–80.
25. Harrington, *New American Poverty*, 81–84.
26. George Gilder, *Wealth and Poverty* (New York: Basic Books, 1981; Bantam edition, 1982), xi, 221–222; Leonard Silk, "A Walk on the Supply Side," *Harvard Business Review* (November-December 1981): 44; Richard Hofstadter, *Anti-Intellectualism in American Life* (New York: Knopf, 1963). For other commentary on Gilder, see Robert Lekachman, "Right Wisdom," *Dissent* 29 (Summer 1981): 373–374; Joseph Sobran, "The Economy of Faith," *National Review* 33 (February 6, 1981): 104–105; Michael Kinsley, "Tension and Release," *New Republic*, February 7, 1981, 25-31; Gordon Tullock, "Two Gurus," *Policy Review* (Summer 1981-Spring 1982): 137–144; Kendall P. Cochran, [review], *Social Science Quarterly* 63 (December 1982): 793–794; Robert Higgs, [review], *Journal of Economic History* 41 (December 1981): 957–959; [anon.], "Blessed Are the Money-Makers," *The Economist*, March 7, 1981, 87–88; Vera Shlakman, [review], *Social Work* (March 1982): 198; Richard N. Farmer, [review], *Business Horizons* 24 (July–August 1981): 90–93; Alan Ryan, "Three Cheers for Capitalism," *Partisan Review* 50 (Spring 1983): 300–303; Barry Gewen, "Gilder's Capitalism Without Tears," *New Leader*, March 23, 1981, 17–19; Ronald A. Krieger, "Supply-Side Economics," *Choice* 19 (November 1981): 341–347.
27. Gilder, *Wealth and Poverty*; Robert Nozick, *Anarchy, State, and Utopia* (New York: Basic Books, 1974); Charles Murray, *Losing Ground: American Social Policy, 1950-1980* (New York: Basic Books, 1984).
28. Gilder, *Wealth and Poverty*, 23, 34, 103–106, 278–279.
29. Gilder, *Wealth and Poverty*, 82, 87, 89, 90–91, 153.
30. Gilder, *Wealth and Poverty*, 82, 87, 89, 90–91, 153.
31. Gilder, *Wealth and Poverty*, 135–136.
32. Gilder, *Wealth and Poverty*, 153, 155, 90, 139–140.
33. Gilder, *Wealth and Poverty*, 304–315.
34. George R. Geiger, [review], *Antioch Review* 36 (Summer 1978): 377; Ernest Van Den Haag, "The Libertarian Argument," *National Review* 27 (July 4, 1975): 729; Michael Sean Quinn, "Defense of a Minimal State," *Southwest Review* 60 (Summer 1975): 312; Sheldon Wolin, [review], *The New York Times Book Review*, May 11, 1975, 31. For other comments on Nozick, see: Virginia Held, "John Locke on Robert Nozick," *Social Research* 43 (Spring 1976): 169-195; R.P.M., [review], *Review of Metaphysics* 30 (Spring 1976): 134–135; Francis Canavan, "False Individualism, Reasons for Hope, Backward Glances," *America*, July 19, 1975, 37; Tibor R. Machan, "The Minimal State," Modern Age (Fall 1975): 434–435; George Kateb, "The Night Watchman State," *American Scholar* 45 (Winter 1976): 816-826; Raziel Abelson, "Is There a Public Interest," *The New Leader*, April 14, 1975, 19–21; Douglas Rae, [review], *The American Political Science Review* 70 (1976): 1289–1291; Steven Lukes,

"State of Nature," *New Statesman*, March 14, 1975, 343–344; Christopher Lehmann-Haupt, "Hard Book That Must Be Read," *New York Times*, August 5, 1975, 29; Michael Harrington, "Misconception of Society," *Commonweal*, November 7, 1975, 534–536; Bernard Williams, "The Minimal State," *Times Literary Supplement*, January 17, 1975, 46-47; Peter Witonski, "New Argument," *New Republic* 172 (April 26, 1975): 29–30; Peter Singer, "The Right to Be Rich or Poor," *New York Review of Books* 22 (March 6, 1975): 19–24.

35. Nozick, *Anarchy, State, and Utopia*, ix–xii.

36. Nozick, *Anarchy, State, and Utopia*, 31.

37. Nozick, *Anarchy, State, and Utopia*, 153, 169.

38. Nozick, *Anarchy, State, and Utopia*, 231.

39. Murray, *Losing Ground*, 196.

40. Murray, *Losing Ground*, 233, 177.

41. Chuck Lane, "The Manhattan Project," *New Republic*, March 25, 1985, 14–15.

42. Lane, "The Manhattan Project."

43. Robert Greenstein, "Losing Faith in Losing Ground," *New Republic*, March 25, 1985, 14; Christopher Jencks, "How Poor Are the Poor?" *New York Review of Books* 32 (May 5, 1985): 41.

44. Jencks, "How Poor Are the Poor?", 46; Greenstein, "Losing Faith," 14.

45. Greenstein, "Losing Faith," 12–13.

46. Lawrence M. Mead, *Beyond Entitlement* (New York: The Free Press, 1986), 1, ix.

47. Mead, *Beyond Entitlement*, 7.

48. Mead, *Beyond Entitlement*, 12. Mead's central themes—distrust of human nature, the need for lowered expectations, a more authoritarian government, and a rejection of equality of condition—are precisely those ascribed by Peter Steinfels to contemporary "neoconservatives." Steinfels, *The Neoconservatives: The Men Who Are Changing America's Politics* (New York: Simon and Schuster, 1979), *passim*.

49. Mead, *Beyond Entitlement*, 7, 9, 10, 18–19, 24, 74, 69.

50. Mead, *Beyond Entitlement*, 13, 84–85.

51. Mead, *Beyond Entitlement*, 200, 6, 10, 87.

52. Mead, *Beyond Entitlement*, 67, 9, 12.

53. Mead, *Beyond Entitlement*, 62–63, 41.

54. Mead, *Beyond Entitlement*, 60. On community action, see Chapter 3.

55. Mead, *Beyond Entitlement*, 18–21, 49.

56. Michael B. Katz, *In the Shadow of the Poorhouse: A Social History of Welfare in America*, tenth anniversary edition, revised and updated (New York: Basic Books, 1996), 107-113; Tracy L. Steffes, *School, Society, and State: A New Education to Govern Modern America, 1890-1940* (Chicago: University of Chicago Press, 2012).

57. Fred Block, "Rethinking the Political Economy of the Welfare State," in Fred Block et al., *The Mean Season: The Attack on the Welfare State*

(New York: Pantheon, 1987), 109-160; "The Obligation to Work and the Availability of Jobs: A Dialogue between Lawrence M. Mead and William Julius Wilson," *Focus* 10 (Summer 1987): 11–19. On the work ethic in American history, see Daniel Rodgers, *The Work Ethic in Industrial America, 1850-1920* (Chicago: University of Chicago Press, 1978).

58. Mead, *Beyond Entitlement*, 6–7.

59. Mead, *Beyond Entitlement*, 24–43.

60. Piven and Cloward, *Regulating the Poor: The Functions of Public Welfare*, 2nd ed. (New York: Vintage, 1973).

61. For the idea that welfare policy assumes a psychology differentiated by class, I am indebted to Piven and Cloward, *The New Class War*, 39.

62. Lawrence Mead, *The New Politics of Poverty: The Non-Working Poor in America* (New York: Basic Books, 1992). I critically examined Mead's arguments in Michael B. Katz, "The Poverty Debate," *Dissent* (Fall 1992): 548–553. The summary list of Mead's argument is from 548–549.

63. See, for example, Ronald Dworkin, "Why Liberals Should Believe in Equality," *New York Review of Books* 30 (February 3, 1983): 57. Amartya Sen, *On Economic Inequality*, expanded edition with a substantial annex by James E. Foster and Amartya Sen (Delhi, Oxford, and New York: Oxford University Press, 1997), 104–105, 210–211.

64. Frank I. Michelman, "On Protecting the Poor Through the Fourteenth Amendment," *Harvard Law Review* 83:7 (1969): 9, 13; "Welfare Rights in a Constitutional Democracy," *Washington University Law Quarterly* 3 (Summer 1969): 678. The latter includes an appendix summarizing important Supreme Court decisions bearing on welfare rights and a commentary on Michelman's argument by other scholars.

65. Raymond Plant, "So You Want to be a Citizen?" *New Statesman* 127, no. 4371 (6 February 1998): 30; Jocelyn Pixley, *Citizenship and Employment: Investigating Post-Industrial Options* (Cambridge: Cambridge University Press, 1993), 201.

66. Linda Kerber, "The Meanings of Citizenship," *Dissent* (Fall 1997): 35; see also Linda K. Kerber, *No Constitutional Right to Be Ladies: Women and the Obligations of Citizenship* (New York: Hill and Wang, 1998); Kuttner, *Everything for Sale: The Virtues and Limits of Markets* (New York: Knopf, 1997), 351. See also Bruce E. Tonn and Carl Petrich, "Everyday Life's Constraints on Citizenship in the United States," *Futures* 30, no. 8 (1998): 783–813; Ralf Dahrendorf, "On the Origin of Inequality Among Men," *Social Inequality* (1969): 39; Anthony Giddens, "T. H. Marshall, the State, and Democracy," in *Citizenship Today: The Contemporary Relevance of T. H. Marshall*, eds. Martin Bulmer and Anthony M. Rees (London: University College of London, 1996), 66–67, 80. For an alternative concept of democracy, see the interesting and provocative C. Douglas Lummis, *Radical Democracy* (Ithaca: Cornell University Press, 1996).

67. Amy Gutmann, "Introduction," 6, and J. Donald Moon, "The Moral Basis of the Democratic Welfare State," 28–29, in *Democracy and the Welfare State*, ed. Amy Gutmann (Princeton: Princeton University Press, 1988). See also J. Donald Moon, ed., *Responsibility, Rights and Welfare: The Theory of the Welfare State* (Boulder and London: Westview Press, 1988).

68. Michael Walzer, *Spheres of Justice: A Defense of Pluralism and Equality* (New York: Basic Books, 1983), 92, 31, 62.

69. Walzer, *Spheres of Justice*, 278, 84, 92–93.

70. Walzer, *Spheres of Justice*, 92–93. See also Walzer, "Socializing the Welfare State," in Gutmann, *Democracy and the Welfare State*, 13–26.

71. National Conference of Catholic Bishops [hereafter cited as NCCB], *Economic Justice for All: Pastoral Letter on Catholic Social Teaching and the U.S. Economy* (United States Catholic Conference, Washington, DC, 1986), 93.

72. NCCB, *Economic Justice*, xi, 8. I am indebted to David Hollenbach for an explanation of the background and intent of the pastoral letter.

73. NCCB, *Economic Justice*, 12, ix, 32.

74. NCCB, *Economic Justice*, 36–37; Dworkin, "Why Liberals Should Believe in Equality," 33–34.

75. NCCB, *Economic Justice*, 57–58, 4–5, 62, 51, 153.

76. Michael B. Katz, *The Price of Citizenship: Redefining the American Welfare State* (New York: Metropolitan Books, 2001; updated edition, Philadelphia: University of Pennsylvania Press, 2008), 26.

77. Jamie Peck, *Workfare States* (New York and London: The Guilford Press, 2001), 9.

78. Peck, *Workfare States*, 85.

79. Peck, *Workfare States*, 81.

80. Richard Nathan, "Will the Underclass Always Be with Us?" *Society* 24 (March-April 1987): 61.

81. Nathan, "Underclass," 61.

82. Fred Block and John Noakes, "The Politics of New-Style Workfare," unpublished paper prepared for PARSS Seminar on Work and Welfare, January 1988, 14–19.

83. Nathan, "Underclass," 61–62.

84. Block and Noakes, "Politics of New-Style Workfare," 33, Table III; 34; 36, Table IV.

85. Katz, *Price of Citizenship*, 57–76.

86. Robert Rector and William F. Lauber, *America's Failed $5.4 Trillion War on Poverty* (Washington, DC: Heritage Foundation, 1995). For an authoritative criticism, see Sharon Parrott, "How Much Do We Spend on Welfare?" Center on Budget and Policy Priorities, 1995.

87. Martin Gilens, *Why Americans Hate Welfare: Race, Media, and the Politics of Antipoverty Policy* (Chicago: University of Chicago Press, 1999).

88. Gilens, *Why Americans Hate Welfare*, 102–153; US House of Representatives, *1996 Green Book*, 474, table 8–28; 483–484, table 8–33.

89. Robert Pear, "Republicans Finish with Welfare Measure, Clinton Ambivalent," *New York Times*, 31 July 1996; Vanessa Gallman, "Republicans Offer Welfare Bill Compromise," *Philadelphia Inquirer*, 31 July 1996; Robert Pear, "Clinton Says He'll Sign Bill Overhauling Welfare System," *New York Times*, 1 August 1996; R. Kent Weaver, "Ending Welfare as We Know It," in *The Social Divide: Political Parties and the Future of Activist Government*, ed. Margaret Weir (Washington, DC: Brookings Institution; New York: Russell Sage Foundation, 1998), 375, table 9-1; *Congressional Record—House*, 31 July 1996, H9396.

90. Lester M. Salamon, *"Holding the Center: America's Nonprofit Sector at a Crossroads,"* (New York: Nathan Cummings Foundation, 1997); Nina Bernstein, "Giant Companies Entering Race to Run State Welfare Programs," *New York Times*, September 15, 1996. Bernstein also wrote about the galloping privatization in the foster care system in "Welfare Bill Has Opened Foster Care to Big Business," *New York Times*, May 4, 1997. See also Barbara Ehrenreich, "Spinning the Poor into Gold: How Corporations Seek to Profit from Welfare Reform," *Harper's*, August 1997, 44; Sam Howe Verhovek, "White House Rejects Texas Plan for Business Role in Welfare," *New York Times*, May 11, 1997; Steven Thomma, "Privatization Jackpot Eyed: Takeover of Texas Welfare," *Philadelphia Inquirer*, March 24, 1997; William D. Hartung and Jennifer Washburn, "Lockheed Martin: From Warfare to Welfare," *Nation*, March 2, 1998; Nina Bernstein, "Squabble Puts Welfare Deal under Spotlight in New York," *New York Times*, February 22, 2000.

91. Jason DeParle, "Tougher Welfare Limits Bring Surprising Results," *New York Times*, December 30, 1997; see also Massing, "The End of Welfare?" *New York Review of Books*, October 7, 1999, 25–26.

92. Barbara Ehrenreich, *Nickel and Dimed: On (not) Getting By in America* (New York: Metropolitan Books, 2001); David K. Shipler, *The Working Poor: Invisible in America* (New York: Knopf, 2004).

93. Mark Rank, *One Nation, Underprivileged: Why American Poverty Affects Us All* (New York: Oxford University Press, 2004), 92, 95.

Chapter 5

1. On the origins of the term "underclass," the definitive account is Herbert J. Gans, *The War Against the Poor: The Underclass and Antipoverty Policy* (New York: Basic Books, 1995), 27–57.

2. "The American Underclass," *Time*, August 29, 1977, 1, 15.

3. Isabel Wilkerson, "New Studies Zeroing in on Poorest of the Poor," *New York Times*, December 20, 1987, 26.

4. "The American Underclass," 14, 16.

5. David Whitman and Jeannye Thornton, "A Nation Apart," *U.S. News and World Report*, March 17, 1986, 18; Myron Magnet, "America's Underclass: What to Do?" *Fortune*, May 11, 1987, 130.

6. Lee Rainwater, "Looking Back and Looking Up," *Transaction* 6 (February 1969): 9. A very good discussion of the origins of the underclass concept in American social science is Robert Aponte, "Conceptualizing the Underclass: An Alternative Perspective," paper presented at the annual meeting of the American Sociological Association, August 26, 1988. The Aponte paper is also one of the two best criticisms of the concept I have read. The other is Nicky Gregson and Fred Robinson, "The Casualties of Thatcherism," paper presented at the annual meeting of the Association of American Geographers, March 20, 1989. For a summary of the most recent social science research on the underclass, see William J. Wilson, ed., "The Ghetto Underclass: Social Science Perspectives," special issue, *Annals of the American Academy of Political and Social Science* 501 (January 1989).

7. Douglas G. Glasgow, *The Black Underclass: Poverty, Unemployment, and Entrapment of Ghetto Youth* (New York: Random House, 1980), 3, 4. Glasgow is a former dean of the School of Social Work at Howard University and vice president of the National Urban League's Washington Operations Office. For his later formulation of the issue, see his "The Black Underclass in Perspective," in National Urban League, *The State of Black America 1987* (Washington: National Urban League, 1987), 129–144.

8. Ken Auletta, *The Underclass* (New York: Random House, 1982), xvi.

9. For a similar example from the nineteenth century, see Michael B. Katz, *Poverty and Policy in American History* (New York: Academic Press, 1983), 134–156.

10. Auletta, *The Underclass*, 260–268.

11. Nicholas Lemann, "The Origins of the Underclass," *The Atlantic Monthly* 257 (June 1986): 31–61, and 258 (July 1986): 54–68. Quotations from 257, 32–33, 35, 258, 59, 61. William J. Wilson points out Lemann's belatedly acknowledged debt to his work in William J. Wilson, *The Truly Disadvantaged: The Inner City, the Underclass, and Public Policy* (Chicago and London: University of Chicago Press, 1987), 197–198, fn. 72.

12. Lemann, *Underclass*, 40, 60, 257–258.

13. Lemann, *Underclass*, 35, 257.

14. Wilson, *Truly Disadvantaged*, 55.

15. Gerald Jaynes, seminar comments, PARSS seminar on the city, University of Pennsylvania, December 15, 1986. See also, Andrew Billingsley, "Black Families in a Changing Society," and Glasgow, "Black Underclass," in National Urban League, *State of Black America*, 105–106 and 132–133.

16. Janice Madden, seminar comments, PARSS seminar on the city, University of Pennsylvania, December 15, 1986.

17. Marian Wright Edelman, *Families in Peril: An Agenda for Social Change* (Cambridge: Harvard University Press, 1987), 73.

18. Martha A. Gephart and Robert W. Pearson, "Contemporary Research on the Urban Underclass," *Items* 42 (June 1988): 3.

19. Wilkerson, "New Studies;" Erol R. Ricketts and Isabel V. Sawhill, "Defining and Measuring the Underclass," unpublished manuscript, December 1986.

20. Douglas S. Massey and Robert J. Sampson, "Moynihan Redux: Legacies and Lessons," *Annals of the American Academy of Political and Social Science* 621 (2009): 18.

21. William Julius Wilson, *The Declining Significance of Race: Blacks and Changing American Institutions* (Chicago: University of Chicago Press, 1978; 2nd edition, 1980). On the controversy, see Joseph R. Washington, ed., *The Declining Significance of Race? A Dialogue among Black and White Social Scientists* (Philadelphia: Joseph R. Washington, Jr., 1979).

22. Andrew Hacker, *Two Nations: Black and White, Separate, Hostile, Unequal* (New York: Scribner's, 1992); Stephan Thernstrom and Abigail Thernstrom, *America in Black and White: One Nation Indivisible* (New York: Simon and Schuster, 1997); Michael B. Katz, Mark J. Stern, and Jamie J. Fader, "The New African American Inequality," *Journal of American History* 92 (June 2005): 75–108.

23. Wilson, *Truly Disadvantaged* vii-viii; William Julius Wilson, *When Work Disappears: The World of the New Urban Poor* (New York: Knopf, 1996); William Julius Wilson, *More Than Just Race: Being Black and Poor in the Inner City* (New York: Norton, 2009).

24. Wilson, *Truly Disadvantaged*, 7–8.

25. Wilson, *Truly Disadvantaged*, 7–8.

26. Wilson, *When Work Disappears*, 243–251.

27. Wilson, *Truly Disadvantaged*, 33–37; Stanley Lieberson, *A Piece of the Pie: Black and White Immigrants Since 1880* (Berkeley and Los Angeles: University of California Press, 1980).

28. Wilson, *Truly Disadvantaged*, 49–56.

29. Wilson, *Truly Disadvantaged*, 46, 55.

30. Wilson, *Truly Disadvantaged*, 56. See also Elijah Anderson, "Of Old Heads and Young Boys: Notes on the Urban Black Experience," unpublished manuscript, University of Pennsylvania, 1986.

31. Wilson, *Truly Disadvantaged*, 60–61.

32. Martha A. Gephart and Robert W. Pearson, "Contemporary Research on the Urban Underclass," *Items* 42 (June 1988): 1–10. The committee's first major "product" was Christopher Jencks and Paul E. Peterson, eds., *The Urban Underclass* (Washington, DC: Brookings Institution, 1991). For an excellent brief history of the SSRC committee see Alice O'Connor, *Poverty Knowledge: Social Science, Social Policy, and the Poor in Twentieth-Century U.S. History* (Princeton: Princeton University Press, 2001), 277–283. I served as archivist to and ex-officio member of the

committee, which funded the volume, *The "Underclass" Debate: The View from History*, which I edited.

33. O'Connor, *Poverty Knowledge*, 277.
34. O'Connor, *Poverty Knowledge*, 278.
35. Quotation in O'Connor, *Poverty Knowledge*, 278, fn. 133.
36. O'Connor, *Poverty Knowledge*, 280.
37. O'Connor, *Poverty Knowledge*, 280.
38. O'Connor, *Poverty Knowledge*, 281.
39. O'Connor, *Poverty Knowledge*, 282.
40. William Julius Wilson, "Social Theory and Public Agenda Research: The Challenge of Studying Inner-City Social Dislocations" (Presidential Address, Annual Meeting of the American Sociological Association, August 12, 1990). For a sophisticated attempt to arrive at a more satisfactory definition, see Martha Van Haitsma, "A Contextual Definition of the Underclass," *Focus* 12 (Spring and Summer 1989): 27–31.
41. William Julius Wilson, "Studying Inner-City Dislocations: The Challenge of Public Agenda Research," *American Sociological Review* 56, no. 1 (Feb. 1991): 1–14. Quotations pp. 4–6.
42. Steve Sailer, "Analysis: Unwed Moms' Birth Rate Up," *United Press International*, July 2, 2003.
43. James T. Patterson, *Freedom is Not Enough: The Moynihan Report and America's Struggle Over Black Family Life—from LBJ to Obama* (New York: Basic Books, 2010), 130.
44. Adam Clymer, "Daniel Patrick Moynihan is Dead," *New York Times*, March 27, 2003, A1; Robert Stacey McCain, "Ex-Sen. Moynihan Dies at 76," *Washington Times*, March 27, 2003, A03.
45. George Will, "Farewell to a Giant Among Public Servants," *The Times* (Albany, NY), March 27, 2003, A11.
46. Peter Edelman, *So Rich, So Poor: Why It's So Hard to End Poverty in America* (New York: New Press, 2012), 37.
47. Edelman, *So Rich, So Poor*, 38.
48. Edelman, *So Rich, So Poor*, 38.
49. Michael B. Katz and Mark J. Stern, *One Nation Divisible: What America Was and What It Is Becoming* (New York: Russell Sage Foundation, 2006).
50. Katz and Stern, *One Nation Divisible*, 135.
51. Edelman, *So Rich, So Poor*, 39.
52. Edelman *So Rich, So Poor*, 36–37.
53. Sara McLanahan and Christine Percheski, "Family Structure and the Reproduction of Inequality," *Annual Review of Sociology* 34 (2008): 257–276. Quotation 264.
54. Charles A. Donovan, *A Marshall Plan for Marriage: Rebuilding Our Shattered Homes*, Heritage Foundation *Backgrounder*, No. 2567, June 7, 2011, 1, 12–13.

55. Charles Murray, *Coming Apart: The State of White America, 1960-2010* (New York: Crown Publishing, 2012), quotation, 148.

56. Sara McLanahan, "Should Government Promote Marriage?" *Journal of Policy Analysis and Management* 26, no. 4 (2007): 951–964. Quotation 951.

57. Kathryn Edin and Maria Kefals, *Promises I Can Keep: Why Poor Women Put Motherhood Before Marriage* (Berkeley: University of California Press, 2005), 6.

58. Wilson, *Truly Disadvantaged*, 83.

59. Paul Tough, *Whatever It Takes: Geoffrey Canada's Quest to Change Harlem and America* (New York: Boston and New York: Houghton Mifflin Harcourt, 2008), 9–17.

60. Katz and Stern, *One Nation Divisible*, 162–163.

61. Elijah Anderson, ed., *Up Against the Wall: Poor, Young, Black, and Male* (Philadelphia: University of Pennsylvania Press, 2008), 3.

62. Anderson, *Up Against the Wall*, ix.

63. Anderson, *Up Against the Wall*, ix.

64. Anderson, *Up Against the Wall*, 3. See also, Elijah Anderson, *Streetwise: Race, Class, and Change in an Urban Community* (Chicago: University of Chicago Press, 1990); Elijah Anderson, *Code of the Street: Decency, Violence, and the Moral Life of the Inner City* (New York: Norton, 1999).

65. Anderson, *Up Against the Wall*, 6.

66. Anderson, *Up Against the Wall*, 8.

67. Harry J. Holzer, "The Labor Market and Young Black Men: Updating Moynihan's Perspective," *Annals of the Academy of Political and Social Science* 621, no. 1 (January 2009): 47.

68. Katz and Stern, *One Nation Divisible*, 88–89.

69. Holzer, "Labor Market and Young Black Men."

70. Katz and Stern, *One Nation Divisible*, 88–89. See also, Bruce Western, *Punishment and Inequality in America* (New York: Russell Sage Foundation, 2006).

71. Holzer, "Labor Market and Young Black Men."

72. Arline Geronimus, John Bound, and Cynthia Colen, "Excess Black Mortality in the United States and in Selected Black and White High-Poverty Areas, 1980-2000," *American Journal of Public Health* 101, no. 4 (April 2011): 720–729.

73. Bill Cosby, "Address at the NAACP on the 50th Anniversary of Brown v. Board of Education," May 17, 2004, American Rhetoric, http://www.americanrhetoric.com/speeches/billcosbypoundcakespeech.htm.

74. Michael Eric Dyson, *Is Bill Cosby Right (Or Has The Black Middle Class Lost Its Mind?)* (New York: Basic Books, 2005), xiii–xv.

75. Dayo Olopade, "Tough Love From the Father-in-Chief," *The Root*, June 19, 2008, http://www.theroot.com/views/tough-love-father-chief, accessed August 11, 2012.

76. Rossi, "First Out, First In," unpublished lecture, August, 1988; 2, 9–16. Mark J. Stern, "The Emergence of Homelessness as a Public Problem," in Erickson and Wilhelm, *Housing the Homeless*, 113.

77. US Department of Housing and Urban Development, "At a Glance: Criteria and Recordkeeping Requirements for Definition of Homeless," http://www.hudhre.info/index.cfm?do=viewResource&ResourceID=4579, accessed 12 December 2012.

78. Mark J. Stern, "Housing and Community Development," in Stern, *Engaging Social Welfare*.

79. Michele Dauber, *The Sympathetic State* (Chicago: University of Chicago Press, 2012), 87–88.

80. Mark J. Stern, "The Emergence of Homelessness," 118–119; Gareth Stedman Jones, *Outcast London* (London: Oxford University Press, 1971), 253.

81. Stern, "The Emergence of Homelessness."

82. Barrett A. Lee, Kimberly A. Tyler, and James D. Wright, "The New Homelessness Revisited," *Annual Review of Sociology* 36 (2010): 501–21.

83. Teresa Gowan, *Hobos, Hustlers and Backsliders: Homeless in San Francisco* (Minneapolis: University of Minnesota Press, 2010), 27–28.

84. Martha Minow, *Making All the Difference: Inclusions, Exclusion, and American Law* (Ithaca: Cornell University Press, 1990).

85. Dennis P. Culhane and Stephen Metraux, "Rearranging the Deck Chairs or Reallocating the Lifeboats?: Homelessness Assistance and Its Alternatives," *Journal of the American Planning Association* 74.1 (2008): 111–121. Available at: http://works.bepress.com/dennis_culhane/51; National Center on Family Homelessness, "The Characteristics and Needs of Families Experiencing Homelessness," update December 2011. On the history of homelessness, see, Kenneth L. Kusmer, *Down & Out, On the Road: The Homeless in American History* (New York: Oxford University Press, 2002).

86. Culhane and Metraux, "Rearranging the Deck Chairs."

87. Mark J. Stern, *Engaging Social Welfare: An Introduction to Policy Analysis* (Boston: Pearson Education, forthcoming 2013).

88. Culhane and Metraux, "Rearranging the Deck Chairs."

89. US Department of Housing and Urban Development, *HUD Strategic Plan FY 2010-2015* (May 2010), 10, http://www.HUD.gov/strategicplan.

90. HUD, *Strategic Plan*, 10.

91. Culhane and Metraux, "Rearranging the Deck Chairs," 112.

92. Mark J. Stern, *Engaging Social Welfare: An Introduction to Policy Analysis* (Boston: Pearson Education Publishing, forthcoming 2013).

93. Dennis P. Culhane, Edmond F. Dejowski, Julie Ibañez, Elizabeth Needham, and Irene Macchia, "Public Shelter Admission Rates in Philadelphia and New York City: The Implications of Turnover for Sheltered Population Counts," *Housing Policy Debates* 5, no. 2 (1994): 107–140; Dennis P. Culhane, Chang-Moon Lee, and Susan

M. Wachter, "Where the Homeless Come From: A Study of the Prior Address Distribution of Families Admitted to Public Shelters in New York City and Philadelphia," *Housing Policy Debate* 7, no. 2 (1996): 327–365.

94. Annie Lowrey, "Homeless Rates in U.S. Held Level Amid Recession, Study Says, but Big Gains Are Elusive," *New York Times*, December 10, 2012, http://www.nytimes.com/2012/12/10/us/homeless-rates-steady-despite-recession-hud-says.html?ref=us.

95. Office of Special Needs Assistance Programs. Office of Community Planning and Development. US Department of Housing and Urban Development, *Homeless Prevention and Rapid Re-Housing Program: Year 1 Summary*, June 2011; Alfred Lubrano, "Shelter and Food Needs Soaring," *Philadelphia Inquirer*, December 12, 2012; U.S. Conference of Mayors, *Housing and Homeless Survey: A Status Report on Hunger and Homelessness in America's Cities. A 25-City Report. December 2012* http://usmayors.org/pressreleases/uploads/2012/1219-report-HH.pdf, accessed April 19, 2013.

96. Susan Saulny, "After Recession, More Young Adults Are Living on Street," *New York Times*, December 18, 2012, http://www.nytimes.com/2012/12/19/us/since-recession-more-young-americans-are-homeless.html?hp&_r=0.

97. Joseph A. Slobodzian, "Parkway Feeding Programs Can Remain—The Judge's Reaffirmation of his Earlier Oral Order Said the Meals 'Benefit the Public Interest.' He Calls for Sides to Settle," *Philadelphia Inquirer*, August 11, 2002; Troy Graham, "Nutter Says He'll Act on Homeless Feeding Report," *Philadelphia Inquirer*, August 29, 2012.

98. Dan Frosch, "Homeless Are Fighting Back Against Panhandling Bans," *New York Times*, October 5, 2012, http://www.nytimes.com/2012/10/06/us/homeless-are-fighting-back-in-court-against-panhandling-bans.html.

99. Katherine Beckett and Steve Herbert, *Banished: The New Social Control in Urban America* (New York: Oxford University Press, 2010); Gowan, *Hobos*, 232–282.

100. Audrey Singer, "Immigrants, Welfare Reform and the Coming Reauthorization Vote," *Migration Information Source*, August 2002.

101. Steven A. Camarota, *Immigrants in the United States: A Profile of America's Foreign-Born Population* (Washington, DC: Center for Immigration Studies, August 2012).

102. Camarota, *Immigrants in the United States*.

103. Audrey Singer, Domenic Vitiello, Michael Katz, David Park, *Recent Immigration to Philadelphia: Regional Change in a Re-Emerging Gateway* (Washington, DC: Brookings Institution, November 2008).

104. John M. MacDonald and Robert J. Sampson, "Don't Shut the Golden Door," *New York Times*, June 19, 2012.

105. See, for instance, Cybelle Fox, *Three Worlds of Relief: Race, Immigration, and the American Welfare State from the Progressive Era to the New Deal* (Princeton: Princeton University Press, 2012).

106. Max Page, *The Creative Destruction of Manhattan, 1900-1940* (Chicago: University of Chicago Press, 1999), 79.

107. Harvey Warren Zorbaugh, *The Gold Coast and the Slum: A Sociological Study of Chicago's Near North Side* (Chicago: University of Chicago Press, 1929), 151.

108. Christopher Jencks and Susan E. Mayer, "The Social Consequences of Growing Up in a Poor Neighborhood" in *Inner City Poverty in the United States*, eds. L. Lynn and M. McGreary (Washington, DC: National Academy Press, 1990).

109. Wilson, *Truly Disadvantaged,* 55, 58.

110. Massey and Denton, *American Apartheid,* 118.

111. Robert J. Sampson, *Great American City: Chicago and the Enduring Neighborhood Effect* (Chicago: University of Chicago Press, 2012), 22, 29.

112. O'Connor, *Poverty Knowledge,* 282.

113. Leila Fiester, *Building a Community of Community Builders: The National Community Building Network 1993-2005* (Oakland, Calif.: Urban Strategies Council, 2007), 4–5; Kristina Smock, "Comprehensive Community Initiatives: A New Generation of Urban Revitalization," COMM-ORG: The On-Line Conference on Community Organizing, 1997. http://comm-org.wisc.edu/papers97/smock/smockintro.htm.

114. Smock, "Comprehensive Community Initiatives."

115. Prudence Brown and Sunil Garg, "Comprehensive Community Initiatives: The Challenges of Partnership," Chapin Hall Center for Children, 1997.

116. Smock, "Comprehensive Community Initiatives."

117. Brown and Garg, "Comprehensive Community Initiatives."

118. Helen Zelon, "Hope or Hype in Harlem?" *City Limits* (March 2010): 15, 30–31. For background on Geoffrey Canada and the HCZ, see Paul Tough, *Whatever It Takes: Geoffrey Canada's Quest to Change Harlem and America* (Boston: Houghton Mifflin, 2008).

119. Zelon, "Hope or Hype," 13–14.

120. Zelon, "Hope or Hype," 28. For a vivid account of the role of test preparation in the daily life of one of the schools, see Tough, *Whatever It Takes.*

121. Zelon, "Hope or Hype," 29.

122. Zelon, "Hope or Hype," 37.

123. Nowak et al., *Religious Institutions and Community Renewal,* I-8-9; Alvis C. Vidal, *Rebuilding Communities: A National Study of Urban Community Development Corporations* (New York: New School for Social Research, Graduate School of Management and Urban Policy, Community Development Research Center, 1992), 34, 87; Robert O. Zdenek, *Taking Hold: The Growth and Support of Community Development Corporations* (Washington, DC: National Congress for Community Economic Development, 1990), 2–6; National Congress for Community Economic Development, *Tying It All Together* (Washington, DC. NCCED, 1995), 1, 19.

124. Zdenek, *Taking Hold*, 7–8; Neal R. Peirce and Carol F. Steinbach, *Enterprising Communities: Community-Based Development in America, 1990* (Washington, DC: Council for Community-Based Development, 1990), 27–30; Randy Stoecker, "The CDC Model of Urban Redevelopment: A Critique and an Alternative," *Journal of Urban Affairs* 19, no. 1 (1997): 1–22; Rachel G. Blatt, "CDCs: Contributions Outweigh Contradictions: A Reply to Randy Stoecker," *Journal of Urban Affairs* 19, no. 1 (1997): 23–38; see also W. Dennis Keating, "The CDC Model of Urban Development: A Reply to Randy Stoecker," and Randy Stoecker, "Should We…Could We…Change the CDC Model? A Rejoinder," *Journal of Urban Affairs* 19, no. 1 (1997): 29–33, 35–44.

125. David J. Erickson, *The Housing Policy Revolution: Networks and Neighborhoods* (Washington, DC: Urban Institute Press, 2009), xii, xix; Christopher J. Walker and Mark Weinheimer, "Community Development in the 1990s" (Washington, DC: Urban Institute, 1998).

126. Jeremy Nowak, "Neighborhood Initiative and the Regional Economy," *Economic Development Quarterly* 11, no. 1 (February 1997): 3–10.

127. Leonard S. Rubinowitz and James E. Rosenbaum, *Crossing the Class and Color Lines: From Public Housing to White Suburbia* (Chicago: University of Chicago Press, 2000), 187, 189.

128. Xavier de Souza Briggs, Susan J. Popkin, and John Goering, *Moving to Opportunity: The Story of an American Experiment to Fight Ghetto Poverty* (New York: Oxford University Press, 2010), 13–14.

129. Xavier de Souza Briggs, Susan J. Popkin, and John Goering, *Moving to Opportunity: The Story of an American Experiment to Fight Ghetto Poverty* (New York: Oxford University Press, 2010), 13–14.

130. Jens Ludwig, Greg J. Duncan, Lisa A. Gennetian, Lawrence F. Katz, Ronald C. Kessler, Jeffrey R. King, Lisa Sanbonmatsu, "Neighborhood Effects on the Long-Term Well-Being of Low-Income Adults," *Science* 337, no. 6101 (September 21, 2012): 1505–1510; Sabrina Taverenise, "Intangible Dividend of Antipoverty Effort: Happiness," *New York Times*, September 21, 2012.

131. Michael B. Katz, *Why Don't American Cities Burn?* (Philadelphia: University of Pennsylvania Press, 2012), 101–150.

132. David J. Bartelt, "Housing the Underclass," in *"Underclass" Debate*, ed., Katz, 118–157.

133. Michael E. Porter, "The Competitive Advantage of the Inner City," *Harvard Business Review* 73, 3 (May 1955): 55–71; Initiative for a Competitive Inner City online, www.icic.org; Initiative for a Competitive Inner City, "State of the Inner City Economies: Small Businesses in the Inner City," *Small Business Research Summary* 260 (October 2005); Julia Sass Rubin and Gregory M. Staniewicz, "The New Markets Tax Credit Program: A Midcourse Assessment," *Community Development Investment Review* 1, no. 1 (March, 2005): 1–11.

134. Ananya Roy, *Poverty Capital: Microfinance and the Making of Development* (Berkeley: University of California Press, 2010).

135. Muhammad Yunus, *Creating a World Without Poverty* (New York: Public Affairs, 2007); Muhammad Yunus, *Banker to the Poor: Micro-Lending and the Battle Against World Poverty* (New York: Public Affairs, 1999); Alex Counts, *Small Loans, Big Dreams: How Nobel Prize Winner Muhammad Yunus and Microfinance Are Changing the World* (Hoboken, NJ: Wiley, 2008).

136. For the operations of Grameen in the United States, see the Grameen America website, www.grameenamerica.com. Kristina Shevory, "With the Squeeze on Credit, Microlending Blossoms," *New York Times*, July 28, 2010. Yunus quoted in Neil MacFarquhar, "Banks Making Big Profits from Tiny Loans," *New York Times*, April 13, 2010. G. S. Radhakrishna, "Suicide Shock for Loan Sharks," *Telegraph* (Calcutta, India), November 23, 2010; Linda Polgreen and Vikas Bajaj, "India Microcredit Sector Faces Collapse from Defaults," *New York Times*, November 17, 2010.

137. Asif Dowla and Dipal Barua, *The Poor Always Pay Back: The Grameen II Story* (Bloomfield, CT: Kumarian Press, 2006).

138. Michael Sherraden, *Assets and the Poor: A New American Welfare Policy* (Armonk, NY: Sharpe, 1991).

139. Reid Cramer, Mark Huelsman, Justin King, Alejandra Lopez-Fernandini, and David Newill, "The Assets Report 2010: An Assessment of President Obama's Budget and the Changing Policy Landscape for Asset Building Opportunities," New America Foundation, 2010; Thomas Shapiro, Tatjana Meschede, and Sam Orso, "Why the Racial Wealth Gap Is Increasing and How to Close It," draft working paper, May 2012.

140. Mark Schreiner and Michael Sherraden, *Can the Poor Save? Saving and Asset Building in Individual Development Accounts* (New Brunswick, NJ: Transaction, 2007); Reed Cramer, "The Big Lift: Federal Policy Efforts to Create Child Development Accounts," Center for Social Development, George Warren Brown School of Social Work, Washington University, St. Louis, CSD Working Papers No. 09-43, 2009; Ford Foundation, "Building Assets to Reduce Poverty and Inequality" (2002); Bill and Melinda Gates Foundation, 2010 Global Savings Forum, November 16-17, Seattle Washington; CFED, "The SEED Initiative," http://cfed.org/programs/abc/initiatives/seed/key_lessons_from_seed/index.htmls

141. New York City Commission for Economic Opportunity, "Increasing Opportunity and Reducing Poverty in New York City" (report to Mayor Michael R. Bloomberg, September 2006), www.Nyd.gov.html/om/pdf/MayorsCommissiononPovertyReport2006.pdf; Laura B. Rawlings, "A New Approach to Social Assistance: Latin America's Experience with Conditional Cash Transfer Programmes," *International Social Security Review* 58, 2–3 (2005): 134; Ariel Fizbein and Norbert Schady, *Conditional Cash Transfers: Reducing Present and Future Poverty* (Washington, DC: World Bank, 2009).

142. James A. Riccio, Nadine DeChuasay, David Greenberg, Cynthia Miller, Zawadi Rucks, and Nandita Verma, *Toward Reduced Poverty Across Generations: Early Findings from New York City's Conditional Cash Transfer Program* (New York: MDRC, 2010); MDRC, "Opportunity NYC Demonstrations," http://www.mdrc.org/project/opportunity-nyc-demonstrations#featured_content; Julie Bosman, "Disappointed, City Will Stop Paying Poor for Good Behavior," *New York Times*, March 31, 2010; Sam Roberts, "New York's Poverty Rate Rises, Study Finds," *New York Times*, April 17, 2012.

143. David Harvey, *Social Justice and the City* (Baltimore: Johns Hopkins University Press, 1973); *A Brief History of Neoliberalism* (New York: Oxford University Press, 2005); *Rebel Cities: From the Right to the City to the Urban Revolution* (New York: Verso, 2012).

144. For an excellent example of the work of geographers applied to poverty, see Jamie Peck, *Workfare States* (New York and London: Guilford Press, 2001).

145. Loïc Wacquant, *Urban Outcasts: A Comparative Sociology of Advanced Marginality* (Cambridge, England and Malden, Mass.: Polity Press, 2008), 3–4.

146. Wacquant, *Urban Outcasts*, 262.

147. Wacquant, *Urban Outcasts*, 233–253.

148. See, for instance, Anderson, *Code of the Streets*, 110–111.

149. Katz and Stern, *One Nation Divisible*, 92–93.

150. Arnold B. Hirsch, *Making the Second Ghetto: Race and Housing in Chicago, 1940-1960* (New York: Cambridge University Press, 1983); Thomas J. Sugrue, *The Origins of the Urban Crisis: Race and Inequality in Postwar Detroit* (Princeton: Princeton University Press, 1996).

151. Michael B. Katz, ed., *The "Underclass" Debate: Views from History* (Princeton: Princeton University Press, 1993).

152. Robert P. Fairbanks II and Richard Lloyd, "Critical Ethnography and the Neoliberal City: The US Example," *Ethnography* 12, no. 1 (2011): 3–11.

153. Robert P. Fairbanks II, *How It Works: Recovering Citizens in Post-Welfare Philadelphia* (Chicago: University of Chicago Press, 2009).

154. Philippe Bourgois and Jeff Schonberg, *Righteous Dopefiend* (Berkeley and Los Angeles: University of California Press, 2009), 16, 17.

155. Teddy Cruz, "Latin American Meander. In Search of a New Civic Imagination," *Architectural Design* 81 no. 3 (May/June 2011): 110–118, quotation 111–112.

156. I realized these ambiguities in Wacquant's use of advanced marginality in the course of discussing the book in a graduate seminar with a group of smart, sharp students.

157. Michael D. Shear and Michael Barbaro, "Romney Calls 47% of Voters Dependent in Leaked Video," *New York Times*, September 18, 2012.

158. http://www.povertytour.smileyandwest.com/.

159. Alfred Lubrano, "Poverty Up in City, Suburbs, U.S. Says," *Philadelphia Inquirer*, September 20, 2012, A1.

160. Mark Robert Rank, *One Nation, Underprivileged: Why American Poverty Affects Us All* (New York: Oxford University Press, 2004), 12.

161. Peter Edelman, *So Rich, So Poor: Why It's So Hard To End Poverty in America* (New York: New Press, 2012), xvi–xviii.

162. Martha F. Davis, "The Pendulum Swings Back: Poverty Law in the Old and New Curriculum," *Fordham Urb. L.J.* 34, no. 4 (2007): 1391.

163. Jeffrey D. Sachs, *The End of Poverty: Economic Possibilities For Our Time* (New York: Penguin Books, 2005), 211–213, 218, 335.

164. Thomas Pogge, ed., *Freedom from Poverty as a Human Right: Who Owes What to the Very Poor?* (New York: Oxford University Press, 2007), vii.

165. Davis, "Pendulum Swings Back," 1413–1414. For information on the advocacy organizations, see www.cesr.org; www.splcenter.org; www.amnestyusa.org; www.economichumanrights.org.

Epilogue

1. Daron Acemoglu and James A. Robinson, *Why Nations Fail: The Origins of Power, Prosperity, and Poverty* (New York: Crown Business Books, 2012). For an informative discussion of this book and the issues it addresses, see Jared Diamond, "What Makes Countries Rich or Poor?" *New York Review of Books*, June 7, 2012, 70–75.

2. Linda Giaonnorelli, Kye Lippold, and Michael Martinez-Schiferl, "Reducing Poverty in Wisconsin: Analysis of the Community Advocates Public Policy Institute Policy Package." Urban Institute. June 2012, 33. The four measures are: senior and disability income tax credit, transitional jobs, minimum wage increase, earnings supplement reform.

3. Bruce D. Meyer and James X. Sullivan, "Dimensions of Progress: Poverty from the Great Society to the Great Recession," conference draft presented at the fall 2012 Brookings Panel on Economic Activity, September 13–14, 2012.

4. Amartya Sen, "Conceptualizing and Measuring Poverty" and Martha C. Nussbaum, "Poverty and Human Functioning: Capabilities as Fundamental Entitlements," in David B. Grusky and Ravi Kanbur, eds., *Poverty and Inequality* (Stanford: Stanford University Press, 2006), 30–75; Jeffrey D. Sachs, *The Ends of Poverty: Economic Possibilities For Our Time* (New York: Penguin Books, 2005).

5. Ananya Roy and Nezar Alsayad, *Urban Informality: Transnational Perspectives from the Middle East, Latin America, and South Asia* (Lanham, MD: Lexington Books, 2004); Sudhir Alladi Venkatesh, *Off the Books: The Underground Economy of the Urban Poor* (Cambridge: Harvard University Press, 2006).

6. Lilian Brandt, "The Causes of Poverty," *Political Science Quarterly* 23, no. 4 (December 1908): 639, 642–645.

7. Edward T. Devine, *Misery and Its Causes* (New York: MacMillan, 1911), 12.

INDEX

able-bodied, as undeserving, 4–5
abortion
    and authoritative public policy,
        167, 181
    black feminism and, 91
    conservative opposition to, 165
achievement gap, 45–46
achievement motive, 11
ACORN, 132–134
active-benefit systems, 195
adaptive role, of culture of poverty,
    12–13, 22
ADC. *See* Aid to Dependent
    Children
ADD. *See* American Dream
    Demonstration
Addams, Jane, 121
adolescent pregnancy, 61, 67
advanced marginality, 256–263, 273
AFDC. *See* Aid to Families with
    Dependent Children
affirmative action, 164, 172

Affluent Society, The (Galbraith),
    104, 115
Affordable Health Care Act (2012),
    136
AFQT. *See* Armed Forces
    Qualification Test
African Americans
    anti-poverty programs and, 17–18
    class stratification among, 212–214
    cycle of poverty and, 19, 20–21
    difficulties of youths, 21–22
    family disintegration and, 19–20
    housing segregation and, 21
    male unemployment and, 20, 63
    matriarchal family structure,
        20–23, 63–64
    migration of southern blacks, 104,
        106–107, 121, 140, 158, 165,
        210–211
    political leadership among,
        118–119
    racism and, 18–19